# The Legal Regulation of Business

*John Ellison LLB (Hons), Grad Cert Ed, MA (Dunelm)*
*Tom Harrison BA (Hons), Grad Cert Ed, LLM (London)*

Harrison Law Publishing 1999

© Tom Harrison   John Ellison

ISBN 1901888 11 8

July 1999

Published in Great Britain by
Harrison Law Publishing
53 South Street
Durham City
DH1 4QP

Tel: 0191 3846218
Fax: 0191 3846218

*British Cataloguing-in-Publications Data*
*A catalogue record for this book is available from the British Library*

Printed and bound in Great Britain at Athenaeum Press, Gateshead

# Preface

This book provides a comprehensive and up to date coverage of the principles of business law contained in the core unit of the HNC/D in Business, the Legal and Regulatory Framework. The authors have also included material found in the other HNC/D core units such as equal opportunity law, health and safety at work and terms and conditions of employment. Practical work related assignments at the end of Chapters provide an opportunity to apply the law, and sets of test questions throughout the text offer an easy means to confirm that the subject matter has been understood. A glossary of the important legal terms is included and an extensive index will help with cross referencing to other units of the HNC/D core.

We hope that the style and approach of the book is student friendly, making the law as accessible as possible so that the study of business law is enjoyable as well as informative. The direct impact that business law has on our personal experiences as consumers and employees should ensure that the book remains of practical value as a reference source long after your formal legal studies have been completed.

For ease of expression the book adopts, in general, the practice of using 'he' for 'he or she' and 'his' for 'his and hers'.

J E
T H

## Acknowledgements

Many thanks to Moira Page who has the ability to decipher woefully handwritten text and had the sole responsibility for the design and type setting of the text and the book cover.

TH  JE
Durham June 1999

## The Authors

John Ellison and Tom Harrison are both law teachers at New College Durham.

John Ellison is Programme Manager for higher education at New College and Director of the full-time HND Business programme. He is also chairman of the AEB committee responsible for 'A' Level Law.

Tom Harrison is course leader for the Music Industry Management stream on the HND course at New College. He is also a visiting lecturer in employment law at Durham University.

# Table of Contents

## Chapter 1   The Legal System

The Legal Framework......................................................................1
The Business Environment ............................................................2
The Purpose of a System of Business Law ...................................3
The Importance of Law to Business .............................................6
Developing Legal Knowledge........................................................8
Law Making Institutions ...............................................................9
Law Making by the Courts ..........................................................11
Statute...........................................................................................14
European Community Law ..........................................................17
The Resolution of Business Disputes .........................................21

## Chapter 2   The Principles of Contract Law

The Idea of Contracts ................................................................. 27
Contractual Liability ................................................................... 28
The Form of Contracts ................................................................ 33
Making a Contract....................................................................... 35
Characteristics of a Valid Offer................................................. 37
Characteristics of a Valid Acceptance ...................................... 43
Consideration............................................................................... 48
Intention to Create Legal Relations .......................................... 53
Issues of Contractual Validity .................................................... 57
Misrepresentation........................................................................ 58
Mistake......................................................................................... 66
Contract Terms ............................................................................ 74
Discharge of Contract ................................................................ 86
Remedies for Breach of Contract .............................................. 94

## Chapter 3   Consumer Protection Law

Sale of Goods.............................................................................109
Unfair Contract Terms...............................................................118
The Transfer of Ownership........................................................120
Remedies of Buyers and Sellers ...............................................123
Consumer Protection Act 126 ...................................................126
Supply of Goods and Services Act ............................................127

*Trade Descriptions Legislation* ....................................................... *129*
*Consumer Credit* ............................................................................ *140*
*Regulatory Agencies* ....................................................................... *141*
*Local Authorities and Consumer Protection* ..................................... *144*
*Food Safety* .................................................................................... *145*
*Data Protection* ............................................................................. *146*

# Chapter 4    The Formation, Management and Dissolution of Business Organisations

*The Classification of Business Organisations* ..................................... *152*
*Sole Traders* ................................................................................... *154*
*Partnerships* .................................................................................. *155*
*Registered Companies* .................................................................... *158*
*Public and Private Companies* ........................................................ *163*
*Forming a Registered Company* ....................................................... *165*
*The Shareholders in a Company* ...................................................... *173*
*Company Borrowing* ....................................................................... *186*
*Business Managers* ......................................................................... *189*
*Directorships* ................................................................................. *190*
*Partners as Business Managers* ....................................................... *207*
*The Dissolution of Business Organisations* ....................................... *213*
*Choosing the Legal Form for a Business* ........................................... *227*

# Chapter 5    The Statutory Regulation of Employment

*Employees and Contractors* ............................................................. *235*
*Distinguishing between the Employed and Self Employed* .................... *237*
*Formation of the Contract of Employment* ....................................... *240*
*Equal Opportunities* ....................................................................... *244*
*Sex and Race Discrimination* .......................................................... *246*
*Disability Discrimination* ............................................................... *248*
*Legal Formalities* ........................................................................... *262*
*The Contents of a Contract of Employment* ..................................... *264*
*Payment of Wages* .......................................................................... *271*
*Health and Safety at Work* .............................................................. *275*
*The Termination of Employment* ..................................................... *290*
*Wrongful Dismissal* ........................................................................ *291*
*Unfair Dismissal* ............................................................................ *298*
*Remedies for Unfair Dismissal* ........................................................ *312*
*Redundancy Payments* .................................................................... *316*

# Table of Cases

## A

Aberdeen Railway Co. v. Blaikie Bros (1854) 1 Macq 461 .................................................201
Ace Mini Cars Ltd. v. Albertie [1990] EAT 262/8915 ....................................................251
Alexander v. Automatic Telephone Co. [1900] 2 Ch. 56 .................................................204
Allen v. Gold Reefs of West Africa [1900] 1 Ch 656 ....................................................180
Aluminium Industrie Vaassen BV v. Romalpa Aluminium Ltd. [1976] 2 All ER 552 .........85, 121
Amalgamated Investment & Property Co. Ltd. v. John Walker & Sons Ltd. [1976] All ER .........70
American Cyanamid v. Ethicon [1975] 1 All ER 504 ....................................................99
Anderson v. Anderson (1857) 25 Beav. 190 ...............................................................216
Associated Dairies v. Hartley [1979] IRLR 171 ..........................................................283
Associated Japanese Bank (International) Ltd. v. Credit du Nord SA [1988] 3 All ER 902 .........70
Atlas Express Ltd. v. Kafco (Importers and Distributors) [1989] 1 All ER 641 ....................74
Re: Attorney-General's Reference (No 2 of 1982) [1984] QB 624 ..................................161
Attorney General v. Lindi St Claire (Personal Services) Ltd 1980 ...................................218
Attwood v. Small (1838) 6 Cl. & Fin. 232 .................................................................62

## B

Re: Bahia v. San Francisco Railway Co. (1868) LR 3.....................................................177
Balfour Beatty Construction (Scotland) Ltd. v. Scotland Power plc [1994] S.L.T. 807 ............97
Barber v. Guardian Royal Exchange Assurance Group [1990] IRLR 240 ...........................20
Barclays Bank plc v. Kapur [1991] IRLR 137 .............................................................250
Barclays Bank plc v. O'Brien [1993] 3 WLR 786 ........................................................73
Barclays Bank plc v. Schwarz 1995 The Times May 31 1995...........................................32
Baxter (Butchers) v. Manley (1985) 4 Tr. L. 219 .......................................................134
Baylis v. Barnett (1988) The Times December 28 ........................................................78
Bentley v. Craven (1853) 18 Beav. 75 .....................................................................211
Blackpool and Fylde Aero Club v. Blackpool B.C. [1990] 1 WLR 1195 .............................39
Boardman v. Phipps [1967] 2 AC 46 ......................................................................159
Bolton v. Mahadeva [1972] 2 All ER 1322.................................................................87
Boston Deep Sea Fishing and Ice Co. v. Ansell (1888) 39 Ch. D. 339 ........................205, 269
Re: Brightlife Ltd. [1986] 3 All ER 673 ...................................................................188
British Aircraft Corporation v. Austin [1978] IRLR 332 ...............................................268
British Car Auctions Ltd. v. Wright [1972] 3 All ER 462 ...............................................38
British Gas plc v. Shama [1991] IRLR 101 ................................................................261
British Railways Board v. Jackson [1994] IRLR 235 ....................................................304
British Steel Corporation v. Cleveland Bridge & Engineering Co. [1984] 1 All ER 504 ..........101
Re: Bugle Press Ltd. [1961] Ch. 270 ......................................................................162
Butler Machine Tool Co. Ltd. v. Ex-Cell-0 Corporation Ltd. [1979] 1 All ER 965 ................44
Byrne & Co. v. Leon van Tienhoven & Co. (1880) 42 L.T. 371 ......................................42

## C

C & B Haulage v. Middleton [1983] 3 All ER 94 .........................................................95
Cammell Laird v. Manganese Bronze & Brass Co. Ltd. [1934] AC 402 ............................117
Carlill v. Carbolic Smokeball Co. [1893] 2 QB 484 ....................................................46
Carlos Federspiel & Co. v. Charles Twigg & Co. Ltd. [1957] 1 Lloyd's Rep. 240 ...............123
Carmichael v. National Power plc [1998] IRLR 301.....................................................239
Carmichael v. Rosehall Engineering Works Ltd. [1983] IRLR 480 ..................................284
Re: Casey's Patents [1892] 1 Ch. 104 .....................................................................52
Cehave NV v. Bremer Handelgesellschaft mbh, The Hansa Nord [1976] QB 44 .................76
Central London Property Trust v. High Trees House [1947] KB 1305 ...............................90
Centrovincial Estates plc v. Merchants Investors Assurance Co. Ltd. [1983] Com. L.R. 158 .....69
Chapleton v. Barry UDC [1940] 1 KB 532 ...............................................................81
Chappell and Co. Ltd. v. Nestle Co. Ltd. [1960] AC 87 ...............................................49
Re: City Equitable Fire Insurance Co. Ltd. [1925] Ch. 407 ...........................................206

Clark v. BET Plc [1997] IRLR 349 ................................................................... 292
Clifford Davies Management v. WEA Records [1975] 1 All ER 237 ............................... 73
Cohen v. Roche [1927] 1 KB 169 ...................................................................... 101
Coleman v. Myers [1977] 2 NZLR 225 ................................................................. 202
Re: a Company [1986] 1 WLR 281 ...................................................................... 223
Re: a Company ex. p Burr [1992] BCLC 724 ......................................................... 185
Re: a Company ex. p Fin Soft Holdings SA [1991] BCLC 737 ..................................... 223
Cook v. Deeks [1916] 1 AC 554 ........................................................................ 205
Cottee v. Douglas Seaton Ltd. [1972] 3 All ER 750 ................................................ 132
Courtaulds Northern Textiles v. Andrew [1979] IRLR 84 ........................................... 295
Couturier v. Hastie (1856) 5 HLC 673 ................................................................ 69
Re: Craig [1971] Ch 95 .................................................................................. 72
Crawford v. Swinton Insurance Brokers [1990] IRLR 42 ............................................ 311
Cresswell v. Board of Inland Revenue [1984] 2 All ER 713 ........................................ 269
Crown Supplies PSA v. Dawkins [1993] IRLR 284 .................................................. 247
Curtis v. Chemical Cleaning and Dyeing Co. [1951] 1 KB 805 .................................... 81
Czarnikow Ltd. v. Koufos (The Heron II) [1966] 2 All ER 593 ....................................

# D

D & C Builders Ltd. v. Rees [1966] 2 QB 617 .............................................. 90, 102
Daniels v. Daniels [1978] 2 All ER 89 ......................................................... 183, 186
Davey v. Cosmos Air Holidays [1989] CLY 2561 ...................................................... 127
David Greig Ltd. v. Goldfinch (1961) 105 S.J. 367 .................................................. 146
Davis Contractors Ltd. v. Fareham UDC [1956] AC 696 ............................................. 93
Decro-Wall International SA v. Practitioners in Marketing [1971] 1 WLR 361 .................... 100
Dekker v. Stichting Vormingscentrum Voor Jonge Volwassenen Plus [1991] IRLR 27 .......... 254
Denard v. Smith and another (1990) The Guardian Aug 21 .................................... 132, 135
Denco Ltd v. Joinson [1991] 1WLR 330 .............................................................. 291
Devis & Sons Ltd. v. Atkins [1977] AC 931 ......................................................... 298
Dixon v. London Fire and Civil Defence (1993) CL 67 .............................................. 287
Dixon Ltd. v. Barnett (1989) 2 TLR 37 .............................................................. 131
Doble v. David Greig Ltd. [1972] 1 WLR 703 ....................................................... 133
Dorchester Finance Co. v. Stebbing [1989] BCLC 498 ............................................. 207
Dryden v. Greater Glasgow Health Board [1992] IRLR 469 ......................................... 266
Dunlop Pneumatic Tyre Co. Ltd. v. Selfridge and Co. Ltd. [1915] AC 847 ....................... 85

# E

Eagleshill Ltd. v. J. Needham (Builders) Ltd. [1972] 3 WLR 789 ................................. 42
East Berkshire Health Authority v. Matadeen [1992] IRLR 336 ..................................... 26
Ebrahami v. Westbourne Galleries [1972] 2 WLR 1289 .............................................. 223
Eley v. Positive Life Assurance Co. Ltd. (1876) 1 Ex D 88 ........................................ 178
Re: Elgindata Ltd. [1991] BCLC 959 .................................................................. 185
Entertainments Ltd. v. Great Yarmouth Borough Council (1983) 134 NLJ 311 .................... 95
Esso Petroleum Co. Ltd. v. Mardon [1976] 2 All ER 5 ............................................. 59
Evans Marshall v. Bertola SA [1973] 1 All ER 992 ................................................ 100

# F

Felthouse v. Bindley (1862) 6 L.T. 157 ............................................................... 45
Ferguson v. John Dawson Ltd. [1976] 1 WLR 346 .................................................. 238
Foakes v. Beer (1884) 9 App.Cas 605 ................................................................. 51
Foss v. Harbottle (1843) 2 Hare 461 ............................................................ 183, 199
Frost v. Aylesbury Dairies Ltd. [1905] 1 KB 608 .............................................. 116, 117
Futty v. Brekkes Ltd. [1974] IRLR 130 ............................................................... 293

# G

Gale v. Dixon Stores Group (1994) 158 J.P.N. 256 ................................................. 135
Gamerco SA v. ICM Fair Warning (Agency) Ltd. [1995] 1 WLR 1226 ............................. 94
Re: Gerald Cooper Chemicals [1978] Ch. 262 ....................................................... 226
Gething v. Kilner [1972] 1 All ER 1166 .............................................................. 202
Gill v. Walls Meat Co. Ltd. [1971] HSIB 22 ......................................................... 308
Goodwin v. The Patents Office [1999] IRLR 4 ....................................................... 249

Godley v. Perry [1960] 1 All ER 36 ............................................................................118
G Percy Trentham Ltd. v. Archital Luxfer Ltd. [1993] 1 Lloyds Rep 25 ........................ 46
Grant v. Australian Knitting Mills Ltd. [1936] AC 85 .................................................116, 117
Greenaway Harrison Ltd. v. Wiles [1994] IRLR 380 ......................................................296
Greenhalgh v. Arderne Cinemas [1951] Ch 286 ...........................................................180
Guinness plc v. Saunders [1990] 1 All ER 652 ............................................................205

## H

Hadley v. Baxendale (1854) 9 Ex. 341 ....................................................................96, 97
Hamilton v. Argyll & Clyde Health Board [1993] IRLR 99 .............................................306
Re: H.R. Harmer Ltd. [1959] 1 WLR 62 ....................................................................184
Harris v. Sheffield United F.C. (1987) The Times March 20 ........................................... 52
Harrison & Jones Ltd. v. Bunten & Lancaster Ltd. [1953] 1 QB 646 ............................... 67
Hartley v. Ponsonby (1857) 7 E & B 872 ................................................................... 50
Hedley Byrne & Co v. Heller and Partners Ltd. [1964] AC 465 ....................................... 63
Hely-Hutchinson v. Brayhead Ltd. [1967] 3 All ER 98 ..................................................197
Hendon v. Adelman (1973) The Times June 16 ............................................................163
Herne Bay Steamboat Co v. Hutton [1903] 2 KB 683 ................................................... 92
Hickman v. Kent or Romney Marsh Sheepbreeders Association [1915] 1 Ch. 881 ...............177
Hilton v. Protopapa [1990] IRLR 376 ........................................................................270
Holliday Concrete v. Woods [1979] IRLR 301 .........................................................78, 241
Hong Kong Fir Shipping Co Ltd. v. Kawasaki Kisen Kaisha Ltd. [1962] 2 QB 26 ................ 77
Horsey v. Dyfed County Council [1982] IRLR 395 ........................................................251
Household Fire Insurance Co v. Grant (1897) 41 L.T. 144 .............................................. 46
Howard Smith Ltd. v. Ampol Petroleum Ltd. [1974] AC 821 ..........................................203
Hughes v. Metropolitan Railway Co (1877) 2 AC 439 ................................................... 90
Hyde v. Wrench (1840) 3 Beav. 334 ......................................................................... 43

## I

Iceland Frozen Foods Ltd. v. Jones [1982] IRLR 439 ...................................................303
Industrial Development Consultants v. Cooley [1972] 2 All ER ......................................205
Insitu Cleaning Co. v. Heads [1995] IRLR 4 ...............................................................255
Irwin v. Liverpool City Council [1977] AC 239 ............................................................ 78

## J

Jarvis v. Swans Tours Ltd. [1973] QB 233 ................................................................. 98
Johnson v. Peabody Trust [1996] IRLR 381 ...............................................................318
Johnstone v. Bloomsbury Heath Authority [1991] IRLR 118 ..........................................288
Jones v. Associated Tunnelling Co. Ltd. [1981] IRLR 477 .............................................267
Jones v. Lipman [1962] 1 All ER 123 ........................................................................162
Jones v. Tower Boot [1997] IRLR 168 .......................................................................255
Jones v. Vernons Pools Ltd. [1938] 2 All ER 626 ......................................................... 53

## K

Kensington and Chelsea Borough Council v. Riley [1973] RTR 122 ..................................131
Kent Management Services v. Butterfield [1992] IRLR 394 ............................................
Kirkham v. Attenborough [1897] 1 QB 201 ................................................................122
Kleinwort Benson Ltd v. Malaysian Mining Corp Bhd [1989] 1 All ER 785 ........................ 54
Krell v. Henry [1903] 2 KB 740 ............................................................................... 92
Kuwait Asia Bank v. National Mutual Life [1991] 1 AC 187 ..........................................202
Kwik-Fit v. Lineham [1992] IRLR 156 .......................................................................297

## L

L. Schuler A G v. Wickham Machine Tool Sales [1974] AC 235 ....................................... 77
Law v. Law [1905] 1 Ch. 140 ..................................................................................211
Lawson and Lawson v. Supasink Ltd. (1984) 3 Tr. L. 37 ................................................ 88
Leaf v. International Galleries [1959] 2 KB 86 ..........................................................63, 70
Lewin v. Rothersthorpe Road Garage (1984) 148 JP 69 ................................................134
Liquidator of West Mercia Safetywear Ltd. v. Dodd [1988] BCLC 250 .............................203
Lister v. Forth Dry Dock [1989] IRLR 161 .................................................................311

Lister v. Romford Ice and Cold Storage Co. Ltd [1957] AC 555...................................................268
Lloyds Bank Ltd. v. Bundy [1975] QB 326 ...........................................................31,,32, 72, 73
Loch v. John Blackwood Ltd [1924] AC 783 ...........................................................................223
Loftus v. Roberts (1902) 18 TLR 532......................................................................................40
Lock v. Cardiff Railway Co. [1998] IRLR 358 .......................................................................309
Luker v. Chapman (1970) 114 Sol. Jo. 788 ..............................................................................97

# M

Macaura v. Northern Assurance Co Ltd. [1925] AC 619.........................................................161
Magee v. Pennine Insurance Co Ltd. [1969] 2 All ER 891 ........................................................71
Malik v. BCCI [1997] IRLR 462 ..............................................................................................270
Mareva Compania Navelia v. International Bulk Carriers [1980] 1 All ER 203 ......................99
Meah v. Roberts [1978] 1 All ER 97 ........................................................................................146
Meer v. London Borough of Tower Hamlets [1988] IRLR 399..............................................256
Mercantile Credit Co v. Garrod [1962] 3 All ER 1103 ...........................................................209
Microbeads v. Vinhurst Road Markings [1975] 1 WLR 218 ...................................................114
Re: Middlesbrough Assembly Rooms (1880) 14 Ch. D. 104....................................................222
Miles v. Clarke [1953] 1 All ER 779 .......................................................................................212
Miles v. Wakefield Metropolitan District Council [1987] IRLR 193 ......................................268
Re: Moore & Co and Landauer & Co [1921] 2 KB 519 ...........................................................114
Mountford v. Scott [1975] 1 All ER 198 ...................................................................................48
Museprime Properties Ltd. v. Adhill Properties Ltd. [1990] 36 EG 144 ..................................62

# N

Napier v. National Business Agency [1951] 2 All ER 264........................................................262
National Carriers Ltd. v. Panalpina (Northern) Ltd. [1981] AC 675 .......................................92
Neptune (Vehicle Washing Equipment) Ltd. v. Fitzgerald [1995] BCC 474 ...........................197
Re: New British Iron Co Ltd. [1898] 1 Ch 342 ........................................................................178
Newham LBC v. Singh (1988) RTR 359 ..................................................................................133
Niblett v. Confectioners Materials Co [1921] 3 KB 387 ..........................................................113
Nicolene Ltd. v. Simmonds [1953] 1 All ER 882 ......................................................................41
Norman v. Bennett [1974] 3 All ER 351 ..................................................................................132
Northampton County Council v. Dattani 1994 IRLB 488.........................................................257
Northern Joint Police Board v. Power [1997] IRLR 610...........................................................247

# O

O'Kelly and Others v. Trusthouse Forte plc [1983] 2 WLR. 605 ...........................................238
Olley v. Marlborough Court Ltd. [1949] 1 KB 532....................................................................82
Re: Othery Construction Ltd. [1966] 1 All ER 145....................................................................222
Owen & Briggs v. James [1982] ICR 618 [1982] IRLR 502 ...................................................251

# P

P v. S [1996] IRLR 347 ............................................................................................................248
Page One Records Ltd. v. Britton [1967] 3 All ER 822 ............................................................99
Panorama Developments (Guildford) Ltd. v. Fidelis Furnishings Ltd. [1971] 3 All ER 16 .....191
Pape v. Cumbria County Council [1991] IRLR 463 1991 .......................................................286
Partridge v. Crittenden [1968] 2 All ER 421............................................................................38
Re: Patrick and Lyon Ltd. [1933] Ch 786 ...............................................................................225
Pavlides v. Jenson and Others [1956] Ch 565..........................................................................183
Pender v. Lushington (1877) 6 Ch. D. 707 ...................................................................183, 186
Pepper v. Webb [1969] 2 All ER 216 ...........................................................................269, 291
Percival v. Wright [1902] 2 Ch 421 ........................................................................................202
Perera v. Civil Service Commission [1983] IRLR 136.............................................................256
Pharmaceutical Soc. of Gt. Britain v. Boots Cash Chemists (Southern) Ltd [1953] 1 QB 401...38
Philip Head & Sons Ltd. v. Showfronts Ltd. [1970] 1 Lloyd's Rep. 140 ................................121
Pickford v. Imperial Chemical Industries plc [1998] IRLR 622...............................................289
Piercy v. S. Mills & Co Ltd. [1920] 1 Ch. 77 ..........................................................................204
Pinnel's Case (1602) 5 Co Rep. 1179 ...........................................................................51, 88, 90
Polkey v. A E Dayton Services Ltd. [1987] 3 All ER 974 .......................................................309
Re: Poly Peck International plc (No.2) [1994] IBCLC 574........................................................196
Price v. Civil Service Commission [1978] 1 All ER 1228 ........................................................256

Re: Produce Marketing Consortium (1989) The Times 7 April ...............................................226

# R

R. v. Associated Octel Co. Ltd. [1994] .......................................................................283
R v. Secretary of State for Trade and Industry ex parte Lonrho plc [1992] BCC 325 ............195
R. v. Thompson Holidays Ltd. [1974] QB 592 .................................................................135
Race Relations Board v. Mecca [1976] IRLR 15 ...............................................................247
Ramsgate Victoria Hotel Co Ltd. v. Montefiore (1866) L.R. 1 Exch. 109..............................43
Raspin v. United News Shops [1999] IRLR 9...................................................................292
Rayfield v. Hands [1960] Ch. 1 ..........................................................................178, 179
Rayford Ltd. v. Drinkwater [1996] IRLR 16.....................................................................273
Read Bros. Cycles (Leyton) v. Waltham Forest London Borough [1978] R.T.R. 397 ................137
Ready Mixed Concrete Ltd. v. Ministry of Pensions [1968] 2 WLR. 775 .............................237
Richards v. Westminster Motors Ltd. [1975] Crim. L.R. 528 .............................................136
Roberts v. Gray [1913] 1 KB 520 ................................................................................56
Roberts v. Leonard (1995) 159 JPN 655 ......................................................................129
Robertson v. Diciccio [1972] R.T.R. 431 .......................................................................131
Robinson v. Graves [1935] 1 KB 597 ...........................................................................110
Rogers v. Parish (Scarborough) Ltd. [1987] 2 All ER 232 ..................................................115
Re: W. & M. Roith [1967] 1 WLR 432..........................................................................204
Roscorla v. Thomas (1842) 3 QB 234 ...........................................................................52
Rose and Frank Co v. Crompton Bros. [1923] AC 445 .......................................................53
Royal British Bank v. Turquand (1856) 6 E. & B. 3.................................................169, 186
Ruxley Electronics and Construction Ltd. v. Forsyth [1995] 3 All ER 268 ..............................96

# S

Sadler v. Whitean (1910) 79 LJKB 786 ........................................................................208
Salomon v. Salomon & Co [1897] AC 22 ......................................................................160
Re: Sam Weller & Sons Ltd. [1990] Ch 682 ...................................................................185
Saunders v. Anglia Building Society [1971] AC 1004 .........................................................68
Saunders v. Richmond on Thames London Borough Council [1978] ICR 75 ..........................253
Saunders v. Scottish National Camps Association [1980] IRLR 174 ....................................304
Scally v. Southern Health and Social Services Board [1991] IRLR 552 .................................271
Scammel v. Ouston [1941] AC 251..............................................................................41
Scottish CWS v. Meyer [1958] 3 WLR 404 ...................................................................184
Secretary of State for Scotland v. Henley 1993 IRLB 476 .................................................259
Seide v. Gillette Industries [1980] IRLR 427...................................................................247
Shepherd & Co. Ltd. v. Jerrom [1986] 3 WLR 801 .........................................................296
Sherratt v. Geralds The American Jewellers Ltd. (1970) 114 S.J. 147 ..................................131
Shine v General Guarantee Corporation [1988] 1 All ER 911 .............................................116
Shuttleworth v. Cox Bros and Co (Maidenhead) Ltd. [1927] 2 KB 9 ...................................180
Sidebottom v. Kershaw, Leese & Co [1920] 1 Ch 154 ......................................................180
Sim v. Rotherham Metropolitan Borough Council [1986] 3 WLR 851....................................267
Singh v. Rowntree Macintosh [1979] IRLR 199 .............................................................251
Sky Petroleum Ltd. v. VIP Petroleum Ltd. [1974] 1 All ER 954 .........................................100
Re: Smith and Fawcett Ltd. [1942] 1 All ER 542 ............................................................175
Smith v. Land and House Property Corporation (1884) 28 Ch. D. 7......................................60
Smith New Court Securities Ltd. v. Scrimgeour Vickers (Asset Management) Ltd. [1994] 4 All ER 225 ...........264
Smith v. Safeway [1996] IRLR 456.............................................................................253
Smith v. Stages and Darlington Insulation Company Ltd [1989] IRLR 177 ..............................13
Sothern v. Franks Charlesley [1981] IRLR 278................................................................297
Spicer (Keith) Ltd. v. Mansell [1970] 1 WLR 333 ...........................................................157
Spriggs v. Sotheby Parke Bernet & Co Ltd. (1984) 272 E.G. 1171 ......................................81
Spurling v. Bradshaw [1956] 2 All ER 121 ....................................................................83
Stapp v. Shaftesbury Society [1982] IRLR 326 ..............................................................300
Stilk v. Myrick (1809) 2 Camp. 317 .........................................................................50, 51
Stirling D C v. Allan [1994] IRLR 208 ..................................................................110, 312
Sumpter v. Hedges [1898] 1 673 ....................................................................86, 87, 88
Sunair Holidays Ltd. v. Dodd [1970] 2 All ER 410 ..........................................................138
Sykes (F. & G.) Wessex v. Fine Fare [1967] 1 Lloyd's Rep. 53 ...........................................41

# T

Taylor v. Alidair Ltd. [1978] IRLR 82 ................................................................ 305
Taylor v. Caldwell (1863) 3 B. & S. 826 .............................................................. 92
Teheran-Europe Co. Ltd. v. S T Belton Tractors ltd. [1968] 2 QB 545 ........................... 117
Tett v. Phoenix Property and Investment Co. Ltd. [1986] BCLC 149 .............................. 175
Thorne v. Motor Trade Association [1937] AC 797 .................................................. 49
Thornton v. Shoe Lane Parking [1971] 2 All ER 163 ................................................ 82
Toyota (GB) Ltd. v. North Yorkshire County Council [1998] ....................................... 136
Treganowan v. Robert Knee & Co [1975] IRLR 1134 ............................................... 308

# U

Underwood v. Burgh Castle Brick and Cement Syndicate [1922] 1 KB 343 ........................ 121
Underwood Ltd. v. Bank of Liverpool [1924] 1 KB 77591 .......................................... 161

# W

Wadham Stringer Commercials Ltd. v. Brown [1983] IRLR 46 ..................................... 295
Walker v. Northumberland CC [1995] IRLR 36 ..................................................... 288
Walton v. TAC Construction Materials Ltd. [1981] IRLR 357 ................................. 61, 241
Waltons & Morse v. Dorrington [1997] IRLR 488 ................................................... 268
Warner Bros v. Nelson [1937] 1 KB 209 ............................................................. 99
Western Excavating (ECC) Ltd. v. Sharp [1978] 2 WLR 344 ...................................... 295
Wheeler v. Patel & J Golding [1987] IRLR 211 ...................................................... 310
White and others v. Jones and others [1995] 1 All ER 691 .......................................... 128
Re: William C. Leitch Brass Ltd [1933] Ch 261 ..................................................... 225
Williams v. Compair Maxim Ltd [1982] IRLR 439 .................................................. 307
Williams v. Roffey Bros and Nicholls (Contractors) Ltd [1990] 1All ER 512 ....................... 50
Wilson v. Best Travel [1993] 1 All ER 353 .......................................................... 128
Wilson v. Rickett Cockerell & Co. Ltd. [1954] 1 QB 598 ............................................ 116
Wings Ltd. v. Ellis [1984] 1 WLR 731 ......................................................... 138, 139
Wishart v. National Association of Citizens Advice Bureaux Ltd. [1990] IRLR 393 ................ 242
Woodar Investment Development Ltd. v. Wimpey Construction U.K. Ltd. [1980] 1 All ER 571 ..... 91
Re: Woodroffes (Musical Instruments) Ltd. [1985] 3 WLR 543 ..................................... 188
Woods v. W H Car Services [1982] IRLR 413 .................................................. 78, 270

# Y

Yates Building Co. v. R J Pulleyn & Son (York) (1976) 119 Sol. Jo. 370 ............................ 44
Re: Yenidje Tobacco Co. Ltd. [1916] 2 Ch. 426 ..................................................... 216
Re: Yorkshire Woolcombers Association Ltd. [1903] 2 Ch 284 ...................................... 187
Yugotours v. Wadsley (1988) CL 852 ........................................................... 130, 138

# Table of Statutes, Statutory Instruments and Treaties

Business Advertisements
(Disclosure) Order 1977 ..................... 127,143
Business Names Act 1985 ....................... 228
Bills of Exchange Act 1882 ....................... 34

Companies Act 1985
  s.1 ........................................... 158,159,163
  s.4 ............................................... 169
  s.5 ............................................... 181
  s.11 ............................................. 164
  s.14 ......................................... 177,178
  s.22 ............................................. 174
  s.26 ............................................. 167
  s.54 ............................................. 181
  s.89 ............................................. 175
  s.183 ......................................... 34,174
  s.186 ........................................... 176
  s.317 ....................................... 197,206
  s.320 ........................................... 198
  s.349 ........................................... 163
  s.428 ........................................... 162
  s.442 ........................................... 163
  s.459 ................................... 184,185,199
  s.461 ........................................... 181
  s.652 ........................................... 218
  s.716 ........................................... 156
  s.741 ....................................... 191,201
Companies Act 1989
  s.35 ..................................... 168,169,186
Company Directors Disqualification
  Act 1986 ................................... 193,194
Consumer Arbitration
  Agreements Act 1988 ........................... 54
Consumer Credit Act 1974 ................ 6,68,107
                                        140,141
  s.65(1) ........................................... 34
Consumer Protection Act 1987 ............. 14,107
                                        126-127
  s.20 ......................................... 135,136
Consumer Transactions
Restrictions on Statements)
(Amendments) Order 1978 ..................... 143
Copyright Designs and Patents Act 1988
  s.90 ............................................... 34
County Courts Act 1984 ........................... 11

Crimimal Courts Act 1973 ........................ 66

Data Protection Act 1984 ....................... 146
Data Protection Act 1998 .......... 14,107,146-148
Disability Discrimination Act 1995 ....... 234,244
Disabled Persons (Employment)
  Act 1958 ........................... 244,248,249

Employment Protection
(Part-time Employees) Regulations 1995
................................... 262,272,274,290
Employment Rights Act 1996 ........ 230,231,237
                                        290-315
  s.1 ......................................... 35,262-264
  s.94 ............................................. 298
  s.95 ......................................... 292,293
  s.98 ......................................... 302-309
  s.111 ........................................... 16,17
Employer's Liability (Defective
  Equipment) Act 1969 ......................... 287
Employment Relations Act 1979 .......... 231,293
                                        300,315
Employment Rights (Disputes
  Resolutions) Act 1998 ..................... 25,301
Equal Pay Act 1970 ........................... 234
Equal Treatment Directive ..................... 234
European Communities Act 1972 ............. 168
Estate Agents Act 1979 ......................... 142
Factories Act 1961 ............................. 282
Fair Trading Act 1973 ......................... 142
Family Law Reform Act 1969 .................. 56
Food Safety Act 1990 ................ 107,145,146

Health and Safety at Work Act 1974 .......... 234
                                        281-285
  s.2 ............................................. 282
  s.3 ............................................. 283
  s.4 ............................................. 284
  s.6 ............................................. 285
  s.7 ............................................. 285
Health and Safety (Display Screen
  Equipment) Regulations 1992 .............. 280

Industrial Tribunals (Extension of
  Jurisdiction) (England and Wales) 1994 ...... 24
Insolvency Act 1986 ...................234,217-227
  s.122 ...........................................185
  s.175 ...........................................226
  s.176 ...........................................226
  s.213 ...........................................163,225,226
  s.214 ...........................................163,225,226
  s.529 ...........................................224

Late Payment of Commercial Debts
  (Interest) Act 1998.............................. 32
Law of Property Act 1925 ....................... 33
Law of Property (Miscellaneous
  Provisions) Act 1989 .......................... 33
  s.1 ................................................. 33
  s.2 ................................................. 34
Law Reform (Frustrated Contracts)
  Act 1943 ......................................... 94
Limited Partnership Act 1907 .................229
Local Government Act 1972 ..............39, 153

Management of Health and Safety at
  Work Regulations 1992 ......................278
Manual Handling Operations
  Regulations 1992 .............................279
Misrepresentation Act 1967..................... 63
  s.2 ........................................... 64,65
  s.3 .................................................

National Minimum Wage Act 1998 ...... 234,240
Package Travel, Package Holidays
  and Package Tours Regulations 1992
  .................................... 208-213,215-217
Partnership Act 1890...................... 155-158
  s.1 ...................................156,157,228
  s.2 .................................................157
  s.4 .................................................155
  s.5 ........................................... 209,229
Personal Protective Equipment at Work
  Regulations 1992 .............................280
Powers of Criminal Courts Act 1973 .........145
Property Misdescriptions
  Act 1991 .....................................60,139
Provision and Use of Work Equipment
  Regulations 1992 .............................279
Public Interest (Disclosure)
  Act 1998................................... 234,240

Race Relations Act 1976 .................. 246-261
Race Relations (Remedies) Act 1994..... 234,260
Redundancy Payments Act 1965 ...............316
Rehabilitation of Offenders Act ...............244
Restrictive Trade Practices Act 1976..............6

Sale of Goods Act 1979 ...........14,107,109-118
  s.3 .................................................56
  s.8 .................................................41
  s.12 ...........................113,114,117,123
  s.13............................ 114,117,123,129
  s.14 ...........................................115,116
  s.15 ...........................................113,118
  s.16 .................................................122
  s.17 .................................................120
  s.18 .................................................121
  s.20 .................................................120
Sale of Goods ( Amendment Act ) 1995 .......122
Sale and Supply of Goods
  Act 1994.................................... 108,115
Sex Discrimination Act 1975 ........234,246-261
Sex Discrimination and Equal Pay
  (Remedies) Regulations 1993 .................260
Single European Act 1986 ..................18, 276
Social Security Act 1975 ....................236
Supply of Goods and Services
  Act 1982 ........................14,107, 127-129
  s.13 .................................................127

Trade Descriptions Act 1968 ................. 14,60
  ............................................107,129-135
  s.1 ........................................... 130-133
  s.14 ...........................................134,135,137
  s.24 .................................................134
Trade Union and Labour Relations
  (Consolidation) Act 1992 ........... 55,244,319
  s.137 .............................................244
  s.168 .............................................273
  s.170 .............................................274
Transfer of Undertakings (Protection of
  Employment) Regulations 1981 .... 15,310,311
Treaty on European Union ......................18
Treaty of Rome 1957 ...........................18
art 118A .............................................276
  art 119 ...........................................20
  art 189 ...........................................20

Unfair Contract Terms
  Act 1977......................31,79,107,109,118
  s.3 ........................................... 119,120
Unfair Terms in Consumer Contracts
  Regulations 1994......................15,79,144
Unsolicited Goods and
  Services Act 1971 .............................145

Working Time
  Regulations 1998....................234,240,277
Workplace (Health and Safety and
  Welfare) Regulations 1992 ..................280

# Glossary of Legal Terms

| | |
|---|---|
| *Acceptance* | • an unconditional assent to an offer |
| *Adjudicate* | • to settle a legal problem by giving judgment |
| *Advocacy* | • the activity of pleading a case before a court |
| *Agent* | • person empowered to make contracts on behalf of another |
| *Appeal* | • asking a higher court to change the decision of a lower court |
| *Appellant* | • a person who appeals |
| *Arbitrate* | • to settle a dispute without court action |
| *Articles of Association* | • rules concerned with the internal administration of a company |
| *Ascertained goods* | • goods which were unascertained and have been identified |
| *Auditor* | • independent financial investigator of a company |
| *Bankruptcy* | • personal insolvency |
| *Barrister* | • lawyer who is an advocate for a client in any court |
| *Bill* | • draft legislation |
| *Binding precedent* | • a precedent which has to be followed |
| *Capacity* | • requirement that parties be capable of contracting |
| *Capital* | • funds raised to finance an organisation |
| *Casual labour* | • workers who are hired only for a short period |
| *Cause of action* | • reason why a case is brought to court |
| *Civil action* | • a case brought by an individual against another alleging a civil wrong |
| *Civil law* | • law dealing with the personal rights and obligations of individuals |
| *Claimant* | • a person or organisation bringing a civil action |
| *Code of practice* | • a statement of trading behaviour produced by a trade association |

| | |
|---|---|
| *Codification* | • bring law together in a formal code |
| *Collective agreement* | • the product of collective bargaining |
| *Company dissolution* | • striking a company off the register of companies by the Registrar |
| *Company secretary* | • the senior administrative officer of a registered company |
| *Compensation order* | • court order requiring a payment of money to the victim of a crime |
| *Complainant* | • an individual presenting a complaint to a tribunal |
| *Compulsory winding up* | • winding up by an order of the court |
| *Conciliation* | • bringing together the parties to a dispute |
| *Conditions* | • major terms in a contract |
| *Consensus ad idem* | • a meeting of the minds |
| *Consideration* | • the idea that the parties to a contract must exchange promises of value |
| *Consolidation* | • bring a number of statutes together into one |
| *Constructive dismissal* | • a contract of employment terminated by the employee |
| *Consumer goods* | • goods which are ordinarily intended for private use or consumption |
| *Contract* | • legally enforceable agreement |
| *Contract for services* | • a contract between an employer and a self employed contractor |
| *Contract of adhesion* | • contract under which a party offer terms which are not up for negotiation |
| *Cooling off* | • a period provided for under statute within which a consumer who has entered into a credit transaction can cancel the agreement |
| *Corporation* | • an organisation treated as an artificial legal person |
| *Criminal law* | • a branch of public law describing rules whose breach results in criminal proceedings |
| *Damages* | • contractual remedy under which a monetary award is made |
| *Data protection* | • legal protection granted to individuals in relation the collection, storage and distribution of personal data about them, using computers |
| *Debentures* | • written statement acknowledging a company's indebtedness and usually supported by some security |

| | |
|---|---|
| *Defendant* | • a party against whom a civil claim is brought |
| *Delegated legislation* | • law produced by individuals and organisations granted the power by Parliament |
| *Deliverable state* | • goods which are in such a condition that the buyer would be bound to accept them |
| *Delivery* | • the voluntary transfer of physical possession of the goods from the seller to the buyer |
| *Direct discrimination* | • less favourable treatment against a particular group |
| *Directive* | • a type of EC law which is in effect an instruction to member states to pass a law giving effect to the rules set out in the directive |
| *Director* | • person responsible for the management of a registered company |
| *Disability* | • a physical or mental impairment which has a substantial long term affect on the person's ability to carry out normal day to day activities |
| *Discharge of contract* | • bringing a contract to an end |
| *Disqualification order* | • court order issued against a named person preventing them from acting as a director or company promoter for the duration of the order |
| *Duress* | • use of threats to force someone into making a contract |
| *Duty of care* | • principle of the tort of negligence recognising the circumstances under which one party has a legal responsibility to another |
| *Economic duress* | • using improper economic pressure to induce a contract |
| *Equitable* | • literally fair and just, but in a legal sense |
| *Estoppel* | • rule of evidence under which a person is prevented from denying the truth of a previous statement of fact |
| *European Union* | • an organisation of 15 European member states which consists of the European Community and two other elements or pillars |
| *Exclusion clauses* | • contract terms seeking to eliminate specified or general contractual liabilities |
| *Express dismissal* | • a contract of employment terminated by the employer with or without notice |
| *Express Terms* | • contractual undertakings expressly agreed orally or in writing by the parties to a contract |

| | |
|---|---|
| *Extortionate credit bargain* | • a credit contract which requires repayments which are grossly exorbitant |
| *Fault liability* | • liability associated with evidence of blameworthiness |
| *Force majeure* | • clause in a contract making provision for events which would otherwise frustrate the contract |
| *Freedom of contract* | • the notion that parties to a contract should be allowed to make their deal without legal interference |
| *Frustration* | • a change in circumstances making contractual performance radically different from that envisaged |
| *Gross misconduct* | • grave misconduct which constitutes a repudiatory breach of the contract of employment |
| *Implied dismissal* | • a contract of employment for a fixed term which terminates when the term expires |
| *Implied terms* | • contractual obligations which are implied into a contract by operation of the common law or statute |
| *Improvement notice* | • an order served by a health and safety inspector requiring a contravention of safety law to be remedied within a specified time |
| *Indirect discrimination* | • less favourable treatment against a particular group by requiring compliance with an unjustifiable condition which is more difficult to satisfy for a member of that group |
| *Injunction* | • court order requiring someone to do something or not to do something |
| *Insolvency* | • condition under which the liabilities of a business exceed its assets |
| *Interlocutory injunction* | • temporary injunction |
| *Judicial precedent* | • a court decision which will act as a guide for future courts and can only be overruled by a higher court |
| *Jurisdiction* | • legal powers of a court or tribunal over particular types of disputes |
| *Law report* | • published report of court proceedings containing the court's judgment |
| *Legal aid* | • state funded scheme providing financial assistance for legal claims |
| *Legislation* | • law made by Parliament |
| *Legislature* | • formal law making body of a state in the UK Parliament |
| *Lien* | • the unpaid seller's right to keep possession of goods against payment in the event of the buyer's insolvency |

| | |
|---|---|
| *Liquidated damages* | • claim for damages where the amount being sought has been quantified |
| *Liquidation* | • corporate insolvency |
| *Liquidator* | • person responsible for managing a company winding up |
| *Litigant* | • a party involved in civil proceedings |
| *Member* | • a company shareholder |
| *Memorandum of Association* | • constitutional document of a company establishing its name, objectives and capital structure |
| *Mens rea* | • 'guilty mind', state of mind required for a criminal offence |
| *Misrepresentation* | • remedy available to a person induced into making a contract by a false statement |
| *Mobility clause* | • a term in a contract of employment which authorises the employer to transfer the employee from one workplace to another |
| *Mutual termination* | • a contractual agreement to terminate a contract of employment |
| *Negligence* | • a legal claim for damages based upon the plaintiff establishing that the defendant has caused loss by breach of a duty of care |
| *Offer* | • an unequivocal undertaking to be bound by an acceptance |
| *Official receiver* | • an officer attached to al courts with insolvency jurisdiction, employed by the DTI and responsible for insolvency matters |
| *Parol contract* | • oral contract |
| *Partnership* | • an unicorporated business association often referred to as a 'firm' |
| *Passing off* | • a legal action in tort available where a business represents its goods or services as those of another business |
| *Persuasive precedent* | • a precedent which a court does not have to follow but should take account of in reaching its decision |
| *Plaintiff* | • person or organisation bringing a civil action |
| *Price variation clause* | • an express term of a contract which allows one of the parties to change the price in certain circumstances after the contract has been concluded |
| *Prima facie case* | • "on the face of it" a case to answer |
| *Principal* | • person who appoints an agent to act on his behalf for the purpose of making contracts |

| | |
|---|---|
| *Private company* | • registered company prohibited from selling its shares to the public |
| *Product liability* | • legal basis upon which a person who suffers harm as a result of a defective product can be compensated |
| *Prohibition notice* | • a statutory notice served on a trader requiring him to stop trading in unsafe goods of a particular description |
| *Prohibition notice* | • an order served by a health and safety inspector requiring that an activity that contravenes safety law should be terminated |
| *Promoter* | • someone involved in setting up a company |
| *Property* | • ownership |
| *Property misdescription* | • expression used to describe the making of false misleading statements by estate agents |
| *Prospectus* | • document providing information to the public about a company which is offering its shares |
| *Protected goods* | • statutory protection granted to debtors under consumer credit agreements |
| *Public company* | • registered company able to sell its securities publicly |
| *Public policy* | • concept guiding judicial decision making based on consideration of the public interest |
| *Punitive damages* | • damages awarded to punish the defendant for the losses caused |
| *Quantum meruit* | • 'as much as he has deserved' |
| *Quoted company* | • company whose securities are traded on the Stock Exchange |
| *Race discrimination* | • discrimination based upon colour, race, nationality, or ethnic or national origin |
| *Receiver* | • person appointed to take control of specified property of a company |
| *Reckless statement* | • a statement made regardless of whether it is true or false |
| *Redundancy situation* | • an employer's requirement for workers of a particular kind have ceased or diminished |
| *Re-engagement* | • to re-employ an employee following a dismissal in the same or similar job |
| *Registered company* | • a corporate body formed under the registration procedures of the Companies Act 1985 |

| | |
|---|---|
| *Reinstatement* | • to re-employ an employee following a dismissal and treat him as if there had been no dismissal |
| *Representation* | • statement which induces the making of a contract |
| *Repudiatory breach* | • a serious breach of contract which allows the innocent party to accept the breach and regard the contract terminated |
| *Rescind* | • to annul or cancel for instance a contract |
| *Respondent* | • an individual defending a complaint before a tribunal or the party |
| *Restitutio in integrum* | • returning everything to the state as it was before |
| *Retention of title clause* | • an express term of a contract under which the seller retains the ownership of goods until certain conditions, such as full payment, have been met |
| *Rights issue* | • an issue of new shares offered first to existing shareholders |
| *Risk assessment* | • a comprehensive survey of organisational, job, workplace and individual factors that affect health and safety at work |
| *Sale of goods* | • a contract involving the exchange of the ownership of goods in return for money |
| *Satisfactory quality* | • statutory standard of quality demanded of goods sold by a seller in the course of business |
| *Securities* | • investments in a company |
| *Sexual harassment* | • conduct of a sexual nature that is unwanted, unreasonable and offensive to the recipient |
| *Shareholder* | • person holding shares in a company who enjoys all the rights attached to the shares |
| *Shares* | • a unit of company capital which a member can own |
| *Solicitor* | • lawyer who is a general practitioner of the law and who has limited rights of audience to represent a client in court proceedings |
| *Specific goods* | • goods which have been identified and agreed upon at the time the contract is made |
| *Specific performance* | • equitable remedy under which the court orders a contracting party to carry out their promises |
| *Statute* | • an Act of Parliament |

| | |
|---|---|
| *Strict liability* | • liability imposed without fault |
| *Summary dismissal* | • instant dismissal without notice |
| *Balance of probabilities* | • standard of proof, "more likely than not" |
| *Tort* | • a civil wrong, the remedy for which is an award of damages |
| *Trade descriptions* | • descriptions applied to goods or services by business sellers |
| *Transfer of risk* | • the passing over from the seller to the buyer the risk of accidental loss or damage to goods |
| *Trust and confidence* | • implied term in a contract of employment signifying mutual respect |
| *Uberrimae fidei* | • a state of utmost good faith |
| *Ultra vires* | • legal doctrine expressing the proposition that corporate bodies cannot act outside their powers |
| *Unascertained goods* | • goods which have been generally described but not specifically identified or singled out at the time the contract is made |
| *Undue influence* | • unlawful pressure put on someone when they make a contract |
| *Unfair dismissal* | • dismissal without good reason contrary to statute |
| *Unilateral action* | • an act done by one party only |
| *Unliquidated damages* | • claim for damages where the amount is not quantified |
| *Vicarious liability* | • legal liability imposed upon one person for the unlawful act of another |
| *Victimisation* | • less favourable treatment because a person has given evidence or brought proceedings under the discrimination legislation |
| *Warranties* | • minor terms which if broken enable only a claim for damages to be brought |
| *Winding up* | • process by which registered company is brought to an end |
| *Working environment* | • arrangements of a workplace including physical and psychological conditions of work |
| *Wrongful dismissal* | • dismissal in a wrongful manner by contravening notice requirements |

# Chapter 1

## The Legal System

## The Legal Framework

The principal objective of a legal system is the establishment of rules designed in the broadest sense to regulate relationships. Human societies are highly complex social structures. Without systems of rules or codes of conduct to control them, such societies have difficulty in maintaining their cohesion, and gradually break up. The interdependence of each member of a community with its other members creates a continuous interaction between individuals and groups and this contact inevitably can lead to occasional disagreement and conflict. In a Western culture like ours, which recognises that people should have the freedom to express their individualism, the realisation of that freedom can result in the infringement of the rights of others. Someone operating a commercial enterprise by selling second hand cars in the street outside his house, or building an extension, or holding regular all night parties may treat these activities as the exercise of basic personal freedoms. They will however give rise to conflict if neighbours resent the street being turned into a used vehicle lot, or find the light to their windows and gardens cut out by the new building, or that they cannot sleep at night for noise. Where interests conflict in this way the law attempts to reconcile differences by referring their solution to established principles and rules which have been developed to clarify individual rights and obligations. The relationships between neighbours are but a small part of the complex pattern of relationships most people are involved in and which the law attempts to regulate.

## Moral Rules

However the law is not the sole binding agent of our social structure. It is not only legal rules which are responsible for guaranteeing social cohesion. Institutions which create legal rules are merely one facet of the wider institutional structure of our society. Political, economic, commercial, cultural and religious institutions are amongst those located in the broader social fabric and which contribute to what we term our *society*. Their contribution also includes the development of rules. Schools and religious institutions for instance recognise a responsibility for the teaching of ethics and morality, and this reminds us that we should not assume rule making to be the sole prerogative of the law. The rules and codes of conduct developed from our sense of moral justice and our perceptions of fairness and unfairness are important determinants of our behaviour. Like legal rules, moral rules guide our conduct and inform us how we should behave in given circumstances. Rules of this kind are described as *normative*. They indicate how we ought to conduct ourselves.

A major difference between legal and moral rules is seen in the sanctions which apply if they are broken. Breach of legal rules carries a potential formal sanction, proceedings before a court followed by a court order. Breaching the moral code does not of itself trigger any formal consequence; we may however feel personally discredited by how we have behaved and find that others who are aware of our conduct avoid or criticise us. So it may be that our neighbour keeps the noise down at night motivated more by a sense of what is fair and reasonable than through any concern over legal sanctions.

In business, ethical considerations also play a role in informing organisational behaviour, although usually in a more diluted form, for the personality of the individuals making up the organisation has a tendency to be subsumed within the personality of the organisation itself. Cynics may argue that businesses which appear to be guided by ethical standards in their business dealings are simply recognising the value of goodwill and cost of legal sanctions and are thus, in effect, protecting their profits. It has also been argued that businesses are keen to self regulate as a way of avoiding the imposition of legal controls which take away their freedom of action by determining their behaviour for them.

## The Business Environment

Our study of these legal rules is of course constrained by the particular field of law we are concerned with, the law applying to the business environment, and a book devoted to a study of this kind focuses specifically on the legal relationships that are a product of business activity and the legal rules which have developed in response to it. Essentially businesses are provider organisations, selling goods and services to anyone who requires them. The customers of a business are usually referred to as consumers. They may be other businesses themselves, but they also include of course individuals, *ultimate consumers*, who use the goods and services for their own private benefit. Examining the business world in any detail reveals far more complex legal relationships than the simple neighbour example given above. We discover an environment in which a richly  diverse range of transactions are constantly performed; where resources of labour, capital, and land are being acquired and disposed of, various forms of property are being bought and sold, information and advice is given and sought, and decisions are regularly being made which have an impact on the owners, managers and customers of the organisations with which they are associated. In short we are seeing a sophisticated market economy conducting its operations.

At first glance the business environment may appear to have little relevance to anyone other than those who are directly associated with it, such as business managers. In practice the impact of business is experienced by everyone. We can see this when we consider ourselves in our role as consumers, that is as users of products and services. Whether we are buying clothes, household goods, holidays, shares, having the car repaired, opening a bank account, taking a job or renting a flat we participate in a business relationship. It does not always have to be a formal matter, and usually will not be. But all these activities are carried on within a legal framework which attempts to set out the responsibilities and obligations of the participants.

Business organisations sit at the centre of a web of relationships which have a strong legal dimension to them. For instance, a business may take decisions on the basis of expert advice provided by a professional advisor in return for payment of a fee or charge. Inaccurate or incomplete advice relied upon by the business may cause it to suffer commercial damage. If this occurs the business may have a legal remedy against the advisor, and will seek to recover any losses it has sustained. Similarly, within the organisation legal relationships exist between managers, owners and staff. Thus, to take one example, directors of a limited company are accountable to the shareholders in general meeting, and can be dismissed from their office by a company resolution in circumstances where they have been guilty of commercial incompetence or malpractice. Exploring the law as it applies to business thus involves examining the legal framework within which all businesses, from the multinational corporations to the one member businesses, pursue their commercial objectives. We have noted that this framework has to do with the relationships their business activity creates, but what are the purposes which underpin legal intervention in business affairs?

## The Purpose of a System of Business Law

Complex, affluent, property owning societies develop detailed and sophisticated rules to regulate themselves, and in the United Kingdom as in most modern states almost every aspect of human activity is either directly or indirectly affected by law. These laws seek to achieve different purposes. One major classification in any legal system involves distinguishing between those legal rules which are concerned with private rights and obligations, a branch of law referred to as *civil* law, and those whose primary purpose is the welfare of society generally, and its protection by means of rules that seek to prevent anti-social forms of behaviour, supported by the power to punish those who break them. This is the *criminal* law.

Legal rules in the field of business are designed to fulfil certain primary purposes. These include the remedying of private grievances, the control of anti-social activities and the regulation of harmful activities.

## The remedying of private grievances

Various branches of law are concerned with recognising personal rights which can be enforced by means of legal proceedings if they are infringed, or where there is a threat to infringe them. One of these branches is the law of *tort*. It is based upon the existence of a set of obligations referred to as *torts*, or civil wrongs, which have been evolved by the courts as a response to the need for established codes of conduct to protect people from certain types of harm. Tortious obligations are imposed by law, rather than arising by agreement between the parties as is the case with contractual obligations. In effect the law of tort recognises specific legal rights, which entitle anyone for whom those rights have been infringed to sue the wrongdoer for compensation. The most significant civil wrong is the tort of negligence which can provide a remedy when an individual suffers harm as a result of the *fault* of another.

The law of contract is a further example of a branch of law dealing in private rights and obligations. Contractual agreements involve the making of promises which are legally enforceable. A party to a contract therefore has the right to take legal action against the other party to the agreement in the event of that person being in breach of his contractual obligations. We will examine the principles of the law of contract in Chapter 2.

Both the law of contract and the law of tort are crucial to the effective functioning of the business environment. Without the ability to enter into binding agreements businesses would be left fully exposed to the risk of their transactions being unilaterally terminated by the other contracting party. Such vulnerability would seriously undermine business confidence and would hamper economic activity generally, and without the ability to seek compensation and redress for wrongs committed against them businesses could suffer significant economic harm. Consider for instance a situation where a small under-insured business could obtain no compensation following the total destruction of its stock and premises due to negligent repair work carried out to an adjoining gas main by the gas company, or where a supplier of goods has delivered them only to find that the buyer refuses to pay for them.

## The control of anti-social activities

This is essentially the task of the criminal law. Whilst it is not possible to prevent crimes from being committed, the presence of penal sanctions, such as imprisonment and fines, which are used to support the criminal code, can act as a deterrent to the commission of an offence.

There is no adequate definition of a crime. Lord Diplock in *Knuller v. Director of Public Prosecutions* 1972 attempted to pin-point the essential differences between civil and criminal law when he said, *"Civil liability is concerned with the relationship of one citizen to another; criminal liability is concerned with the relationship of a citizen to society organised as a state."*

Businesses, like individuals, are subject to the criminal law. Of the wide range of offences that an organisation might commit in the course of its business, the following provide some illustrations:

- offences in the field of consumer protection. These are many and varied. They include offences connected with false trade descriptions applied to goods and services, consumer credit arrangements such as engaging in activities requiring a licence but where no licence has been granted, and safety obligations for certain manufactured items, for instance oil heaters and electric blankets, which must meet standards laid down under government regulations; (considered in Chapter 3)

- offences in the field of employment, such as a contravention of the obligations owed to employees under health and safety legislation; (considered in Chapter 5)

- offences connected with the operation of registered companies, such as failure to file accounts or the insertion of untrue statements in a prospectus; (considered in Chapter 4)

- offences in relation to tax liability, such as the making of false returns.

Enforcement of the criminal code is a duty imposed upon a range of agencies. The *Crown Prosecution Service* (the CPS), set up in 1985, is responsible for the prosecution of all criminal offences which have resulted from police investigations. Investigation of potential liability in certain specific fields of the criminal law, and the bringing of prosecutions where appropriate, is placed in the hands of specialised agencies. *Trading Standards Officers* employed by local authorities are responsible for investigation and prosecution of that part of the criminal code dealing with consumer protection, the *Health and Safety Executive* through its inspectorate, deals with criminal aspects of health and safety law, and the *Department of Trade and Industry* has the task of investigating breaches of company legislation where criminal offences are involved. These agencies investigate complaints made to them. They also rely on inspection as a method of systemised investigation.

## The regulation of harmful activities

Methods of legal regulation include licensing, registration and inspection. These are useful mechanisms for exercising effective control over a range of activities, which, if uncontrolled, could be physically, economically and socially harmful. As we have noted above powers of inspection, supported by enforcement mechanisms, are granted to factory inspectors working for the Health and Safety Executive. The inspection of work places such as factories and building sites enables inspectors to ascertain whether safety legislation is being complied with, and that employees' physical requirements are thus being met. Certain types of trading practices which are potentially anti-competitive can only be pursued legitimately if the agreements in which they are contained are registered with the Director General of Fair Trading, under the Restrictive Trade Practices Act 1976. Even then they are only legally permissible if they are approved by the Restrictive Trade Practices Court. Additionally anyone in the business of providing credit facilities is obliged to register under the Consumer Credit Act 1974 with the Director General of Fair Trading before being legally permitted to lend money. The aim is to eliminate unscrupulous finance dealers from the credit market, overcoming the social problems which arise when poorer members of society borrow at high rates of interest which they are unable to afford, often in an effort to extricate themselves from other debts. And in cases of alleged malpractice in the management of registered companies the Department of Trade and Industry has the power to carry out investigations into the affairs of companies, for instance to establish the true ownership of shares in a company.

## The Importance of Law to Business

The legal system affects businesses and individuals alike. Every aspect of business life, from formation and operation to dissolution, occurs within an environment of legal regulation. We have seen that many purposes are being pursued in applying legal regulation to business activity. In broad terms the underlying characteristics of business law may be seen as the dual aims of:

(a)    providing a practical and comprehensive framework of legal rules and principles to assist the organisation in its commercial affairs; whilst at the same time

(b)    ensuring a sufficient level of protection for the legitimate interests of those who come into direct contact with it. This includes not only members of the public in their capacity as consumers, but also business creditors and the employees and owners of business enterprises.

There appears to be one fundamental and compelling reason why business organisations are likely to seek to comply with the law. If they fail to do so it will cost them money, either directly or indirectly. A business which is in breach of law, whether the civil law or the criminal law, will in most cases suffer from the breach commercially.

The commercial consequences to an organisation which has been found to have broken or otherwise failed to comply with the law includes the possibility of:

- an action for damages against the business, brought by someone seeking financial compensation from it. Such an action may be the result of a breach of contract committed by the business, or be in respect of some form of tortious liability it has incurred. An alternative claim brought against it could be for an injunction restraining it from pursuing a particular course of action;

- a claim that the action of the business is devoid of legal effect because it has failed to follow procedures which bind it. For instance, a limited company cannot act unless it has correctly followed the registration procedures laid down by statute, and has received a certificate of incorporation. Nor can it alter its own constitution, its memorandum and articles of association, unless this is done in accordance with relevant statutory procedures regarding notice periods, the holding of a meeting and the need to secure an appropriate majority of votes cast;

- the loss of an opportunity to take some form of legal action, because the time limit for doing so has passed, for instance bringing a late appeal against an unfavourable planning decision;

- a prosecution brought against it alleging breach of the criminal law, resulting in a fine, or in certain circumstances the seizure of assets;

- the exercise of enforcement action against it for its failure to comply with some legal requirement, for example to take steps to remedy a serious hazard to health, as a result of which its business operations are suspended;

- the bringing of a petition to have the organisation brought to an end. A registered company can for example be wound up compulsorily by its unpaid creditors.

As most commercial enterprises are profit maximisers these outcomes can be seen as interfering in the pursuit of basic organisational aims.

Thus at an organisation level there are sound commercial reasons for keeping properly informed about the law and complying with it as it affects business, apart from any moral or social responsibility for acting within the law. Moreover, legal proceedings often attract public attention and result in adverse publicity to the organisations involved. At a personal level individuals engaged in managing a business may find themselves dismissed and facing civil and/or criminal liability if they are responsible for serious errors of judgment which carry legal consequences, such as negligent or dishonest performance in handling a company's financial affairs.

## Developing Legal Knowledge and Skills

Usually it is not possible for people in business to find the time to develop the skills to cope with all the legal demands of operating a business, however there will remain sound reasons for acquiring at least a basic level of legal knowledge and skills and devoting some time to legal issues as and when they arise. This is because:

- many straightforward legal problems can be resolved simply by means of a letter or a telephone call to the other party involved. Legal advice has to be paid for, and in some situations will be both an unnecessary expense, and a time consuming activity;

- certain legal problems require immediate action, for example, what rights the employer has to dismiss an employee against whom an allegation of sexual misconduct has been made; or what rights a buyer has to reject goods delivered late by the seller;

- the daily routine of a business involves frequent encounters with matters of a legal nature, such as examining contracts, signing cheques, health and safety, negotiating deals and organising the workforce. It would be impractical to seek professional advice regularly in these routine areas;

- many business activities are closely legally regulated, and a working knowledge of them is essential if the business is to function effectively. For example a business providing credit facilities needs to employ staff who are fully aware of the strict legal requirements regulating such transactions;

- when expert advice and assistance is being sought the effectiveness of the process of consultation is assisted if the precise issues can be identified from the outset, and relevant records and materials can be presented at the time. In addition, when the advice is given it will be of little value in the possession of someone who can make no real sense of it;

- managing a business effectively demands a working knowledge of the legal implications not only of what is being decided, but also of the processes by which it is decided. For instance company directors ought to be familiar with the basic principles of the law of company meetings, since it is by means of such meetings that important decision making is achieved.

# Law Making Institutions

Until the 1st January 1973 English law was created by two, separate, law making institutions, the courts and Parliament. However in 1973 the United Kingdom became a member of the European Economic Community, the effect of which in legal terms was to introduce a new, third, law making source. The impact of this fundamental change has been considerable, even though there are many areas of activity which remain outside the jurisdiction of the law making bodies of the European Union (EU). Business operations however fall squarely within the remit of the work of the European Union.

To acquire a proper understanding of the law it is necessary to consider the work of the law makers, and examine the methods by which they create law. In an historical context it was the courts which laid down the original foundations of our law, and so it is appropriate to consider their law making role before examining the contribution of Parliament and the European Union as law makers.

## The Courts of England and Wales

For the purpose of the administration of justice in England and Wales two separate court structures exist, one dealing with civil law matters and the other criminal matters. Some courts exercise both a civil and criminal jurisdiction. An example is provided by the Magistrates courts, which are primarily criminal courts but which also exercise a limited but nevertheless important civil jurisdiction in family matters.

An appeals structure gives the parties involved in any form of legal proceedings the opportunity to appeal against the decision of the trial court on points of law or fact. The trial court is the court in which the case is first tried, and in which evidence is given on oath to the court by witnesses appearing for the parties involved, to enable the court to establish for the purposes of the case the relevant material facts. The court in which a case is first tried is known as a court of *first instance*. Usually *leave to appeal* must be granted either by the trial court or the appellate court although certain appeals are available as of right.

## The Civil Courts

In a civil court an action is commenced by a *plaintiff* (now a claimant) who sues the other party, called the *defendant*. If either party takes the case before a higher court on appeal that party is known as the *appellant* and the other as the *respondent*.

Before commencing proceedings the plaintiff must decide whether the case is worth bringing. This is likely to involve a number of considerations including costs, time, the complexity of the action, and the resources of the defendant. In 1999 new procedures are being introduced to promote early settlement of cases and where possible direct cases from the courts towards cheaper and quicker resolutions. The main thrust of the reforms is to encourage greater openness between opponents and require lawyers to follow agreed steps from the moment a claim is envisaged. The aim is to reduce spiralling costs and delays in legal action. Judges as trial managers will be required to set strict timetables for cases and ensure that deadlines are met. In an attempt to make administration of justice more understandable to the layman, new terminology has also been introduced for example:

- a *plaintiff* is now a *claimant*;

- a *High court writ* is now a *claim form*;

- *minors* are now called *children*;

- witnesses are no longer *subpoenaed* but *summoned*;

- *pleadings* are replaced by a *statement of claim*.

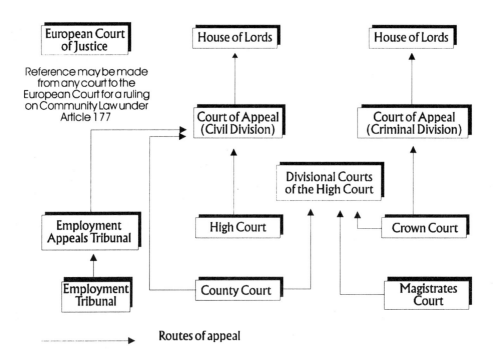

**Figure 1.1**  *Civil and Criminal Courts structure in England and Wales, including Employment Tribunals*

# Small Claims Arbitration

For the purpose of determining small claims, that is those claims not exceeding £8,000, rules made under the County Courts Act 1984 require that the matter must be referred to the arbitration procedure operated by the County Courts. In brief this provides for a relatively informal method for considering the claim, which will usually be heard before a district judge (previously known as a Registrar) rather than a circuit judge, the title given to the senior judge attached to the Court. Although the parties may be legally represented they must normally pay for their own lawyers' fees themselves, whatever the outcome of the case. This is sometimes referred to as the *no costs* regime. Thus a successful plaintiff cannot recover from the defendant the costs of being legally represented.

Most claims can be dealt with under the arbitration procedure if the claim can be quantified in financial terms, and it is not considered that the factual issues are too complex or the point or points of law too difficult. If they are the case is referred to a full trial. A claim for more than £8,000 may be reduced by the party bringing the action to keep the matter within the arbitration procedure. A claim in excess of £8,000 can only be heard within the procedure if both parties agree. The loser will usually bear the costs of the action. This is not the case where the claim is within the £8,000 limit. A sting in the tail for plaintiffs who successfully bring a county court claim estimated as in excess of £8,000, but which is found to be within the small claims jurisdiction, is that such plaintiffs may find that they are not awarded their costs.

# Law Making by the Courts

The two major domestic sources of law making are the courts and the legislature. Whereas the legislature creates law through the introduction of statutes, the law making role of the courts is quite different. Parliament enjoys a virtually unlimited lawmaking capacity. The courts on the other hand are subject to significant restrictions in their role as lawmakers. This is entirely proper since the courts are manned by members of the judiciary, the judges, who are neither elected by the public to this office nor are accountable to the public for the way in which they discharge their responsibilities.

The primary role of the courts, and the various tribunals which supplement the courts system, is the resolution of legal disputes which are brought before them. This process has a history dating back to Norman times.

In order to resolve a dispute it is necessary to have a reference point; some identifiable rule or principle which can be applied in order to solve the problem. One approach is simply to treat each case on its own merits, but such a system would hardly be just for decisions would turn on the character of the individual judge, whose values, prejudices, qualities of analysis and reasoning power would dominate the decision making process. Such a system would be unpredictable and capricious. English law, in common with other law making systems, adopted an approach that sought to achieve a level of certainty and consistency. It did this by means of a process referred to as *stare decisis*, literally *standing by the decision*. Today we talk of the doctrine of judicial precedent. Under the doctrine of judicial precedent, the successor to the stare decisis system, judges when deciding cases must take into account relevant precedents, that is earlier cases based upon materially similar sets of facts. Whether a court is bound to follow an earlier case of a similar kind can be a matter of considerable complexity, however the general rule is that the decisions of higher courts are binding on lower courts within the hierarchical courts structure seen. This structure can be seen in Figure 1.1.

English law became enshrined in the precedent system, and much of our modern law is still found in the decisions of the courts arrived at by resolving the cases brought before them. Not surprisingly this body of law is referred to as case law. It is these cases, or precedents, which make up the contents of the law reports, the published reports of court proceedings containing the judgment given in the case. The bulk of the law of contract and the law of tort is judge made law, or, as it is more usually known, the common law.

In addition to developing and refining the common law, the judges in modern times have played an increasingly important role in the task of interpreting and applying statutory provisions.

## The meaning of common law

In its modern usage the expression common law has come to mean law other than that contained in statutory provisions. Common law in this sense means judge made law embodied in case decisions. However, the expression common law is also sometimes used to describe, in a broader sense, the *type* of legal system that operates in England and Wales, a system which has been adopted by countries all over the world and especially those in the Commonwealth.

The common law of England dates back to the Norman Conquest and has its origins in the decisions of the royal judges who attempted to develop and apply principles of law *common* to the whole country. This they did by modifying and adapting rules of Norman law, and rules contained in Saxon local custom. The development of the common law has involved an evolutionary process extending over hundreds of years. Through the process England and Wales was rewarded with a unified and coherent body of law which remains the foundation upon which significant areas of our law, such as the law of contract and tort are based.

## The judgment of the court

Whatever the nature of a case coming before a court the most vital legal aspect of the legal proceedings comes at the end of the trial when judgment is delivered. Whereas certain parts of the judgment will be binding for the future, other parts of the judgment will have merely persuasive authority whenever the case is considered by a future court. These ideas need further explanation.

When a decision is reached on a dispute before a superior court, such as the High Court, Court of Appeal or House of Lords, the judges will announce their decision by making speeches known as judgments. Within a judgment, the judges will refer to numerous matters, such as the relevant legal principles which are drawn from existing cases or statutes, a review of the facts of the case, their opinion on the relevant law, their actual decision and the reasons for it. For the parties to an action, the matter they are most concerned with is the actual decision, that is who has won the case. The main issue of relevance to the law, however, is the reason for the decision. This is known as the *ratio decidendi* of the case (the reason for deciding). The *ratio* expresses the underlying legal principle relied on in reaching the decision and it is this which constitutes the binding precedent. As we have seen this means that if a lower court in a later case is faced with a similar dispute it will in general be bound to apply the earlier *ratio decidendi*.

All other matters referred to in a judgment are termed *obiter dicta* (things said by the way). The *obiter* forms persuasive precedent and may be taken into account by a court in a later similar case, however the court is not bound to follow it.

The decision of the House of Lords in *Smith v. Stages and Another* 1989 illustrates the distinction between *ratio* and *obiter*. In this case it was necessary to determine the extent to which an employer may be made liable for the actions of an employee, and in particular when an employee can be said to be acting in the course of his employment. The action was brought on behalf of an employee, who as a passenger in the defendant's car, suffered personal injuries as a result of the negligent driving of the defendant, a fellow employee. Despite the fact that the employers neither required nor authorised the journey by car to and from their particular workplace they were joined as second defendants on a claim that they were vicariously liable for the driver's negligence. The House of Lords held that here the employers were vicariously liable for the employee's negligent driving. The court decided that employees who are required to travel to and from non regular workplaces, and are in receipt of wages for doing so, remain within the course of their employment, even if they have a choice as to the mode and time of travel. This statement forms the *ratio* of the judgment and is binding on a lower court if faced with a similar factual situation.

In the course of the judgment however a number of suggestions were made by the House of Lords in relation to the question as to when an employee is acting in the course of his employment during travelling time. The receipt of wages would indicate that an employee was travelling in his employer's time, and acting in the course of his employment. Equally so would an employee travelling in the employer's time between different workplaces. An employee travelling in his employer's time from his ordinary residence to a workplace, other than his regular workplace, to the scene of an emergency such as a fire, accident or mechanical breakdown of plant, would also be acting in the course of his employment. Deviations or interruptions of a journey undertaken in the course of employment unless merely incidental would normally take an employee outside the course of his employment. All of these suggestions are *obiter dicta,* persuasive authority which may or may not be followed by a lower court dealing with a similar case.

A court with suitable jurisdiction has the power to declare the decision in a previous case no longer good law. This can be done when there is evidence that the previous court did not accurately interpret the law, or when the later court is of the view that the ratio of the earlier case is no longer sustainable or desirable. Where overruling takes place, the case which has been overruled is considered 'bad law' and does not have to be followed by the present court or any future court.

Reversing occurs when an appeal court overturns the decision of the court below it from which the appeal came. If the appeal court agrees with the lower court's decision it is said to affirm it.

# Statute

Within the United Kingdom the primary source of law is made by Parliament in the form of Statutes. Statutes or Acts of Parliament are also referred to as legislation and in the fields of commercial, company and employment law there are numerous examples of major statutes that contain the ever fundamental rules. The Sale of Goods Act 1979, the Trade Descriptions Act 1968, The Supply of Goods and Services Act 1982, the Consumer Protection Act 1987 and the Data Protection Act 1998 all contain provisions conferring rights on consumers in commercial transactions. The Employment Rights Act 1996 and the Employment Relations Act 1999 confer rights on employees and the Companies Act 1985 contains the rules relating to the formation and operation of companies. These statutes are explored in Chapters 3, 4 and 5.

While primary legislation is a major source of law, many statutes contemplate further law making by means of delegated legislation. Numerous Statutory Instruments contain a multitude of regulations which have the force of law, and provide a convenient means of amending previous statutory provisions. Under the umbrella of the Health and Safety at Work etc. Act 1974 the Secretary of State for Employment is given authority on the advice of the Health and Safety Commission to make regulations on a wide range of matters. It is by this means that the previous law on health and safety at work is in the process of being replaced and refined.

Later in the chapter we will focus on how Statutory Instruments may be used to incorporate European Community legislation into the domestic law of the United Kingdom. The Unfair Terms in Consumer Contract Regulations 1994 were introduced to give effect to the 1993 European Directive on Unfair Terms in Consumer Contracts. The Transfer of Undertakings (Protection of Employment) Regulations 1981 were passed to give effect to obligations which arose under the European Directive 77/187 (the Acquired Rights Directive). Statutes and Statutory Instruments are only enacted of course after undergoing a strict parliamentary process. In addition, draft Codes of Practice require the approval of both Houses of Parliament and only come into effect on such date as the Secretary of State appoints.

Codes of Practice have an increasingly important role in the regulation of employment relationships and industrial relations generally. Their primary function is to provide guidance to employers, employers' associations, workers, and trade unions with the aim of improving industrial relations. While a failure to observe the provision of a code of practice does not of itself make a person liable to legal proceedings before a court or tribunal, compliance or non compliance with a code is admissible in evidence.

When a dispute comes before a court it is the task of the court to hear the evidence, identify the relevant law and apply it. The legal principles which the court has to apply may be common law principles. Often however they will be principles, or rules, which are contained in statutes. Where this is so, the court has to ascertain the meaning of the statute in order to apply it, and sometimes this can cause problems for a court because it discovers that the language of the statute is not entirely clear. The courts take the view that their responsibility is to discern Parliament's will or intention from the legislation under consideration.

## Statutory Interpretation

In relation to statutes the primary role of the courts and tribunals is to apply the legal rules within them to conflict situations. Inevitably this function involves interpreting the meaning of particular legal rules and so setting precedents which provide guidance to future courts and tribunals as to how these rules should be applied. The task of the courts in interpreting statutory provisions is to attempt to discover Parliament's intention and this should be achieved primarily by examining the specific words of the statute.

An example of a statutory provision may help to illustrate this judicial function. In the Employment Rights Act 1996 there are numerous provisions which confer rights on employees. In particular if a qualified employee believes that he has been dismissed without good reason he may under section 111 present a complaint of unfair dismissal against his employer before an Employment Tribunal. The Act provides however that there are strict time limits to be complied with, otherwise the right to present a complaint will be lost.

Section 111(2) of the Act states that .... *"an employment tribunal shall not consider a complaint under this section unless it is presented to the tribunal before the end of the period of three months beginning with the effective date of termination or within such further period as the tribunal considers reasonable in a case where it is satisfied that it was not reasonably practicable for the complaint to be presented before the end of the period of three months."*

The legal rule is stating therefore, in relatively straightforward terms, that if a dismissed employee wants to complain of unfair dismissal before an Industrial Tribunal he must start the proceedings within three months, but if he fails to do so the tribunal still has a discretion to hear the case if it was not reasonably practicable for him to present it within the time limit. If a legal dispute arises over whether an unfair dismissal claim has been presented within the time limits it is the function of the courts and tribunals to attempt to resolve the conflict by applying the exact wording of s.111(2) to the factual situation before it. The subsection requires the Industrial Tribunal therefore to ask itself one or possibly two questions:

1.    Has the complaint been brought within the three months time limit prescribed in the section?

2.    If not, was it reasonably practicable to present the complaint within the time limit?

If the answer to the first question is no and the answer to the second question is yes then the tribunal should not proceed to hear the complaint of unfair dismissal. If the reverse is true however and either the complaint is within the time limits or it was not reasonably practicable to present it in time then the tribunal does have jurisdiction to proceed.

There are many case decisions which over the years have provided guidance to Industrial Tribunals as to the approach to be adopted in addressing these questions.

If a tribunal decide that the complaint was not presented within the time period it would still proceed to hear it if it was not reasonably practicable to present the complaint in time. Parliament has left it to the courts and tribunals therefore to determine the issue of reasonable practicability in any given case. Reasons for late claims brought before tribunals have included postal delays, bad advice from lawyers or civil servants, and obstructive employers. Case decisions made in relation to these reasons provide guidance and in some cases lay down precedents for future cases.

To summarise therefore it is possible to say that the law on time limits for presenting a complaint of unfair dismissal is most certainly contained within s.111(2) of the Employment Rights Act 1996 but also as interpreted in the numerous decisions of our courts and Industrial Tribunals.

# European Community Law

The United Kingdom has been a member of the European Community since January 1st 1973. Currently the European Union has fifteen member states, with a population of 370 million, which form a single economic region in which goods, services, people and capital can move almost as freely as they do within national boundaries.

As a Member State of the European Community the United Kingdom is bound by Community Law. In the field of business this is of enormous significance because the European Community is essentially economic in nature, and the community objective of the completion of a single European market is based upon the actual harmonisation of laws relating to business and trade between Member States.

Inevitably therefore there are significant examples of measures which have been adopted and implemented by the UK government as a consequence of European legislation. Examples can be seen in the fields of:

- company law harmonisation and investor protection;

- consumer rights and consumer protection;

- data protection;

- environmental protection;

- intellectual property rights;

- employment law.

In each of these fields European law has been active in amending and adding to existing UK law, as well as requiring the introduction of new law. For example in employment law the Community has been active in the following areas:

- pregnancy dismissals and maternity leave;

- statutory rights for part-time workers;

- collective redundancy procedures;

- dismissals and detrimental conduct relating to health and safety;

- acquired rights on a business transfer;

- health and safety at work regulations;

- sex discrimination and equal pay.

The framework of Community law is set out in the Treaty of Rome 1957 as amended by the Single European Act of 1986 and the Treaty of European Union signed at Maastricht in 1992. The institutions of the Community must operate within and give effect to these Treaties.

The Treaty on European Union which was negotiated in Maastricht in November 1991 came into effect at the beginning of November 1993, after completing the difficult process of ratification in each of the member states.

The Treaty creates a European Union which has three main elements, often described as *pillars*. The first is the European Community itself, the powers and decision making procedures of which are extended and modified. The second element relates to foreign and security policy, and the third to justice and home affairs.

We are concerned only with the first pillar of the Treaty which provides for closer European integration within the framework of Community law. This part of the Treaty expands the areas of Community activity. Under the Treaty the task of the European Community will be to promote a harmonious and balanced development of economic activities, sustainable and non-inflationary growth respecting the environment, a high degree of convergence of economic performance, a high level of employment and of social protection, the raising of the standard of living and quality of life, and economic and social cohesion and solidarity.

The UK, however, negotiated to opt out of two important parts of the Treaty, the *Social Chapter* and the third stage of economic and monetary union which is the adoption of a single currency. The remainder of the Treaty applies with full effect to the UK and the Labour Government is committed to adopting its Social Chapter and potentially monetary union following a referendum.

It is clear that under the European treaties the Community has power to legislate over a very broad range of issues which embrace the entire area of business law. It is in practice by far the most important source of new law in this sphere. It should also be appreciated, however, that there are areas of legal regulation which remain exclusively within the domain of national law making powers. These include, for example, major parts of the criminal law, control over the direct taxation of income, family law, the law of inheritance and numerous other important fields of law.

## Types of Community Law

The major sources of Community law are *primary* legislation found in the treaties establishing and developing the EC; *secondary* legislation made on an ongoing basis by the Community institutions; judgments of the Court of Justice and unwritten general principles of law. In relation to treaty provisions and secondary legislation it is useful to distinguish between the concepts of *direct applicability* and *direct effect.*

A Community law is said to be directly applicable when it is of a type which is directly incorporated in its entirety into the laws of the members states without the need for further legislative or administrative action on the part of the member state or the Community institutions. Such rules create immediate rights and obligations as between individuals and or organisations and as against member states. These rights or obligations are directly enforceable in the ordinary courts within the member states. EC regulations are directly enforceable in the ordinary courts of member states.

A Community law which is not directly applicable may nonetheless have direct effects in terms of conferring rights upon individuals which may be enforced in the domestic courts. Such provisions usually will not have direct applicability because they are not self-contained, in the sense that they require some action, usually by the member state, in order to implement them. Typically this will apply where directives have not been implemented in full or at all, and the deadline for implementation has passed. In these circumstances the directive may produce direct effect provided it is sufficiently clear, unconditional and precise. One significant limitation on the doctrine of direct effect is that directives are only directly effective as against the state.

## Primary Legislation

The primary legislation of the European Community is the European Treaties. It is these Treaties that set out the framework of Community law, and create the institutions:

* The Commission

- The Council of Ministers of the European Union

- The European Parliament

- The Court of Justice

The European Treaties also lay down procedures for making secondary legislation on an ongoing basis.

Whilst certain provisions in the treaties lay down broad or vague policies which need to be fleshed out in secondary legislation, the Court of Justice has held that others can be directly applicable. Article 119 of the Treaty of Rome, for example, provides that *"Each member state shall ... maintain the application of the principle that men and women receive equal pay for equal work"*.

> In *Barber v. Guardian Royal Exchange* 1990 the Court of Justice applied article 119 in its decision that occupational pension schemes, as opposed to state retirement pension, and the benefits conferred under them on employees, are pay for the purpose of article 119. It is therefore unlawful to discriminate between men and women in relation to them. Mr Barber claimed to be entitled to benefit under his company pension scheme on the same basis as female employees and objected to the fact that he could not receive benefits under the scheme until he reached the age of 65 whereas his female counterparts could benefit at 60. The Court of Justice's decision in his favour caused major changes in many occupational pension schemes to give effect to the equalisation of pension ages and benefits as between men and women.

Many articles of the Treaty have been held to be directly effective, including, for example, article 12 prohibiting member states from introducing new customs duties on imports or exports from other member states, and articles 85 and 86 prohibiting anti-competitive practices.

## Secondary legislation

The Treaties confer significant law making powers on the Institutions of the Community. These powers are limited in that they extend only to areas where the Community has competence to legislate. There are some areas which remain within the exclusive domain of the national sovereignty of the member states. As we have seen, however, the Community's law making competence extents to virtually all aspects of business law.

Under Article 189 of the Treaty of Rome the Council and the Commission can make regulations, directives and decisions.

A regulation has general application. It is binding in its entirety and directly applicable in all member states. Regulations are the equivalent of UK statutes on a community scale. They apply to everyone in all fifteen member states and there is no requirement for action at a national level to bring them into effect.

## Directives

A directive shall be binding, as to the result to be achieved, upon each member state to which it is addressed but shall leave to the national authorities the choice of form and methods. Directives are the major instrument for achieving the harmonisation of national laws as between the member states. They operate by setting out the objectives which the proposed new laws must achieve, giving a time limit within which member state governments must achieve them. The resulting law will be in the form of a domestic law within the member state. In the UK directives are implemented either by a new Act of Parliament or by delegated legislation. There are many examples of directives and their implementation throughout this text, notably in such areas as consumer protection, employment rights and health and safety at work.

## Decisions

A *decision* is binding in its entirety upon those to whom it is addressed. They may be addressed to a member state, a business or other organisation or an individual. There is no discretion as to the manner of implementation, and decisions take effect upon notification.

## Recommendations and opinions

*Recommendations* and *opinions* are not legally binding or enforceable. They are often addressed to member states and may give a view on a particular matter or set out guidelines to be followed in relation to an issue, sometimes with the implication that if they are not followed proposals for a stronger type of Community law may be made at a later date.

# The Resolution of Business Disputes

While the High Court has an important role to play in hearing civil disputes concerning large sums of money the vast majority of civil legal actions which go to court are dealt with at County Court level. Changes in the jurisdiction of the County Courts, has increased their workload by passing over to them cases which previously would have been heard before the High Court.

Not all civil disputes however are resolved by means of court proceedings. Many cases are dealt with instead before tribunals. The workload of tribunals has been steadily increasing. Collectively tribunals now handle in the region of six times more work than the High Court and County Court combined. One important field in which they are used is in the handling of employment disputes. These are heard before Employment Tribunals.

We begin by looking at the organisations and individuals who are available to assist those with a legal problem.

# Sources of Legal Advice and Information

Many sources of legal advice and information are available to a consumer or a trader who has a legal problem. He may be able to research it himself by looking at law books in a library, but more usually he will seek outside help. If the trader is a member of a trade or professional association it is probable that he will be able to obtain legal guidance from such a body, particularly if the question is one which is closely associated with the operation or regulation of his business.

In relation to legal enquiries of a general nature, the Citizen's Advice Bureau (CAB) may be able to point a consumer in the right direction, or provide the information which he requires. In addition, there are a number of law centres which provide a similar, though more specialist, role in giving legal advice and acting on behalf of clients. Law centres, however, tend to deal with legal problems arising in relation to social issues such as housing, immigration, consumer and employee rights. They do not usually take on the role of advising businessmen in relation to commercial matters.

## Lawyers

The most obvious source of advice and legal information is the solicitor. Larger business organisations may have their own legal department or in-house solicitor to provide a comprehensive legal service for the business. These permanently employed lawyers will deal with such matters as conveyancing, drawing up contracts, registering intellectual property rights, advising management on day to day legal matters, designing procedures to ensure compliance by the business with its legal requirements and conducting litigation on its behalf.

Smaller business organisations cannot usually justify the expense of a legal department and will use *solicitors* in private practice to deal with their legal affairs. Solicitors are the general practitioners of the law, although within any particular firm individual solicitors will usually specialise in one or two areas of law. If a businessman refers a legal problem to solicitor and the solicitor requires further specialist help or advice in order to deal with it, the solicitor can obtain the opinion of a *barrister*. The barrister, or counsel, usually specialises in a much narrower field of law than the solicitor. A businessman cannot approach a barrister directly for legal help but must first use a solicitor. The solicitor can refer the matter to a barrister if he feels that it is necessary. The main functions of the barrister are to provide legal opinions, to draw pleadings in preparation for litigation, and to act as an advocate in court. A solicitor cannot always act as an advocate without a barrister because the solicitor has only limited rights of audience before the courts. He is allowed to appear before a Magistrates Court, a County Court and, in certain circumstances, a Crown Court without a barrister. He is unable to appear in the High Court or any of the appeal courts and must use a barrister if he intends to conduct a case in one of these courts.

Communications between a client and a solicitor or barrister are subject to legal professional privilege. This means that the lawyer is duty bound not to disclose the communication to any other party without the authority of the client. In practice the effect of legal professional privilege is that the client can disclose all of the information which is relevant to his legal problem without fear that the information may be used against him at some later stage. The purpose of the rule is to ensure that the client does not hold back information which might be relevant to the legal problem which has arisen. This allows the lawyer to have all of the facts and to make a proper decision as to the course of action which is in the client's best interests.

In July 1995 *conditional fee arrangements*, often referred to as no win no fee arrangements became available for personal injury, insolvency and human rights cases. If the case is won solicitors can charge a success fee of up to double their normal fee. This is to compensate for the risk of not being paid if they lose. The amount of the success fee is reflected by the degree of risk involved. Should the case be lost the plaintiff, under conditional fee arrangements, will have no liability for his own solicitors costs but is still potentially liable for his opponent's costs. This risk for prospective plaintiffs can and should be covered by after-the-event insurance. The Law Society has developed and approved an insurance package called Accident Line Protect, designed to be used in conjunction with conditional fees. At the cost of £85 this insurance cover is however only available where the solicitors are members of the *Law Society's Accident Line Scheme so* guaranteeing that they are experts in personal injury work .The Law Society recommend that the conditional fee charged should not in any event exceed 25% of the damage recovered. There is no doubt that through this scheme many more accident victims particularly those at the workplace, have been encouraged to seek and obtain legal redress, when otherwise they would have been discouraged to do so because of the risk of substantial legal costs. One notable case commenced in September 1996 under conditional fee arrangements was personal injury claim brought against the tobacco industry. Here solicitors had been prepared to accept the risk of an estimated two million pounds in costs in proceedings which are expected to take years to get to court.

# Bringing a Claim Before an Employment Tribunal

Tribunals are an alternative method to the courts used to handle certain types of specific disputes. In general they tend to be quicker, less formal and therefore cheaper than the ordinary courts. The vast majority of individual employment rights and duties are legally enforceable by means of presenting a complaint before an Industrial Tribunal. Originating under the Industrial Training Act 1964 with only a restricted function, the Employment Tribunal is now the focus for dealing with statutory employment law disputes. Employment Tribunals have a wide jurisdiction extending to unfair dismissal, redundancy, wage deductions, discrimination and numerous other statutory employment rights (see Chapter 5). The Industrial Tribunals (Extensions of Jurisdiction) (England and Wales) Order 1994 provides that Tribunals may also determine wrongful dismissal claims which previously were exclusively heard in the County Court. The Tribunal is composed of three members, a legally qualified chairman and two lay members, one of whom is usually a nominee of an employer's organisation, and the other the nominee of a trade union.

Its role has been described as acting as that of "an industrial jury". As such it is the final arbiter on questions of fact. While the aim of conferring jurisdiction on a Tribunal is to encourage decision-making which is both inexpensive and speedy, the reality is that there has been increasing legal complexity introduced into Tribunal proceedings.

It is of crucial importance that a complainant to an Employment Tribunal presents the claim within the appropriate time limits. In a complaint involving unfair dismissal the claim must be presented within three months of the effective date of the termination of employment. The Employment Tribunal does have a discretion to allow an application out of time where it was not reasonably practicable to present it before the end of the three month period.

One of the functions of ACAS is in relation to conciliation when a complaint is presented alleging that a statutory right has been infringed. The role of a conciliation officer in an unfair dismissal claim for instance, is to endeavour to promote a settlement of the complaint without the dispute having to go before an Employment Tribunal. The officer is required to promote a settlement if requested to do so by either party or if he feels that he could act with a reasonable prospect of success. The Employment Rights (Dispute Resolution) Act 1998 encourages the use of internal procedures and voluntary arbitration developed by ACAS. Either party may apply for a *pre-hearing review* to take place, or the Tribunal may arrange an review in the absence of an application. The pre-hearing review is carried out by the

Tribunal Chairman examining the papers, assessing the strength of the claim and deciding whether the respondent's defence has any merit.

An appeal from the Employment Tribunal on a question of law or a mixed question of law and fact with usually lie to the Employment Appeal Tribunal. The President of the EAT will be a High Court judge or a Lord Justice of Appeal who will normally sit with two lay members drawn from a panel of persons who have proven industrial relations experience. The time limit for submitting an appeal from a Tribunal decision is 42 days and this involves submitting a notice of appeal together with the reasons for it and a copy of the Tribunal decision. Appeal from the decision of the EAT lies to the ordinary courts, namely the Court of Appeal and from there, in rare cases, an appeal lies to the House of Lords.

The Employment Appeal Tribunal in *East Berkshire Health Authority v. Matadeen* 1992 attempted to resolve the uncertainty in relation to the power of the EAT to overturn a decision of the Industrial Tribunal. The EAT held that it can allow an appeal against the Tribunal decision if:

- there is an error of law on the face of the decision; or

- there is a material finding of fact relied upon by the tribunal which is unsupported by the evidence; or

- there is a finding that the Tribunal's decision is perverse.

An error of law involves a misinterpretation or misapplication of the law. An unsupported finding of fact involves a misunderstanding of the evidence before the Tribunal. Perversity is reaching a decision which is not a permissible option for it is *"a conclusion which offends reason or is one to which no reasonable Industrial Tribunal could reach"*. The EAT cannot therefore simply overturn a Tribunal decision with which it disagrees or substitute its own views of fairness or reasonableness for that of the Employment Tribunal. The role of the Tribunal as the final arbiter on questions of fact is best illustrated in relation to dealing with complaints of unfair dismissal.

# Chapter 2

## The Principles of Contract Law

### Introduction

This chapter explores the law of contract. It begins with an examination of the background to contract making, then goes on to consider how a contract is set up. It concludes by looking at the main legal principles which apply to contracts once they have been created, in particular how a contract may be broken or declared invalid, and what the legal consequences are if this should happen.

### The Idea of the Contract

#### Why a law of contract?

The idea of the contract owes its existence to a concept which is central to economics, that of the market. Market activity, the interaction of buyers and sellers of goods and services, has origins going back to the early civilisations and the emergence of the first forms of trading activity within and between societies. One of the conditions necessary for trade to function effectively is the existence within the market place of a code of trading behaviour which provides a framework of rules within which trading parties can transact and to which they are willing to adhere. Without such a framework trading anarchy would prevail, and such a condition would be too uncertain and unstable a climate for individuals and businesses to make investment decisions and financial commitments. In a market free for all where no remedy is obtainable to repair a broken bargain few would have the confidence to trade. The contract has developed as a legal mechanism to provide a formalised set of rules of trading. Modern contract law has increasingly reflected a significant social dimension also. Examples we shall come across later include the limitations placed upon excluding certain types of contractual liability, and the rights of consumers injured as a result of defective manufactured goods, but there are many others. The objectives of social justice can also be seen reflected in the various rights granted to employees within the contract of employment.

The law of contract may thus be regarded in broad terms as a set of rules and principles which:

- provide a legal framework offering a measure of trading security to anyone engaging in the process of buying and selling;

- seek to achieve a measure of social justice by restricting activities which are seen as unfair or harmfu';

- identify and control economic practices which are regarded as contrary to the public interest;

- establish the technical means by which parties who wish to make legally enforceable transactions can do so.

## A Definition of Contract

A contract is simply a legally enforceable agreement. As it stands this is not a definition which takes us very far, for it raises further questions. We need to establish what the components are of an agreement, and what conditions have to be satisfied in order that an agreement can become legally recognised. Making an agreement does not automatically result in the making of a contract, for there are many other factors that are taken into account before a contract can materialise. For instance the parties to the agreement must have the legal capacity to contract, and there must be evidence that they intend their transaction to be legally binding.

An agreement which does not achieve contractual status will, in consequence, contain undertakings which the parties have exchanged with each other that do not bind them in a legal sense. Non-contractual agreements of this kind may still be honoured by the parties making them out of a sense of moral or social obligation. The observance of rules and principles is frequently based upon a sense of duty or responsibility and does not always have to be underpinned by legal sanctions to be carried out. When friends agree to meet in town in the evening for a drink it is unlikely the law would see the arrangement as legally binding. We would nevertheless expect them to honour their arrangement because they will not want to let each other down, and break their promises.

## Contractual Liability

Whenever a contract is made it produces contractual liabilities. The content of such liabilities depends upon the substance of the contract in question, but all contractual liabilities are based upon a simple common element. They involve people entering into agreements consisting of legally enforceable promises exchanged between them. Such promises may be simple or complex; they may be single promises or sets of promises. But in whatever form they emerge contractual promises give rise to contractual liabilities. The result is that if a promise of this kind is not carried out, or is carried out improperly, a legal obligation has been broken and the injured party may choose to seek a remedy from the contract breaker before the courts.

## The Concept of Freedom of Contract

Contracting parties have never enjoyed unlimited freedom to make whatever deal they choose. No court, for example has ever been prepared to enforce a contract whose purpose is unlawful, such as an agreement to commit a criminal offence. But how interventionist should the law be?

Eighteenth and nineteenth century capitalists philosophy advocated a *laissez-faire* economic approach, leaving the markets for goods and services, as far as reasonably practicable, to regulate themselves. The idea of a free market, left to control itself unhindered by the interventions of the courts or Parliament, found its legal expression in the concept of *freedom of contract*. The advocates of freedom of contract considered that as few restrictions as possible should be placed upon the liberty of individuals to make agreements. The Master of the Rolls, Sir George Jessel, expressed it in the following way in 1875: *"If there is one thing which more than any other public policy requires it is that men of full age and understanding shall have the utmost liberty of contracting and their contracts when entered into freely and voluntarily shall be held sacred and shall be enforced by the courts of justice."*

There are compelling reasons for allowing a wide measure of contractual freedom, for example:

- *market needs:*

  in the interests of healthy markets the participants in market activity should be allowed to trade unhindered. The able will survive and the weak will flounder. External intervention in this process will tend to weaken rather than strengthen economic performance by the artificial distortion of the bargaining process;

- *personal liberty:*

  interference in contract making is an infringement of individual liberty. In the same way that a person chooses when to marry, or for whom to vote, they should be free to negotiate their own bargains. The contract is a private, not a public event;

- *knowledge:*

  it should be assumed that contracting parties act in a rational manner so that the contract they make is the contract they want. Nobody else is better placed to identify contractual wants and needs than the parties themselves.

Closer analysis, however, suggests these factors reflect more a theoretical ideal than the reality of modern contract making. This is most strikingly apparent when we look at the role of consent in contract making.

## The Role of Consent in Contract Making

In a sense we enjoy complete contractual freedom, for individuals and organisations alike are free to choose whether or not to enter into a contractual relationship. It cannot be forced on them for consent is a precondition of the relationship. But what precisely does consent mean? To answer this question we need to examine how the courts discriminate between those situations where consent is regarded as genuine, and those in which the consent is in reality artificial. Where the consent given to an agreement is not genuine consent there is said to be no *consensus ad idem,* or meeting of the minds of the parties. Circumstances in which the courts will be prepared to consider a claim that the consent is unreal are in cases of misrepresentation, mistake, fraud, duress and undue influence. They are referred to technically as *vitiating elements.* Once established they have the effect of either invalidating the contract in its entirety, in which case the contract is said to be *void,* or of entitling the injured party to escape from the contract if he or she wishes to do so. In such circumstances the contract is said to be *voidable* in the injured parties favour. To vitiate literally means to make invalid or ineffectual.

The presence of a vitiating factor in an agreement can defeat the entire contract. By granting relief where consent is a sham because a person has been misled, tricked, coerced or mistaken, the courts are demonstrating that they will look at what the parties believed they were agreeing to when the contract was made. Equally of course, the notion of freedom carries with it responsibility. It is not the role of the courts to repair bad bargains made through lack of prudence. The balance between intervening in an attempt to right legitimate wrongs, whilst leaving the parties to learn from their trading mistakes is not easily achieved. The point is that the courts are prepared in appropriate cases to untie the bond that has been made, thereby protecting parties in a limited way from the consequences that complete freedom of contract would otherwise produce.

## Bargaining Inequality

An equally important element in exploding the myth of freedom of contract is the issue of bargaining strength. True consensus is only possible where parties meet as bargaining equals. In practice such equality is generally elusive; the commercial reality is an inequality of bargaining power where one party is able to dominate the other. The result is that far from arriving at agreement through a process of negotiation, the contract is a one sided arrangement in which the dominant party presents terms to the weaker party on a take-it-or-leave it basis. Commonly the dominant party will only be prepared to do business on the basis of standard terms designed to provide it with a high level of commercial protection. If the dominant party is a monopoly supplier, like a railway company, the consumer is unable to shop around for a better deal or a different set of terms. Even in a reasonably competitive market suppliers of goods or services trade invariably on the same or very similar terms, for instance by using a contract designed by the trade association of which they are a member. Contracts arising in this way are sometimes referred to as contracts of *adhesion*, for the weaker party is required to adhere all the terms imposed by the stronger party.

## Legal Intervention in the Market Place

To help overcome market place imbalances Parliament and the courts have been prepared to intervene in appropriate circumstances, to produce a kind of externally manipulated commercial justice. Parliament has for example legislated to strengthen the rights of *consumers*, business consumers as well as individuals. The range of legislative measures which seek to create a more level playing field for contracting parties is now very extensive. They are considered later in the book, but the most notable examples are the Consumer Credit Act 1974, the Unfair Contract Terms Act 1977, and Sale of Goods Act 1979, the Supply of Goods and Services Act 1982 and the Consumer Protection Act 1987. Parliament has also sought to protect the interests of *employees*. The major statutory employment rights are found in the Employment Rights Act 1996.

In addition the courts have been prepared to intervene in circumstances of exceptional exploitation, drawing on an equitable principle known as *undue influence*.

> This is well illustrated by the decision of the Court of Appeal in *Lloyds Bank Ltd. v. Bundy* 1975. Here an elderly farmer, who was ill and had little business knowledge, agreed with the bank to guarantee the account of his son's company. The company was in difficulties, and over a period of time the father increased the size of the guarantee, which was secured by a

mortgage on his house, so that eventually the mortgage on the property was for more than the property was worth. This arrangement had been made by the father in consultation with the bank manager, upon whom he implicitly relied. The company's debts remained outstanding, and the bank sought to sell the father's house in order to realise the guarantee. The Court of Appeal unanimously set aside the agreement between the father and the bank, Lord Denning MR observing that: *"no bargain will be upset which is the result of the ordinary interplay of forces. There are many hard cases which are caught by this rule ... yet there are exceptions to this general rule ... in which the courts will set aside a contract, when the parties have not met on equal terms, when the one is so strong in bargaining power and the other so weak that, as a matter of common fairness, it is not right that the strong should be allowed to push the weak to the wall .... English law gives relief to one who, without independent advice, enters into a contract on terms which are very unfair..."*

However the mere fact that one party is weaker than the other is not enough, in itself, to escape the contract. The agreement must be unconscionable to obtain equitable relief. In *Barclays Bank plc v. Schwarz* 1995 the defendant, the principal director of a number of property companies, argued before the Court of Appeal that he was not liable to make good debts of over £1/2 m which his companies owed the bank. He had signed personal guarantees in favour of the bank regarding these debts. His defence was his poor understanding of English, something the bank was aware of, and that the bank should have explained to him the nature of the documents he was signing. The court rejected these arguments, finding that his weakness in the English language was not a sufficient ground to set aside the guarantees. Illiteracy was not a defence. Simon Brown LJ was not convinced that a man with a number of property companies could argue that *"his understanding of the ... English language, and the nuts and bolts of ordinary commercial life, was so deficient that he could thereby escape the consequences of signing routine legal instruments."*

There are many other examples of market interventions which parliament and courts have introduced and which are not included here. What is certainly clear is that the practice of responding to perceived market inadequacies or injustices by judicial or legislative activity is not a process that is yet complete. New examples continue to emerge. A recent illustration is the Late Payment of Commercial Debts (Interest) Act 1998, a measure introduced to give effect to the Governments desire to grant a statutory right for businesses to interest on late payment of debts. The Act grants the rights to interest payments on certain commercial debts, without the need to establish that a contract term provides for this, and without the need to have brought legal proceedings in respect of such debts.

# The Form of the Contract

At common law no restriction is placed upon the way in which a contract can be expressed. The parties are free to make the contract orally, or in writing, or if they wish by using a combination of these methods. In appropriate cases a contract can even be inferred from the conduct of the parties. The term *simple* contract, suggesting a transaction that does not have to meet special technicalities of form, is therefore used to describe such arrangements.

It is a commonly held view, although an entirely erroneous one, that written evidence of the transaction is essential if a contract is to be valid. In fact the only circumstances in which writing is a legal requirement occur where Parliament demands it. Allowing oral contracts is based upon practicalities. For most transactions written agreements would be cumbersome, time consuming, and most unnecessary. However there are good reasons for expressing a contract in writing. In particular:

(a)    the writing will stand as evidence of the transaction, should anyone challenge its existence, and

(b)    the task of reducing the agreement into writing is likely to help the parties focus more precisely on what each is promising the other, in other words the terms or obligations that have been agreed between them. Most of the simple contracts we make regularly as individual consumers are oral agreements; buying food, petrol, a record or tape, clothes and so on. The existence of a contract may also be *inferred* when the facts support it.

There is however a type of contract which is expressed in very formal terms. This is the *deed*, sometimes referred to as a speciality contract. Under the Law of Property (Miscellaneous Provisions) Act 1989 a deed must be contained in writing, and be signed by the parties making it, with their signatures being witnessed.

There are relatively few circumstances in which the law demands a deed to give effect to a contract. Under the Law of Property Act 1925 a deed is required to transfer legal ownership in land from one party to another, and to create a lease of more than three years duration.

## Contracts Where Writing is Necessary

Certain contracts are required by statute to be made in writing. In some cases, the objective is to protect the consumer by requiring a clear statement of rights and responsibilities under the contract to be contained in the written agreement. In others it is required to oblige parties involved in technical transactions, particularly those involving non-tangible property such as shares and copyright, to formally record the making and content of the transaction.

The most important examples include:

(a)    hire purchase and conditional sale agreements. Under s.65(1) of the Consumer Credit Act 1974 such agreements cannot been enforced unless they are properly executed. This occurs when a legible document containing all the express terms of the agreement and in the prescribed form is signed by the parties;

(b)    the transfer of shares in a registered company, a requirement under s.183 Companies Act 1985, which states that a *"proper instrument of transfer"* must be delivered to the company. The company cannot register the transfer until this is done;

(c)    an assignment of copyright, under s.90 Copyright Designs and Patents Act 1988;

(d)    cheques, bills of exchange and promissory notes, under the Bills of Exchange Act 1882; and

(e)    contracts for the sale or other disposition of land under the Law of Property (Miscellaneous Provisions) Act 1989. S2(1) of the Act provides that, *"a contract for the sale or other disposition of an interest in land can only be made in writing and only by incorporating all the terms which the parties have expressly agreed in the document or, where contracts are exchanged, in each."* S2(3) provides that, *"the document incorporating the terms... must be signed by or on behalf of each party to the contract."*

Failure to comply with the any of these statutory requirements renders the contract *invalid*.

Other than for merchant seaman and apprentices, there is no legal requirement that a *contract of employment* be in writing. Given the fluid nature of a contract of employment there is no guarantee that a requirement to reduce the original contract to writing would solve all the problems of interpreting its content.

Under s.1 of the Employment Rights Act 1996 there is however a statutory requirement on employers to provide their employees within eight weeks of the commencement of employment with a written statement of the main terms and conditions of employment.

## Test Questions

1.   What is the purpose of a contract?

2.   Provide a simple definition of a contract.

3.   Distinguish between a void contract and a voidable contract.

4.   Why is it in the public interest to allow freedom of contract?

5.   How does Parliament assist the weaker party to a contract?

6.   Give two reasons for expressing a contract in writing.

7.   Give five examples of contracts where writing is necessary.

## Making a Contract

We have seen that a contract is a legally enforceable agreement. But what exactly is an agreement, and what is needed for an agreement to become legally enforceable?

## Agreement

A contract cannot occur without an agreement, and so the idea of agreement is central to an understanding of the law of contract. Agreements are undertakings to do, or sometimes refrain from doing, specific things.

Perhaps most people can rely on instinct or common sense to assess whether they have an agreement or not, but for legal purposes it is not sufficient to rely upon subjective judgments to decide events of such significance. If a disputed agreement comes before a court, obviously the court cannot get inside the minds of the parties to discover their actual intentions. At best it can look at the way they have conducted themselves, examining what they have said and what they have done, in order to decide the matter on the basis of what a reasonable person would assume their intentions to be.

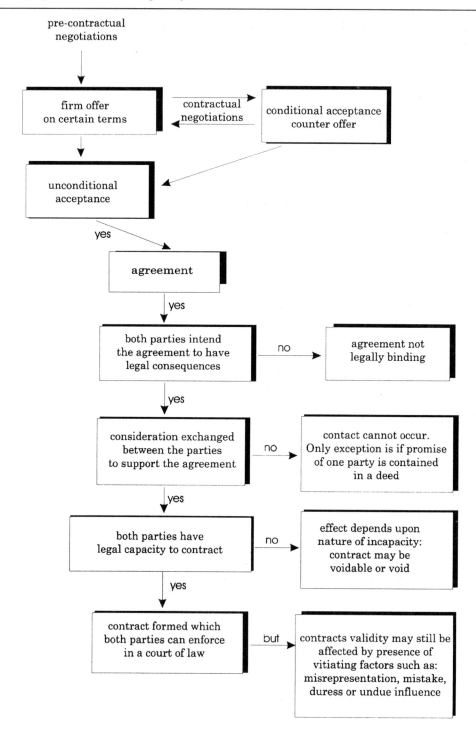

**Figure 2.1** *Elements in the formation of contract*

An agreement contains two elements:

(i)     an *offer*, made by one party to the other; and

(ii)    an *acceptance* by the other of the terms contained in the offer.

If a court cannot identify the presence of these two components in a transaction, a simple contract cannot arise.

## The process of negotiation

The person making an offer is referred to as the *offeror*, and the person to whom it is addressed the *offeree*. In business the parties usually reach agreement following a period of negotiation. Negotiations will focus the details of the proposed transaction, and include such matters as price, specifications concerning the subject matter of the agreement, and the time and place for performing it. Often during these negotiations offers will be made by one party to the other which are rejected, or met by a fresh offer. Either of the parties to the transaction is able to make an offer, not just the one who wishes to sell the goods or services in question or who is the owner or supplier of them.

Examining the negotiating process is important for many reasons. For instance it enables us to identify which party made the final offer, and thus the terms upon which the offer was based and hence which make up the terms of the; in addition during negotiations false statements may sometimes made by one of the parties which induce the other to enter into the contract. These are referred to as *misrepresentations*, and are actionable.

## Characteristics of a Valid Offer

To be legally effective an offer must satisfy the following general requirements:

*   it must be firmly made;

*   it must be communicated;

*   its terms must be certain; and

*   it must not have terminated.

## Firm offer or invitation to treat

The offeror must intend the offer to be unequivocal, so that when acceptance occurs he will be bound. It is sometimes difficult to distinguish firm offers from statements which do not carry the full legal status of offers. What appears to be a firm offer may merely be an incentive or encouragement designed by the person making it to encourage the making of offers to him and not intended to be legally binding. A statement of this kind is known as an *invitation to treat*. It is an indication that the person is willing to do business with anyone who is interested.

> In *Pharmaceutical Society of Great Britain v. Boots Cash Chemists (Southern) Ltd.* 1953 one of the shops in the company's chain had been converted into a self-service supermarket. Some of the shelves carried poisons which by statute were required to be sold in the presence of a qualified chemist. The chemist was in attendance at the checkout. The Pharmaceutical Society, which had a duty to enforce the statutory provisions, claimed that the company was in breach of them. The Society argued that the contract was made at the shelves where there was no pharmacist in attendance. The court however held that the goods displayed on the shelves were merely invitations to treat. The contract was made at the checkout. The customers made the offer when presenting the goods for payment and the offer was accepted by the cashier passing them through the checkout.

> Advertisements are also generally regarded as constituting invitations to treat. In *Partridge v. Crittenden* 1968 the Divisional Court of the Queens Bench Division was asked to determine whether an advertisement in a magazine which read, *"Bramblefinch cocks, bramblefinch hens 25/- each"*, constituted the offence of offering to sell wild birds contrary to the Protection of Birds Act 1954. The court quashed the conviction against the defendant which had been issued in the Magistrates Court. The advertisement was simply an encouragement to stimulate the market into making offers. Members of the public responding to the advert made the offers, but of course they could not commit an offence since they were offering to buy, not to sell. The defendant should have been charged with the separate offence contained in the Act of selling wild birds.

> In *British Car Auctions Ltd. v. Wright* 1972, an unroadworthy car had been sold at auction. The auctioneers were convicted in the Magistrates Court of offering to sell an unroadworthy vehicle, contrary to the Road Traffic Act 1972. In quashing the conviction Widgery LCJ stated: *"The auctioneer when he stands on his rostrum does not make an offer to sell the goods on behalf of the vendor; he stands there making an invitation to those present at the auction themselves to make offers to buy"*.

Further examples of the invitation to treat are advertisements inviting suppliers of goods and services to submit tenders, and prospectuses issued by limited companies inviting members of the public to subscribe for shares.

## Tenders

The use of tenders is a common commercial practice. Indeed local authorities are required by the Local Government Act 1972 to contract in this way. Under the tendering process a tender is an offer and an invitation to tender is an invitation to treat. It is merely an invitation by an individual or organisation wishing to purchase goods or services to request suppliers to submit a contractual offer in the form of a tender.

In appropriate circumstances an invitation to tender can give rise to a binding contractual obligation. If there is clear evidence from what the parties have said and done that a contractual obligation to consider a particular tender in conjunction with all other tenders meeting the tendering requirements was intended, the court will enforce it.

> In *Blackpool and Fylde Aero Club v. Blackpool Borough Council* 1990 the local authority owned and managed an airport. The plaintiff flying club had for some years operated pleasure flights from the airport. When the grant of the club's concession came up for renewal the council prepared invitations to tender. These were then sent to the club and six other parties. The forms sent out stated that the council did not bind itself, *"to accept all or any part of any tender"*. The form added, *"No tender which is received after the last date and time specified shall be admitted for consideration."*

The plaintiffs delivered their tender to the council offices before the deadline, however because council staff failed to empty the council letter box when they should have done the council received the tender too late to be considered, and accepted a tender from another tenderer lower in value than the plaintiff's tender. The club sued for damages alleging breach of contract and negligence. The court held that although contracts in such circumstances should not be freely implied, the evidence here was of a clear intention that the council was contractually obliged to consider the plaintiff's tender with the other tenders, or at least that it would be considered if all the others were. The claim for breach of contract was successful.

An invitation to treat is not however devoid of legal effect. It can give rise to legal liability in the following ways:

- as a statement it can amount to an actionable misrepresentation (see later); and

- it may also give rise to criminal liability under the Trade Descriptions Act 1968, if it constitutes a false trade description, or under the Consumer Protection Act 1987 if it gives a false or misleading indication as to the price of goods or services.

## Communicating the offer

The party to whom an offer is directed must be aware of it. Although an offer will normally be made to a single individual or organisation, there is nothing to prevent an offer being directed to a specific group of individuals, anyone or more of whom may choose to accept it. For instance a private limited company that is going public may offer some of its shares at favourable rates to the members of its workforce.

It is possible to make an offer to the public generally, without at the time being able to identify who all the possible recipients may be. One of the most celebrated instances of an offer made to the public at large, occurred in *Carlill v. Carbolic Smokeball Co.* 1893 which is considered below.

What constitutes communication is a question of fact for the court. Letters, telephone calls, voice mail messages, faxes and emails are all recognised methods of communication.

## Certainty of terms

If the parties disagree about the meaning of a term it will ultimately fall to the court to decide the question. The courts always endeavour to find certainty but a term which is obscure or meaningless will fail. This will not prove fatal to the contract if the term constitutes only a minor part of the overall obligations, but an uncertain term that is central to the functioning of the contract, will inevitably defeat the contract as a whole.

In *Loftus v. Roberts* 1902 an agreement provided for the appointment of an actress by another person at a *"West End salary to be mutually agreed between us."* Subsequently the parties were unable to arrive at a salary which satisfied them both. The court held that the contract must fail. Even if it were possible to assess a suitable salary by reference to West End rates of pay, the court could not impose such a figure since the parties had already stated that it had to be mutually agreed, something they had been unable to achieve. What they had was an agreement to agree at a further date. The contract failed.

In *Scammel v. Ouston* 1941 an agreement for the sale of a van where the balance of the price was to be met *"on hire purchase terms over a period of two years"* also failed. Since there was no previous course of dealing between the parties to enable the court to identify what these "hire purchase" terms might be, the only alternative would have been to treat the terms as standard hire purchase terms. Unfortunately, as the court observed, hire purchase terms are not standardised and identical, but vary from agreement to agreement, for example by charging different rates of interest.

A meaningless term can however often be ignored.

In *Nicolene Ltd. v. Simmonds* 1953 a contract was made for the sale of 3000 tons of steel bars. The seller later broke the contract. When the buyer sued for damages the seller argued there was no contract between them, relying on a statement in one of the contractual documents that, *"we are in agreement that the usual conditions of acceptance apply"*. The court, whilst recognising that there are no *"usual conditions of acceptance"*, found that the contract was in every other respect clear as to the obligations of the parties. The meaningless term could be cut out from the rest of the contract. In the course of his judgment Lord Denning MR commented that, *"A clause which is meaningless can often be ignored . . .; whereas a clause which has yet to be agreed may mean there is no contract at all."*

Some issues of uncertainty are overcome by statutory mechanisms. S.8 Sale of Goods Act 1979 is an example. It provides that if a contract for goods the parties have not agreed a price, the buyer is bound to pay a *reasonable* price (usually the going market price).

Sometimes the contract will have a mechanism which can be used to fix the price, or indeed resolve any other aspect of uncertainty.

In *Sykes (F & G) Wessex v. Fine Fare* 1967 a supplier of chickens undertook to supply a supermarket chain with between 30,000 and 80,000 birds each week over a period of one year. The agreement also provided that for a further four years the supplier would provide chickens in quantities *"as might be agreed"*. The meaning of this expression subsequently led to a dispute between the parties. The court held that since the contract provided for arbitration to settle disagreements, the contract was not void on the basis of the uncertainty of the term as to quantity.

## The offer must not have terminated

If the offer has come to an end in some way before the offeree accepts it, the acceptance is ineffective for there is no longer an offer to accept. An offer will be regarded as terminated where:

(a)    the offeror has *revoked* the offer; or

(b)    it has *lapsed*; or

(c)    it has been *accepted* or met with *a counter offer*.

## Where the offeror has revoked the offer

Revoking, or withdrawing, the offer is permissible at any time before the offeree has accepted it, and the revocation can be effective even if it is not communicated directly by the offeror, provided it is communicated through some reliable channel. However, like an offer, a revocation is only effective when it is actually communicated by being brought to the attention of the offeree. The following case illustrate the point.

> In *Byrne & Co. v. Leon Van Tienhoven & Co.* 1880 an offer to sell tin plate was received by the offeree on 11 October, and immediately accepted by telegram. The offeror however had posted a revocation which the offeree received on 20 October. It was held the revocation was only effective when actually received, and was therefore too late.

Does actual receipt mean physical delivery to the business premises of the offeree or must it in addition be opened and read? In *Eagleshill Ltd. v. J Needham (Builders)Ltd.* 1972 the House of Lords suggested that it will be effective even if it has not been opened, provided that it would have been opened, *"if the ordinary course of business was followed"*.

## Where the offer has lapsed

When an offer is made it will not remain open indefinitely, but will lapse. This occurs automatically in certain circumstances, for example

- after a stated time limit for which the offer was to be held open has passed; or if there is no such time limit, after a reasonable time;

In *Ramsgate Victoria Hotel Co. Ltd. v. Montefiore* 1866 the defendant offered by letter on 8 June to buy shares in the company, and was allotted the shares on 23 November. It was held that the defendant was entitle to refuse the shares on the grounds that his offer had lapsed before the company had made the allotment. Clearly the market value of shares can fluctuate widely over a period of six months;

- if the situation on which it was based has fundamentally changed, for instance if the property which has been offered for sale has been destroyed by fire or has been stolen, before acceptance occurs;

An offeror is not obliged to keep the offer open for any particular length of time, unless a separate contract is made by the parties to achieve this. So if A is interested in buying goods from B, and B promises to hold open the offer to sell A the goods at a particular price for a fixed period of time, the promise is only binding if A has given a valuable promise in return – probably by agreeing to pay B for the benefit of the offer being kept open.

# Characteristics of a Valid Acceptance

Acceptance is defined as the unconditional assent to all the terms of the offer. It must be unequivocal.

The following points indicate how the courts determine whether an acceptance will be regarded as valid.

## It must be unconditional

Often people believe they have accepted the offer, when in fact they have made a fresh offer themselves by introducing new conditions.

An acceptance which is qualified by containing new terms constitutes a *counter offer,* and a continuation of the negotiating process. A counter offer both rejects and extinguishes an original offer.

In *Hyde v. Wrench* 1840 the defendant offered his farm to the plaintiff for £1,000. The plaintiff replied offering £950. The defendant subsequently rejected this, so the plaintiff purported to accept the original £1,000 offer. It was held that there was no contract since the original offer had been extinguished by the counter offer. Although expressed as an acceptance, it was in fact a fresh offer.

Any alteration to the terms of the offer will render the acceptance invalid, and in commercial negotiations between parties, each trading on their standard terms, the terms which apply to the contract will often be those belonging to the party who fired the last shot. This situation has become known as the *battle of the forms*.

> In *Butler Machine Tool Co. v. Ex-Cell-O Corporation (England)Ltd.* 1979 the plaintiffs offered to sell a machine tool to the defendants in a quotation. The quotation contained a price variation clause, which by means of a specific formula enabled the plaintiffs to raise the quoted price between contract and delivery if their own costs rose. The defendants ordered the goods but on their own standard terms which did not include a price variation clause. The plaintiffs, on receipt of the order form, signed and returned an acknowledgement slip contained on the order form.

> The plaintiff's costs rose considerably between contract and delivery and they sought to apply the price variation clause. The defendants disputed that it was part of the contract. The Court of Appeal treated the defendant's order as a counter offer, and the return of the acknowledgement slip as the plaintiff's acceptance, consequently the contract between them did not contain the price variation clause.

## Communicating the acceptance

The offeror is free to stipulate the method by which acceptance may be made. If no stipulation is given, anything that achieves communication will suffice; words, writing or conduct. Where it is clear that the offeror demands a particular method of acceptance then no other method will be effective. In most cases however, the offeror is likely to do little more than to give a general indication of the form of acceptance to be used. Where this occurs but the offeree adopts a different method of acceptance which is as quick or quicker than the specified method, the acceptance will be effective, since the offeror will have suffered no disadvantage.

> Consequently the Court of Appeal in *Yates Building Co. v. R J Pulleyn & Son (York)* 1976 held that an acceptance by means of ordinary post was effective, despite the offeror directing that registered post or recorded delivery should be used.

Since contractual communications require positive action silence can never amount to an effective acceptance of the offer. This holds true even if the parties have, in advance, agreed such an arrangement. For instance, if following an interview, an employer says to the interviewee that the job is his or hers if they hear nothing from the employer in the next seven days, the interviewee agrees this arrangement, and the seven days elapse without word from the employer, a binding contract will not have come into existence. What the law requires is some positive act.

> In *Felthouse v. Bindley* 1862 an uncle wrote to his nephew offering to buy the nephew's horse for £30.15s. and stating *"If I hear no more about him I shall consider the horse mine at that price"*. The nephew gave instructions to the defendant, an auctioneer, not to sell the horse as he intended it for his uncle. The defendant inadvertently sold the horse, and the uncle sued him in the tort of conversion. The court held that action must fail. Ownership in the horse had not passed from the nephew to the uncle for there was not a contract between them. Actual communication of acceptance never occurred.

There are two circumstances in which acceptance can operate without communication occurring at the same time, firstly in cases where the post is used to create the contract and secondly where the nature of the offer makes formal notification of acceptance unrealistic.

## Transactions using the post

Transactions effected by means of correspondence in the form of letters, fax's, email, invoices, quotations and share applications are obviously very common forms of commercial activity. Business organisations need to keep records of their commercial activities, and the use of written correspondence is an effective way of achieving this.

Where the post is used there is of course the period whilst the letter is in transit when the person to whom it is addressed is unaware of its contents. Whereas an offer or revocation of an offer made by post is effective only when it is received by the party to whom it is sent, in the case of an *acceptance* by post the courts have laid down a rule that the letter is effective at the time and place of posting, provided it was correctly addressed and pre-paid. This remarkable rule, which is completely at odds with he normal requirements regarding communication, applies even if the letter of acceptance is lost or destroyed in the post.

The parties are free to vary these rules if they wish to do so, and it may be prudent for an offeror to stipulate that an acceptance in writing which is posted to him shall not be effective until it is actually received. It is common to find terms in standard form business contracts to this effect, and the courts seem willing to infer a variation of the post rules whenever possible.

The post rules can produce some surprising results. In *Household Fire Insurance Co. v. Grant* 1879 the defendant applied for 100 shares in the plaintiff company. The company received his application form, and the company secretary completed and posted a letter of allotment to the defendant, and entered his name on the register of shareholders. The letter never arrived. The company later went into liquidation, and the liquidator claimed the payment outstanding on the shares from the defendant. By a majority the Court of Appeal held that the defendant was liable to pay. The shares became his when the letter of allotment was posted, even though he never received it and was therefore unaware that he had become a shareholder.

## Formal acceptance unrealistic

Sometimes the circumstances of an offer are such that the courts will regard conduct which occurs without the knowledge of the offeror as a sufficient method of acceptance. Where an offer has been made to the public at large the courts may take the view that the offeror could not possibly have expected to receive an acceptance from every person who has decided to take up the offer. This would be a commercial nonsense.

In *Carlill v. Carbolic Smokeball Co.* 1893 the defendant company advertised a medical preparation they manufactured, and claimed in the advertisement that they would pay £100 reward to anybody who contracted *"the increasing epidemic of influenza"* after purchasing and using the product as directed. The advertisement added that £1000 was deposited with the Alliance Bank *"showing our sincerity in the matter"* The plaintiff purchased the product, used it as directed, then caught influenza. She sued for her £100 reward. The court held that the advertisement constituted a firm offer intended to be legally binding since the bank deposit indicated an intention to meet claims, the offer could be made to the public at large, and acceptance of the offer in such circumstances could be implied by the conduct of those like the plaintiff, who performed the stated conditions. In consequence the company were held liable.

In *G Percy Trentham Ltd. v. Archital Luxfer Ltd.* 1993 the Court of Appeal found itself having to review the whole question of contractual agreements. The plaintiffs were the main contractors engaged in a building contract, and they had negotiated with the defendants a sub-contract under which the defendants were to supply and fit architectural furniture, such as doors and windows. The sub-contract was satisfactorily performed, but a dispute arose when the plaintiffs, who were obliged to make a penalty payment under the main contract, sought a contribution from the defendants. The defendant's response was that no contract had ever been concluded between the parties. Telephone calls had been made and letters exchanged but no discernible offer and acceptance could be identified. As a result it was not possible to determine whose standard terms of trading applied to the agreement.

The Court of Appeal held that a contract had been made between the parties. In carrying out the work the defendants had agreed to an offer from the plaintiffs. Steyn LJ took the view that the test to determine whether a contract has been formed is an objective one, and in this case one should look to *"the reasonable expectations of sensible businessmen"* rather than the *"subjective and unexpressed mental reservations of the parties."* Although the usual mechanism of contractual formation is offer and acceptance in some circumstances this is not necessary. The instant case was an example, which concerned *"a contract alleged to have come into existence during and as a result of performance."* The contract was an executed one (i.e. had been carried out) making it very difficult to argue either lack of intention to create legal relations, or invalidly based upon uncertainty of terms. *"If a contract comes into existence during and as a result of performance of the transaction,"* said his Lordship, *"it will frequently be possible to hold that the contract impliedly and retrospectively covers pre-contractual performance."*

## Test Questions

1. State the two elements of a binding agreement.

2. What are the characteristics of a valid offer?

3. Distinguish between an offer and an invitation to treat.

4. What is an invitation to tender and how can it lead to a contract?

5. Give an example of an ambiguous offer.

6. When will an offer terminate?

7. What is meant by an unconditional acceptance?

8. When is an acceptance by post legally effective?

9. What happened in *Carhill v. Carbolic Smokeball Co* 1893?

# Consideration

Under English law the simple contract has always been seen as a bargain struck between the parties. The bargain is arrived at by negotiations and concluded when a definite and certain offer has been made which has been met with an unequivocal acceptance. Millions of transactions of this kind are made each day.

Making an agreement, as we have seen, involves giving undertakings or promises. The offeror makes a promise, and indicates what the offeree must do in return. The idea of a contract as an exchange of promises is fundamental to an understanding of the simple contract.

Lawyers refer to the promises exchanged under a contract as the consideration each party is providing the other. A number of important principles of consideration exist, and which we need to examine. Of these the most fundamental is that consideration is needed to support all simple contracts, and so in any case where valid consideration has not passed between the parties the general rule is the agreement they have made will be of no legal effect.

## Consideration need not be adequate but must have some value

The word *adequate* in this context means equal to the promise given. The principle of adequacy of consideration has developed to cope with contractual disputes in which one of the parties is arguing that the contract is bad because the value of the consideration provided by the other party is not the economic equivalent of the value of the promise given in return.

The courts are not prepared to defeat an agreement merely on the grounds that one of the parties has, in effect, made a bad bargain. Bad bargains are a fact of commercial life. A deal that is struck where one of the parties has entered it in haste, or without proper enquiry, or has been swayed by convincing salesmanship, may be bitterly regretted subsequently, but it is certainly not possible in such circumstances to escape liability on the grounds that *"I gave more than I got"*. Consequently there is no relief for the business or the individual who is at the receiving end of a hard bargain.

> In *Mountford v. Scott* 1975 the defendant made an agreement with the plaintiff, granting the plaintiff an option to purchase the defendant's house for £10,000 within six months. The plaintiff paid £1 for the option, and later sought to exercise it. The value of the defendant's property had risen by this time and he refused to sell. The court was prepared to grant an order for specific performance, compelling the defendant to transfer the property for the

agreed price. It was for the defendant to fix the value of the option. Some consideration was provided and this was enough. The trial judge commented: *"It is only necessary, as I see it, that the option should have been validly created"*.

However apparently insignificant the consideration may be, as long as it has some discernible value it will be valid.

In *Chappell and Co. Ltd. v. Nestlé. Ltd* 1960 the defendants, as part of a sales promotion, offered a record at a reduced price if their chocolate bar wrappers accompanied the payment. The plaintiffs held the copyright in the record, and argued that the royalties they were entitled to should be assessed on the price of the record plus the value of the wrappers, which the defendants in fact simply threw away when they had been received. The House of Lords agreed with the plaintiffs, seeing the subsequent disposal of the wrappers as irrelevant, since each wrapper in reality represented the profit on the sale of a bar of chocolate, and was therefore part of the consideration.

Adequacy is not determined solely by economic criteria. It is enough that the promise is a promise to refrain from doing something which the promisor is legally entitled to do. It may be a promise not to take legal proceedings, or not to exercise a legal right such as a right of way. Even where the promise is related to a positive act the act may have little to do with anything capable of economic valuation, yet still be good consideration in the eyes of the law. A parent may undertake to pay a sum of money to a son or daughter in the event of them marrying, or graduating, and the marriage or graduation will be valid consideration in these circumstances.

The question of whether a forbearance will operate as adequate consideration may sometimes concern those engaged in business and commercial activity. Suppose the owner of the only retail travel agency in a small town is approached by a larger company, with a number of agencies in the area. The owner is told that in consideration of the payment of £30,000 by him to the company, it will not set up a competing business in the town. Would this be a valid agreement? In *Thorne v. Motor Trade Association* 1937 Lord Atkin, commented, *"it appears to me that if a man may lawfully, in the furtherance of business interests, do acts which will seriously injure another in his business he may also lawfully, if he is still acting in the furtherance of his business interests, invite that other to pay him a sum of money as an alternative to doing the injurious acts"*.

## Consideration must be sufficient

Consideration is treated as insufficient, and therefore incapable of supporting a contract, when it involves the promisor undertaking to do something he is already obliged to do legally. The rationale is that since the promisor is bound to carry out the promise anyway, there can be no true bargain in using performance of this promise to support another contract. Consideration is insufficient therefore in the two circumstances. The first is where the promisor has an existing contractual obligation to carry out the promise offered as consideration.

> In *Stilk v. Myrick* 1809 a promise by a ships captain to pay sailors an additional sum for working the ship on the return voyage as unenforceable, even though they had to work harder due to the desertion of two crew members. The court found that their existing contracts bound them to work the ship home in such circumstances, thus they had provided no new consideration to support the promise of extra wages.

In dramatically changed circumstances it may be possible to show a fresh contract has been negotiated.

> In *Hartley v. Ponsonby* 1857, a ships crew was so depleted that the ship was dangerous to work. In these circumstances the promise of the captain to pay extra wages was held to be enforceable.

> In *Williams v. Roffey Bros. & Nicholls (Contractors) Ltd.* 1990 the defendants had a contract with a housing association for the refurbishment of a number of flats. They subcontracted the joinery work to the plaintiff. After performing most of his obligations under the contract the plaintiff found himself in financial difficulties, for the agreed price of £20,000 was too low. The defendants were anxious for their contract with the housing association to be completed by the agreed date, since under a penalty clause they would suffer financially for late completion. The defendants met the plaintiff and agreed to pay him an additional £10,300 for completion of the joinery work. He then carried out most of the remaining work, but refused to finish it when the defendants indicated that they would not pay him the additional agreed sum. They argued that he was under a contractual obligation to carry out the work arising from the original contract. He had given no new consideration for the promise of extra payment.

> The Court of Appeal held that the new agreement was binding on the defendants. By promising the extra money they had received a benefit, namely the avoidance of a penalty payment, or alternatively the need to employ another sub-contractor. This benefit was consideration to support the new

agreement even though the plaintiff was not required to any more work than he had originally undertaken. The court approved the decision in *Stilk v. Myrick* , however on its facts the Williams case seems to suggest that the courts are now prepared to take a more liberal approach in their willingness to recognise a fresh contract and what can be properly regarded as good consideration.

Of further relevance to the question of how to assess sufficiency is the old common law principle that payment of a lesser amount to a creditor than the full debt cannot discharge the debtor from liability for the full amount even though the creditor agrees it, and accepts the lesser amount. This is known as the rule in *Pinnel's Case* 1602, a rule subsequently confirmed by the House of Lords in *Foakes v. Beer* 1884. It is based upon the view that there can be no real bargain in a person agreeing to accept a lesser sum than they are legally entitled to. But if the varied agreement contains an additional element, such a promise to pay the reduced sum earlier than the date on which the full debt is due, then provided the creditor agrees it, this will be binding. It may be of considerable commercial advantage to receive a smaller amount immediately than have to wait for the full sum, where, for example, the creditor is experiencing cash flow problems.

In addition to early payment of a reduced amount if agreed by the creditor, there are certain other exceptions to the rule in Pinnel's case. They include:

- Substituted performance. This arises where the creditor accepts some other form of consideration instead of money, such as the delivery of goods. Alternatively payment of a lesser sum together with an additional element, such as a promise to repair the creditor's car, would suffice.

- Payment of a lesser sum where the debtor is disputing the value of the work that has been performed, and the creditor accepts the reduced amount. The reason why the creditor is bound by such an arrangement is that if the dispute were to be resolved by court action, the court might determine the value of the work performed as worth even less than the debtor has offered to pay. Accepting the reduced sum may be seen as a new bargain.

- When the equitable doctrine of promissory estoppel applies (see later).

The second example of insufficiency is where the promisor has a public obligation to carry out the act.

Performance of a public duty as a means of providing consideration is insufficient to support the contract. However if the promisor performs some act beyond the public duty, this will operate as valid consideration.

In *Harris v. Sheffield United F C* 1987 the football club challenged its contractual liability to pay for the policing of its football ground during home matches. It was held however that the contract between itself and the police authority was valid. The number of officers provided was in excess of those who would have been provided had the police simply been fulfilling their public obligation to keep the peace and prevent disorder.

## Consideration must not be past

A party to contract cannot use a past act as a basis for consideration. Therefore, if one party performs an act for another, and only receives a promise of payment after the act is complete, the past act would be past consideration. What is required is that the promise of one of the parties to the alleged contract is given in response to the promise of the other. If an act is carried out with no promise of reward having been made, it will be treated as purely gratuitous.

In *Roscorla v. Thomas* 1842 the seller of a horse, after the buyer had purchased it, promised the buyer that it was sound and free from vice. It was not, and the buyer sued the seller on the promise. The action failed. The promise was supported by no new consideration.

There are exceptions to the past consideration rule, for example where the work has been performed in circumstances which carry an implication of a promise to pay.

In *Re Casey's Patents, Stewart v. Casey* 1892 the joint owners of a patent agreed with Casey that he should manage and publicise their invention. Two years later they promised him a third share in the patent, as *"consideration of your services as manager"*.The court rejected the view that this promise was supported by past consideration from Casey. The request to him to render his services carried an implied promise to pay for them. The promise of a third share was simply the fixing of the price.

Only the parties to the agreement who have provided each other with consideration can sue on the contract. A person who has provided no consideration does not have the right to sue on the contract, for that person is not a party to it. This principle, known as *privity of contract*, is examined later.

# Intention to Create Legal Relations

A valid agreement supported by consideration may still fail as a contract unless it is able to satisfy a further legal test, namely that the parties intended their agreement to have legal consequences. In many agreements it is obvious from the context the parties did not intend a legal relationship. A court distinguishes between those arrangements where the parties did intend their agreement to be legally enforceable, and those where this was not the intention, by looking at all the available evidence, and in particular whether the parties have expressly indicated their intention. For instance a written agreement may suggest a more formal type of relationship.

## Common law presumptions regarding intention

At common law certain presumptions regarding intention are applied by the courts. In an agreement of a *social* or *domestic* kind, the courts will presume there was no intention to create a contract. This does not mean, for example, that it is impossible for members of the same family to contract each with the other. They may well be participants in joint business ventures such as partnerships which are founded on a contractual relationship. Rather it is simply a requirement of the common law that there is clear evidence of such an intention. This must be sufficient to overcome the presumption that the parties did not intend a contract.

In *commercial* transactions the courts will presume an intention that they are intended to be legally binding. Indeed whenever there is a business dimension to the agreement the only way to prevent the judicial presumption from operating is to indicate clearly that the agreement is *not* intended to be a contract. The inclusion of the phrase *"binding in honour"* on a football coupon was held by the court in *Jones v. Vernons Pools Ltd*. 1938 to amount to clear evidence that there was no intention to create a contract.

> In *Rose and Frank Co. v. Crompton Bros* 1923 a written agreement entered into by two commercial organisations included the following clause *"This arrangement is not entered into, nor is this memorandum written, as a formal or legal agreement... but... is only a definite expression and record of the purpose and intention of the ... parties concerned, to which they each honourably pledge themselves"*. This clause, the court held, was sufficient evidence to overturn the presumption that the commercial agreement was intended to be legally binding.

Since *honour clauses* have the effect of making an otherwise legally enforceable agreement unenforceable by means of court action, they need to be treated with some care.

A particular commercial practice which can sometimes give rise to questions of contractual intention is the use of the so called *letter of comfort*. These are letters which are designed to provide commercial reassurance, and their use is illustrated in the following case.

> In *Kleinwort Benson Ltd. v. Malaysia Mining Corporation Bhd* 1989 the plaintiff bank agreed to make loan facilities of up to £10M available to a subsidiary company owned by the defendants. The defendants were not prepared to give the bank a formal guarantee to cover the loan facility to the subsidiary, MMC Metals Ltd., however they wrote to the bank stating, *"It is our policy to ensure that the business (of MMC Metals) is at all times in a position to meet its liabilities to you...,"* and, *"We confirm that we will not reduce our current financial interest in MMC Metals Ltd.".*
>
> Subsequently MMC Metals, a tin dealer, went into liquidation following the collapse of the world tin market. The bank looked to the defendants to make good the loss suffered by it on the loans it had made to MMC. The Court of Appeal held that on the facts the defendants letter did not give rise to a binding contract, for on a proper construction of it, it showed no intention to create a legal relationship. In particular the use of the expression "policy" indicated that the defendants were making it clear they were not to be legally bound. Companies are free to change their policies, and often do. The parties were trading equals, and the bank ought to have been aware of the implications of being offered a letter of comfort rather than a letter of guarantee.

## Clauses ousting the courts jurisdiction and arbitration clauses

A term contained in an agreement which attempts entirely to exclude the court's jurisdiction will be void on the grounds that its effect would be to prevent a court from even determining the preliminary issue of the nature of the agreement itself. It is quite legitimate to insert an arbitration clause into the contract. Arbitration clauses are a common feature of business agreements providing a dispute solving mechanism which is generally cheaper, quicker and more private than court proceedings. The rights of consumers under agreements they have made which contain arbitration clauses are now protected under the Consumer Arbitration Agreements Act 1988. The Act is designed to deal with contracts where an arbitration clause is being used by a business as a mechanism for preventing a dispute from being heard before the courts, so that the consumer is bound to follow arbitration arrangements which may well be weighted against him. The Act provides that where a consumer has entered into a contract which provides for future differences between the parties to be referred to arbitration, the arbitration arrangements cannot be enforced against him unless, under s.1:

(a) he has consented in writing after the difference has occurred to the use of the arbitration; or

(b) he has submitted to the arbitration; or

(c) the court has made an order under s.4. This enables the court to determine that the consumer will not suffer a detriment to his interests by having the difference determined by the arbitration arrangements rather than by court proceedings.

The court must consider all relevant matters, including the availability of legal aid.

For the purposes of the Act, a consumer is someone who enters into the contract without either making the contract in the course of a business or holding himself out as doing so. The other party must have made the contract in the course of a business, and if the contract is a sale of goods transaction the goods must be of a type ordinarily supplied for private use or consumption.

## Collective agreements

Contractual intention is also of significance in relation to collective agreements, A *collective agreement* is one between trade unions and employers' organisations by which an agreement or arrangement is made about matters such as terms and conditions of employment. It is estimated that as many as 14 million employees within the United Kingdom are employed under contracts which are regulated in part by collective agreements. The Trade Union and Labour Relations (Consolidation) Act 1992 provides that a collective agreement is presumed not to have been intended by the parties to be a legally enforceable contract unless the agreement is in writing and contains a statement that the parties intend it to be legally enforceable.

## Capacity to contract

Capacity is an expression that describes a person's ability to do something. In legal terms it covers the ability to make contracts, commit torts and commit crimes.

The general rule under English law is that anyone can bind themselves by a contract, as long as it is not illegal, or void for public policy. There are however exceptions to the rule. The most significant are contracts made by corporations and contracts made by minors.

## Corporations

The nature of corporate bodies is dealt with in Chapter 4. Corporations are regarded as legal persons in their own right, thus enabling then to make contracts, commit torts (and some crimes), and hold land. Since they enjoy legal rights and are subject to legal obligations they can sue, and be sued, in respect of these rights and obligations.

## Minors (Children)

The law has always sought to protect minors (Children) from the consequences of making transactions detrimental to themselves. The aim has been to provide them with some protection from their lack of commercial experience, whilst at the same time recognising circumstances where it is appropriate that they should be fully accountable for the agreements they make. The result is a mixture of common law and statutory rules which seek to achieve a balance between these conflicting objectives. The expression *minor* refers to anyone under the age of eighteen, this being the age of majority under the Family Law Reform Act 1969. Categories of contracts a minor can make include beneficial contracts of employment, and contracts for necessaries. A beneficial contract of employment is one which is substantially for the minor's benefit. Benefit is invariably taken to mean that the contract must include some element of training or education, although this can usually be easily established. The court will set aside a contract of employment which viewed overall is not beneficial.

> In *Roberts v. Gray* 1913 the defendant, a minor, with a view to becoming a professional billiards player, had entered an agreement with the plaintiff, himself a leading professional, to accompany the plaintiff on a world tour. The plaintiff spent time and money organising the tour, but following a dispute the defendant refused to go. The plaintiff sought damages of £6000 for breach of contract. The Court of Appeal held that the contract was for the defendant's benefit, being in the nature of a course of instruction in the game of billiards. The plaintiff was awarded £1500 damages.

Necessaries are defined in s.3 Sale of Goods Act 1979 as *"goods suitable to the condition in life of the minor ... and to his actual requirements at the time of sale and delivery."* This is a subjective test of the minors needs, found by reference to his economic and social status.

Some contracts made by minors are said to be voidable. They bind the minor until he repudiates them. Repudiation is the expression used to describe the act of rejecting a contract. Repudiation must occur before reaching majority or within a reasonable time thereafter. If a repudiation has not taken place after this time the contract becomes valid. Contracts falling within this category are those of a long term nature, such as non-beneficial contracts of employment, contracts for a lease, contracts to take shares in a company, and partnership agreements.

## Test Questions

1. Give a simple definition of 'consideration'.

2. Explain what is meant by 'consideration need not be adequate'.

3. When is consideration insufficient?

4. What is the rule in Pinnel's Case 1602 and state the exceptions to it?

5. Explain what is meant by 'consideration must not be past'.

6. What are the common law presumptions regarding intention to create legal relations?

7. What is the purpose of an arbitration clause?

8. What is a collective agreement?

9. Which contracts are binding on a minor?

## Issues of Contractual Validity

So far we have concentrated on how a contract is made. It might be supposed that no further contractual issues are likely to emerge. The parties to the agreement, having met the basic legal requirements and formed their contract, carry out their respective responsibilities to their mutual satisfaction and performance will have been completed. This is indeed what usually happens. The contract is made and performed. Each side is satisfied and transaction is completed.

But contracts do not always run so smoothly. They can go wrong, sometimes for technical reasons and sometimes for practical reasons. Among the more common claims that are asserted are that:

- the contract is not binding because there was not true consent given to it. It may be alleged that the contract was induced by the making of false statements, or that one or even both parties were mistaken in reaching their agreement. A further possibility is an allegation that one side exerted unfair influence over the other, or perhaps even made threats against the other;

- the contract is invalid because its purpose is something contrary to the public interest, for instance because it imposes an unreasonable restraint upon trading freedom;

- some event has occurred which has brought the contract to an end, without performance having been completed.

- the obligations arising under the contract have not been performed either partially or in total, so that there has been a breach of contract;

Of these various possibilities the most frequent are claims of breach of contract. Whatever the nature of the claim may be, however, it will always involve the innocent party seeking some remedy; perhaps financial compensation in the form of damages, or a court order to prevent a threatened breach of contract or enforcing the performance of the contract.

Sometimes what appears to be a properly constituted contract, proves on closer examination to be one containing a defect which was present when the agreement was made. Certain defects of this kind the law recognises as sufficiently serious to invalidate the contract either partially or wholly. Such defects are referred to as *vitiating* factors, and they occur in circumstances of misrepresentation, mistake, duress and undue influence. To vitiate means to invalidate.

## Misrepresentation

Before reaching contractual agreement the parties will often be involved in a process of negotiation. Negotiations can range over any issues which the parties think are relevant to the protection of their interests, but are likely to cover questions of payment, when and how the contract is to be performed, and what terms will be attached to it. The aim of negotiating is both to obtain information and to drive a good bargain, and negotiating skills are a valuable commodity in most areas of commercial and industrial life. Not all contracts are preceded by negotiations however, and as a general rule the more marked the imbalance in trading strength between the parties the less likely will be serious negotiation of terms and conditions. Thus transactions between large organisations on one side, and small organisations or private consumers on the other tend to be characterised by the dominant party presenting the weaker party with a set of terms which are not open to discussion but have to be accepted in their entirety if a contract is to be made.

## The nature of representations

Statements made during the bargaining process may become a part of the contract itself, that is, they may become *terms* of the contract and give rise to an action for breach of contract if they prove untrue. But in many cases there will be no intention by the maker of the statement that the statement should be absorbed into the contract at all. It will be made merely to induce the other party to make the contract. Statements of this sort are known as *representations*. If a representation is untrue for any reason it may constitute a *misrepresentation*, and as such it will be actionable. The injured party (*the misrepresentee*) will base a claim not on breach of contract, but on the law applicable to misrepresentation.

A representation is a statement or assertion of fact made by one party to the other before or at a time of the contract, which has the effect of inducing the other to enter into a contract. The statement can be in any form. It can be in writing, such as a company prospectus containing details of the company's trading activities, or it can be spoken, or be implied from conduct. The definition enables us to distinguish a number of statements whose form or content excludes them from being treated as representations.

## Statements of opinion

Often during negotiations statements are made which are based purely upon the opinion of the person making them. Since a representation must be a statement of fact, a statement expressed as an opinion cannot become a representation. It can be a difficult task to discriminate between what is, or can be fairly regarded as an issue of fact rather than opinion.

> In *Esso Petroleum Co. Ltd. v. Mardon*. 1976 Mardon took a tenancy of a filling station owned by Esso, having been given a forecast by an experienced Esso sales representative of the quantity of petrol the station could be expected to sell annually. This quantity was never reached during the four years Mardon remained as tenant, and the business ran at a loss. The Court of Appeal decided that the company had made a misrepresentation, since the

sales representative's knowledge of such matters made the forecast a statement of fact rather than opinion, and the sales representative was acting in the capacity of an agent of the company. Mardon's claim for damages was successful. The misrepresentation was regarded as a negligent one, and the court also took the view that the representation amounted to a contractual warranty, that is a contractual promise. In his leading judgment Lord Denning MR commented: *"it was a forecast made by a party, Esso who had special knowledge and skill. It was the yardstick by which they measured the worth of a filling station. They knew the facts. They knew the traffic in the town. They knew the throughput of a comparable station. They had much experience and expertise at their disposal. They were in a much better position than Mr. Mardon to make a forecast. It seems to me that if such a person makes a forecast – intending that the other should act on it and he does act on it – it can well be interpreted as a warranty that the forecast is sound and reliable in this sense that they made it with reasonable care and skill. That warranty was broken. Most negligently Esso made a fatal error in the forecast they stated to Mr. Mardon, and on which he took the tenancy. For this they are made liable in damages"*.

Clearly it is not possible to avoid liability for a statement which is expressed as, or is subsequently claimed to be an opinion, when the knowledge and experience of the representor in the matter is far greater than that of the representee.

### Advertising and sales boasts

Much advertising and sales patter falls outside the rules on misrepresentation because the statements made are not capable of substantial verification. They do not attract any legal consequences. Examples include the holiday tour company's, *holiday of a lifetime,* and the carpet company's *We cannot be equalled for price and quality.* However to advertise that *interest free credit is available on all items bought this month,* or that a motor vehicle has returned *31 m.p.g. at a constant 75 m.p.h* are clearly statements of fact. If untrue they give rise to a criminal offence under the Trade Descriptions Act 1968 as well as amounting to misrepresentations. In respect of descriptions applied to *properties* the Property Misdescription Act 1991 has introduced stringent controls over the language that may be used in their sale.

### Statements of law

A false statement of law cannot constitute a misrepresentation. This principle is based upon the general legal proposition that ignorance of the law does not excuse an otherwise unlawful act. The assumption is that the representee knows the law, and cannot therefore rely upon a plea that he relied upon inaccurate statements of law. Of course it would be quite different if these statements were being made by his legal adviser, upon whom he is placing reliance.

Distinguishing statements of law from statements of fact can in some cases be a difficult task. A single statement may be one of mixed law and fact.

> In *Smith v. Land and House Property Corporation* 1884 in a contract for the sale of an hotel the seller stated that it was leased to *"a most desirable tenant"*. In fact the tenant was far from desirable and the purchaser attempted to terminate the contract on the grounds of misrepresentation. The court held that the statement was not one of law, for its principal observation was not the evidence of the person being a tenant, but rather that the tenant was a person who had qualities of value to the purchaser.

## Silence

Although generally a non-disclosure cannot amount to a representation, there are some important exceptions to this rule. In contracts *uberrimae fidei* (of the utmost good faith) duties of full disclosure are imposed. In general these are contracts where one party alone has full knowledge of all material facts. Insurance contracts and contracts for the sale of shares through the issue of a prospectus are examples of contracts *uberrimae fidei*. If full disclosure is not made in such cases the injured party can rescind the contract. Thus before entering into an insurance agreement the party seeking cover must disclose all facts which are material to the nature of the risk which is to be insured.

In contracts for the sale of land the vendor is under an obligation to disclose any defects in his title, that is in his *ownership* of the property, although the obligation does not apply to defects in the property *itself*, for instance dry rot or damp.

In relation to a contract of employment there is no duty on a job applicatant to volunteer information which is not requested during the recruitment process, including the completion of an application form.

> In *Walton v. TAC Construction Materials Ltd.* 1981 the complainant was dismissed after working for thirteen and a half months when the employer discovered that he was a heroin addict. During a medical inspection prior to employment the employee had answered *"none"* when asked to give details of serious illnesses, and failed to reveal that he was injecting himself with heroin. While the tribunal decided that it was fair to dismiss him because of the deception *"it could not be said that there is any duty on the employee in the ordinary case, though there may be exceptions, to volunteer information about himself otherwise than in response to a direct question"*.

If a statement is true when made but becomes untrue before the contract is concluded, the representor will be under a duty to disclose this alteration to the other party.

## Inducement

The representation must induce the person to enter into the contract. There can be no inducement where the other party is unaware of the representation or does not believe the statement, or has relied on his own skill and judgement. In such cases no action will lie in misrepresentation.

> In *Attwood v. Small* 1838 during the course of negotiations for the sale of a mine, the vendor made exaggerated statements of its capacity. The buyers subsequently appointed their own experts to investigate the mine, and the agents reported back to the buyers that the vendor's statements were true. As a result the buyers purchased the mine, only to discover that the statements were inaccurate. It was held that the buyers had no remedy in misrepresentation. They placed reliance upon their own independent investigation.

No test of reasonableness is applied to an inducement so a claim is not prevented by evidence that a reasonable person would not have been induced by the statement, *Museprime Properties Ltd. v. Adhill Properties Ltd.* 1990, provided the belief in the statement is genuine.

## Types of misrepresentation

Actions for breach of contract and for misrepresentation differ in an important respect. If a term of a contract is broken the state of mind of the contract breaker is irrelevant in establishing the existence and extent of liability. If however a mere representation has proved to be untrue and has become a misrepresentation, the effect this has on the liability of the misrepresentor depends on the state of mind accompanying it. A misrepresentation may be made *innocently*, *negligently* or *fraudulently*.

It is *innocent* if the person making it had reasonable grounds for believing it to be true, and negligent where there was a lack of reasonable care taken to determine the accuracy of the statement. In contrast, a *fraudulent* misrepresentation is a representation which a person makes knowing it to be untrue, or believing it to be false, or which is made recklessly where the person making it does not care whether it is true or false. Thus it is a representation which is not honestly believed by the person making it, or where there has been complete disregard for the truth.

At common law it has been possible since 1964 to claim damages in the tort of negligence for a *negligent* misrepresentation under the principle laid down in *Hedley Byrne v. Heller* 1964. *Hedley Byrne* provides that where there is a special relationship between the person making a statement and the recipient of it, a duty of reasonable care is owed in making it. If the duty is broken damages can be claimed, representing the loss suffered. The special relationship concept is central to the decision. The quality of this relationship was referred to by Lord Morris when he stated: *"Where in a sphere in which a person is so placed that others could reasonably rely on his judgment or his skill or on his ability to make careful inquiry, a person takes it on himself to give information or advice to, or allows his information or advice to be passed on to another, who, as he knows or should know, will place reliance on it then a duty of care will arise"*.

The reliance placed on the statement by the recipient of it must be reasonable. In *Hedley Byrne* itself, a disclaimer of liability was enough to prevent reliance on a financial reference that had been given by a bank to a third party being reasonable.

## Remedies available for misrepresentation

A variety of remedies are available. They include common law and equitable remedies, and under the Misrepresentation Act 1967. At common law, as we have seen, damages are available in the tort of deceit for fraudulent misrepresentation, and in the tort of negligence for negligent misrepresentation. In equity *rescission* is available in any case of misrepresentation. It is a remedy which seeks to put the parties back to their pre-contractual position. If this cannot be achieved, for instance where the subject matter of the contract has been altered, lost, or sold to a third party, rescission is not available. Nor can it be claimed if it would be inequitable to grant it. Thus if a person knowing of the misrepresentation *affirms* the contract, so indicating that that he intends to continue, the right to rescind will be lost. Affirmation can occur through delay in bringing an action.

In *Leaf v. International Galleries* 1959 the plaintiff bought from the defendants a picture described as a Constable, but was unable to rescind the contract some five years later when he discovered on trying to re-sell it that it was not a Constable after all. The plaintiff also argued, unsuccessfully, that the contract was affected by mistake. It can be of advantage to a plaintiff to plead alternative legal arguments in this way, for if one proposition fails the other might succeed, and clearly a plaintiff would not choose to bring two separate actions, or even more, if the matter can be dealt with in one trial.

Unlike the common law remedy of damages, which are available as of right once liability has been established, rescission, being an equitable remedy, is discretionary. The court exercises this discretion in accordance with certain principles, referred to as *equitable maxims*. Essentially these principles are concerned with ensuring that in awarding equitable relief the court should be satisfied not only that the plaintiff has acted fairly, but also that the defendant will not be unfairly treated if the remedy sought by the plaintiff is granted. This is the justification for the restrictions on the granting of rescission which have previously been referred to.

> The appropriate measure of damages in a misrepresentation case is illustrated. In *Smith New Court Securities Ltd. v. Scrimgeour Vickers (Asset Management) Ltd.* 1994. The plaintiffs made a successful bid for shares in the company called FIS Ltd. They paid 82.5 pence per share. There were two factors regarding price which they were unaware of when they made their bid. Firstly a fraudulent misrepresentation had been made to them on behalf of the defendants, that other parties were putting in competing bids. This was a fabrication. Had the plaintiffs known the truth the real market value of the shares would have been 78 pence. Secondly FIS Ltd. had suffered a massive fraud committed against it by another person party which at the time of the bid had not become common knowledge. If the market had been aware of the fraud it would have reduced the share price to 44 pence The question for the Court of Appeal was the measure of damages available to the plaintiffs. The court concluded that damages should be assessed by reference to the general knowledge of the market at the time the transaction occurred. The unrelated fraud was not common knowledge when the bid was made consequently the price the plaintiffs would have paid if the defendants had not made their misrepresentation was 78 pence instead of 82.5 pence per share. They were awarded £1,176,010 damages. This was a major blow to them for the trial judge had treated the measure of damages as the difference between 82.5 pence and 44 pence a share, and awarded them £10,764,005 damages.

Damages are available under the Misrepresentation Act 1967 in respect of negligent and innocent misrepresentation. Under s.2(1) damages are available for negligent misrepresentation. It is a defence for the maker of the statement to show that up to the time of the contract he believed that the statement was true and that there was reasonable cause to believe this. Obviously such a belief will depend upon the steps taken by representor to verify the statement. Under s.2(2), damages are also claimable for an innocent misrepresentation; however, the section requires that the party seeking relief must ask the court to rescind the contract. If the court is satisfied that grounds for rescission exist it may award damages instead, if it is of the opinion that it would be equitable to do so.

| | Fraudulent misrepresentation | Negligent misrepresentation | Innocent misrepresentation |
|---|---|---|---|
| **At Common Law** | Damages in the tort of deceit | Damages in the tort of negligence under the rule in *Hedley Byrne v Heller* (1964), if a special relationship exists | |
| **In Equity** | Rescission (and damages). If the contract is executory the fraud is a defence if the misrepresentor brings action for specific performance | Rescission | Rescission |
| **Under the Misrepresentation Act 1967** | | In addition to rescission, or, at the court's discretion instead of rescission, damages under s.2(1) if the misrepresentee has suffered loss. If the defendant can prove that up to the time of the contract he believed, with reasonable cause, that his statements were true, this will be a defence. | If the grounds for rescission exist, the court, in its discretion, may award damages instead under s.2(2) |

## Remedies for Misrepresentation

A person cannot exclude liability in respect of claims brought under the Act, unless the court, in its discretion, considers that use of the exclusion is fair and reasonable in the circumstances of the case. The section applies a test of reasonableness to such an exclusion clause.

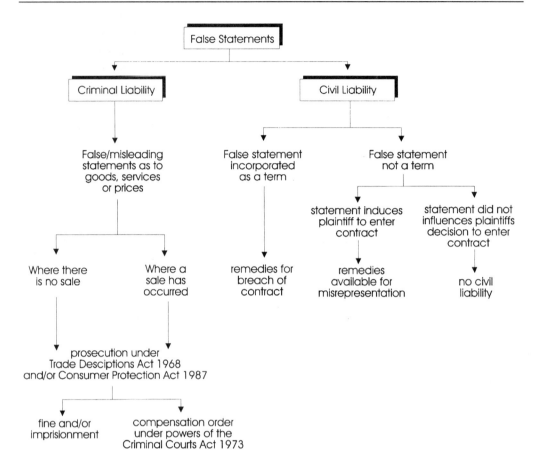

**Figure 2.2** *Liability for False Statement*

## Mistake

The courts have always been reticent about treating mistake as a ground for the avoidance of contractual liabilities. Previously we have seen that a contract will remain valid despite its proving to be economically disadvantageous to one of the parties because of what is, in effect, a mistake as to the value or quality of the subject matter. Provided the parties have made their deal openly and voluntarily the courts will enforce it. In contracts for goods the common law traditionally has taken the view it is the buyers responsibility to ensure the transaction is worth making. This is summed up in the expression *caveat emptor* (let the buyer beware). Modern consumer legislation, notably the Sale of Goods Act 1979 (as amended) readjusts this responsibility by imposing obligations on sellers regarding the quality, suitability and description of the products they sell. However these obligations attach only to business sellers, for the legislation is designed to prevent business from sheltering behind the *caveat emptor* rule. In private sales, where it is assumed the parties can bargain as equals, caveat emptor still applies. They must live with errors of judgment they make about the transaction they make. Of course if their error was engineered by the seller making false statements the situation is different, for in these circumstances a misrepresentation claim will lie. It can sometimes be difficult to distinguish between mistake and misrepresentation, and they often overlap, but they do involve different principles of liability. Part of the confusion lies in the terminology itself. A misrepresentation involves mistaken belief, because the representee has gone ahead with the contract believing certain statements to be true when they are not true. The essence of misrepresentation is that the false statement simply induces the transaction, but it does not become a part of it. Where however a person is seeking a remedy on the grounds of contractual mistake, the argument being put forward is that the substance of the contract itself is tainted by the mistake, and the remedy is a contractual one.

Some types of mistake do not effect the validity of a contract; notably:

- a mistake of law;

- an error of judgment about the value of the subject matter of the contract, unless a misrepresentation was made;

- a mistake about the meaning of a trade term. In *Harrison & Jones Ltd. v. Bunten & Lancaster Ltd.* 1953 a buyer purchased 100 bales of *Sree brand* kapok from the seller. Both parties believed that this type of kapok was pure, but when the buyer discovered that Sree brand was a mixture of different types of kapok he claimed that the contract was void for mistake. The court, however, held that the contract was valid, being unaffected by the mistake; and

- a mistake about ability to perform the contract within a certain time, e.g. in a building contract.

Other, however, are regarded as so fundamental to the transaction that the courts will take account of them. Such mistakes are known as *operative* mistakes, and they render the contract void. The following is an outline of the types of operative mistakes which are recognised.

## Mistake about the nature of a signed document

The law does not permit a person to escape liability from a document they have signed simply because they have not read it, or have read but not understood it. A defence, known as *non est factum* (not my deed), is however available if all the following conditions can be satisfied:

(i)     that the document signed is fundamentally or radically different from the one the signatory believed it to be;

(ii)    that the signatory exercised reasonable care in signing the document;

(iii)   that fraud was used to induce the signature.

Collectively these factors are very demanding, and the defence is thus rarely successful.

> In *Saunders v. Anglia Building Society* 1974 the House of Lords indicated the narrow limits of the defence of non est factum. The facts were that a 78 year old widow had signed a document which a Mr. Lee had told her was a deed of gift of her house to her nephew. She did not read the document as her glasses were broken when she signed it. The document in fact transferred her property to Lee, who subsequently mortgaged the property to a building society. The widow now sought to recover the deeds, pleading non est factum. The action failed. The document had been signed with carelessness, and furthermore it was not substantially different from the one she believed she was signing: they were both assignments of property.

There will sometimes be grounds other than mistake on which a person who has signed a contractual document can rely to avoid the contract. For example, in the case of consumer credit agreements such as hire-purchase agreements, the Consumer Credit Act 1974 grants a five-day period after the agreement is made within which the debtor can cancel the agreement, provided it was signed somewhere other than on the creditor's premises. Signing a contract which is void at law, such as an illegal contract, will incur no contractual liability at all.

## Mistake as to the identity of the other party

Mistake of this kind is usually *unilateral*, where only one of the parties is mistaken about the identity of the other party to the contract. When this occurs the contract will be void only if the mistaken party can show that the question of identity was material to the making of the contract, and that the other part knew or ought to have known of the mistake. The majority of cases in which this type of mistake occur involve fraud, so the requirement of knowledge of the mistake will have been satisfied, leaving the mistaken party with the difficult task of trying to show that he would not have made the contract if the true identity of the other party had been known.

An example of the limited extent to which a unilateral mistake may affect the validity of a contract is provided by *Centrovincial Estates plc v. Merchant Investors Assurance Co. Ltd.* 1983 a case involving a business tenancy between the plaintiffs, the landlords, and the defendants who were the tenants. The issue concerned the fixing of a new rent, under a rent review clause in the lease. The mistake in question was made by solicitors acting for the plaintiffs who wrote to the defendants on June 22 1982 asking them to agree to a new rent of £65,000 per annum to operate from the rent review date. The defendants were happy to agree to the new rent by letter the following day, for the figure suggested was a reduction of over £3,000 per annum on the current rent. The plaintiff's solicitors, when they discovered the error a few days later attempted to persuade the defendants to accept the true figure of £126,000 per annum. The plaintiffs claimed the mistake had prevented any *consensus ad idem* between the parties. The Court of Appeal, applying strict contract law, held that acceptance of an unambiguous offer resulted in a contract. The mere assertion of a mistake, of which the offeree was unaware, did not affect the contract's validity.

## Bilateral mistakes

The instances of mistake considered so far have concerned mistakes made by just one of the parties, unilateral mistakes. In cases of bilateral mistake however both the parties are mistaken, either about the same thing, *common* mistake, or about something different, *mutual* mistake.

Where a mutual mistake occurs the parties are at cross purposes, and in cases of fundamental error arguably there can be no contract in existence anyway, on grounds of the uncertainty of their agreement. Thus if one company agrees to sell a machine to another, and the description of it is so vague that the seller believes he is selling an entirely different machine to the one the buyer believes he is buying, there is no effective agreement within the process of offer and acceptance.

An example of a common mistake occurred in *Couturier v. Hastie* 1856. A contract was made for the sale of some wheat which at the time was being carried on board a ship. Unknown to both parties, when they made the agreement the wheat had already been sold by the ship's captain because during the voyage it had started to overheat. The court held the contract to be void, since it was a contract of impossibility.

There are some significant exceptions to this type of claim. At common law relief from a contract affected by a common mistake will not be available where the mistake:

(a)    occurs after the contract is made. In *Amalgamated Investment & Property Co. Ltd. v. John Walker & Sons Ltd.* 1976 the defendants sold the plaintiffs a warehouse for £1.7m. The defendants knew the plaintiffs intended to redevelop the site, and both knew planning permission would be necessary. Contracts were exchanged on 25 September. On 26 September the defendants were informed by the Department of the Environment that the building had become 'listed'. This made development consent most unlikely, and without it the property was worth £200,000. The plaintiffs sought to rescind the contract. The Court of Appeal rejected the claim. There was no mistake in the minds of the parties when the contracts were exchanged sufficient to set the contract aside;

(b)    is as to quality. An example of a mistake about quality occurred in *Leaf v. International Galleries* 1950 (see earlier).

The doctrine of common mistake was reviewed by the court in *Associated Japanese Bank (International) Ltd. v. Credit Du Nord SA* 1988. The facts of the case were that an individual, Bennett, purported to sell specified items of machinery to the plaintiff bank, which the bank then leased back to him. Under the transaction Bennett received approximately £1 million. The plaintiff bank required Bennett to provide a guarantee from another bank, and this he obtained from the defendants. The machinery was non-existent. Bennett disappeared with the money, and the plaintiffs claimed under the guarantee against the defendants. The defendants argued that (a) the guarantee was subject to an express or implied condition that the machinery existed, or alternatively (b) that the guarantee was void from the outset on the grounds of the mistaken belief of both parties that the machinery existed. The plaintiff's claim failed. On the facts the judge, Steyn J took the view that the guarantee agreement included an express condition that the machinery existed. Even if it had not, he was of the view that it would contain an implied term to this effect for a reasonable man would regard this as so obvious as hardly to require saying. The guarantee was also void from the outset for the mistake, at common law. The judge summarised the common law approach to mistake as follows:

(i)    the courts should seek to uphold rather than defeat apparent contracts;

(ii)   the rules regarding mistake are designed to deal with the effect of exceptional circumstances upon apparent contracts;

(iii)  the mistake must concern existing facts at the time of the contract, and both sides must substantially share the mistake;

(iv)   the mistake must render the subject matter of the contract essentially and radically different from what was in the minds of the parties; and

(v)    there must be reasonable grounds for the belief of both parties.

# Remedies

## At common law

The effect of an operative mistake at common law is to render the contract void *ab initio* - from the outset. The true owner is thus entitled to the return of goods, or damages, from whoever is in wrongful possession.

## In equity

The position in equity is different however, for equity recognises certain types of operative mistake which the common law does not grant relief for, in particular in cases involving mistake as to quality. The following cases illustrate the position.

> In *Magee v. Pennine Insurance Co. Ltd.* 1969 a proposal for insurance of a motor car had been incorrectly completed without the insured's knowledge. Following a crash, a claim was made and the insurance company agreed to pay £385 which the insured was willing to accept. On discovery of the material inaccuracy in the policy however, the company withdrew their offer of payment and the insured sued them to obtain it. The Court of Appeal held that under the common law the common mistaken belief that the policy was valid was inoperative and the contract of the insurance was valid. In equity however the agreement to pay £385 would be set aside as there had been a fundamental misapprehension, and the party seeking to rescind was not at fault.

## Test Questions

1.    Give a simple definition of misrepresentation..

2.    Give an example of a statement of opinion and a statement of fact.

3.    Can silence ever be misrepresentation?

4.    What are the three types of misrepresentation?

5.    Are damages available as a remedy for misrepresentation?

6.    How can a trader be made liable for false statements in a transaction?

7.    Which mistakes do not affect the validity of a contract?

8.    What is meant by non est factum?

9.    Distinguish between common mistake and mutual mistake.

## Duress and Undue Influence

At common law coercing a person into making a contract by means of actual or threatened violence to them is referred to as *duress,* and if it can be proved the contract is treated, not surprisingly, as void. Because of its narrow limits the plea of duress is an extremely unusual one.

Equity however goes much further than the common law. The doctrine of *undue influence* which it has developed recognises more subtle forms of improper pressure that are sometimes relied on to create agreements. Where undue influence is shown to have occurred equity will allow the innocent party the opportunity to rescind the contract. In certain relationships a presumption of undue influence arises, for example in fiduciary relationships, and in those where one person is in a position of dominance over the other. Parent and child, solicitor and client, doctor and patient, and trustee and beneficiary are classic illustrations. The courts are still prepared to recognise new relationships where the doctrine can be applied, for example an influential secretary companion and his elderly employee in *Re Craig* 1971, and a banker who sought to obtain a benefit from his customer in *Lloyds Bank v. Bundy* 1975. The dominant party who attempts to uphold a transaction entered into in such a relationship must rebut the presumption of undue influence by showing that he has not abused his position in any way. Evidence that the innocent party has taken independent advice will go a long way to achieving this and saving the contract.

In *Barclays Bank plc v. O'Brien* 1993 Mr. O'Brien, who was a shareholder in a manufacturing company, wanted to increase the overdraft available to the company from its bank, Barclays. The bank agreed to an overdraft facility of £135,000. The O'Brien's matrimonial home, jointly owned by Mr. & Mrs. O'Brien, was used as security for the loan, and the O'Briens executed a legal charge in favour of the bank. The bank did not advise Mrs. O'Brien as to the effect of the charge; nor did she read the documents she signed. Her husband had told her merely that the charge was to secure £60,000, and would last for only a short time. The company's debts increased, and the bank sought to enforce its security. The House of Lords unanimously held that Mrs. O'Brien was entitled to set aside the legal charge on the matrimonial home. The court restated the law applying in surety cases involving marriage partners and cohabitees. In a case such as this, where the spouse placed trust and confidence in the principal debtor (the husband) and acted as surety on the basis of a misrepresentation or through undue influence, the legal position would be as follows. If the surrounding circumstances were such as to put the creditor on inquiry, for instance where on the face of it the transaction was not to the wife's benefit, then the creditor should take reasonable steps to establish that her consent had been properly obtained. This could be done by discussing the matter with her privately, warning her of the risks, and suggesting she take independent legal advice. A creditor put on inquiry, who failed to take such reasonable steps would take the security subject to the equitable rights of the wife to have it set aside, for the creditor would have constructive notice of those rights.

There have been a number of subsequent cases which have explored the implications of the *O'Brien* decision. Essentially they have all involved questions of what the duty of a bank is taking into account its knowledge or its potential knowledge of misrepresentation or undue influence occurring between the parties to the relationship.

In modern times the courts have demonstrated an increased willingness to see the principles underlying duress and undue influence as elements in a broader principle of law which Lord Denning referred to in *Lloyds Bank v. Bundy* 1975 as *inequality of bargaining power*.

In *Clifford Davies Management Ltd. v. WEA Records Ltd.* 1975 this inequality approach was clearly demonstrated. Two composer members of a pop group (Fleetwood Mac) had entered into an agreement with their manager to assign the copyright in all their work to him for a period of ten years. In return they received a very small financial consideration and his promise to use his best endeavours to publish the work they composed. The Court of Appeal found that on the basis of bargaining inequality the contract could be set aside at the option of the composers. The factors cited by the court that pointed to the inequality were: the overall unfairness of a ten year tie, supported by vague consideration offered in return by the manager; the conflict of interest arising from the manager acting as the business adviser to the composers, whilst at the same time representing his own company's interests in negotiating with them; and the absence of any independent advice available to the composers, and their reliance upon the manager, who exerted undue influence over them.

Further development of this approach has lead to the recognition of *economic duress*. Economic duress is a plea based upon a claim that the weaker party gave their consent to the agreement as a result of improper commercial influence or pressure put on them. The following cases illustrate situations in which the courts have been prepared to recognise economic duress as a ground for contractual relief.

In *Atlas Express v. Kafco (Importers and Distributors)* 1989 the defendants were a small company involved in the import and distribution of basketware. They sold a quantity of their goods to Woolworths, and agreed with the plaintiffs, a national road carrier, for deliveries to be made by the plaintiffs. The plaintiffs depot manager quoted a price for deliveries based upon his guess as to how many cartons of goods would be carried on each load. In the event he overestimated this figure and refused to proceed with the contract unless the defendants agreed to a minimum payment for each load of £440, in substitution for the original arrangement of £1.10 per carton. Anxious to ensure the goods were delivered on time, and unable in the circumstances to find an alternative carrier, the defendants agreed to the new arrangement, but later refused to pay. The plaintiff's claim for breach of contract failed. The court took the view that the plaintiff's threat to break the contract together with their knowledge of the defendants dependency on them represented a clear example of economic duress.

## Contract Terms

The terms of a contract are the promises which the parties make to each other. These promises, sometimes referred to as legal obligations, are of course legally enforceable.

All contracts contain terms, sometimes complex and detailed sets of undertakings, more often simple comprehendable statements of what each side to the transactions is promising the other. These undertakings may be oral, or contained in a written document. Businesses generally regard a written contract as an essential safeguard against subsequent disagreements over what has actually been agreed.

By inserting a range of terms into the contract the parties will seek to clarify their mutual obligations. In a well constructed contract they will anticipate all eventualities, so that no issue can emerge later which cannot be resolved by reference to the contract itself. Different types of contract obviously reflect different sets of terms appropriate to the nature and purpose of the agreement, but whatever the objective is always to ensure that the terms cover all the issues associated with the performance of the contract.

The terms of a contract constitute a kind of index of the parties responsibilities. It is an important index because it is the means by which performance of the contract is measured. If a term has not been carried out properly, or not carried out at all, a breach of contract has occurred giving rise to a potential claim by the injured party, probably for financial compensation. If you take any contract and examine it, it becomes possible to list out all its terms, and so identify which of the parties has to do what to fulfill their side of the bargain.

## The classification of terms

The terms of a contract vary in importance. Sometimes the contract itself will say how much importance is attached to a certain term, while in other cases it may be left to the court to decide because the parties to the contract have not made it clear themselves. The value that is attached to each term is of great significance because it determines what the consequences will be if the particular term is broken.

Major terms are called *conditions*. A condition is a term which is said to go to the root of the contract, and whose performance is therefore essential to the contract. Because a condition is so important, if it is broken the innocent party has the right to treat the contract as repudiated and to refuse to perform their obligations under it. In addition the injured party may sue for damages.

Minor terms are called *warranties*. They are terms which are said to be collateral to the main purpose of the contract. In consequence, if a warranty is broken the contract still stands, and the innocent party does not have the right to treat the contract as being at an end, merely the right to damages.

Where breach of a condition occurs the injured party is not bound to repudiate the contract. As an alternative the injured party can elect to treat the contract as continuing, treating the breach of condition as if it were a warranty. The obligation that has been broken is then referred to as an *ex post facto* warranty, and only damages will be available. Sound commercial reasons may justify treating a breach of condition as one of warranty, and letting the contract stand. The innocent party may realise that if the contract is repudiated it will be difficult to obtain an alternative supplier of the goods and services in question, or undue delay and inconvenience will be caused if the goods have to be disassembled, removed from the premises and returned to the supplier.

Sometimes it is impossible to say whether a term is a condition or a warranty when it is first created because it has been so broadly framed that it could be broken in a major respect or a minor respect, in such cases therefore it is only possible to say after the event what effect the particular breach should have on the contract. Such terms are referred to as *innominate*, meaning intermediate, terms.

> The position is illustrated in *Hong Kong Fir Shipping Co. Ltd. v. Kawasaki Kaisen Kaisha Ltd.* 1962. Here a ship was chartered on terms that stated what it would be *"in every way fitted for ordinary cargo service"*. Inefficient engine-room staff and old engines contributed to a number of breakdowns so that during the first seven months of the charter the ship was only able to be at sea for eight and a half weeks. The charterers repudiated the contract. The Court of Appeal decided that this particular breach did not entitle the charterers to repudiate. Diplock J stated that the terms in the contract were not really either a condition or a warranty but rather *"an undertaking, one breach of which may give rise to an event which relieves the charterer of further performance ... if he so elects and another breach of which may not give rise to such an event but entitle him only ... to damages."*

A further illustration is provided by the case of *Cehave NV v. Bremer Handelsgesellschaft, mbh, The Hansa Nord* 1975. A term in a contract under which the defendants agreed to sell citrus pulp pellets to the plaintiffs stipulated *"shipment to be made in good condition"* . Delivery was by consignments. On delivery of one of the consignments, of the 3293 tons supplied 1260 tons were found to be damaged. The market price for such goods had now fallen, and the buyers used the damaged goods as an opportunity for repudiating the whole contract on grounds of breach of condition. In fact they later bought exactly the same cargo at well below half the original contract price from a third party who had obtained it from the original sellers. The buyer then used it to make cattle food, exactly what they had bought it for in the first place. The Court of Appeal held the term to be an intermediate one, and damages rather than repudiation was an appropriate remedy. Lord Denning commented *"if a small portion of the whole cargo was not in good condition and arrived a little unsound, it should be met by a price allowance. The buyer should not have the right to reject the whole cargo unless it was serious or substantial."* In the later case of *Bunge Corporation, New York v. Tradax Export SA Panama* 1981 the

House of Lords emphasised that parties cannot artificially create intermediate terms. Whether a term is to be regarded as intermediate is a matter of construction.

## Express terms

These are the terms which have been specifically agreed by the parties. They can classify them as conditions or warranties when they are made if they wish. If they fail to do so the court has to decide how significant a particular breach is by looking at the term in relation to the contract as a whole. Even where the contract itself classifies a term or terms, the court still reserves the right to construe the meaning of the term by looking at the contract as a whole.

In *L Schuler AG v.Wickham Machine Tool Sales* 1973 the German appellant company, granted sole selling rights over their panel presses in England to the respondents, Wickham. Their agreement provided that Wickham's representatives should visit six named firms every week for the purpose of seeking orders. Clause 7(6) indicated the status of this particular term stating that *"it shall be a condition of this agreement"*. On certain occasions Wickham's employees failed to satisfy the term. Schulers responded by claiming repudiation of the contract, arguing that a single failure would be sufficient to constitute a breach. The House of Lords rejected this argument. Such a construction was so unreasonable that the parties could not have intended it.

A question sometimes faced by the Court is whether statements made during contractual negotiations, referred to as representations, have become incorporated into the contract as actual terms. The test usually applied is whether the person making the statement was promising its accuracy. If so, the statement is usually treated as a term.

If the parties to a contract of employment have included their respective rights and obligations under it in a signed document called the contract of employment, then this document will contain the express terms of the agreement. In many cases however the express term of a contract of employment can only be determined by establishing the content and status of the various documents transferred during the *recruitment* process and what the parties orally agreed at the inteview. Express terms will be found in the statutory statement of the main term and conditions of employment, the details contained in the job application form and in rare cases even a job advertisement.

In *Holliday Concrete v. Wood* 1979 a job advertisement indicated that a fifteen month contract was available and this was held to be the period of employment.

In *Joseph Steinfeld v. Reypert 1979* the fact that a post was advertised as *"sales manager"* indicated the contractual status of the successful applicant.

## Terms implied by the courts

The courts are sometimes willing to imply a term to give a contract *business efficacy*.

In *Irwin v. Liverpool City Council* 1977 the defendant council let a flat in an upper floor of a block of flats to the plaintiff tenant. A term was implied by the court into a tenancy agreement between the plaintiff and the defendant council to the effect that the defendants had an obligation to keep in repair the stairs and the lift in the block of flats which they owned, thus ensuring that the plaintiff could gain effective access to his property.

In *Baylis v. Barnett* 1988 the plaintiff lent the defendant a sum of money. The defendant knew this involved the plaintiff in borrowing the money from a bank. Although the parties did not discuss the question of interest the court held there was an implied term that the defendant would indemnify the plaintiff for any interest he owed to the bank.

A field in which the courts have been active in implying terms is in the relationship between employers and employees. The common law implies a number of important terms into the contract of employment; for instance that the *employee* owes a duty of good faith to the employer, and that the *employer* has an obligation to provide for the employee's safety.

In *Woods v. W H Car Services Ltd.* 1982 the court acknowledged that in every employment contract there is an implied term of great importance, that of trust and confidence between the parties. Such a term requires that employers *"will not without reasonable and proper cause, conduct themselves in a manner calculated or likely to destroy the relationship of trust and confidence between employer and employee"*.

The need to imply terms in this way occurs where there is a dispute between the parties in which one of them is claiming it was implicit in their agreement that an unexpressed term was nevertheless intended to make the contract work properly.

## Statutory implied terms

Parliament has been particularly active during the last thirty years or so in the use of legislation to introduce specific terms into certain types of contractual agreement. Statutory implied terms are nowadays found in an enormous range of different kinds of contract. Being statutory terms they are specific about the obligations being imposed. In many cases statutory terms are implied as a legislative attempt to counter-balance the inequalities that exist in a particular bargaining situation. In other cases statutory terms can be seen as a vehicle for effecting profound social and economic change, such as the insertion of the *equality clause* in contracts of employment. Yet again, there are those statutory terms which simply represent a codification of judicially recognised mercantile custom, for example those within the Sale of Goods Act 1979. Detailed examples of statutory implied terms can be found in Chapters 4 and 5.

# Exclusion Clauses

Legal liability can arise in a variety of different ways, for example through misrepresentation, breach of contract or negligence. One way of trying to reduce or extinguish this liability is by the use of exclusion or limitation clauses. An *exclusion clause* in a contract is an express term which attempts to exempt one party from all liability for failure to perform some part of the contract.

A *limitation clause* on the other hand is slightly different for it aims to *reduce* rather than extinguish the liability. These clauses may be drafted to place an overall financial limit on the liability of one party for breach of contract, or to limit liability to the replacement of goods supplied, or to deprive the other of a particular remedy for the breach. For convenience, references made to exclusion clauses used here can be taken to mean both total or partial exclusion of liability.

The principle of freedom of contract permits the use of exclusion clauses. The courts however have developed a number of common law principles designed to rob such clauses of effect in certain circumstances. These principles were developed because the courts recognised that the use of exclusion clauses could result in unfairness to one of the contracting parties. Judicial controls were developed largely by the application of existing principles of contract law and are limited in scope. It was not until the 1970's that legislation was introduced. The Unfair Contract Terms Act 1977 now provides a comprehensive set of rules which regulate both the use of exclusion clauses in contracts and the use of non-contractual notices. These rules have been supplemented by the Unfair Terms in Consumer Contracts Regulations 1994 which were introduced to give effect to the 1993 European Council Directive on Unfair Terms in Consumer Contracts. The Regulations do not alter the operation of the 1977 Act, which remains unchanged, but provide an additional set of rules designed to strengthen consumer protection in this area. The content of the 1977 Act and the supplementary regulations can be found in Chapter 3.

In determining the validity of an exclusion clause, several legal principles have to be applied. The first step is to make sure that legal liability of one type or another would arise if the exclusion were not present. Next the common law rules of incorporation and interpretation (discussed below) must be applied. If the exclusion survives the application of the common law rules, we must then apply the provisions of the 1977 Act and the 1994 Regulations are then applied. The figure below summarises these steps in diagrammatic form.

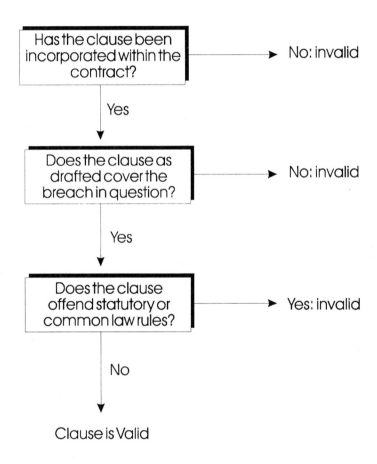

**Figure 2.3** *Legal control over exclusion and restriction of contractual liability*

# Incorporation – Is the Term Part of the Contract?

## Signed documents

A person who signs a document containing an exclusion clause will be bound by the terms it contains whether or not they have actually been read or understood. The only exceptions are where the signature is induced by fraud or misrepresentation. Otherwise the exclusion clause will automatically be part of the contract.

> In *Spriggs v. Sotheby Parke Bernet and Co. Ltd.* 1984 the plaintiff handed over to Sothebys a diamond which they were to auction for him. They gave him a document to sign, which he signed without reading. Immediately above the space for signature a printed declaration in bold type said "*I have read and agree to the instructions for sale as detailed on the reverse of this form*". The reverse of the form contained an exclusion clause. It was held that the clause had been validly incorporated into the contract.

If the contents of a contract have been misrepresented before it is signed, an exclusion clause in the document will be ineffective to the extent of the misrepresentative effect of the clause.

> In *Curtis v. Chemical Cleaning and Dyeing Co.* 1951 the plaintiff took a wedding dress to the defendant company for cleaning. An assistant asked her to sign a receipt. Before she did so she was told that her signature on the receipt excluded the company's liability for any damage to the beads and sequins on the dress. The dress was stained during cleaning, however no damage was done to the beads and sequins. The signed receipt actually excluded the defendants' liability for any damage to the dress "*howsoever caused*". The Court of Appeal held that the defendants were liable for the damage to the dress and could not rely on the full exclusion clause because they had misrepresented its effect to the plaintiff.

## Unsigned documents

A term contained in an unsigned document, or displayed on a notice, is only effective if the person relying on it took reasonable steps to bring it to the attention of the other party, and where the document or notice might reasonably be regarded as likely to contain contractual terms.

> In *Chapelton v. Barry U.D.C.* 1940 the plaintiff hired a deck chair from the defendant for use on a beach. He paid an attendant and was given a ticket in return. He was injured when the chair collapsed as he sat down on it. There was an exclusion clause printed on the back of the ticket which the plaintiff had not read. The Court of Appeal held that the ticket was merely a receipt and not the sort of contractual document which a reasonable person might

have expected to contain contractual terms. The exclusion clause was therefore ineffective and the defendants were liable.

Where a term is particularly onerous or unusual, then even if it has been incorporated within a contractual document, the party seeking to enforce it must nevertheless show that it has fairly and adequately been drawn to the other party's attention.

## Terms introduced after the contract is made

An exclusion clause will not be effective unless it is adequately brought to the attention of the other party before the contract is made. It must be part of the contractual offer, and the rules of offer and acceptance can be used to determine whether the clause is actually part of the contract.

In *Olley v. Marlborough Court Hotel Ltd.* 1949 the plaintiff booked into an hotel and paid for the room in advance. She went up to her hotel room where there was a notice which stated *"The proprietors will not hold themselves responsible for articles lost or stolen unless handed to the Manageress for safe custody"*. The plaintiff left her fur coat in the room and it was stolen. The Court of Appeal held that the defendant was not entitled to rely on the exclusion clause as it was not a term of the contract. The contract was concluded at the reception desk and the plaintiff had no notice of the clause at that stage.

In *Thornton v. Shoe Lane Parking* 1971 the plaintiff drove into a car park which he had not used before. At the entrance there was a machine which issued a ticket to him before raising a barrier to allow entry. On the back of the ticket there was a statement that it was issued subject to terms and conditions displayed within the car park. One of these conditions purported to exclude the defendant's liability for injury to customers howsoever caused. The plaintiff was injured by the defendant's negligence when he came to collect his car. The Court of Appeal held that the exclusion clause was ineffective because it had been introduced after the contract was concluded. Lord Denning analysed the process of contract formation in the following way. *"The customer pays his money and gets a ticket. He cannot refuse it. He cannot get his money back. He may protest to the machine, even swear at it; but it will remain unmoved. He is committed beyond recall. He was committed at the very moment when he put his money into the machine: the contract was concluded at that time. It can be translated into offer and acceptance in this way. The offer is made when the proprietor of the machine holds it out as being ready to receive the money. The acceptance takes place when the customer puts his money into the slot. The terms of the offer are contained in the notice placed on or near the machine stating what is offered for the money. The customer is bound by these terms as long as they are sufficiently brought to his notice beforehand, but not otherwise. He is not bound by the terms printed on the ticket, if they differ from the notice, because the ticket comes too late. The contract has already been made"*

Where there is a previous course of dealing between the parties the court may be prepared to recognise the incorporation of an exclusion clause into a contract even though it was not specifically referred to at the time the contract was made. This will occur where the past dealings between the parties have consistently been made on the same terms and with the exclusion clause.

In *Spurling v. Bradshaw* 1956 the plaintiffs were warehousemen who had dealt with the defendant for many years and always on the plaintiff's standard contractual terms. These terms excluded the plaintiff's liability for *"negligence, wrongful act of default"*. The defendant delivered eight barrels of orange juice to the plaintiff for storage and a few days later received an acknowledgement which referred to the standard terms of contract. When the defendant came to collect the barrels they were found to be empty. He refused to pay the storage charges and the plaintiff sued. It was held that the exclusion clause, although on this occasion introduced after the contract was made, was part of the contract. This was because the parties had regularly dealt with each other in the past and had done so consistently on the same contractual terms. The defendant was therefore well aware of these terms when he deposited the goods. The exclusion of liability was valid and the plaintiff's claim for storage charges succeeded.

## Test Questions

1.  What is meant by 'undue influence'?

2.  What is meant by 'economic duress'?

3.  How are contract terms classified?

4.  Why are the courts prepared to imply terms into a contract?

5.  Give two examples of statutes that imply terms into contracts.

6.  Explain what is meant by an exclusion clause.

7.  How does an exclusion clause become a contractual term?

# Standard Form Contracts

The value of expressing the terms of a contract in writing has already been discussed. In most cases written contracts are of a standard form kind. A standard form contract is a printed document containing a set of uniform terms designed to regulate all aspects of an agreement. Businesses favour them for two reasons:

- firstly because standardising terms avoids the need to negotiate fresh terms each time a new agreement is made; and

- secondly because such a contract can be designed to protect the business against a wide range of contingencies which would otherwise damage it commercially if they were to occur. An obvious example of this is the use of exclusion clauses designed to shield a business from the consequences of breaching its contractual undertakings.

Standard form contracts are found in all fields of commercial activity. Banks, package tour operators, motor vehicle dealers, telephone companies, electricity, water and gas suppliers and train operators are amongst those businesses who always do business with their domestic customers on standardised terms of trading.

If a standard form contract is analysed, it will usually be found to contain terms designed to deal with a range of well recognised eventualities. Of course a standard form agreement under which a service is being provided, such as a package holiday, will not look the same as one in which a product, say a car, is the subject matter of the agreement. These contracts are about very different things. We can however identify the types of standard terms which are most frequently encountered in standard form agreements, and some examples of them are set out below, together with a brief commentary explaining what each term is designed to do.

**Exclusion clause** (the example given is taken from an agreement between a customer and the supplier of a mobile phone service).

*"We have no liability other than the duty to exercise the reasonable care and skill of a competent mobile tele communications service provider. We do not accept liability for indirect loss, such as loss of profits, business, or any other form of economic loss."*

The supplier is seeking in this clause to limit any liability which might arise where the customer has suffered a financial loss due to a failure to provide the service. This could occur where, for instance, a business person looses an order being placed over the mobile phone because of poor reception. Such a loss is indirect, or consequential. This limitation of liability is only legally valid if the supplier can show it to be fair - Unfair Terms in Consumer Contracts Regulations 1994. The regulations also require all written terms in contracts between sellers and suppliers of goods and services, and consumers, to be expressed in plain English. The reference to reasonable care and skill is a reference to the duty imposed on a supplier under s.13 Supply of Goods and Services Act 1982. This section cannot be lawfully excluded. (See Chapter 3)

**Force majeure** (the example given comes from an agreement between a holiday company and a customer to provide holiday home accommodation).

*"In the event of 'force majeure' we regret we cannot pay any compensation. Force majeure means unusual and unforseeable circumstances beyond our control, the consequences of which neither we nor our suppliers could avoid, for example war, threat of war, riots, civil*

*strife, terrorist activity, industrial disputes, natural or nuclear disaster, fire, adverse weather conditions, level of water in rivers or similar events beyond our control."*

Notice that the company, probably as a consequence of the plain English requirement, has set our fully what the technical expression 'force majeure' means. Without excluding force majeure eventualities the company could find itself liable to a holiday maker whose holiday has been affected or prevented by any of items listed. Force majeure eventualities may also frustrate the contract.

**Price variation** (the example given is taken from a contract of sale).

*"Where the date for the delivery of the goods is more than three months from the date of this agreement, the seller reserves the right to increase the price of the goods by an amount not to exceed 2½% of the contract price, to reflect any increase in costs to the seller of materials and labour in the period between the date of the agreement and delivery date."*

Using a clause of this type the seller seeks protection from a possible reduction in profits on a sale where additional costs are incurred between the date of the agreement and the date of delivery, by having the capacity to pass these costs on to the buyer such a clause is particularly useful in periods of high inflation.

**Retention of title** (the example given is taken from a contract of sale).

*"Property in the goods subject to this agreement shall remain with the seller until such time as the seller has received payment in full for the goods and all other sums owing to the seller from the buyer on whatever grounds."*

Such a term is known technically as a Romalpa clause (from the case in which the validity of such a clause was first upheld). Its effect is to enable an unpaid seller who has physically delivered the goods to the buyer to remain the owner of the goods until they are paid for. In the clause above the seller continues in ownership until all monies owed to the seller from the buyer have been met. S.17 Sale of Goods Act 1979 allows for the parties to a contract of sale to make express provision for the passing of property i.e. the transfer of ownership, in goods, and this is what a Romalpa clause is doing. Often such clauses include additional provisions requiring the buyer to mark the unpaid goods as belonging to the seller and requiring the buyer to seek the sellers approval before dealing with the goods in any way.

**Liquidated damages** (again the example is taken from a contract of sale).

*"In the event of the cancellation of this contract by the buyer for any reason the buyer hereby agrees to pay the seller by way of liquidated damages the sum of 10% of the contract price."*

A liquidated damages clause is designed to set in advance the level of compensation payable in the event of a breach of contract, in the above example a failure by the buyer to proceed with the contract. The common law allows such a clause as long as it represents a genuine pre-estimate of the loss that would be suffered if the breach were to occur. If however the figure of compensation set is disproportionate to the loss likely to occur on a breach the clause will be a penalty and void.

In *Dunlop Pneumatic Tyre Co. v. New Garage Motor Co.* 1915, Lord Dunedin stated that a liquidated damages clause:

*"will be held to be a penalty if the sum stipulated for is extravagant and unconscionable in amount in comparison with the greatest loss that could conceivably be proved to have followed from the breach."*

# Discharge of Contract

Since a contract gives rise to legally enforceable obligations, contracting parties need to know how and when these obligations have been discharged and cease to be binding on them. Discharge is thus a technical term used to describe the ending of contractual liabilities. No legal claim will lie once a contract is discharged. Discharge can occur in any of the following ways:

## Discharge by performance

The general rule is that complete performance, in which both parties comply precisely with the contractual terms they have agreed, is necessary to discharge the contract.

> This common law rule was applied in the case of *Sumpter v. Hedges* 1898, where the plaintiff builder had agreed to erect some houses for a lump sum of £565. Having carried out half the work to the value of £333 the builder was unable to complete the job because of financial difficulties. In an action by the builder to recover compensation for the value of the work he had already carried out, the Court of Appeal confirmed that he was not entitled to payment, Smith, LJ observing that *"The law is that where there is a contract to do work for a lump sum, until the work is completed, the price of it cannot be recovered"*.

This appears to be a very harsh decision, for the builder was unable to recover for any work he had performed, whilst the purchaser obtained a half completed contract for nothing. The difficulty for the court in such a case is that a single sum has been arranged in consideration for the completion of specified works. If these works are not completed in their entirety the court would be varying the clearly expressed intentions of the parties if it was to award payment of a proportionate part of the lump sum. In other words, by agreeing a lump sum the parties have impliedly excluded that possibility of part payment for partially fulfilled building work. Such a contract is said to be an *entire* contract.

The obligation on a contracting party to provide precise, complete performance of the contract before the contractual obligations can be treated as discharged can obviously produce injustice, and there are two exceptions that grant limited relief to the party obliged to perform. These are in cases where the contract is *divisible*, and in cases where there has been *substantial performance*.

## A divisible contract

In some circumstances the courts are prepared to accept that a contract is a divisible one, that is a contract which can be broken down into a series of specific parts, so that partial performance of the contract can be set off against partial consideration to be given in return. Had the parties in *Sumpter v. Hedges* agreed a specified sum to be paid on completion of certain stages of the house building, then the builder could have recovered compensation for part of the work done. In practice it is usual in a building contract to provide for payment of parts of the total cost at various stages of completion.

It is not necessary for the parties to formally specify that the contract is a divisible one. The courts seem willing to recognise a divisible contract wherever possible, and will, for example, regard an agreement based upon an estimate or quotation given in advance, which itemises the work to be performed and with a breakdown of the costs, as a divisible contract.

## Substantial performance

If a party to a contract has substantially performed his contractual obligations subject only to minor defects, the courts have recognised that it would be unjust to prevent him recovering any of the contractual price. Therefore under this exception the contractual price would be recoverable, less a sum representing the value of the defects. It must be stressed that the exception will only operate where the defects are of a trifling nature, an issue determined by considering not only the character of the defects but also the cost of rectifying them in relation to the total contract price.

A claim of substantial performance of the contract was made in *Bolton v. Mahadeva* 1972. The plaintiff, a heating contractor, had agreed to install a central heating system in the defendant's house for £560. On completion of the work the system proved to be so defective that it would cost £174 to repair. The defendant refused to pay the plaintiff any of the cost of the work and the plaintiff sued. The County Court accepted the plaintiff's claim of substantial performance and awarded him the cost of the work less the cost of the repair. On appeal however, the Court of Appeal held that in the circumstances the plaintiff had not substantially performed the contract and he was not therefore entitled to recover any of the cost of the work. The substantial performance plea would not succeed where there were numerous defects requiring a relatively high cost of repair.

From the consumer's point of view it can be difficult to ascertain whether incomplete performance of the contract is nevertheless sufficient on the facts to amount to substantial performance. Refusal to pay may well be met with a legal action by the contractor to recover the debt owed. Further complications may be caused where the contractor offers to remedy the customer's complaint free of charge and the customer refuses to accept the offer. In the event of a dispute concerning the value of work performed, an offer of reduced payment by the debtor to the creditor will be binding on the creditor, an example of one of the exemptions to *Pinnel's case.*

In *Lawson v. Supasink Ltd.* 1982 the plaintiff's employed the defendants to design, supply and install a fitted kitchen. The total cost was £1,200, and the plaintiffs had to pay a deposit. After the kitchen units had been fitted, but before work on the kitchen was completed, the plaintiffs informed the defendants of their dissatisfaction with the standard of workmanship. In response the defendants undertook to remedy the faults free of charge, but the plaintiffs later rejected this, asked for the units to be removed and for the return of their deposit. The defendants refused. The Court of Appeal, having accepted that the shoddy work did not amount to substantial performance, then considered the offer to remedy made by the defendants. The question was whether they had failed to mitigate their loss, that is minimise the damage they had suffered. In *Fayzu Ltd. v. Saunders* 1919 Scrutton LJ commented, "*... in commercial contracts it is generally reasonable to accept an offer from the party in default.*" In *Lawson* the Court held that the plaintiffs had not acted unreasonably for, in the words of Shaw LJ " *I do not see how the plaintiffs could be required ... to afford the defendants a second opportunity of doing properly what they singularly failed to do adequately in the first instance.*"

## The acceptance of partial performance

If a party to a contract partially performs his obligations and the other party accepts the benefit, then he is obliged to pay a reasonable price for it. In such circumstances the courts allow an action on a quantum meruit basis an equitable principle literally meaning as much as he deserves. This exception however will only apply where the party receiving the benefit has the option of whether or not to accept or reject it. In *Sumpter v. Hedges* the owner had no choice but to accept the work done on the half completed houses and was therefore not obliged to pay for it, whereas in *Lawson v. Supasink* the units were capable of being removed and returned.

## Where performance is prevented

Obviously if a party to a contract is prevented from fulfilling his contractual obligations by the other party then he will not be in default. In a building contract should the owner prevent the builder from completing, for example by locking him out of the site, the builder can recover a reasonable price for the work done on what is called a *quantum meruit basis* (a concept discussed later in the chapter).

As well as the above exceptions to the general rule that the performance of contractual obligations must be precise, it is well settled that if a party to a contract makes a valid tender (offer) of performance this may be regarded as equivalent to performance. The refusal of the other party to allow performance to take place will discharge any further obligations on the part of the tenderer. Thus if a seller of goods tries to deliver them at the agreed time and place and the goods meet contract description, the refusal of the buyer to accept them will,

- amount to a valid tender of performance; and

- entitle the seller to sue the buyer under s.50 Sale of Goods Act 1979 for damages for non-acceptance of the goods.

Despite the problems that can sometimes occur in performance, most contracts are nevertheless satisfactorily discharged in this way.

## Discharge by agreement

This method of discharge occurs where the parties mutually agree to waive their rights and obligations under it. It is called bilateral discharge. To be an effective *waiver* the second agreement must be a contract, the consideration for which is the exchange of promises not to enforce the original contract.

Each party is agreeing to release the other from the original contractual promises and not to use on the grounds of non-performance. The situation however is more complex where one party to a contract has already executed or partly executed his consideration under it. Here for a waiver to be effective it must be embodied within a speciality contract or be supported by fresh consideration. This is called unilateral discharge and can only be achieved by *accord* and *satisfaction*. The accord is simply the agreement to discharge and the satisfaction is the consideration required to support it. An example occurs when a football manager with three years of a £100,000 per year contract still to run is asked by the club after a poor season to leave. If the two sides agree to a new deal (the accord) in which the manager will receive a £200,000 lump sum to go, both sides obtain a new benefit (satisfaction). The manager receives a substantial payment and the club can bring in a new manager. By contrast suppose X contracts to sell goods to Y for £50. X then delivers the goods to Y but hearing of Y's financial difficulties agrees to waive payment. Here the agreement of X to waive payment (the accord) is not enforceable unless supported by fresh consideration furnished by Y (the satisfaction). The fresh consideration of course must be of value but need not be adequate. As we saw in our examination of the principles of consideration, at common law the rule in *Pinnel's case* provides that there is no value in a creditor taking as satisfaction payment of a lesser sum than he was due under the original agreement.

A creditor's promise to accept a reduced amount may however be binding on him, through the operation of the equitable doctrine of promissory estoppel, established in *Hughes v. Metropolitan Railway Co.* 1877 by the House of Lords, and by Denning J as he then was in *Central London Property Trust Ltd. v. High Trees House Ltd.* 1947. In the High Trees case the defendant company took a 99-year lease on a block of flats from the plaintiff company at an annual rent of £2,500. The lease was granted in 1937. By 1940 the evacuation of large numbers of people out of London because of war meant that the defendant company was unable to let all the flats and could not meet the annual rent out of the profits it was making. As a result, the plaintiff company agreed to accept a reduced annual rent of £1,250. By the beginning of 1945 the flats were fully let again. An action was brought by the plaintiff company to recover the difference between the reduced rent and the full rent for the last two quarters of 1945. The action succeeded, for the court considered that the agreement of 1940 would continue only as long as wartime conditions prevailed. The Court also considered whether the plaintiffs could recover the remaining arrears from the defendants, relying on *Pinnel's case*. It took the view that such action would be inequitable, even though permissible at common law. In equity the creditor would be estopped, or denied the right of disowning his promise to accept the reduced amount, where the debtor had to the creditor's knowledge relied on the promise, and acted on it to his detriment. This rule is consequently referred to as promissory estoppel. The doctrine only arises within the context of a pre-existing contractual relationship, and does not remove consideration as a requirement of the contract.

Being a form of equitable relief, promissory estoppel can only be used as defence by those who have acted in an equitable manner themselves.

In *D & C Builders v. Rees* 1965 Mr. & Mrs Rees exacted a promise from D & C Builders to accept a reduced amount than that originally agreed, for building work carried out to the Rees's home. They claimed the building work was substandard, but in fact they were simply attempting to escape the full payment due, using their knowledge that the builders were in financial difficulties and desperate for cash. Sometime after the reduced payment had been made the company sued for the outstanding balance, and the defendants pleaded promissory estoppel. The court refused to allow Mr. & Mrs Rees the equitable defence, on the grounds of their own lack of equity.

## Discharge by breach

A party to a contract who completely fails to perform their obligations under it or performs them defectively is in breach of contract. Generally, the remedy of an innocent party to a contract who has suffered as a result of a breach is to sue for damages. For some breaches of contract however, the innocent party is given the additional remedy of treating the contract as repudiated, in other words terminated, thus discharging any remaining obligations arising under it. Terms in a contract have different status and it is only when a condition has been broken that repudiatory breach can occur. If a breach of contract takes place before the time set for performance of the agreement it is called an *anticipatory breach*. This will occur where a party to a contract expressly declares they will not perform their part of the bargain. Once an anticipatory breach has arisen the innocent party does not have to wait for the date set for performance but has the option of immediately suing for breach of contract. In such circumstances the injured party has the choice of commencing legal action at the time of the anticipatory breach, or of waiting until performance is due to see if it is in fact carried out, and if it is not, commence action thereafter. Which approach is adopted is likely to have an effect upon the level of any damages awarded. Crucially of course it has to be decided whether the words or actions that have given rise to the assumption of repudiation are in the circumstances sufficient. In *Woodar Investment Development Ltd. v. Wimpey Construction Ltd. 1980,* Lord Willberforce said the test was, " *whether, objectively speaking* (the defendants) *conduct showed an intention to abandon the contract. "*

## Discharge by frustration or subsequent impossibility

Discharged by frustration occurs where as a result of an event subsequent to making the contract, its performance can no longer be carried out. The event must arise after contracting since if the contract is impossible to perform at the time it is made there can be no contract. Originally the common law did not take such a lenient view of changes in circumstances and required that the parties to a contract should provide for all eventualities. If because of a subsequent event performance of an obligation became impossible, the party required to perform it would be liable to pay damages for non performance. Today however the courts recognise that certain supervening events may frustrate a contract and thus release the parties from their obligation under it.

In *National Carriers Ltd. v. Panalpina (Northern) Ltd.* 1981 the plaintiffs leased a warehouse in Hull to the defendants. The lease was for ten years, however for a period of twenty months the only access road to the premises was closed by the local authority due to the poor state of a listed building nearby. The defendants refused to pay any further rent to the plaintiffs. The House of Lords accepted the defendant's argument that a lease could, in law, become frustrated, but felt that twenty months out of a ten year period, was not sufficiently substantial to frustrate the contract.

There are a number of grounds upon which a contract may become frustrated. They include:

- *Changes in the law.* If because of new legislation performance of the contract would become illegal this would be a supervening event to frustrate the contract.

- *Destruction of subject matter.* If the subject matter or means of performance of the contract is destroyed this is an event which frustrates a contract.

In *Taylor v. Caldwell* 1863 the plaintiff agreed to hire the defendant's music hall to give some concerts. Prior to performance the hall was destroyed by fire and this event, the court held, released the parties from their obligations under the contract.

- *Inability to achieve main object.* If as a result of change in circumstances performance of the contract would be radically different from the performance envisaged by the parties then the contract is frustrated. It must be shown that the parties are no longer able to achieve their main object under the contract.

In *Krell v. Henry* 1903 the defendant hired a flat for two days to enable him to watch Edward VII's Coronation procession. Due to the King's illness the Coronation was cancelled and the defendant naturally refused to pay. The Court of Appeal held that as the main object of the contract was to view the procession, and this could no longer be achieved, the foundation of the contract had collapsed. The contract was thus frustrated and the parties released from their obligations under it.

A further claim of frustration as a consequence of the cancellation of the Coronation was brought in *Herne Bay Steamboat Co. v. Hutton* 1903. Here a steamboat had been chartered to watch the naval review as part of the

Coronation celebrations and also for a day's cruise round the fleet. The Court of Appeal had to determine whether the cancellation of the naval review released the defendant from his obligation to pay the hire charge. The Court held that there has not been a sufficient change in circumstances to constitute a frustration of the contract. Here the defendant could have derived some benefit from the contract and was therefore liable to pay the hire charges. Frustration is not available in a commercial transaction merely because the contract turns out to be less profitable than one of the parties expected.

- *Death or illness.* In a contract for personal services the death or illness of the person required to perform will frustrate the contract. Temporary illness or incapacity will generally not release a party from his obligations. The illness must be such that it goes to the root of the contract.

## Non frustrating events

The common law doctrine of frustration will not apply in the following circumstances:

(a)   If performance of the contract has become more onerous on one party or financially less rewarding.

In *Davis Contractors Ltd. v. Fareham UDC* 1956 the plaintiff building company claimed that a building contract should be regarded as discharged by frustration due to the shortage of available labour and resultant increased costs. The House of Lords rejected the arguments that frustration had discharged the contract. Performance of the contract had simply been made more onerous than originally envisaged by the plaintiffs.

(b)   If the parties to a contract have made express provision for the event which has occurred.

(c)   If it can be shown that a party to the contract caused the supposed frustrating event by his own conduct then there will be no frustration however there may be a contractual breach. This is self induced frustration.

## Consequences of frustration of contract

To determine the rights and duties of the parties following frustration it is necessary to consider the position at common law and under statute. As we have seen frustration will terminate a contract. However under common law it does not discharge the contract *ab initio* (from the outset) but only from the time of the frustrating event. Therefore, if before that date work had been done or money transferred, the common law rule is simply that losses lie where they fall. It is thus not possible to recover money due or paid prior to frustrating events, except if there is a total failure or consideration, for example if there has been performance of consideration by one party and non performance of consideration by the other.

This common law position was altered by the Law Reform (Frustrated Contracts) Act 1943. The Act however does not apply to certain contracts such as insurance, charter-parties (shipping contracts) and contracts for the sale of specific goods, so the common law position remains to some transactions relevant. Under the Act the following conditions apply:

- Money transferred prior to the frustrating event may be recovered.

- Money due prior to the frustrating event is no longer due.

- Expenses incurred prior to the frustrating event may be deducted from money to be returned.

- Compensation may be recovered on a quantum meruit basis where one of the parties has carried out an act of part performance prior to the frustrating event and thus conferred a benefit on the other party.

In *Gamero SA v. ICM/Fair Warning (Agency) Ltd.* 1995 the plaintiffs had agreed with the defendants to promote the defendants rock concert. It was to be held in a Madrid stadium, however a few days before the concert the plaintiff's licence to hold it was taken away by the public authority following safety concerns about the stadium and the concert did not take place. Both the parties had incurred preliminary expenses, and the plaintiffs had made an advance payment to the defendants, which they sought to recover under the 1943 Act. The court found the contract to be frustrated because the stadium could not be used. The plaintiffs could recover the advance payment. The court decided not to deduct the defendants expenses from this sum, as the plaintiffs had also suffered loss and to make the deduction would be unfair.

## Remedies for Breach of Contract

Whenever a breach of contract arises the innocent party is likely to seek a remedy against the contract breaker. We saw at the beginning of our study of contract law that the fundamental quality of contracts is their legally enforceability, and in the law on remedies that enforceability is realised. The options available are to claim damages and/or treat the contract as discharged under the common law, or to pursue an equitable discretionary remedy.

## Damages

Damages is the technical term used to describe monetary compensation. The usual claim is for *unliquidated* damages under the common law. Unliquidated damages are damages whose level is determined by the court, exercising its own discretion. It is sometimes possible for a plaintiff to quantify the measure of damages being sought concisely, in which event the plaintiff will claim a *liquidated* amount e.g.: three weeks' loss of salary where the salary is of a fixed amount, or loss of profit on a sale.

### The aim of awarding damages

Damages awarded under an unliquidated claim should amount to a sum which will put the innocent party in the position he would have been in had the contract been performed properly, that is the loss resulting from the breach directly and naturally. Consequently a plaintiff should not be awarded damages when the result would be to put him in a better position financially than would have been the case if the contract had not been broken. The aim of awarding contractual damages is not to punish the contract breaker.

> In *C & B Haulage v. Middleton* 1983 the Court of Appeal refused to grant damages to an engineer who was evicted from the business premises he occupied before the contractual licence he held had expired. The reason for the refusal was that he was working from home, and thus relieved from paying any further charges under the licence. Damages would make him better off.

Damages may be refused where the court is of the view that they are too speculative.

> On this basis the court awarded only nominal damages to the plaintiffs in *Entertainments Ltd. v. Great Yarmouth Borough Council* 1983. The council had repudiated an agreement under which the plaintiffs were to put on summer shows in the town. The judge, Cantley J took the view that as it had not been established as probable that the shows would have made the plaintiffs a profit, to award anything other than nominal damages would be speculative.

If as a result of a breach of contract the innocent party does not obtain what he expected under the contract, but the value of the performance is not affected, what is the level of damages that a court should award to compensate for the loss?

This was the issue faced by the courts in *Ruxley Electronics and Construction Ltd. v. Forsyth* 1995. Builders had agreed to build a swimming pool with a maximum depth of 7ft 6ins for £70,178. When the work was completed the customer discovered that the maximum depth was only 6ft 9 ins and only 6ft at the point that people would dive in. As is usual in this type of building contract certain sums had been paid by the owner towards the cost of the work during the construction and £39,072 remained outstanding. The builders claimed the balance and the customer counterclaimed for breach of contract. The High Court held that despite the builders breach of contract there had been no reduction in the value of the pool and ordered the customer to pay the balance less £2,500 for the loss of amenity. This decision was reversed by the Court of Appeal who decided that it was appropriate to award £21,560 damages to reflect the cost of replacing the pool to remedy the breach, even though the depth of the pool had not decreased its value. On final appeal the House of Lords held that in this type of case involving defective building work the court was entitled to take the view that it would be unreasonable to insist on reinstatement if the expense of the work involved would be out of all proportion to the benefit obtained. A relevant factor in determining reasonableness was the intention of the customer to rebuild. In this case as the customer did not intend to reinstate, his loss was restricted to the difference in value. The original judgment of £2,500 damages for the loss of amenity was restored and the decision of the Court of Appeal reversed.

## Remoteness of damage

The consequences of a contractual breach can often extend well beyond the immediate, obvious losses. A failure to deliver goods may for example result in the buyer being unable to complete the work on a particular job, which will in turn put him in breach with the party who had contracted him to carry out the job. That party may in turn suffer further consequences, thus the original breach leads to a chain of events which become increasingly remote from it. Damages will only be awarded for losses which are *proximate*. The courts take the view that it is unfair to make a contract-breaker responsible for damage caused as a result of circumstances of which he was unaware.

In *Hadley v. Baxendale* 1854 the plaintiff mill owner contracted with a defendant carrier who agreed to take a broken millshaft to a repairer and then return it. The carrier delayed in delivery of the shaft and as a result the plaintiff sought to recover the loss of profit he would have made during the period of delay. The court held that this loss was not recoverable as it was too remote. The possible loss of profit was a circumstance of which the carrier was unaware at the time of the contract. The result would have been different however had the plaintiff expressly made the defendant aware that this loss of profit was the probable result of a breach of contract.

The decision in *Hadley v. Baxendale* has been approved by the House of Lords on many occasions and knowledge of the circumstances which could produce the damage it still a crucial factor in determining the extent of the liability for the breach.

In *Czarnikow v. Koufos (The Heron II)* 1969 a shipowner delayed in delivering a cargo of sugar to Basrah. The sugar was to be sold by the cargo owners at Basrah, where there was an established sugar market. During the nine days the ship was delayed the market price fell. The cargo owners successfully sued for their loss. The House of Lords considered that the loss ought to have been within the reasonable contemplation of the shipowners as a consequence of the delay. It was felt that the shipowners should have appreciated that a market for goods is something which by its nature fluctuates over time.

In *Balfour Beatty Construction (Scotland) Ltd. v. Scottish Power plc* 1994 the defendants were supplying electricity to the plaintiffs under an agreement linked to a construction project the plaintiffs were carrying out. A break in the supply prevented the completion of a concrete pour. As a result prior construction work was rendered useless and had to be demolished, and then rebuilt. On the grounds that the defendants neither were aware, nor ought reasonably to have been aware of the full effect of interruption to a concrete pour, the House of Lords held the losses to be too remote.

## Other principles applicable to a claim for damages

Where a breach has occurred the innocent party, if he accepts that the breach discharges the contract, must take all reasonable steps to mitigate the loss resulting from the breach. There is no requirement for the injured party to act immediately to take on a risky venture but rather act reasonably in order to minimise the loss rather than *sitting on the breach*. For instance an hotel would be expected to try and relet a room that a customer, in breach of contract, had failed to use.

In *Luker v. Chapman* 1970 the plaintiff lost his right leg below the knee following a motor accident partly caused by the negligence of the defendant.

This injury prevented him from continuing his work as a telephone engineer, but he was offered clerical work as an alternative. He refused it, choosing instead to go into teacher training. It was held that he could not recover as damages the loss of income suffered whilst he underwent the teacher training.

Damages are not limited to the pure economic cost of the loss of the bargain but may also be recovered for inconvenience, discomfort, distress or anxiety caused by the breach.

In *Jarvis v. Swans Tours Ltd.* 1973 the Court of Appeal held that the plaintiff was entitled to damages for mental distress and disappointment due to loss of enjoyment caused by breach of a holiday contract.

In substantial contracts involving large sums, such as building contracts, it is usual to attempt to liquidate damages payable in the event of a breach. This is achieved by the parties expressly inserting a clause into the contract providing for a sum of compensation to be payable on a breach. Generally, provided such clauses represent a genuine pre-estimate of the future possible loss rather than amounting to a penalty to ensure performance of contract, they are enforceable by the courts.

The right to treat a contract as discharged will depend upon the nature of the breach. For breaches of condition the innocent party may sue for damages and/or treat the contract as repudiated, whereas for less important terms the innocent party is limited to an action for damages.

Quantification of damages in relation to goods or land is essentially a question of assessing the market price and then determining the actual loss. The Sale of Goods Act 1979 provides for a number of remedies, including damages, available to an injured party to a sale of goods transaction.

## Discretionary remedies

Historically these remedies became available through the intervention of the Court of Chancery. They include the injunction, specific performance and the remedy of quantum meruit.

## Injunctions

An injunction is an order of the court which directs a person not to break his contract, and is an appropriate remedy where the contract contains a negative stipulation.

This can be seen in *Warner Bros. Pictures v. Nelson* 1937. The defendant, the actress Bette Davis, had agreed to work for the plaintiff company for twelve months, and not to act or sing for anyone else or be otherwise employed for a period of two years, without the plaintiff's written consent. It was held that she could be restrained by injunction from breaking the negative aspects of her undertaking, thus preventing her from working under a new acting contract in England where she was earning more money. The injunction was however confined to her work as an actress, for it was recognised that if the negative terms in her contract were fully enforced it would have the effect of either forcing her to work for Warner Bros. or starve, and this would mean the injunction acting as a device for specific performance of the contract. Equity will not order specific performance of contracts of a personal kind which would involve constant supervision, and which, by their nature, depend upon the good faith of the parties. Similarly in *Page One Records Ltd. v. Britton* 1968 an injunction was applied for to prevent the Troggs pop group from engaging anyone as their manager other than the plaintiff. An injunction on these terms was refused, for to grant it would indirectly compel the pop group to continue to employ the plaintiff.

## Types of injunction

There are three types of injunction which may be applied for:

(a)   *an interlocutory injunction.* This is designed to regulate the position of the parties pending trial, the plaintiff undertaking to be responsible for any damage caused to the defendant through the use of the injunction if in the subsequent action the plaintiff is unsuccessful. In *American Cyanamid v. Ethicon* 1975 the House of Lords said that an interlocutory injunction should only be granted where the plaintiff can show that the matter to be tried is a serious one and that the balance of convenience is in his favour. One rarely used option for an employee who feels that his employer is unreasonably requiring him to do work which is not part of his contactual obligations is to seek an injunction to maintain the status quo at work.

In certain circumstances a specialised kind of interlocutory injunction, known as a *Mareva injunction,* may be sought. The Mareva injunction takes its name from the case in which it was first successfully applied for, *Mareva Compania Naviera v. International Bulk Carriers* 1980, and it is used when the subject matter of a contract is in danger of being removed from the area of the courts jurisdiction. If the action which is to be heard involves a claim for damages and the sale of the subject matter is likely to be used to pay them, a Mareva injunction can be used to restrict the removal of these assets from the courts' jurisdiction. This is a valuable protection in cases where the defendant is a foreign organisation. Section 37 of the Supreme Court Act 1981 grants the High Court the power to issue such injunctions.

(b)    *a prohibitory injunction.* This orders a defendant not to do a particular thing. The injunction sought in the *Nelson* case (above) was of this kind. Much of the case law concerning prohibitory injunctions is concerned with employment contracts, and as we have seen such an injunction can only be used to enforce a negative stipulation. In addition the remedy of a prohibitory injunction will not be given where a court is of the opinion that damages would be an adequate remedy, although in the words of Sachs LJ in *Evans Marshall v. Bertola SA* 1973 *"The standard question in relation to the grant of an injunction, are damages an adequate remedy? might perhaps, in the light of the authorities of recent years, be rewritten: is it just, in all the circumstances, that a plaintiff should be confined to his remedy in damages."*

A prohibitory injunction was used in *Decro-Wall International v. Practitioners in Marketing* 1971 where a manufacturer was restrained from breaking a sole distributorship agreement by an order preventing him from disposing of the goods to which the agreement related in any other way. The Court was not however prepared to order him to fulfil the positive part of the agreement which was to maintain supplies of the goods to the distributor, for this would have amounted to specific performance of the contract (see below).

(c)    *a mandatory injunction.* This is used to order that a positive act be done, for example that a fence blocking a right of way be taken down.

In *Sky Petroleum Ltd. v. VIP Petroleum Ltd.* 1974 the parties entered into a ten year agreement in 1970 under which VIP undertook to supply all Sky's petrol requirements. Following a dispute in 1973 VIP refused to continue its supplies to Sky, and because of an oil crisis at the time Sky found itself unable to secure any other source of supply. The Court granted a temporary injunction against VIP restraining it from withholding a reasonable level of supplies.

## Specific performance

The decree of specific performance is an order of the court requiring a party who is in breach of contract to carry out his promises. Failure to comply amounts to a contempt of court. As an equitable remedy it will only be granted if certain conditions apply. These are:

- *Where damages would not provide an adequate remedy.* Usually in commercial transactions damages will be adequate, and will enable the injured party to purchase the property or obtain the services from some alternative source. However where the subject matter of the contract is unique, for example a painting, specific performance will lie. The item must however be unique, and in *Cohen v. Roche* 1927 specific performance was not ordered of a contract to sell some rare Hepplewhite chairs since it was difficult, but not impossible, to buy similar chairs on the open market.

Land is always regarded as unique, and it is in the enforcement of contracts for the sale of land that specific performance is most commonly used.

A contract for the purchase of shares or debentures can also be specifically enforced.

- *Where the court can properly supervise the performance.*

- *That it is not just and equitable to grant the order.*

In addition the plaintiff must satisfy the various equitable maxims which demand high standards of behaviour if relief is to be granted. Thus for example it is said that *"he who comes to equity must come with clean hands"*, meaning that the plaintiff's behaviour must be beyond reproach.

## Quantum meruit

A *quantum meruit* claim ( for as much as is deserved) is available where:

- *damages is not an appropriate remedy.* This could occur where performance of a contract has begun, but the plaintiff is unable to complete the contract because the defendant has repudiated it, thus preventing the plaintiff from obtaining payment.

- *where work has been carried out under a void contract .*

In *British Steel Corporation v. Cleveland Bridge and Engineering Co. Ltd.* 1984 steel had been supplied to the defendants by the plaintiffs whilst the parties were still negotiating terms. The negotiations subsequently failed, and no contract was concluded between them. The court held that the plaintiffs were entitled to claim on a quantum meruit for the price of the steel supplied to the defendants and used by them.

## Test Questions

1.  How is a contract discharged?

2.  Explain what is meant by substantial performance.

3.  What is accord and satisfaction?

4.  What happened in *D & C Builders v. Rees* 1965.

5.  Explain what is meant by a frustrated contract.

6.  Give three examples of non frustrating events.

7.  What is meant by unliquidated damages?

8.  When is damage too remote?

9.  What discretionary remedies are available for breach of contract?

10. Explain what is meant by a quantum meruit claim?

# Assignment - Are we Agreed?

You work as a legal assistant in the legal department of Anglo-Swedish Metal Industries plc. On returning from your summer holiday you find two files in your in-tray, accompanied by a memorandum from your superior, Jane West, one of the company's lawyers, which states, "Please respond to the letters contained in the attached files. See me if you have any difficulties."

The first file contains the following letter from a solicitor:

> I represent Miss Sally Goldwell. I understand from my client that she was interviewed for a clerical post with your company. Following the interview she was asked if she would be willing to accept the post, and she indicated that she would. A week later, on 10th September 199X, she received a formal offer of the post from your company's Personnel Officer. She was asked to reply in writing within five days. She was ill at the time and arranged for a friend to notify you of her acceptance by phone. Her friend telephoned sometime after 7 pm on 13th September 199X. This was a Friday, and her friend had to leave a message on the Personnel Department's answerphone. I gather that the Personnel Department closes from 4.30pm on Friday, until 8.30 the following Monday, and that the message only reached the Personnel Officer at midday on Monday 16th September. He had that morning telephoned another interviewee to offer her the job, which she accepted. My client subsequently heard from you that the post was no longer available for her.
>
> I am of the opinion that a contract exists between my client and yourselves, in respect of which you are in breach. I look forward to your prompt response.
>
> Yours faithfully,
>
> Roger Major

The second file contained the following letter from one of the company's suppliers, Humberside Steels Ltd.:

We refer to our offer to supply you with 40 tonnes reinforced steel bars, to which you responded with an order (68747/5/NX) for the goods to be delivered to you on 1st May. We replied immediately informing you that due to circumstances beyond our control delivery would be on the 24th May. We heard from you, and delivered the goods on 24th May, only to find that you rejected them on the basis that they had not been ordered. We are at a loss to understand your action, particularly as we have often varied the delivery date with you in this way in the past, without complaint by you.

We should be grateful therefore to receive your remittance in due course.

Yours faithfully

*James Leach*

James Leach pp
Humberside Steels Ltd.

## Tasks

1. In the form of a memorandum to your superior, Jane West, indicate any weaknesses you have been able to identify regarding the company's legal position in respect of the two claims.

2. Draft replies to each of the letters, in which you state the legal basis upon which the company challenges the contractual claims they make.

## Guidance

These tasks explore the law relating to the making of agreements, and so you should concentrate upon applying the rules of offer and acceptance in order to determine whether or not a contract has occurred in each case. The use of counter offers can be seen in one of the problems. You may find that you face ambiguities that emerge from the facts; what for example does "5 days" mean?

# Assignment - The Brothers

Tim and Anthony O'Brien are brothers who set up together in business as builders some years ago. The business was based in Dagenham where they both lived. In 1985 Tim married and moved some miles away to Colchester. As as a result the business was dissolved, each brother re-establishing a business in his own right. Tim was more successful than Anthony, who was not such a good businessman. Anthony acquired a reputation as a bad credit risk, and found it increasingly difficult to find suppliers who were prepared to deliver building materials without payment in advance. He told Tim about the problem.

Tim's main supplier was a company called Anglian Associated Materials Ltd. Tim knew the managing director well, since they both belonged to the local golf club and were District Councillors together. Tim mentioned his brother's problem to Charlie, the managing director, and Charlie agreed to supply Anthony. "Obviously I'll see you all right Charlie, if anything goes wrong", responded Tim.

Earlier this year Anthony placed an order with Charlie's company for £4,000 worth of timber, and £8,000 of scaffolding. Due to acute cashflow problems he subsequently found himself unable to pay the full debt when it was demanded, and contacted Charlie direct to discuss the matter. Charlie reluctantly agreed to accept £2,000 for the timber, but insisted the scaffolding had to be paid for in full. Charlie then approached Tim, reminding him of his earlier promise, and requesting him to meet the outstanding £2,000 debt. Tim subsequently replied by letter as follows:

```
Dear Charlie,

I have been advised that I have no legal liability
regarding payment of the outstanding amount of my brothers
indebtedness to your company. However, in recognition of
our friendship and all the help you have given me in the
past I am prepared to make a payment of £1000 towards the
bill.

Yours sincerely,

       T OBrien.

Tim O'Brien
```

Later that week Tim wrote again:

> Dear Charlie,
>
> I understand that my brother's business is in credit again. In the circumstances I feel I must withdraw my offer to you, and suggest that you pursue him for the outstanding amount.
>
> Yours sincerely,
>
> *Tim O'Brien*
>
> Tim O'Brien

## Task

As an administrative assistant to the Company Secretary of Anglian Associated Materials Ltd. you often deal with legal problems involving facing the company, and Charlie, the managing director, has asked you to consider whether the company has a legitimate claim for payment against either of the brothers.

Draft an informal report for the managing director in which you indicate the company's legal position in the matter.

# Chapter 3

## Consumer Protection Law

The aim of this chapter is to identify and explain some of the key provisions relating to consumer protection from the main statutory sources of consumer protection law. The table on the following page provides an overview of UK consumer protection legislation and how it is enforced. The table clearly shows the division between civil and criminal liability, and in the case of the latter the significant enforcement role of trading standards officers employed by local authorities throughout the UK. Aggrieved consumers have in addition numerous civil law remedies, particularly when suppliers of goods and services fail to fulfill contractual obligations. Civil proceedings may be taken through small claims arbitration or court action by consumers seeking legal redress.

The chapter focuses on the key provisions of consumer protection legislation and on the role of agencies concerned with consumer protection. The following statutes and regulations make up the law of contemporary consumer protection law and each is considered in the chapter.

- Sale of Goods Act 1979

- Sale and Supply of Goods Act 1994

- Unfair Contract Terms Act 1977

- Trade Descriptions Act 1968

- Property Misdescriptions Act 1991

- Consumer Credit Act 1974

- Data Protection Act 1998

- The Food Safety Act 1990

- Consumer Protection Act 1987

- Supply of Goods and Services Act 1982

- Unfair Terms in Consumer Contracts Regulations 1995

# Consumer Protection Law

## Civil Law

| Legal Source | Unlawful Act | Enforcement |
| --- | --- | --- |
| Contract Law | Breach of contract misrepresentation | Contracting party sues in the Civil Courts |
| Sale of Goods Act 1979 Sale and Supply of Goods Act 1994 | Breach of sale of goods contract | Buyer or seller sues in the Civil Courts |
| Supply of Goods and Services Act 1982 | Breach of contract for the supply of service | Buyer or seller sues in the Civil Courts |
| Package Travel Regulations 1992 | Tour organiser falsely describes package causing loss | Consumer sues in the Civil Courts |
| Consumer Credit Act 1975 | Creditors failure to comply with formalities or extortionate credit bargain | Debtor has right of cancellation, termination, and court redress, and possible interest rate deduction |
| Consumer Protection Act 1987 | Defective product put into circulation by producer/supplier | Injured party sues in the Civil Courts |

## Criminal Law

| Legal Source | Unlawful Act | Enforcement |
| --- | --- | --- |
| Trade Descriptions Act 1968 and Consumer Protection Act 1987 | False description of goods and services | Trading Standards Officers prosecute in the Criminal Courts |
| Food Safety Act 1980 | Sell, offer for sale food injurious to health | Trading Standards Officers and Environmental Health Officers may serve orders or bring prosecutions |
| Consumer Protection Act 1987 | Supply consumer goods which are not reasonably safe | Trading Standards Officers may serve orders or prosecute in the Criminal Courts |
| Consumer Credit Act 1974 | Failure to comply with duties imposed on the suppliers of credit | Trading Standards Officers |
| Package Travel Regulations 1992 | Tour organiser falsely describes a package holiday or fails to provide information | Trading Standards Officers prosecute in the criminal courts |

# The Sale of Goods Act 1979

This Act regulates all contracts for the sale of goods. The importance of the Sale of Goods Act 1979 to the commercial activity of the United Kingdom cannot be underestimated, for it provides the framework of rights and obligations applicable to all buyers and sellers of goods. The original Sale of Goods Act of 1893 sought to regulate the contract of sale only to the extent that the parties themselves had failed to do so, and as a result subsequently found themselves in disagreement. It was not for Parliament to dictate to a businessperson what the contract should be. This freedom to exclude is still contained in the Sale of Goods Act 1979, but it is now a very limited freedom. This is because it is subject to the provisions of the Unfair Contract Terms Act 1977, which restricts, and in certain cases, prohibits a seller from excluding his liabilities which arise under the 1979 Act. The effect of such restrictions is that the 1979 Act is not simply an aid to the business world, it is also a creator and defender of the rights of the economically weaker sections of the community, and thus qualifies for inclusion in the growing body of legislation which grants protection to the consumer and which is consequently referred to as consumer law.

## Definition of a Sale of Goods Transaction

The Act defines a contract for the sale of goods as one by which the seller transfers or agrees to transfer the *property* in goods to the buyer for money consideration called the price. To understand this definition and therefore identify those transactions which fall outside the Act, an explanation of the terms *property*, *goods* and *money consideration* is necessary.

*Property* is ownership. It follows that the Act does not apply to transactions in which ownership does not pass from one party to the other, for example where goods are hired or borrowed, for the hirer or borrower is simply obtaining possession, not ownership. Hire purchase agreements are excluded from the Act. This is because a hire purchase agreement consists of a simple hiring of goods, to which there is attached an option to purchase. Since the hirer is not compelled to purchase the goods he or she is not a 'buyer' for the Act defines a buyer as a person who *buys* or *agrees to buy* goods.

In *Helby v. Matthews* 1895 the House of Lords made it clear that an option does not give rise to a firm commitment. In that case a piano dealer agreed to hire a piano to a customer for a period of 3 years by monthly repayments. The agreement provided that on completion of all the monthly payments the customer would become the owner of the piano, being liable to pay any arrears of the monthly payments outstanding at the date of termination. During the hire period the customer disposed of the piano to an innocent third party. The Court held that the dealer was entitled to recover the piano from the third party for the customer was not an owner and therefore could not pass a *good title* (i.e. ownership) to the third party.

The expression goods includes all personal property including such things as cars, furniture, tools, and books - but not land which forms a separate category of property. Things which are attached to or form part of the land and which are agreed to be removed from the land either before the sale or under the contract of sale are treated as goods. However such goods must be identifiable from the land itself and not classified as fixtures, such as machinery bolted to the floor.

In *Morgan v Russell and Sons* 1909 a sale of slag and cinders was considered not to be a sale of goods because these materials had merged into the land upon which they had been deposited.

In *St Albans District Council v. ICL* 1996 the court held that the sale of computer software to be used by the council administering the community charge (the poll tax) did not constitute a sale of goods because as a program it was intangible. The result would be different however if the program had been supplied on a disk for then of the Sale of Goods Act 1979 would imply a term in the contract requiring it to be fit for the purpose for which it was bought.

Annual growing crops such as barley, and industrial growing crops, like pine trees, are also goods within the meaning of the Act. However the following do not constitute goods:

* shares and patents;

* money, unless sold as something other than currency, such as a collector's item;

* contracts whose substance is the supply of labour and materials where the value of the materials supplied under the contract is of lesser value than that of the labour involved. In *Robinson v. Graves* 1935 a commission to paint a portrait was held to be a contract for labour and materials. In contrast the following have been held to the contracts of sale: a contract to supply and lay a carpet (*Philip Head & Sons Ltd v. Showfronts Ltd* 1970), a contract to make a fur coat, and a contract to prepare and supply food in a restaurant.

The expression *money consideration* excludes from the definition of contract of sale gifts, and any transaction where goods are exchanged for other goods - a *barter* -

although where the consideration is partly in goods and partly in money the contract will be one of sale.

# Price

It might be expected that in a commercial transaction the parties will at very least determine the price of the goods. The Act says that the price may be fixed under the contract or left to be fixed in a manner agreed by the contract, or where the parties have dealt with each other before, by reference to their previous course of dealing. In the event of no price being fixed the buyer must pay a *reasonable* price. Although this is likely to be the *market* price it is necessary to consider the circumstances of each particular case.

# The Transfer of Property

The object of a sale is the transfer of property (i.e. ownership) in the goods from the seller to the buyer. The Act lays down a set of rules for determining when this vitally important event takes place, but these rules apply only if the parties have not expressed their own intention as to when property shall pass. The rules are examined later but it is helpful at this stage to identify why the time at which property passes is so important.

(i)    The Act states that *risk* passes with property, unless the parties agree otherwise. This means that it is the owner of the goods who bears the risk of them being stolen or accidentally damaged. A person may be an owner although not in actual physical possession or control of the goods, as for example where a buyer of a painting leaves it at the auction rooms for collection at a later date, or where a seller allows the buyer to take possession of the goods, but provides in the contract that ownership shall only pass to the buyer when all outstanding sums owed by the buyer to the seller have been paid - a *Romalpa clause*. A prudent owner will usually insure the goods, and this will be especially important where the goods are not under his or her own control. The Act also provides that if delivery of the goods has been delayed through the fault of one of the parties the goods are then at the risk of the party at fault.

(ii)   It is a general rule of law that a non-owner of goods cannot transfer ownership in them to another. This is expressed by the Latin maxim *nemo dat quod non habet* (no one can give what he has not got). The rule is subject to a number of exceptions, but as a broad principle a seller who is not an owner is unable to transfer a valid title.

(iii)   The seller can sue for the price of the goods only after the property in
them has passed, unless the parties have agreed that payment should be
made at some other time.

It will be recalled that the definition of a contract for the sale of goods makes
reference to the transfer of property. It goes on to add that where property in the
goods is transferred at the time the contract is made, there has been a *sale*, whereas
if the transfer is to take place at some future time or subject to some condition to be
fulfilled later the contract is called an *agreement to sell*. In this connection two
points relating to the passing of property are worth noting. Firstly the Act provides
that if a seller sells goods to a buyer and is unaware that the goods had *perished* at
the time the contract was made the contract will be void on the grounds of
*impossibility*. They may for instance have been stolen, or destroyed by fire while in
a warehouse, without the seller's knowledge. Secondly the Act provides that where
the goods perish *after* the contract has been made, but before the risk was passed to
the buyer, then the contract becomes *frustrated* and void, (frustration was examined
in Chapter 2). Exactly when the goods reach a stage at which they can be said to
have perished is not clear, however in *Asfar v. Blundell* 1896 a consignment of dates
that became unsaleable through contamination with sewage were held to have
perished.

## Conditions and Warranties

Even the most simple type of contract contains promises given by one party to the
other. Most will include a variety of mutual undertakings. These undertakings are
the contractual obligations which each party owes to the other and they represent the
terms of the agreement - its *contents*. They generally arise through express
agreement, however certain terms are implied into specific types of contract by
statute, and the courts will sometimes be prepared to imply terms which the parties
have not expressly agreed. If a term is broken the consequences for the contract will
depend upon the importance of the term in relation to the contract. Obviously the
more important it is the more serious will be the effect if it is broken. Terms are
classified into conditions, warranties and innominate terms.

In relation to sales the Act defines conditions and warranties by looking at the effect
on the contract if they are broken. A condition is an undertaking, the breach of
which gives rise to a right on the part of the innocent party to treat the contract as
repudiated (i.e. rejected) and/or to recover damages. A warranty on the other hand
is an undertaking whose breach entitles the innocent party to claim only damages,
but the contract still stands. A warranty is therefore of less importance to the
purpose of the contract. Where there has been a breach of condition there may still
be sound reasons for continuing the contract. For instance the buyer may have no
other source of supply than the seller and is unlikely therefore to repudiate when the

seller advises that for example the goods cannot be delivered on time. It should be added that the courts will usually regard the delivery date in a commercial transaction as being a condition, or of the essence of the contract as it is sometimes expressed.

> In *Richards (Charles) Ltd v. Oppenheim* 1950 the seller agreed to build the buyer a car. When it had not been completed by the agreed delivery date the buyer requested the seller to complete it as soon as possible. Over three months later the car was still not ready, and the buyer told the seller that if it was not ready at the end of a further four weeks the contract would terminate. It was held that since the car was still incomplete at the end of the period the buyer was under no obligation to buy. He had waived the original delivery date, but had replaced it by serving a reasonable notice on the seller to complete the work.

Whether a particular term is to be treated as a condition or a warranty is a matter of interpretation for the courts. The label placed upon a term by the parties, for instance goods sold 'warranted free of all defects', does not mean that the court is bound by that label. In the example above defects in the goods would more likely be regarded as breaches of condition, enabling the buyer to repudiate, than warranties limiting the claim to damages alone.

Under sections 12-15 of the Sale of Goods Act 1979 a wide range of conditions (and two warranties) are implied into all sales of goods. Taken together these provisions impose upon business sellers stringent trading and quality standards and represent key consumer rights. These occur notably in relation to the descriptions applied in the marketing of goods, in the emphasis placed upon customer reliance on a seller's skill and judgment, and in respect of product standards.

## The Right to Sell

Under section 12 a condition is implied into a contract of sale that the seller has *a right to sell the goods*. If there is an agreement to sell it is an implied condition that the seller will have the right to sell by the time ownership is to pass. The words 'right to sell' mean that the seller must have the legal *power* to sell the goods if the seller does not own them (unless the true owner has authorised the seller to sell them) or exceptionally if he or she is the owner but can be prevented by legal means from selling them.

In *Niblett v. Confectioners Materials Co* 1921 a buyer purchased 3000 tons of preserved milk in tins, some of which bore labels marked 'Nissly Brand'. This constituted an infringement of the trade mark used by the Nestlé Company, who could have obtained an injunction restraining the sale of the tins by the purchaser.

The purchaser suffered a loss of profits by selling the tins without the offending labels, and it was held that the original sellers were in breach of the condition under s.12. *'If a vendor can be stopped by process of law from selling he has no right to sell,'* said Lord Justice Scrutton.

Section 12 also implies a warranty that the buyer will enjoy *quiet possession* of the goods.

> The meaning of this expression can be seen *in Microbeads v. Vinhurst Road Markings* 1975. Buyers of road-marking machines found that shortly after purchasing them, another company, not the seller, had become the patent holder of such machines, enabling it to bring action against the buyers to enforce the patent. The sellers were held liable in damages to the buyers, since the buyers ownership rights over attempting to exclude the machines were the subject of the rights of the patent holders.

Any clause attempting to exclude s.12 is treated as absolutely void by virtue of the Unfair Contract Terms Act, 1977.

## Sale by Description

When goods are sold it is usual to find the seller has described them in some way. The description may be verbal, or by reason of labelling on the goods 'Low Fat Natural Yoghurt'. Weight, size, quantity, contents and packing may also constitute part of the description. If goods are sold by description there is an implied condition, under s.13, that the goods shall correspond with the description. The following case illustrates the commercial importance of this condition and demonstrates how liability under it is strict.

In *Re: Moore & Co Ltd and Landauer & Co* 1921 the buyers of a quantity of canned fruit, which the contract required to be packed in cases each containing thirty tins, sought to reject the whole consignment when on delivery it was found that half the consignment was packed in cases containing twenty-four tins. The buyer's action was successful despite the fact that no commercial loss had been suffered by the buyer through the incorrect packing.

As a counter balance despite a buyer who purchases on the basis of a *trade* description applied to goods cannot rely on s.13 if the goods correspond to that description while failing to comply with its literal meaning. Thus when buyers of 'safety glass' to be fitted into goggles discovered that the glass splintered on impact they were unable to reject the glass since it conformed to the technical trade meaning of safety glass. They had assumed safety glass was glass that would not splinter. In addition microscopic deviations as to size, weight, etc. will in general be disregarded.

## Satisfactory Quality

Goods may of course correspond with description but still suffer from some major defect of substance. A leaking washing machine is still a washing machine, even though it is not of sound quality. S. 14(2) assists the buyer in such a situation by implying a condition on the part of the seller that the goods shall be of *satisfactory quality,* an expression introduced by the Sale and Supply of Goods Act 1994 to replace the somewhat old fashioned expression merchantable quality contained in the 1979 Act. The 1994 Act seeks to clarify the obligations of a supplier of goods in relation to the quality of the goods and to express the consumers rights in a clear and accessible way using plain English.

Section 14(2) of the 1979 Act, as amended, provides:

> *"Where the seller sells goods in the course of a business there is an implied condition that the goods supplied under the contract are of satisfactory quality".*

Even if the particular goods in question are not regularly sold by a business seller there is still a sale in the course of a business for the purposes of s.14(2) of the Sale of Goods Act 1979.

> In *Stevenson v Rogers* 1998 the Court of Appeal held that a one off sale of a fishing boat by a seller in business as a fisherman was subject to the implied condition of merchantability. This was despite the fact that it was clearly not a sale of trading stock but rather a capital asset, the court stressing the wide protection for buyers that the section was intended to introduce.

Under s.14(2)A, goods are of satisfactory quality if they *"meet the standard that a reasonable person would regard as satisfactory, taking account of any description of the goods, the price (if relevant) and all other relevant circumstances".*

> In *Rogers v. Parish (Scarborough) Ltd.* 1987 the plaintiff bought a new Range Rover from the defendant's garage. Although it was driveable and roadworthy the car had a number of defects in its engine, gearbox, oil seals and bodywork. The defendant argued that the car was of merchantable quality within the definition as it could be driven in safety on a road and therefore was *"fit for the purpose for which goods of that kind are commonly bought".* The Court of Appeal rejected the defendant's argument on the grounds that it was based upon too narrow an interpretation of s.14(2)A. *"The purpose for*

*which goods of that kind are commonly bought would include not merely the
purpose of driving the vehicle from one place to another but of doing so with
the appropriate degree of comfort, ease of handling, reliability and pride in
the vehicle's outward and interior appearance.*

It should be stressed that in determining whether goods are of satisfactory quality,
price and description are crucial factors. A £1000 pound used car may have many
defects and yet still be of satisfactory quality.

> In *Shine v. General Guarantee Corp Ltd* 1988 a secondhand car which had
> been submerged in water for 24 hours and written off was nevertheless
> described by the seller as *"superb, a good runner, and having no problems"*.
> The Court of Appeal felt that a reasonable purchaser knowing the true
> position *"would not touch it with a barge pole"* unless it was sold at a
> substantially reduced price. This secondhand car did not meet the standard of
> merchantable quality and there was a breach of condition.

The seller is not bound by the condition if the defect has been pointed out to the
buyer prior to the contract, or where the buyer has examined the goods before
purchasing them, and ought to have discovered the defect.

The case law regarding merchantability is still relevant in deciding whether goods
would pass today's test of satisfactory quality. Thus the following have been held to
constitute breaches of s.14(2) as non-merchantable items: beer contaminated by
arsenic (*Wren v. Holt* 1903), woolen underpants containing a chemical that caused
dermatitis (*Grant v. Australian Knitting Mills* 1936), 'Coalite' containing a detonator
which exploded when thrown into a fire (*Wilson v. Rickett Cockerell & Co* 1954),
and a plastic catapult which splintered on use causing the child who bought it to lose
an eye (*Godley v. Perry* 1960).

> Liability under the section is strict. In *Frost v. Aylesbury Dairies Ltd* 1905, the
> dairy supplied milk containing typhoid germs and was held to be in breach of
> the section despite establishing that it had taken all reasonable precautions to
> prevent such contamination.

## Reasonably Fit

An additional benefit to a buyer is granted by s.14(3) which states that where a seller
sells goods in the course of a business and the buyer, either expressly or impliedly,
makes known to the seller any particular purpose for which the goods are being
bought, then there is an implied condition that the goods supplied under the contract
are reasonably fit for that purpose. The condition is not implied in circumstances
which show that the buyer did not rely, or that it was unreasonable to rely, on the

seller's skill and judgment. For instance if goods are purchased by their trade name and in such a way as to indicate that the buyer is satisfied that they will fulfill the purpose, the condition will not apply. Nor will it apply where the buyer has knowledge about particular market conditions which the seller does not possess.

In *Teheran-Europe Co Ltd v. S T Belton (Tractors) Ltd* 1968 the buyer purchased air compressors from the seller for export and resale in Iran. In fact the goods infringed Iranian import regulations, the buyer was fined, and sued the seller. The action failed. As an Iranian incorporated company, The buyer must have been relying on its own knowledge and judgment of the suitability of the goods for the Iranian market.

However it may happen that the buyer places only partial reliance on the seller. If this occurs the buyer will only have a claim against the seller where the unfitness relates to a matter on which the buyer did rely on the seller.

In *Cammell Laird & Co Ltd v. Manganese Bronze & Brass Co Ltd* 1934 The buyers supplied the sellers with a specification for ships' propellers which the sellers were to manufacture for the buyers. Reliance was placed upon the sellers regarding matters outside the specification, such as the appropriate thickness of the metal to be used. On delivery the propellers were unsuitable, being too thin. The sellers were held liable, because the unfitness concerned a matter on which the buyers relied on the sellers' skill.

It will be noticed that even if there has been reliance, the standard required of the goods is only that they should be *reasonably fit*, and that like s.14(2) the provisions of s.14(3) apply only where the seller sells in the course of a business. Although a buyer may expressly state to the seller the particular purpose for which the goods are required, it is clear that if the goods have only one usual purpose, for example a CD player, then merely by purchasing the goods the buyer will be implicitly making known that purpose.

Goods may be merchantable under s.14(2) while failing to be fit for their purpose under s. 14(3), although in practice there is considerable overlap between them. The contaminated milk in *Frost v. Aylesbury Dairies* 1905 was both unmerchantable and unfit for its purpose, namely to drink.

The implied conditions imposed upon sellers under the Act, in particular ss.13 and 14, can provide consumers with substantial protection. Many years ago Lord Wright in *Grant v. Australian Knitting Mills* 1935 noted this when he observed that in retail sales '...*a buyer goes to the shop in confidence that the tradesman has selected his stock with skill and judgment*'. This is sometimes expressed by the principle *caveat venditor,* let the seller beware. Sellers are expected to know something of their own business.

## Test Questions

---

1.    Give five examples of statutes designed to provide consumers with legal rights against suppliers of goods and services.

2.    Define a sale of goods transaction.

3.    What is meant by 'goods' under the Sale of Goods Act 1979?

4.    Why is it important to know when the buyer becomes the owner under a sale of goods contract?

5.    Distinguish between conditions and warranties.

6.    Identify the implied conditions in a sale of goods contract.

7.    When are goods of satisfactory quality?

8.    Explain the implied condition in s.14(3) of the Sale of Goods Act.

---

# The Unfair Contract Terms Act 1977

A breach of the implied conditions will in most cases mean lost profit for the seller, since one remedy for breach of a condition is to terminate the contract because of the repudiatory breach. It is hardly surprising that with this in mind the natural reaction of a seller will be, in most cases, to attempt to exclude or restrict liability under ss. 12-15. The seller may do so by trying to exclude the provisions in their entirety, or limit liability to a fixed sum. The seller may impose a time limit upon the buyer's right to reject, or reduce the buyer's remedies (e.g. obliging the buyer to have the defective goods repaired). The Unfair Contract Terms Act 1977 limits the seller's freedom to exclude and restrict liability. Significantly the Act distinguishes business transactions (non-consumer deals) from consumer deals; under the 1977 Act a person deals as a consumer if he or she does not make the contract in the course of a business, the other party *does* make the contract in the course of a business, and the contract goods are of a type ordinarily supplied for private use or consumption. If the contract satisfies these criteria any attempt by the seller to exclude or restrict ss.12-15 of the Sale of Goods Act 1979 is void. If the contract does not satisfy these criteria, for example where both parties are acting in the course of business, then the effect is that the seller is unable to exclude or restrict liability under s.12 of the Sale of Goods Act 1979. The seller may however exclude or restrict liability in relation to ss.13-15, provide the term by which it is done satisfies a further test, that of reasonableness. In determining whether this test had been satisfied the 1977 Act lists a number of matters or *guidelines* to which reference must be made in reaching a decision. These are:

- The respective *bargaining strengths* of the parties relative to each other. This involves considering possible alternative sources of supply, hence a monopolist seller may have difficulty in establishing the reasonableness of a widely drafted exclusion clause.

- Whether the customer received an *inducement* to agree to the term, or in accepting it had an opportunity of entering into a similar contract with other persons, but without having to accept a similar term. The reference to *other persons* involves account being taken of other suppliers within the market and their terms of trading. Sometimes suppliers combine to produce standardised terms of trading, giving buyers no opportunity of finding improved terms.

  A customer may receive an *inducement* by an adjustment of the contract price.

- Whether the customer knew or ought reasonably to have known of the existence of the term. This involves the customer's knowledge of the seller, with whom the customer may have previously traded on the same terms.

- Where the term excludes or restricts any relevant liability if some condition is not complied with, whether it was reasonable at the time of the contract to expect that it would be practicable to comply with the condition. It might not be practicable, for example, to oblige the buyer to notify the seller of defects occurring in a large consignment of goods within a limited time period and to couple that requirement with a term excluding liability if it is not complied with.

- Whether the goods were manufactured, processed or adapted to the special order of the customer.

If a contract term excluding or restricting liability under ss.13-15 fails to satisfy the test of reasonableness then it will be void.

A seller may also seek to exclude or restrict liability for failure to comply with other terms of the contract, such as time and place of delivery, delivery of the wrong quantity, or even the rendering of no performance at all.

S.3 Unfair Contract Terms Act 1977 applies in such cases where the seller's liability is a *business liability*. It provides that where goods are purchased by a buyer who either *deals as a consumer*, or who purchases on the seller's written standard terms of business the seller cannot exclude or restrict liability for personal breaches of contract. Nor can the seller claim to be entitled to either (i) render contractual performance substantially different from that which was reasonably expected of him, or (ii) in respect of the whole or any part of the contractual obligations, to render no performance at all, unless the exemption clause satisfies the test of reasonableness. The guidelines used to determine the question of reasonableness are not required to be applied under s.3, although they are likely to be taken into account by the court. The following points arising from the section are worth bearing in mind:

- a buyer who purchases on the seller's written standard terms can of course include business organisations as well as private consumers;

- the meaning of standard terms is not defined, but it seems likely that even if the only standard part is the exclusion clause or clauses that the section will still apply;

- the section will apply to the seller's fundamental breaches of contract. A fundamental breach of contract is a breach which deprives the innocent party of substantially the whole benefit that it was intended should be obtained under the contract, and such breaches have been the object of considerable judicial discussion over the years. Exclusion of fundamental breach of contract is now only valid to the extent that it can be shown to be reasonable - generally something which will be difficult to establish.

# The transfer of ownership

At some stage after the contract between the buyer and the seller has been concluded ownership will transfer from the seller to the buyer. This transfer of ownership is the principal obligation of the seller under the contract. Earlier, reference was made to the rule under s.20(3) that risk is borne by the owner of the goods. It is obviously important to know who owns the goods for other reasons. For instance if either party becomes bankrupt that person's *trustee in bankruptcy* is obliged to gather all the property belonging to the estate of the bankrupt (in the same way that a liquidator collects the property of a company that is wound up) in order to sell it and pay off debts. The trustee or company liquidator must know which property he can lawfully realise. Also the buyer can be sued for the price of the goods once he or she has become the owner of them.

Section 17 says that if the goods are *specific* or *ascertained*, ownership in them passes when the parties intend it to pass. Specific and ascertained goods are those *identified and agreed upon at the time the contract is made*, such as a motor vehicle by its registration number. The question of intention is determined by looking at the contract itself and all the surrounding circumstances. Because ownership is such a vital concept it will often be expressly referred to under the terms of the agreement.

A good illustration is provided *by Aluminium Industries Vaasen DV v. Romalpa Aluminium Ltd* 1976 where a reservation of title clause was inserted into a contract under which the plaintiffs sold aluminium foil to the defendants. The defendants would use the foil in their manufacturing process for the purposes of resale, and the plaintiffs clause provided firstly that ownership would only pass to the defendants when all payments owing by the defendants had been met, and secondly that if the foil was processed into other articles, that ownership in these articles would pass to the plaintiffs. The Court upheld the validity of the clause.

If the clear intention of the parties regarding the passing of property cannot be found, five rules to ascertain this question come into operation. The rules are contained in s.18.

## Rule 1

When there is an *unconditional contract* for the sale of *specific goods* in a *deliverable state* the property in goods passes to the buyer when the contract is *made*, and it is immaterial whether the time of payment or the time of delivery, or both, be postponed. Goods are in a deliverable state when the buyer would be bound to take delivery of them. In *Philip Head & Sons v. Showfronts* 1969 the plaintiffs had sold the defendants a quantity of carpet which the plaintiffs had agreed to lay. After the carpet had been delivered to the defendants' premises in bales, prior to being laid, it was stolen. Since it was not in a deliverable state at the time of the theft it was held that property was still with the plaintiffs under Rule 1 and the defendants were not liable to pay the price. Although Rule 1 enables property to pass even though payment and/or delivery occur at a later date, in the case of sales in supermarkets and cash and carry stores the implied intention is that ownership shall only pass when the price is paid.

## Rule 2

In a contract for the sale of specific goods where the seller is bound to do something to the goods to put them into a deliverable state, the property does not pass until that thing is done, and the buyer has notice of it.

In *Underwood v. Burgh Castle Brick & Cement Syndicate* 1922 a 30 ton condensing machine was to be sold under the terms that the seller would be responsible for removing it from its site and loading it on to a train for delivery to the buyer. During the removal it was damaged and the Court held that the seller's action to recover the price must fail since, applying Rule 2, ownership had not passed. This was because something remained to be done to the engine.

## Rule 3

In a contract for the sale of specific goods in a deliverable state, but where the seller is bound to weigh, measure or do something to the goods in order to ascertain the price, ownership will not pass until that thing has been done and the buyer has been given notice of it.

## Rule 4

When goods are delivered to the buyer on approval or on sale or return property passes to the buyer when he or she either signified his or her approval or acceptance or does some act adopting the transaction, or alternatively if the buyer retains the goods without giving notice that he or she is rejecting them within the time specified (e.g. goods delivered on 14-day approval) or if there is none, within a reasonable time. In cases where the buyer resells the goods he or she will be treated as having *adopted* the transaction. By the resale the buyer is asserting rights of ownership over the goods. In *Kirkham v. Attenborough* 1897 the pledging of goods with a pawnbroker was held to constitute an adopting of the transaction.

## Rule 5

This rule applies only to *unascertained goods*, unlike the four previous rules which apply to specific goods. Specific goods, it will be remembered, are those that are identified and agreed upon at the time the contract of sale is made. If the contract of sale is not for specific goods, then it must be for unascertained goods. Examples of such transactions include the purchase of 100 tons of coal, or 500 tons of wheat out of a cargo of 1000 tons of wheat on board a named ship, or animal feedstuff to be produced by the seller according to a formula supplied by the buyer. In each of these examples it is impossible to identify at the time of the contract the particular goods which are to become the buyer's property, even though they have necessarily been described.

Under s.16 in a contract for the sale of unascertained goods no property is transferred to the buyer unless and until the goods are ascertained. If the goods become ascertained then s.17 applies and ownership will pass when the parties intend it to pass. Under the Sale of Goods (Amendment) Act 1995 protection was conferred upon the buyer of an undivided share of goods e.g. 500 computers in a warehouse storing 5000. If the buyer pays for the computers he aquires property in an undivided share of the bulk e.g. 10% of the computers

Under Rule 5 ownership in such goods passes to the buyer when goods as described, and in a deliverable state, are unconditionally appropriated to the contract either by the seller with the buyer's assent or vice-versa. The expression *unconditionally appropriated* is vital.

> In *Carlos Federspiel v. Charles Twigg & Co* 1957 the plaintiffs bought from the defendants a quantity of eighty five bicycles. The contract required the seller to deliver them to the ship they were to be carried in and load them. Before they had left the seller's premises a Receiver was appointed who claimed the bicycles which were packed and marked with the plaintiff's name. The Court held that property had not passed to the plaintiffs, firstly because in a contract of this type (known as an f.o.b. - free on board contract) the intention is that property shall pass when the goods are loaded, and secondly because in any event there had not been an unconditional appropriation. Pearson J stated that *"To constitute an appropriation of goods to the contract the parties must have had, or be reasonably supposed to have had, an intention to attach the contract irrevocably to those goods"*.

Rule 5 requires that the appropriation must be made by one party with the assent of the other. This may be *implied*. A clear illustration is provided in the case of purchasing petrol. It has been held that if petrol is put into a car by a forecourt attendant the petrol is being unconditionally appropriated with the implied assent of the buyer and if it is the buyer who personally fills the car at a self-service petrol station there is an unconditional appropriation with the implied assent of the garage as seller when the petrol is being poured.

Under Rule 5, delivery of the goods by the seller to the buyer, or to a carrier for delivery to the buyer, amounts to an unconditional appropriation.

## Remedies available to buyers and sellers

In the event of a breach of the obligations owed by one party to the other under a sale of goods contract the injured party may seek redress against the other. The principal obligations that arise may be summarised as follows:

(a)   *the seller must transfer ownership in the goods to the buyer*; physically deliver them to the buyer unless the contract provides otherwise; and fulfill the implied conditions and warranties contained in ss.12-15 of the 1979 Act.

(b)    *the buyer must accept the goods and pay for them.* Payment and delivery are concurrent obligations, unless the parties agree otherwise. This means they occur at the same time, for instance cash sales in shops.

## The remedies of a seller

If the seller is owed money by the buyer the Act gives the seller the following rights, even if the buyer has become the *owner* of the goods:

(i)    *a lien over the goods*, i.e. a right to retain possession until he of she is paid;

(ii)    *if the goods are in transit and in possession of a carrier, a right to regain possession of them during the transit if the buyer has become insolvent;*

(iii)    *a right of resale* in certain circumstances, for instance when the goods are of a perishable nature, or where the seller gives the buyer notice of the intention to resell and the buyer does not with a reasonable time pay for the goods. In the event of a resale the seller can claim damages, representing any loss suffered. Such a loss could be the reduced profit on a resale because of a drop in the market price of the goods, including the cost of advertising them, etc;

(iv)    *an action for the price of the goods;*

(v)    *an action for damages* where the goods are still owned by the seller and the buyer refuses or simply fails to accept them. Damages awarded will represent the loss directly and naturally resulting from the non acceptance. Prima facie, this will be the difference between the contract price, and the market price or current price at the time when the goods should have been accepted, assuming of course there is an available market. So if supply exceeds demand and there is a fixed retail price for the goods damages will then represent the loss of profit that would have been made on the sale, but if demand exceeds supply then damages will only be nominal as the goods can be readily resold.

## The remedies of a buyer

(i)    *an action to recover damages when the seller wrongfully fails or refuses to deliver the* goods. Again damages are measured in the same way as outlined above in a seller's action for non acceptance. It should be stressed that in the case of a non delivery by the seller, or a non acceptance by a buyer it is the market *price when the breach occurs* that is used to determine the measure of damages.

In *Pagnan v. Corbisa* 1970 Lord Justice Salmon made it quite clear that other market fluctuations are not relevant, *'...the innocent party is not bound to go on the market and buy or sell at the date of the breach. Nor is he bound to gamble on the market changing in his favour. He may wait if he chooses; and if the market turns against him this cannot increase the liability of the party in default. Similarly, if the market turns in his favour, the liability of the party in default is not diminished'.*

(ii)     *recovery of the price paid* if the goods are not delivered.

(iii)    *rejection of the goods* where there has been a breach of condition, and damages for breach of warranty - the amount being the difference between the value of the goods as delivered, and their value if the warranty had been complied with. A buyer may elect to treat a breach of condition as a breach of warranty.

# Test Questions

| | |
|---|---|
| 1. | What is the purpose of the Unfair Contract Terms Act 1977? |
| 2. | What is the test of reasonableness in relation to an exclusion clause? |
| 3. | When is it not permissible to exclude liability under the Unfair Contract Terms Act? |
| 4. | Distinguish between specific and unascertained goods. |
| 5. | When does ownership pass under section 17 and Rule 1? |
| 6. | When does ownership pass when goods are sold on sale or return under Rule 4? |
| 7. | What is meant by 'unconditional appropriation'? |
| 8. | Identify five remedies of the seller in a sale of goods contract? |

# Consumer Protection Act 1987

This statute was passed by the UK Parliament to implement the Product Liability Directive 1985, a European Directive concerning liability for defective products.

The aim of the Act is to impose strict liability for defects in consumer products on the *producer*. The 'producer' is defined as the person who manufactures the product, an importer of the product into the European Union or a person who represents himself as the supplier by putting his name or trademark on the product. The product is defective if it does not meet the requirements of safety that people generally are entitled to expect in the context of risks of damage to property as well as death or personal injury. Measuring safety can only be achieved by considering all the circumstances including the making of the product, instructions as to use, warnings and the use to which you would reasonably expect the product to be put.

## Civil liability

If civil proceedings are brought against a producer of a defective product under the Act for damages in respect of injury or damage there are a number of defences available, the most controversial of which is the *development risks defence*. Adopting this defence the producer would have to prove that the state of scientific and technical knowledge at the time that the producer supplied the product was such that no producer of that type might have been expected to discover the defect. Certainly it would be insufficient for a producer to argue that high cost or the difficulty in establishing the defect are relevant factors. The producer may be made liable for damages caused to any property by the defective product or death or personal injury to the consumer. Inevitably if there is more than one producer of the defective product liability could be joint or they could be solely responsible.

## Criminal liability

The provisions of the Consumer Protection Act also impose criminal liability on the suppliers of unsafe consumer products, this replacing and amending previous legislation on consumer safety.

Under the Act it is an offence to supply consumer goods which do not comply with general safety requirements. For this purpose suppliers would include manufacturers, importers or distributors. Retailers may also incur potential liability but only if they know or had reason to believe that the goods fail to comply with general safety requirements. Knowledge includes the situation where the retailer shuts his eyes to the obvious or deliberately fails to make inquiries. Measuring general safety requirements can only be achieved by determining that in all the circumstances the goods are not reasonably safe bearing in mind marketing, instructions, warnings, published safety standards and the means by which the goods could have been made safer. There are various alternatives to prosecution for a guilty trader, including the service prohibition notices or suspension notices to prevent trading in the unsafe product.

# The Supply of Goods and Services Act 1982

If a consumer contracts for the supply of a service such as car hire, laundry, holidays, financial service, and professional advice, and the service provider does not fulfill their contractual obligations, then the consumer may seek redress for breach of the express contractual term.

The tour operator who fails to provide the agreed holiday and the removal firm that damages the customers belongings could potentially be sued for breach of contract subject of course to any exclusion or limitation of liability.

Usually however the consumer's complaint in relation to the supplying of services relates to the quality of the service provided due to lack of care from the service provider. The claim is that the service has been supplied negligently with insufficient care by the solicitor, hairdresser, surveyor, banker etc. In these circumstances the Supply of Goods and Services Act 1982 may provide assistance by implying terms into service contracts for the benefit of the consumer.

Under section 13 in a contract for the supply of a service where the supplier is acting in the course of a business there is an implied term that the supplier will carry out the service with reasonable skill and care.

In all service contracts this term sets the standard of the reasonably competent professional. The lawyer, dentist or hairdresser must exercise a reasonable degree of skill and care.

In carrying out their functions this standard of care can be achieved even if the doctor fails to cure your ailment or the lawyer loses the case provided that as suppliers they can demonstrate they have acted competently.

Two holiday cases illustrate how s.13 may be implied to provide the consumer with a remedy.

> In *Davey v Cosmos Air Holidays* 1989 the plaintiff and his family contracted diarrhoe and dysentery on a two week package holiday in the Algarve. The evidence established that the illness was caused by a general lack of hygiene at the resort particularly shown by the practice of pumping raw effluent into the sea near the beach. While the tour operators were not the cause of the hygiene risk the fact that they were aware of it and had failed to warn their clients of

the danger meant that they were at fault. The court held they were liable for a breach of s.13 by failing to take reasonable care to avoid exposing their clients to a significant risk of injury.

Alternatively in *Wilson v. Best Travel Ltd.* 1993 the plaintiff suffered serious injuries after tripping and falling through glass patio doors at a hotel in Greece. The glass doors were fitted with glass which complied with Greek safety standards but would not have met equivalent British standards. The plaintiff claimed damages against the defendant tour operators, arguing that the hotel was not reasonably safe for use by the defendants' customers and that they were in breach of their duty of care under s.13 of the Supply and Goods and Services Act 1982. It was held that the tour operators were not liable because they had confirmed that local safety regulations had been complied with. It was not necessary for the operator to ensure that the Greek hotel came up to English safety standards.

The Supply and Goods and Services Act 1982 may also imply terms into a service contract in relation to time set for performance of the contract and the prices. These terms are implied into a contract where the parties fail to set a price or the dates for performance. It is not unusual of course in the supply of a service such as car repairs, or professional advice, that the parties will not have fixed the price or the date set for performance. In such cases the Act provides in s.14 that there is an implied term that the supplier will carry out the service within a reasonable time. In section 15 the implied term is that the party contracting with the supplier will pay a reasonable charge. What is a reasonable time and a reasonable charge is a question of fact and will depend on the nature of the service that is provided.

If there is no contractual relationship between the supplier of the service and the consumer then any action for financial loss caused by the professional's fault must be based upon the tort of negligence.

The important decision of the House of Lords in *White and another v. Jones and others* 1995 considered the potential liability of the defendant solicitors who caused the plaintiff's financial loss as a result of a negligent omission. The plaintiffs had originally been cut out of their father's (the testator) will but then reinstated on the testator's instructions to the defendant solicitors. The solicitors had delayed in carrying out the instructions to change the will for over six weeks and unfortunately, meanwhile, the testator died. As there was no contractual relationship between the plaintiffs and the defendants the action for financial loss could only be based on the tort of negligence. The central issue in the dispute was whether a solicitor in drafting a will owes a legal duty of care in the tort of negligence to a potential beneficiary. The High Court thought not. This decision was reversed on appeal and the solicitors then made a final appeal to the House of Lords. By a three to two majority decision their Lordships held that the potential loss to the plaintiffs in these circumstances was reasonably foreseeable and the relationship of a solicitor, called upon to draft a will, and the potential beneficiary, should be brought within the established categories of relationship under which a duty of care arises. This duty of care had been broken by the solicitor's negligence causing financial loss for which the defendants were liable.

# Trade Descriptions Legislation

The Trade Descriptions Act 1968 is an early example of the use of the criminal law to promote consumer protection. The Act introduces criminal sanctions which may be imposed on business traders who mislead the public by falsely describing goods and services for sale. The use of the criminal law within the field of consumer protection demonstrate parliaments recognition of harmful effects on market activity unscrupulous and rogue trading can have. It is also acknowledgment of the failure of civil sanctions to provide adequate redress and the desirability of achieving a change in attitude in business suppliers whose trading standards are unacceptable. One of the most important features of the legislation is that there can be no liability under the 1968 Act unless the person applying the false description does so within the course of a trade or business rather than a private sale. This is one reason why the Business Advertisements (Disclosure) Order 1977 requires a trader to identify himself as such when he advertises in the classified advertisements in newspapers. The fact that a business organisation is the vendor or purchaser does not automatically mean that a sale is in the course of a trade. The transaction must be of a type that is a regular occurrence in that particular business, so that a sale of business assets would not normally qualify as a sale in the course of a trade or business.

> In *Roberts v. Leonard* 1995 veterinary surgeons were held to be carrying on a trade or business, the court deciding that there was no sufficient reason to exclude the professions from the scope of the Act.

Where there is a genuine private sale and, for example, the seller falsely describes the goods, the buyer's remedy will be to rescind the contract. As we saw earlier he may also claim damages in a civil law action for misrepresentation or breach of the term implied into the contract by s.13 of the Sale of Goods Act 1979. A buyer from a business seller can also exercise these remedies, but in addition may report the trader to the trading standards department with a view to a prosecution for a breach of the criminal law under the 1968 Act. In all trade descriptions cases there is potentially liability under the civil law which illustrates the fact that here consumer protection law is founded upon the interrelationship between civil and criminal activities. Prosecutions for trade description offences are brought in the Magistrates Court and exceptionally in the Crown Court with the possibility of an appeal to the Divisional Court of the Queen's Bench Division of the High Court.

The two principal offences under the Trade Descriptions Act 1968 relate to false description of goods, and making misleading statements about services. A number of defences are also provided for. Further offences of giving misleading price indications were originally contained in the Act, but are now found in the Consumer Protection Act 1987, and are considered separately below.

## False Description of Goods

The 1968 Act provides, in s.1(1) that: *"Any person who, in the course of a trade or business:*

(a)    *applies a false trade description to any goods; or*

(b)    *supplies or offers to supply any goods to which a false trade description is applied;*

*shall, be guilty of an offence"*.

Two different types of conduct will amount to offences under this section. The first is where the trader himself applies the false trade description contrary to s.1(1)(a). This offence could be committed, for example, by a trader who turns back the mileometer of a car to make it appear that the car has not travelled as many miles as it actually has. The second, under s.1(1)(b), involves supplying or offering to supply goods to which a false trade description has been applied by another person, for example where a retailer sells a garment to which the label *pure new wool* has been attached by the manufacturer, where the garment is partly composed of manmade fibres. There is a strict duty therefore not to pass on false trade descriptions applied by another, subject to a defence which we will consider later.

This is an example of a strict liability offence for there is no requirement to prove that the supplier acted with guilty intent.

A false trade description may be applied verbally or in writing, for example in a label on goods or in an advertisement, communicated by pictorial representation or even by conduct.

In *Yugotours Ltd. v. Wadsley* 1988 a photograph of a three-masted schooner and the words *"the excitement of being under full sail on board this majestic schooner"* in a tour operator's brochure was held to constitute a statement for the purpose of the Act. By providing customers who had booked a holiday relying on the brochure with only a two masted schooner without sails the tour operator was guilty of recklessly making a false statement contrary to the Trade Descriptions Act.

The meaning of the term *trade description* extends, to statements relating to quantity, size, composition, method of manufacture, fitness for purpose, place or date of manufacture, approval by any person or other history including previous ownership of goods.

In *Sherratt v. Geralds The American Jewellers Ltd.* 1970 the defendant sold a watch described by the maker as a diver's watch and inscribed with the word *"waterproof"*. The watch filled with water and stopped after it had been immersed in water. It was held that the defendant was guilty of an offence under s.1(1)(b).

To constitute an offence under the Act the trade description must be false or misleading to a material degree.

In *Robertson v. Dicicco* 1972 a second-hand motor vehicle was advertised for sale by a dealer and described as *"a beautiful car"*. The car, although having a visually pleasing exterior was unroadworthy and not fit for use. The defendant was charged with an offence under s.1(1)(a). He argued that his statement was true as he had intended it to refer only to the visual appearance of the vehicle. It was held that he was guilty because the description was false to a material degree. A reasonable person would have taken the statement to refer to the mechanics of the car as well as its external appearance.

A similar approach was taken in *Kensington and Chelsea Borough Council v. Riley* 1973 where the trader was convicted of an offence under s.1(1)(a). It was held that the description *"in immaculate condition"* was false when applied to a car which required repairs costing £250 to make it roadworthy.

A trade description applied to goods for sale can be false for the purpose of s.1(1)(b) even when it is scientifically correct if it is likely to mislead a customer without specialist knowledge.

In *Dixon Ltd. v. Barnett* 1989 a customer was supplied with an Astral 500 telescope which was described as being capable of up to *"455 x magnification"*. The evidence showed that the maximum useful magnification was only 120 times, although scientifically 455 times magnification could be achieved. The Divisional Court held that the store was nevertheless guilty of an offence despite the fact that the statement was scientifically sound. An ordinary customer would have been misled by the statement because he would be interested in the maximum useful magnification rather than a blurred image produced at 455 times magnification.

A half truth is false for the purpose of the Act, so that while it was technically true to describe a vehicle as only having one previous owner in *R v. Inner London Justices and another* 1983 the fact that the owner was a leasing company and the car had had five different keepers meant that the statement was grossly misleading and false.

In *Denard v. Smith and another* 1990 the Divisonal Court considered whether it is a false trade description to advertise goods in a shop at the point of sale as items offered for sale when they are temporarily out of stock and are not immediately available. The court held that unless customers are informed of the non-availability of the goods at the  time of purchase the advertisement constituted a false trade description of offering to supply goods.

Where defects in goods are disguised and the trader has no reason to realise or suspect that they are present, he will not be guilty of an offence under s.1(1)(b).

In *Cottee v. Douglas Seaton Ltd.* 1972 the bodywork of a car which had been in very poor condition was repaired using plastic body filler. This was smoothed down and the car repainted before it was sold to the defendant. The defendant was unaware of the fact that the bodywork was defective. He resold the car to a purchaser who subsequently discovered the defect. It was held that the disguised defects amounted to a false trade description as the goods, in effect, told a lie about themselves. The defendant was not guilty of an offence, however, because he was unaware that the description had been applied to the goods.

A person may be guilty of an offence under s.1(1)(b), even though he does not know the description is false, provided he knows that the description has been applied to the goods by another person. This situation may arise for example where a car dealer sells a car which records an incorrectly low mileage on its mileometer. If a dealer is uncertain as to the accuracy of the recorded mileage, he may try to ensure that a false trade description is not applied by displaying a notice disclaiming the accuracy of the mileage reading.

In *Norman v. Bennett* 1974 a customer bought a second-hand car with a recorded mileage of 23,000 miles. In fact the true mileage was about 68,000 miles. He signed an agreement containing a clause which said that the reading was not guaranteed. It was held that this was not an effective disclaimer. Lord Widgery, the Lord Chief Justice, stated that, in order to be effective, a disclaimer: *"must be as bold, precise and compelling as the trade description itself* and *must be as effectively brought to the notice of any person to whom the goods may be supplied. In other words, the disclaimer must equal the trade description in the extent to which it is likely to get home to anyone interested in receiving the goods"*.

The use of a disclaimer will be an effective defence provided it complies with the test laid down in *Norman v. Bennett*. The Motor Trade Code of Practice, approved by Director General of Fair Trading in 1976, recommends the use of the following form of wording in these circumstances:

> *"We do not guarantee the accuracy of the recorded mileage. To the best of our knowledge and belief, however the recording is correct/incorrect".*

Clearly a disclaimer will only be an effective defence to a charge under s.1(1)(b). If the trader himself has turned back the mileage he will be unable to rely on this defence.

A disclaimer cannot exclude liability once it has arisen and is only effective to the extent that it prevents the commission of a criminal offence. The disclaimer could:

- prevent an indication being regarded as a trade description; or

- qualify a description so that it does not mislead; or

- qualify a description so that it is not false to a material degree.

Certainly it would be pointless to attempt to disclaim liability after an offence has already been committed.

In *Doble v. David Greig Ltd.* 1972 the defendants displayed bottles of Ribena for sale in their self service store at a particular price with an indication that a deposit on each bottle was refundable on its return. At the cash till however, a different notice stated that in fact no deposit would be charged because in the interest of hygiene the store would not accept the return of empty bottles. The retailer was convicted of the offence of offering to supply goods with a false price indication. The court held that the offence of offering to supply was committed when the goods were displayed and the subsequent notice at the cash till was ineffective in disclaiming liability.

While a disclaimer may prevent the commission of an offence of offering to supply goods, it will not apply to an offence of applying a false trade description.

> In *Newham LBC v. Singh* 1988 as the defendant car dealer had not been aware that a car mileometer had been altered and had not been the person applying the false trade description to the car, he could successfully rely on a disclaimer when charged under s.1.

Finally, an important feature of disclaimers is that it is for the prosecution to establish the offence and prove that the disclaimer is ineffective, whereas the specific defences under the Act must be established by the defendant.

## Defences

It is a defence to any charge under the 1968 Act that the defendant, perhaps a newspaper or magazine publisher innocently published a misleading advertisement received by him for publication in the ordinary course of his business.

A number of separate defences are contained in s.24. These are available to a defendant who can prove:

> *"(a)   That the commission of the offence was due to a mistake or to reliance on information supplied to him or to the act or default of another person, an accident, or some other cause beyond his control; and*
>
> *(b)   that he took all reasonable precautions and exercised all due diligence to avoid the commission of such an offence by himself or any person under his control"*

In order to have an effective defence under s.24, the onus is on the defendant to prove any one of the reasons listed in paragraph (a) above and all of the elements in (b). He must also supply to the prosecution, at least 7 days before the hearing, a written notice giving such information as he has to enable the other person to be identified.

In *Baxters (Butchers) v. Manley* 1985 the defendant was accused of offences under the 1968 Act in relation to the pricing and weight of meat exposed for sale in his butcher's shop. He claimed that the offences were due to the act or default of the shop manager. This claim was accepted by the court, but the defence under s.24 failed because he was unable to prove that he had taken reasonable precautions to avoid the commission of the offence by his manager. In particular he had failed to give the manager any detailed instructions or guidelines on the requirements of the Act; there was no staff training; and the standard of supervision by a district manager was inadequate.

In *Lewin v. Rothersthorpe Road Garage* 1984 the s.24 defence was raised in response to a prosecution for selling a motor car to which a false trade description had been applied. The defendant was a member of the Motor Agents Association, and had adopted the code of practice drawn up by the Association in consultation with the Office of Fair Trading. Staff had been instructed in the contents of the code of practice. The court held that he had taken reasonable precautions to avoid the commission of an offence by his employee.

Alternatively in *Gale v. Dixon Stores Group* 1994 the defendant committed a s.1 offence when he supplied as new a computer that had already been returned by another customer as defective. This constituted a s.1 offence. The Magistrates accepted that the statutory defence under s.24 had been established on the basis that the defendants intended to introduce a procedure that would prevent such an occurrence in the future. On appeal it was held that the new procedure was a reasonable precaution but the fact that it was not in place at the time of the incident meant that the statutory defence could not stand.

To establish that he took all reasonable precautions and exercised all due diligence the defendant needs to show that he has an effective system in operation. A court should also bear in mind the size and resources of the organisation in determining the steps you would expect a reasonable business to take.

In *Denard v. Smith* 1990 the defendant attempted to establish a s.24 defence when charged with falsely advertising at the point of sale that particular goods were offered for sale when in fact they were out of stock and not available. The court found that an elementary requirement of due diligence would have been to issue some instructions that some amendment should be made to the point of sale literature. A simple notice hung over or beside the advertising placard would have been sufficient to show reasonable precautions and due diligence for the purposes of s.24.

In relation to enforcement of the 1968 Act, as we have seen, wide investigatory powers are conferred on local authority trading standards officers. Before a prosecution is brought, however, the local authority is required to inform the Department of Trade. This is to prevent numerous unnecessary prosecutions for the same false trade description.

The legality of bringing a second prosecution where there are a number of complaints in relation to the same false statement was at issue in *R. v. Thomson Holidays Limited* 1973. In this case a misleading statement in a travel brochure constituted an offence under s.14. The Court of Appeal held that a separate offence was committed every time someone read the brochure, and that it was not necessarily improper to bring more than one prosecution in these circumstances.

## Misleading price indications

The offence of giving a misleading price indication is contained in s.20 of the Consumer Protection Act 1987, which provides: *"A person shall be guilty of an offence if, in the course of any business of his, he gives (by any means whatever) to any consumers an indication which is misleading as to the price at which any goods, services, accommodation or facilities are available".*

The types of statements which would be caught by s.20 include:

- false comparisons with recommended prices, for example a false claim that goods are £20 less than the recommended price; or

- indications that the price is less than the real price, for example where hidden extras are added to an advertised price; or

- false comparisons with a previous price, for example a false statement that goods were £50 and are now £30; or

- where the stated method of determining the price is different to the method actually used.

Failure to correct a price indication which initially was true, but has become untrue, is also an offence.

Case law suggests that the courts have interpreted s.20 with consumer protection in mind. In *Toyota (GB) Ltd v North Yorkshire County Council* 1998 a conviction under s.20 against a car dealer was upheld as appeal for a misleading price indication. This was despite the fact that the price indicated was subject to negotiations and invariably reduced. The price was misleading because it did not include a delivery charge which would be added to it and a reference to the charge in small print at the bottom of the advertisement was insufficiently prominent to give a fair indication of the price.

The Secretary of State, after consulting the Director General of Fair Trading, has issued a code of practice designed to give practical guidance on the requirements of s.20. It aims to promote good practice in relation to giving price indications. Breach of the code will not, of itself, give rise to criminal or civil liability, but may be used as evidence to establish either that an offence had been committed under s.20, or that a trader has a defence to such a charge.

The following cases, decided under previous legislation, illustrate the type of behaviour which will constitutes an offence.

In *Richards v. Westminster Motors Ltd.* 1975 the defendant advertised a commercial vehicle for sale at a price of £1,350. When the buyer purchased the vehicle he was required to pay the asking price plus VAT, which made a total price of £1,534. It was held that the defendant was guilty of giving a misleading indication as to the price at which he was prepared to sell goods.

In *Read Bros. Cycles (Leyton) v. Waltham Forest London Borough* 1978 the defendant advertised a motor cycle for sale at a reduced price of £540, £40 below the list price. A customer agreed to purchase the motor cycle and negotiated a £90 part exchange allowance on his old vehicle. The defendant charged him the full list price for the new cycle, and stated that the reduced price did not apply where goods were given in part exchange. It was held that the defendant was guilty of giving a misleading price indication.

## False Description of Services

Suppliers of services, such as holiday tour operators, hairdressers and dry cleaners will be liable to prosecution under s.14 of the Trade Descriptions Act 1968 if they make false statements knowingly or recklessly in the course of their business.

*Under s.14(1):*

*"It shall be an offence for any person in the course of any trade or business:*

(a)   *to make a statements which he knows to be false; or*

(b)   *recklessly to make a statement which is false;as to any of the following matters:*

(i)   *the provision ... of any services, accommodation or facilities;*

(ii)   *the nature of any services, accommodation or facilities;*

(iii)   *the time at which, the manner in which or persons by whom any services, accommodation or facilities are provided;*

(iv)   *the examination, approval or evaluation by any person of any services, accommodation or facilities;or*

(v)   *the location or amenities of any accommodation.*

The main difference between this offence and the offence in relation to goods is that in order to obtain a conviction under s.14, the prosecution must show *mens rea* (guilty mind) either that the trader knew that the statement was false, or that he was *reckless* as to its truth or falsity. You will remember that in relation to goods, liability is strict.

A statement is made recklessly if it is made regardless of whether it is true or false. It need not necessarily be dishonest. The knowledge or recklessness must be present at the time the statement is made.

In *Sunair Holidays Ltd. v. Dodd* 1970 the defendant's travel brochure described a package holiday in a hotel with *"all twin bedded rooms with bath, shower and terrace"*. The defendant had a contract with the hotel owners under which they were obliged to provide accommodation of that description. A customer who booked the package was given a room without a terrace. The defendant had not checked with the hotel to make sure that its customers were given the correct accommodation of that description. It was held however, that the statement was not false when it was made, and therefore the defendant was not guilty of an offence under s.14.

It must be shown that the trader, at the time the statement is made, either knows that it is false or is reckless as to its truth or falsity; and that the statement actually *is* false. Subsequent developments are irrelevant if these elements are present at the time the statement is made.

Conduct of the defendant subsequent to the false statement is relevant however to determine whether an inference of recklessness can be maintained.

In *Yugotours Ltd. v. Wadsley* 1988 the fact that statements in a holiday brochure were clearly false and known to be so by the company meant that when the company failed to correct the statement, it was guilty of an offence. The court stated that there was sufficient material before the court to infer recklessness on the part of the maker of the statement. *"If a statement is false and known to be false, and nothing whatever is done to correct it, then the company making the statement can properly be found guilty of recklessness notwithstanding the absence of specific evidence of recklessness"*.

In *Wings Ltd. v. Ellis* 1984 the false nature of a statement in their travel brochure was not known by a tour operator when its brochure was published. Some 250,000 copies of the brochure contained an inaccurate statement that rooms in a hotel in Sri Lanka were air conditioned. The brochure also contained a photograph purporting to be a room in the same hotel which was of a room in a different hotel. When the mistake was discovered, reasonable steps were taken to remedy it by informing agents and customers who had already booked by letter. Despite this, a holiday was booked by a customer on the basis of the false information. It was held by the House of Lords that the tour operator was guilty of an offence under s.14 because the statement was made when the brochure was read by the customer, and at the time the defendant knew that it was false. The fact that the tour operator was unaware that the uncorrected statement was being made to the customer did not prevent the offence being committed. As a result of this judgment the offence under s.1(1)(a) has been described rather crudely as a *"half mens rea offence"*. Knowledge that a statement is false is necessary but there is no need to show mens rea as to the making of the statement.

For corporate liability under s.14 the prosecution must establish that a high ranking official of the company had the necessary mens rea. The Chairman of a company would certainly suffice but not the Contracts Manager in *Wings Ltd. v. Ellis* who had approved the photograph of the hotel which gave a wrong impression.

The Property Misdescriptions Act, passed in 1991, imposes criminal liability for making false statements in relation to the sale of residential and commercial land and buildings, is similar in many respects of the Trade Descriptions Act 1968.The offence only applies to statements made in the course of an estate agency business or a property development business. Those made by a private seller or a seller in a different line of business are not caught by the Act. Statements made in the course of providing conveyancing services, for example by solicitors or licensed conveyancers, are also outside the scope of the offence. The offence covers statements made by estate agents in advertisements or in written particulars describing a property for sale. It also applies to statements made in the course of a property development business. This covers builders of new commercial and residential premises and those who renovate old properties to sell.

# Test Questions

1.   What is the aim of the Consumer Protection Act 1987?

2.   Describe what is meant by the development risks defence.

3.   How could a tour operator incur liability under the Supply of Goods and Services Act 1982?

4.   Why did the Trade Descriptions Act 1968 introduce criminal sanctions into consumer protection law?

5.   State the s.1(1) offence under the Trade Description Act 1968.

6.   Explain what is meant by strict liability under the 1968 Act

7.   How is the term 'false' interpreted under the 1968 Act?

8.   What are the defences to a prosecution under the 1968 Act?

9.   Give three examples of false trade descriptions in relation to price.

10.   How does the law on false description relating to services differ from the law on false description in relation to goods?

# Consumer Credit Act 1974

The Consumer Credit Act 1974 is the most significant piece of legislation designed to give protection to the consumer in a credit transaction. It sets up a licensing system administered by the Director General of Fair Trading to regulate businesses that supply credit. The Act also contains the rules relating to the supply, formation, content and termination of consumer credit agreements. For the Act to apply and regulate the agreement the creditor who supplies the finance may be a company but the debtor must be an individual and the credit must not exceed £15,000. *'Credit'* includes a cash loan and any other financial accommodation including hire purchase, credit sales and credit cards.

The the rules relating to the formation of credit agreements ensure that the debtor is made aware of the rights and duties imposed under the agreement, in particular

- the amount and rate of the total charge for credit

- the protection and remedies available.

The agreement must be properly signed, contain all the required terms and be in the prescribed form. The debtor must be supplied with a copy of the agreement and given the opportunity to cancel the agreement where the agreement is signed at a place other than the creditor's place of business e.g. at home.

Usually a trader will supply the goods and arrange for a finance company to supply the credit under a hire purchase agreement. This is known as a debtor - creditor - supplier agreement. If the supplier defaults in some way through breach of contract or misrepresentation the creditor may be made equally liable and the debtor can choose to sue either or both of them. By making finance companies potentially liable for the defaults of traders the Act is effectively ensuring that financiers will only deal with suppliers who are reputable. One advantage of purchasing goods with a credit card is that if the supplier breaks the contract the credit card company is also potentially liable.

If the debtor is in default and fails to make the credit payments then the agreement may be enforced against him subject to the provisions of the Act. The creditor in such circumstances is required to serve a *default notice* on the debtor specifying the breach of contract and giving the debtor at least seven days to take remedial action. Under a hire purchase agreement the creditor retains the ownership of the goods until the debtor exercises the option to purchase by payment of the final installment. As owner therefore the creditor may retake the possession of goods if the debtor is in breach of the agreement. However the goods become *protected* once the debtor has paid more than one third of the total price. The creditor can only recover possession of protected goods with the approval of the debtor or the court. Usually possession will be sought because the debtor has defaulted in making payments.

If the debtor has difficulty in making the repayments he can terminate the agreement by giving notice to the creditor and returning the goods. The debtor may also be made liable for further repayments to represent the creditor's loss and this is why formal termination by the debtor is not an advisable course of action. If the court feels that the credit bargain is extortionate in that it is grossly exorbitant or offends the principles of fair dealing then it may reopen the credit agreement and do justice between the parties. Effectively the court could change the agreement by rescheduling repayments and/or set aside the whole or part of the debt.

# Regulatory Agencies

To ensure high standards and consumer protection where there is potential for abuse by unscrupulous traders there are some fields, in particular, where statutory licenses are required to enable suppliers to trade. Only advisors licensed under the Financial Services Act 1986 may provide consumers with financial advice and those who provide credit in the course of a business are required to be licensed under the Consumer Credit Act 1974. Withdrawal of a license would be an effective sanction against a trader guilty of abuse.

In addition most professionals are members of professional bodies who administer compliant procedures against their members. Such bodies control solicitors, accountants, surveyors, doctors etc. and can exercise disciplinary powers over their members.

Trade Associations can also be very powerful and often exercise a high degree of control. Membership of the Association of British Travel Agents (ABTA) is a mark of status in the travel industry and conflict between consumers and tour operators is usually dealt with by the ABTA arbitration scheme rather than legal action in the courts. Trade Associations also lay down codes of practice for their members giving guidance as to good practice in straightforward terms. They are self regulatory providing a quick inexpensive means of setting high standards and possible a means of redress for the consumer.

Both central and local governments have important roles to play in consumer protection. The Department of Trade and Industry has responsibility for the promotion and implementation of consumer legislation in conjunction with a number of national consumer protection bodies such as:

- The Office of Fair Trading

- The National Consumer Council

- The Consumer Protection Advisory Committee

- The Directors-General in consumer fields such as electricity and gas.

Enforcement of consumer legislation is in the hands of local authority trading standards officers usually based in consumer protection departments.

## The Office of Fair Trading

The Office of Fair Trading, created by the Fair Trading Act 1973, has a significant national role in relation to the broad task of protecting the interests of the consumer. The 1973 Act created the post of Director General of Fair Trading. The Director has wide powers under the 1973 Act and other legislation, notably the Consumer Credit Act 1974 and the Estate Agents Act 1979.

The duties of the Director are:

- to review commercial activities and report to the Secretary of State;

- to refer adverse trade practices to the Consumer Protection Advisory Committee;

- to take action against traders who are persistently unfair to consumers;

- to supervise the enforcement of the Consumer Credit Act 1974 and the administration of the licensing system under that Act;

- to arrange for information and advice to be published for the benefit of consumers in relation to the supply of goods and services and consumer credit;

- to encourage trade associations to produce voluntary Codes of Practice; and

- to superintend the working and enforcement of the Estate Agents Act 1979.

## Referral of adverse trade practices to the Consumer Protection Advisory Committee

The Director has power to refer to the Consumer Protection Advisory Committee any consumer trade practice which in his opinion adversely affects the economic interests of consumers. The type of activity which can give rise to such a reference include trade practices relating to:

(i)     the terms or conditions on which goods or services are supplied,

(ii)    the manner in which those terms or conditions are communicated to the consumer,

(iii)   promotion of goods or services by advertising, labelling or marking of goods, or canvassing,

(iv)    methods of salesmanship employed in dealing with consumers,

(v)     the way in which goods are packed, or

(vi)    methods of demanding or securing payments for goods or services supplied.

A reference by the Director may include proposals for the creation of delegated legislation by the Secretary of State.

Examples of regulations made under this procedure include the Consumer Transactions (Restrictions on Statements) Order 1976 and (Amendment) Order 1978, and the Business Advertisements (Disclosure) Order 1977. Another example is the Mail Order Transactions (Information) Order 1976, which applies to goods sold by mail order which have to be paid for in advance. Under the regulations, any advertisement for such goods must state the true name or company name of the person carrying on the mail order business, as well as the true address of the business. Thus, for example, an advertiser giving only a P.O. Box number would be committing an offence if he required payment in advance.

## Taking action against persistently unfair traders

The Director has power to bring proceedings in the Restrictive Practices Court against any person who persistently maintains a course of conduct which is unfair to consumers. Before making a reference to the Court, the Director must first attempt to obtain a written assurance from the trader that he will refrain from the unfair trade practice. If the trader refuses to give an assurance, or breaks an assurance once it has been given, the Director must apply for an order restraining the continuance of the unfair conduct. If the trader does not comply with the order, he will be in contempt of court and liable to imprisonment.

A course of conduct will be regarded as being unfair to consumers if it involves a breach of any legal obligations, either criminal or civil, by the trader. Examples of unfair conduct include persistently giving short measure or applying false trade descriptions, or repeatedly delivering unmerchantable goods.

## Unfair Terms in Consumer Contract Regulations 1998

The Unfair Terms in Consumer Contract Regulations 1998 were designed to encourage the elimination of exemption clauses and other unfair terms from consumer contracts. The Office of Fair Trading has a monopoly over its enforcement and can apply to the High Court for an injunction to prohibit the use of an oppressive term. While a large number of investigations have been carried out there is little evidence of the Director General seeking High Court injunctions. Most businesses will respond to a request to change a term however, following an investigation. Terms which could be classified as unfair are not limited to exemption clauses but could include unilateral price variation clauses and terms require excessive notice periods to terminate the contract e.g. mobile phone contracts. It is possible for a party in litigation to claim that the regulations made a contract term ineffective.

In February 1999 the Director General of Fair Trading wrote to the *Guardian newspaper* and stressed the extent to which the Unfair Terms in Consumer Contracts Regulations 1995 had been enforced by his Office. Following 3400 complaints from consumers over 2000 unfair terms had been modified or dropped from contracts for the supply of goods and services to the advantage of the consumer. He answered the criticism that no court actions had been pursued by emphasising the fact that the Office of Fair Trading is empowered to accept undertakings from suppliers in lieu of court proceedings. The lack of contested cases did not indicate inertia on behalf of his office which stood *"ready to take action against any unfair terms in standard contracts which meet the criteria of the regulations."*

## The Role of Local Authorities in Consumer Protection

Responsibility for the enforcement of most consumer protection legislation, other than that which gives the consumer a right to sue for damages, rests with local authorities. It is carried out by trading standards or consumer protection departments. In practice, these departments see their major role as one of giving guidance to traders. This is done by a combination of education and persuasion. Prosecution for criminal offences is seen as a last resort when other measures fail.

Trading standards officers have wide investigatory powers to enable them to carry out their enforcement functions effectively. They can make sample purchases of goods or services; enter premises; require suppliers to produce documents; carry out tests on equipment; and seize and detain property. A person who obstructs a trading standards officer, or makes a false statements to him commits a criminal offence.

Many Acts of Parliament and regulations made under them are enforced by trading standards officers including the Consumer Credit Act 1974, the Food Safety Act 1990, the Trade Descriptions Act 1968, the Unsolicited Goods and Services Act 1971, and the Consumer Protection Act 1987.

Most, but not all, of the criminal offences designed to protect the consumer apply only to persons supplying goods or services in the course of a trade or business. Traders who are charged with criminal offences will be prosecuted in the Magistrates or the Crown Court. If convicted, they will be liable to a fine or, in some cases, imprisonment. Following a conviction the criminal courts also have power to make a *compensation order* to the victim of the crime. In this context the victim will be the consumer who has suffered loss as a result of the offence. The power to make a compensation order is contained in s.35 of the Powers of Criminal Courts Act 1973. This provides that any court convicting a person of an offence may, in addition to its sentencing power, make an order requiring the offender to pay compensation for any personal injury, loss or damage resulting from the offence or any other offence taken into consideration.

The power to make compensation orders is particularly useful from the point of view of the consumer. It saves him the trouble and expense of bringing proceedings in the civil courts. It will be used only in relatively straightforward cases, however. It is not designed to deal for example with complicated claims involving issues of causation or remoteness of damage.

## The Food Safety Act 1990

The Food Safety Act 1990 is designed to strengthen consumer protection in relation to food safety, an area of increasing concern in recent years. The Act consolidates existing provision in this areas, adds a number of new regulatory powers and substantially increases the penalties for offences relating to the quality and safety of foods. It is an offense, to process or treat food intended for sale for human consumption in any way which makes it injurious to health. Food is injurious to health if it causes any permanent or temporary impairment of health. The offense can be committed by food manufacturers, food handlers, retailers or restaurants. The offense may be committed, for example, by adding a harmful ingredient, or subjecting food to harmful treatment such as storing it at an incorrect temperature or storing cooked meat alongside uncooked meat. Also, food intended for human consumption must satisfy *the food safety requirement*. It is an offense to sell, offer or have in one's possession for sale, prepare or deposit with another for sale any food which fails to meet this requirement.

> In *David Greg Ltd. v. Goldfinch* 1961 a trader was convicted of selling food which was unfit for human consumption (under an equivalent provision in the Food and Drugs Act 1955). He sold a pork pie which had small patches of mold under the crust. The fact that the mold was of a type which was not harmful to human beings was held to be no defense to the charge.

It is also an offense for a supplier to sell, to the prejudice of the consumer, any food which is not of the nature, substance or quality demanded.

> In *Mead v. Robbers* 1978 an employee of a brewery cleaned the beer pumps and taps in a restaurant with caustic soda. He placed the remaining fluid in an empty lemonade bottle labeled 'cleaner' which he left for use by the restaurant. The caustic soda was mistakenly served to a customer who order lemonade. The customer became seriously ill as a result. It was held that the restaurant proprietor was guilty of the offence because the food was not of the nature demanded.

As with many other statutes creating criminal offences of strict liability, a number of defences are available, for example it is a defence to a show that the commission of the offence was due to the act or default of another or, that it was committed as a result of reliance on information supplied by another. Similarly, if the defendant can show that he exercised all due diligence and all reasonable precautions to avoid the commission of the offence, he will escape liability.

## The Data Protection Act 1998

Inevitably it is in the interests of suppliers of goods and services to collect and store information about their clients/customers. Usually the information is stored on computer files and concerns about its accuracy and the use to which it could be put led to pressure for legislation in the mid 1980s to protect consumers. The Data Protection Act 1984 was passed with the aim of providing a legal framework governing the collection, storage and distribution of personal data about individuals stored on computers. The fact that the vast majority of individuals who are protected by the Act are consumers of goods and services means that the Act can be classified as consumer protection legislation. The 1984 Act has now been repealed and replaced by the Data Protection Act 1998 which is now the principal means by which the law regulates the gathering of information about individuals including employees. It will come into force in 1999.

The 1998 Act goes further than the Data Protection Act 1984, protecting against the disclosure of private information, and may be viewed as an attempt to regulate surveillance at work. There are new possibilities for workers and unions to discover and object to information held on them by their employers. Under the 1984 Act the control of information held on computers was limited to entitling individuals to copies of the information. The Data Protection Act 1998 was passed to implement the Data Protection Directive 1995 aimed at regulating the dissemination and holding of information about individuals. The Directive requires *"Member States to protect the fundamental rights and freedoms of natural persons, in particular their rights to privacy with respect to the processing of personal data"*.

Some matters are categorised as sensitive personal data and that is given special protection. Thus in data consisting of matters such as ethnic origin, political opinion, racial origin, religion beliefs, criminal record, sex life and trade union membership. The 1998 Act follows the line of the 1984 Act by making reference to the Data Protection principles. It is the duty of the data controller to comply with the data protection principles in relation to all personal data with respect of which he is the data controller.

The Data Protection Principles are set out in the Act:

- personal data shall be processed fairly and lawfully;

- personal data shall be obtained only for one or more specified and lawful purposes;

- personal data shall be adequate, relevant and not excessive in relation to its purpose;

- personal data shall be accurate and where necessary kept up to date;

- personal data shall be processed in accordance with the rights of the data subject;

- appropriate technical and organisational measures shall be taken against unauthorised or unlawful processing of personal data and against accidental loss or destruction of personal data; and

- personal data shall not be transferred to a country outside the European Economic Area; unless that country ensure an adequate level of protection for the rights of data subjects.

The 1998 Act gives data subjects access to personal data by making provisions enabling individuals to be informed of and in some circumstances gaining access to personal data being processed by a data controller. Certain personal data is exempt from the rights of access such as that relating to national security, tax or duty collection, criminal activities, mental or physical health. A failure to supply information without good reason is a contravention of one of the data protection principles. An individual who suffers damage or distress as a result would maintain a claim for compensation.

The Data Protection Registrar created under the 1984 Act continues to exist under the new Act but becomes the Data Protection Commissioner. He is required to maintain a register of notified information and make it publicly available for inspection. There is a duty on data controllers to register with the commissioner before processing personal data, and failure to do so is a criminal offence.

The court has power on the application of a data subject to rectify, block, erase or destroy inaccurate personal data about the data subject. This would be because of the incomplete or inaccurate nature of the data held.

# Test Questions

1.   What is the aim of the Consumer Credit Act 1974?

2.   What are 'protected goods' under the Act?

3.   Give five examples of regulatory agencies that enforce consumer protection law.

4.   What are the duties of the Director General of Fair Trading?

5.   What action can be taken against persistently unfair traders?

6.   State the purpose of the Unfair Terms in Consumer Contract Regulations 1998.

7.   What are the main offences under the Food Safety Act 1990?

8.   How does the Data Protection Act 1998 differ from the 1984 Act.

9.   What are the duties of the Data Protection Commissioner?

# Assignment - Espana Greenhouses

Tom Cooper, a keen gardener and a member of the local gardening club, has for a number of years specialised in growing tomatoes on a small scale in the 'lean-to' on his allotment. He sees the following advert in the April edition of 'Gardening World'.

---

### Introducing the *ESPANA*

A new revolutionary greenhouse which will bring Mediterranean conditions to your garden. This greenhouse is ideal for growing all types of hot house fruit and vegetables. Each greenhouse is supplied in kit form with full instructions for easy erection within three hours.

Size - Length 4 metres
Width 1.5 metres
Height 2 metres

giving 360 cubic metres of growing space.

Price £995 inclusive of delivery.

*Available from your local gardening centre. Imported into the UK by J Sandford Ltd.*

---

Tom, is considering purchasing a new greenhouse as he hopes to improve the quality and size of his tomato crop.

The two reasons for this are:

(a)   he is keen to exhibit show tomatoes at his local gardening club,

(b)   the price of commercially grown tomatoes has recently increased substantially and he hopes to make savings on the family budget.

Tom visits Todd's his local gardening centre, who have the 'Espana' in stock and he is advised by the manager, Mr. Massey, as to the suitability of the 'Espana' for growing tomatoes. Tom decided to take the plunge and buy the greenhouse, which the gardening centre agrees to deliver the next day. He also purchases 10 dozen tomato plants from the gardening centre. The greenhouse and plants are delivered the following day and Tom and his friend, Jim, a market gardener, spent the morning erecting the greenhouse paying close attention to the manufacturer's instructions.

After completing the erection, Tom and Jim install heating equipment, a propagating frame and then the tomato plants. On standing back to admire the finished job, Tom and Jim suspect that the dimensions of the greenhouse are not as specified and, on checking this, they discover that its dimensions are in fact - length 3.5 metres width 2 metres and height 2 metres. Tom immediately returns to the centre and complains to Mr. Massey that the greenhouse does not match the advertised dimensions. Mr. Massey, however, maintains that there is really no problem as the cubic metreage of the greenhouse, is in fact, equivalent to that advertised and, in any case, Tom should take it up with the manufacturer. Determined to take further action on the matter, Tom returns home to find to his horror that the greenhouse roof has totally collapsed for no apparent reason, injuring his wife Joanne who was inside the greenhouse at the time, and completely destroying all his installed equipment and tomato plants.

Tom has written to the local Consumer Protection Department of his council explaining that neither the garden center, nor the greenhouse manufacturer, are prepared to consider the complaints he has made to them. In his letter he has provided the Department with all the information contained above. His wife is also anxious to establish if she can bring a legal claim for her injuries.

## Tasks

In your role as an assistant to the Trading Standards Officer you have arranged to interview Tom in order to advise him as to the legal position in relation to his complaint. You are required to produce a set of notes for your own assistance in the interview with Tom. These notes should deal with:

(a) Tom's contractual rights against the garden center;

(b) any legal rights he may have against the manufacturer;

(c) the possibility of the Department taking legal proceedings against the garden center or the manufacturer in relation to the Espana advertisement.

# Chapter 4

# The Formation, Management and Dissolution of Business Organisations

## Introduction

Business is a broad and loosely defined term. Perhaps it is most generally understood to mean a commercial enterprise which aims to generate a profit for its owners, a profit achieved by the sales of its goods or services. But like most simple definitions this one is not entirely satisfactory. There are business enterprises which certainly aim to trade profitably, but whose overriding purpose is charitable, or educational, and which therefore do not seek to distribute profits to their members. The National Trust is just one example.

Whatever the economic or social objectives a business organisation is established to pursue however, the one common characteristic they all share is that they trade, and preceeding chapters have explored a range of legal considerations applying to the trading activity business organisations carry out. This chapter, however, takes as its theme the organisations themselves, looking at how they are set up and run, and how they come to an end. This is a study which is crucial to an understanding of business law, for without trading organisations the only economic activity that would be carried out would be between individuals, the kind of activity associated with simple agrarian societies.

Trading is an economic activity, and as such is undertaken in accordance with the principles and practices of economics. The legal implications of trading emerge from legal recognition of different forms of trading organisations, and the consequential rules and principles applicable to such organisations which the law imposes upon them.

Businesses of all kinds reveal certain common characteristics, and it is useful to note these characteristics for they assist in understanding the organisational framework around which the law is constructed.

## Common Characteristics of Business Organisations

The following characteristics are exhibited by most businesses:

(a)    *Defined business aims and objectives*. In general organisations are set up for a specific purpose; selling particular products, providing a service, and so on. Successful businesses are those which evolve as the commercial environment changes and new commercial opportunities present themselves;

(b)    *A distinct identity*. This identity is associated with who owns the organisation, who it employs, what it calls itself, who it trades with and what its markets are;

(c)    *An organisational structure displaying levels of authority*. Leadership will be provided in the form of a system of management with senior management levels located at the top of the structure;

(d)    *Accountability for its actions*. The organisation as a whole will possess accountability. It will be accountable to those who own it, those whom it employs, and those with whom it trades. Similarly those people it employs are legally accountable to the organisation to fulfil their obligations towards it. This idea of legal accountability is fundamental to the principles and practice of English business law.

## The Classification of Business Organisations

It is easy to create elaborate charts and diagrams which classify business organisations according to different criteria, but as a starting point a simple diagram showing how these organisations relate to each other is useful. The figure on the next page does so. It distinguishes organisations according to ownership and then breaks down private sector business organisations, which form the subject matter of this chapter, into their specific legal categories.

Two features of the figure require special attention. These are the distinctions between:

• corporate and unincorporated bodies; and

• private and public sector organisations.

It is outside the scope of a law textbook to examine the differences between public and private sector organisations in any detail, however it is important to be clear about the significance of the distinction. Essentially what distinguishes a public sector from a private sector organisation is who owns, and therefore controls it. Whereas in the public sector this will be the state; in the private sector it will be private individuals and other organisations.

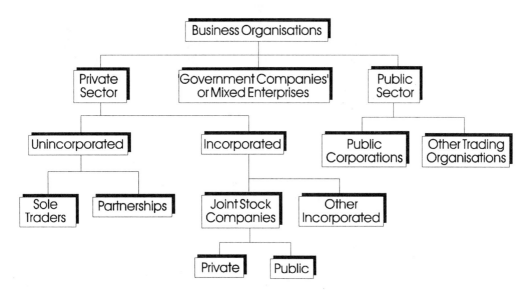

**Figure 4.1** *General Classification of Business Organisations*

Most of the work carried out by organisations in the public sector is not principally concerned with commercial trading, but rather with the provision of public services such as health, education and housing, and the management of a wide range of social welfare benefits such as pensions. The state does however engage in limited commercial trading. Despite privatisation plans the Post Office a state trading organisation; so too is Her Majesty's Stationery Office (HMSO). Much of the law contained in this book is as applicable to these state organisations as to those trading in the private sector.

A further distinguishing feature is the method used to create a public sector organisation. Usually they are created by a specific Act of Parliament, thus local authorities in England and Wales are established under the Local Government Act 1972. The use of an Act of Parliament to create a private sector organisation, although possible, is most unusual.

## Corporate and Unincorporated Bodies

Under English law all business enterprises can be classified into one of two basic legal forms. They are either *corporate* or *unincorporated* bodies. An unincorporated body is usually a group of individuals, who have joined together to pursue a common business purpose. The body and the individuals who compose it are not separate from each other under the law. They may however trade under a business name, rather than using their own names, creating the appearance that the business is in some way separate from them. The most important example of the unincorporated association is the partnership.

A corporate body, or *corporation*, is also generally made up of a group of individuals who have joined together for a common purpose, but who through the process of legal incorporation have created an artificial legal person which has a legal identity separate from themselves. The distinction between corporate and non-corporate bodies is fundamental to understanding the law as it applies to organisations.

The corporation has proved itself to be the most significant form of business for the pursuit of commercial activity in the United Kingdom, for reasons that are explained below. Unlike unincorporated associations, which are not generally subject to legal control over their formation, corporate bodies can only be established by way of formal mechanisms used to set them up. They can be created by Royal Charter, by means of a particular Act of Parliament, or by registration under the Companies Act 1985. This is the method used to create almost all private sector corporate bodies. The 1985 Act recognises two basic forms of registered company, public limited companies and private limited companies. In so doing it recognises an important commercial distinction which we shall be considering.

Although registered companies are the dominant form of commercial enterprise in the United Kingdom, and therefore warrant particular attention, unincorporated businesses remain the significant form of business in a number of fields, notably the professions, in consultancy, and in relation to many small business operations.

There are two types of unincorporated business we need to consider, the sole trade and the partnership.

# Sole Traders

The term *sole trader* describes a person operating an unincorporated business alone and thus having sole responsibility for its management. In such business people rarely work entirely alone and will usually employ staff to assist them in the operation of the business. There are no specific legal formalities relating to the creation of such businesses. The law which a sole trader needs to be aware of is that associated with trading, employing staff and acquiring and operating business premises. Some types of business enterprise must also acquire a licence to permit them to operate. For instance a publican requires a licence to sell intoxicating drinks and a turf accountant a betting and gaming licence.

Such a business will normally be financed by the owner himself, which means that the opportunities for raising business capital are necessarily restricted. The sole owner is entitled to all the profits of the business, but also has unlimited liability in relation to its losses and so must bear them personally. The sole trader form of business is therefore most suitable for an individual who wishes to retain absolute control of the sort of business enterprise which requires only a modest amount of financial investment. Obvious examples include retail shops and service trades such as plumbing and hairdressing. Collectively, sole traders provide a valuable service to the community by making a wide range of goods and services available in a personal way, meeting needs which might otherwise be unfulfilled.

Responsibility for decision making in such a business rests with the owner. There is no individual or group to whom the trader is directly accountable. This is very attractive to those who wish to *be their own boss*. Of course there are those who will be affected by the owner's actions; the customers or clients, the creditors to whom the business owes money, and especially the employees of the business. Such groups have a valid interest in the decisions made by the sole trader and may ultimately seek to hold the trader legally accountable for commercial decision making. An employee may complain that employment rights have been infringed, or a customer that consumer rights have been abused. Ultimate accountability arises where the sole trader becomes insolvent, that is unable to meet the debts of the business and has bankruptcy proceedings commenced against him or her.

# Partnerships

The other major form of unincorporated business organisation is the partnership. Lawyers refer to partnerships as *firms* for the Partnership Act 1890 which is the main source of partnership law states under s.4 that: *"Persons who have entered into a partnership with one another for the purposes of this Act are called collectively 'a firm', and the name under which their business is carried on is called the firm-name"*.

There are no detailed legal formalities required when individuals agree to operate a business together and thus form a partnership, and the advantages to a business enterprise of forming a partnership are somewhat similar to those enjoyed by the sole trader. The partners are capable of managing their own firm as they see fit, of sharing the profits and being able to deal directly with their customers or clients.

The partnership provides the compromise of allowing an extension of skill and expertise and the possible influx of additional capital by the introduction of extra partners. This extra potential for capital allows many partnerships to grow to become substantial business enterprises.

Although it has always tended to be overshadowed by the limited company, the partnership remains a significant form of business organisation in the United Kingdom, and is the choice of many people either setting up a new business or modifying an existing one.

## Forming a partnership

An agreement between two or more persons to form a partnership constitutes a contract between them but there is no legal requirement as to the form of this contract, so it can be oral, in writing, contained in a deed, or even implied by the law from the surrounding circumstances. The Partnership Act 1890, which contains most of the legal rules relating to partnerships, defines a partnership under s.1 simply as the *"relation which subsists between persons carrying on business in common with a view of profit"*. This definition shows that it is possible for a business to be run as a joint venture without the participants being aware that their business is in law a partnership. This may be of no consequence to them as long as they are able to work together in harmony, but in a dispute it is important to them to ascertain whether their relationship constitutes a partnership. If it does the provisions of the 1890 Act will apply, carrying significant consequences regarding the rights and obligations the partners owe each other.

The main risk in operating a business as a firm is that if the business should get into financial difficulties, the liability of the partners is not limited in any way. The individual members are liable to the extent of their personal wealth to pay off partnership debts. In extreme cases they may loose almost all their personal property through bankruptcy proceedings.

Although the 1890 Act lays down no formation requirements, it is of course commercially desirable, and certainly common practice, for partners to execute a deed of partnership, in which they provide for matters such as the capital contribution required from each member of the firm, and how profits and losses are to be divided. If the partners do *not* agree such details then the rights and duties laid down under the Act will apply to the partnership.

S.716 Companies Act 1985, provides that a partnership cannot validly consist of more than twenty members. An exception is made however for certain professions, such as accountants and solicitors, who are prevented by statute from practising as limited companies. No restriction is placed upon the size of such firms. Some of the largest firms of lawyers and accountants have hundreds of partners.

Partners can choose any name they please for their firm provided it is not similar to an existing name and therefore not likely to mislead others. However the name cannot end in the word *limited* or any abbreviation of it, for this would indicate that the organisation is a company having limited liability. The words *and Co* at the end of the partnership name refers to the fact that there are partners in the firm whose names do not appear in the firm name. If a firm uses a trading name which does not consist of the surnames of all the partners the Business Names Act 1985 requires that their names must appear on their business stationery, and their true names and addresses must be prominently displayed at their business premises in a place to which the public have access. Non-compliance with these provisions is a criminal offence.

## The definition of partnership

Under the s.1 definition there must be:

- a business;

- carried on in common by its members;

- with a view to making a profit.

Under the Act *"business"* includes every trade, occupation or profession. Although business is a broad term it does imply the carrying on of some form of commercial activity. This may be for a single purpose. It is the court, looking at the facts, to resolve any doubt about whether a business is being conducted.

> In *Spicer (Keith) Ltd. v. Mansell* 1970 the Court of Appeal held that two persons who were working together for the purpose of forming a limited company, and had opened a bank account and ordered goods in this connection were not in partnership prior to the incorporation of the company (which in fact was never formed). The reason was that at that time they were preparing for business, rather than operating an existing one.

A thin line often exists between a mere hobby and a business.

The business must be a joint venture, which implies mutual rights and obligations existing between the members of it. There may still be a joint venture even though one (or more) of its members is a sleeping partner who does not take an active part in the management of the business but simply contributes capital.

There must also be a profit motive underlying the business. It will be a question of fact whether the partners aim to make a profit.

Help in determining when a business may be treated as a partnership is provided by s.2. It says that where a person receives a share in the profits of a business, this will be *prima facie* evidence that he is a partner, although the presumption can be shifted by other conflicting evidence. The section goes on to state a list of situations which do not, of themselves, make a person a partner, for instance: where a person working as an employee or agent of the firm is paid out of a share of its profits, or when people are co-owners of land, even where profits are shared from the use of the land.

## Registered Companies

We saw earlier that a registered company limited by shares is a corporate body, an artificial person recognised by the law, with an identity separate from the members which compose it. The members of such an organisation are referred to as its shareholders.

The limited company is the most common type of business enterprise operated as a corporation. Many thousands of registered limited companies function in the UK between them employing the majority of the nation's workforce and generating about two thirds of the income made by the private sector. Companies can be formed which have only one member. They can also develop into massive multi-national UK registered enterprises which have thousands of shareholders holding millions of shares. Such is the diversity of these organisations that it is difficult to generalise on their structure and behaviour but most have been formed with the expectation of future expansion financed by the raising of capital through the issue of shares. As separate legal entities they also give the owners the protection of limited liability and it is this feature more than any other that has contributed to their popularity. Another appealing feature is that ownership can be divorced from management, thus an investor can stake capital in a company without having to be involved in the actual running of it, whilst maintaining control over the managers by means of their accountability in the general meeting.

Limited liability means that where a company is unable to pay its debts its shareholders' legal liability to contribute to the payment of debts is limited to the amount, if any, unpaid on their shares. Thus, someone buying twenty £1 shares in a company who pays 25p on each share (these are called partly paid shares) is only liable to contribute the amount of the share value remaining unpaid, in this case 20 x 75p, a total of £15.

It is of course only the shareholders whose liability is limited. The company itself is fully liable for its debts, and may be brought to an end through the process of winding-up if it cannot meet them.

The liability of the members of a registered company may be limited either by shares or guarantee, or in rare cases be unlimited. This is provided for by s.1(2) of the Companies Act 1985 which states that a company may be:

(i)    limited by *shares,* where the liability of the company members, the shareholders, is limited to any amount as yet unpaid on their shares; or

(ii)    limited by *guarantee,* where the members' liability is limited to an amount they have guaranteed to contribute in the event of the company being brought to an end, a process known technically as winding up; or

(iii)    *unlimited,* where the members are fully liable for the debts of the company, in the event of it being wound up.

Unlimited companies can only operate as private companies. They are used primarily as service and investment companies. Although the number of public limited companies is relatively small (they are numbered in thousands, whilst private companies are numbered in hundreds of thousands), their commercial importance places them at the heart of the private sector economy. They include the major banks, multinational organisations such as ICI, British Airways and Marks and Spencer, and a range of other household names. Commonly, public companies began life as private companies, becoming sufficiently successful commercially to warrant *going public,* and thus able to offer their shares on the open market.

Statutory registration was first introduced under the Companies Act 1844, to provide a quick cheap method of incorporation. Statutory registration proved immediately popular and helped to provide the capital which the growth of business activity at that time urgently needed. Capital was provided by investors attracted not only by the investment prospects offered by newly formed registered companies but also by the financial protection available through limited liability. The registered company remains just as popular with investors today, and has been further stimulated by the privatisation programmes of the 1980s and 90s and the idea of popular capitalism.

Companies can expand and diversify by raising additional capital as needed, through the issue of more shares. The growth of this form of business enterprise and the recognition of the company as a separate legal entity has however posed many problems and led to many abuses. The law has recognised these difficulties. Various Companies Acts, now consolidated in the Companies Act 1985, have sought to regulate corporate behaviour, bearing in mind not only the interests of the shareholders themselves but also the interests of outsiders who trade with them.

## The concept of corporate personality

As an artificial legal person, the registered company has some although not all the powers and responsibilities of a natural person. It can own property, enter into contracts such as trading contracts and contracts of employment, and sue or be sued in its own name. But its artificial nature imposes obvious limitations upon its legal capacity. It cannot generally be held liable for criminal acts, since most crimes involve proving a mental element such as intention or recklessness and a corporation has as such no mind. Nevertheless sometimes the collective intention of the board of directors can be regarded as expressing the will of the corporation. Lord Denning has spoken of the company as having a human body, the employees being the hands that carry out its work while *"others are directors and managers who represent the directing mind and will of the company and control what it does"*. The development of this line of reasoning has enabled companies to be convicted of manslaughter.

Because the members and the company are legally separate changes in the membership, including the death or bankruptcy of members, will have no effect upon the company, which may have an almost perpetual life span if there remain investors willing to become or to remain members of it.

> The legal separation of a company from its members was confirmed in the leading case of *Salomon v. Salomon & Co.* 1897. Salomon owned a boot and shoe business. His sons worked in the business and they were anxious to have a stake in it so Salomon formed a registered company with himself as managing director, in which his wife, daughter and each son held a share. The company's nominal capital was £40,000 consisting of 40,000 £1 shares.
>
> The company resolved to purchase the business at a price of £39,000. Salomon had arrived at this figure himself. It was an honest but optimistic valuation of its real worth. The company paid him by allotting him 20,000 £1 shares treated as fully paid, £10,000 worth of debentures (a secured loan repayable before unsecured loans) and the balance in cash. Within a year of trading the company went into insolvent liquidation owing £8,000 to ordinary creditors and having only £6,000 worth of assets. The plaintiff, Mr. Salomon, claimed that as a debenture holder with £10,000 worth of debentures he was a secured creditor and entitled to repayment before the ordinary unsecured creditors. The unsecured creditors did not agree. The House of Lords held that despite the fact that following the company's formation, Salomon had continued to run the business in the same manner and with the same control as he had done when it was unincorporated, the company formed was a separate person from Salomon himself. When the company was liquidated therefore, and in the absence of any fraud on the creditors and shareholders, Salomon, like any other debenture holder, was a secured creditor and entitled to repayment before ordinary creditors. The court thus upheld the principle that a company has a separate legal existence from its membership even where one individual holds the majority of shares and effectively runs the company as his own. In his leading judgment Lord Macnaghten stated, *"The company is at law a different person altogether from the subscribers to the memorandum; and, though it may be that after incorporation the business is precisely the same as it was before, and the same persons are managers, and the same hands receive the profits, the company is not in law the agent of the*

*subscribers or trustee for them. Nor are the subscribers as members liable, in any shape or form, except to the extent and in the manner provided by the Act.*"

Many consequences flow from this basic proposition of company law. For example the company's bank account is quite separate and independent from the account of the majority shareholder.

In *Underwood Ltd. v. Bank of Liverpool & Martins Ltd.* 1924 it was held that a managing director who held all except one of the shares in his company was acting unlawfully in paying company cheques into his own account, and drawing cheques on the company's account for his own personal benefit.

The application of the Salomon principle makes it possible for a shareholder/director to be convicted on a charge of theft from his own company: *Re: Attorney General's Reference (no. 2 of 1982)* 1984.

A company is also the owner of its own property in which its members have no legal interest, although clearly they have a financial interest.

In *Macaura v. Northern Assurance Co. Ltd.* 1925 it was held that a majority shareholder has no insurable interest in the company's property. A fire insurance policy over the company's timber estate was therefore invalid as it had been issued in the plaintiff shareholder's name and not the company's name.

## Lifting the corporate veil

Both the courts and Parliament have accepted that in some situations it is right and proper to prevent the members from escaping liability by hiding behind the company. The result has been the creation of a number of exceptions to the principle of limited liability. These exceptions seem to be based broadly upon public policy considerations, and many of them are associated with fraudulent practices. If for instance a company is wound up and the court is satisfied that the directors have carried on the business with an intention to defraud the creditors, they may be made personally liable for company's debts.

## The common law position

In special cases, the courts are prepared to disregard the separate legal personality of a company because it was formed or used to facilitate the evasion of legal obligations. This is sometimes referred to as lifting the veil of incorporation, meaning that the court is able to look behind the corporate, formal identity of the organisation to the shareholders which make it up. It is a very significant step, since it is effectively denying the protection which the members have sought to obtain by incorporation.

In *Jones v. Lipman* 1962 the defendant agreed to sell land to the plaintiff and then decided not to complete the contract. To avoid the possibility of an order of specific performance to enforce the sale the defendant purchased a majority shareholding in an existing company to which he then sold the land. The plaintiff applied to the court for an order against the defendant and the company to enforce the sale. It was held that the formation of the company was a mere sham to avoid a contract of sale, and specific performance was ordered against the vendor and the company.

In *Re: Bugle Press Ltd.* 1961 the company consisted of three shareholders. Two of them, who together had controlling interest, wanted to buy the shares of the third, but he was not willing to sell so the two of them formed a new company which then made a take-over bid for the shares of the first company. Not surprisingly the two shareholders who had formed the new company accepted the bid. The third did not. However since he only held 1/10 of the total shareholding, under what is now s.428 Companies Act 1985, the new company was able to compulsorily acquire the shares. The Court of Appeal however held that this represented an abuse of the section. The minority shareholder was in effect being evicted from the company. The veil of the new company was lifted and, in the words of Harman LJ: this revealed a *"hollow sham"*, for it was *"nothing but a little hut built round"* the majority shareholders.

The courts are sometimes prepared to lift the veil in order to discover the relationship within groups of companies. It is a common commercial practice for one company to acquire shares in another, often holding sufficient shares to give it total control over the other. In these circumstances the controlling company is referred to as a *holding* company, and the other company its *subsidiary*. In appropriate cases a holding company can be regarded as an agent of its subsidiary, although it is more usual to find the subsidiary acting as an agent for the holding company.

## The statutory position

In addition to this common law strategy there are a number of provisions contained in the Companies Act 1985 which have the effect of lifting the veil. They include the following:

(a)  a fall in the membership of a *public* company to below 2, under s.24. In these circumstances if the condition continues for more than six months, the sole shareholder becomes personally liable for the company's debts incurred after that time. Note that to be a member of a company it is only necessary to hold a single share.

(b)  Under s.349(4) if an officer of a company such as a company secretary or any person on its behalf:

   (i)   issues or authorises the issue of a business letter or signs a negotiable instrument and the company name is not mentioned, or

   (ii)  issues or authorises the issue of any invoice, receipt or letter of credit of the company and again the company name is not mentioned;

         that person shall be personally liable for debts incurred unless they are paid by the company.

In *Hendon v. Adelman* 1973 directors of a company whose registered name was L & R Agencies Ltd. signed a cheque on behalf of the company omitting the ampersand between 'L' and 'R'. The bank failed to honour the cheque and the court found that this omission was sufficient to make the directors personally liable for the cheque.

(c)  Under powers granted to the Department of Trade and Industry to investigate the affairs of any company within the same group as one primarily under investigation by a DTI Inspector.S442(1) provides that where there appears to be good reason to do so, the Department may appoint inspectors to investigate and report on the membership of any company in order to determine the true identity of the persons financially interested in its success or failure, or able to control or materially influence its policy.

(d)  Under sections 213 and 214 Insolvency Act 1986. These important provisions are considered in more depth at the end of the chapter.

## Public and Private Companies

S1 Companies Act 1985 provides that a registered company limited by shares may be either a *public* or a *private* one. The most significant distinction between them is that a public limited company is permitted to advertise publicly to invite investors to take shares in it. A private company cannot advertise its shares in this way. Once purchased, shares in a public company can then be freely disposed of by the shareholder to anyone else who is willing to buy them. By contrast private companies commonly issue shares on terms that if the member wishes to dispose of them they must first be offered to the existing members. Where such rights are available to members they are known as *pre-emption* rights.

All companies are now treated as though they are private ones, unless certain requirements have been met which allow the company to be registered as a public limited company. This change was introduced to make it easier to define public companies for the purpose of complying with EC company law directives applicable to public companies. To register as a public company, the company must:

- state both in its name, and in its memorandum that it is a public company. Thus its name must end in the words *"public limited company" "plc."* The name of a private company ends with the word *"limited"* or *"Ltd."*;

- register an appropriate memorandum of association;

- satisfy s.11 of the 1985 Act. This requires the company to have an authorised share capital figure of at least £50,000 with at least one quarter of this amount paid up before the company can commence trading, or exercise its borrowing powers. Consequently a plc. must have at least £12,500 paid up share capital before it starts trading, and be able to call for an additional £37,500 from its members.

An explanation of the terms regarding company capital may be helpful.

The *authorised share capital* is the amount that the company is legally permitted to raise by the issue of shares, the *paid-up share* capital is the amount the company has received from the shares it has issued, and the *uncalled capital* is the amount remaining unpaid by shareholders for the shares they hold; e.g. a company may issue £1 shares but require those to whom they are allotted to pay only 50p per share for the present.

The expression *allotment of shares* describes the notification by the company, usually in the form of a letter, that it has accepted an offer for the shares, and that the new shareholders name will be entered on the register of shareholders.

A registered company which does not meet the three requirements listed above will be treated as a private company. Private companies differ from public companies in a number of respects. They are less heavily regulated, and enjoy a number of advantages over public companies, which include being able to: operate with a single member; avoid holding formal company meetings and publishing full accounts; exclude in their articles s.89 Companies Act 1985. The section provides that ordinary shares issued for cash by a company must first be offered to existing shareholders (a rights issue).

The only disadvantage a private company has is its inability to advertise publicly its shares. If it wishes to do so, as a way of funding growth, then it must re-register as a public company.

## Single Member Companies

The Companies (Single Member Private Limited Companies) Regulations 1992, implementing the Twelfth Company Law Directive, allow for the formation and operation of private limited companies having a *single* member. This amends s.1 CA 1985 which requires a company to have at least two members. Now the rule only applies to public companies. The register of members of a single member company must state that it is such a company, and provide the name and address of the sole member; company resolutions must be evidenced in writing; and any contract between the sole member and the company (unless made in the ordinary course of its business on the usual terms and conditions) must be expressed in writing. A single member company must however have two officers, a director and a secretary. Normally the sole member is likely to be the director, and the non-member the secretary.

## Forming a Registered Company

A company is incorporated and so comes into being when the Registrar of Companies in Cardiff issues it with a document called the certificate of incorporation. This certificate is issued following an application by the persons who wish to form the company. They are known as the company's *promoters*. The two main documents which must be included in the application are the *memorandum of association* and the *articles of association*. Once the certificate of incorporation has been granted a private company can commence trading immediately, however a public company must be issued with a further document, a *trading certificate*, before it is authorised to start trading.

## The Memorandum of Association

The memorandum of association and the articles of association set out the constitution of a registered company. They are the two major documents within a group of documents to be sent to the Registrar of Companies prior to incorporation. The Companies Act 1985 requires the memorandum to include: the name of the company with *limited* as the last word in the case of a private company, or *public limited company* in the case of a public company; the situation of the registered office identifying whether the company is situated in England or Scotland; the objects of the company; the liability of its members; and its nominal capital divided into numbers of shares and denominations.

The Registrar of Companies maintains a file for all registered companies, which is open to public inspection on payment of a fee. The file for each company includes the company memorandum.

Stating the country in which the company is situated determines whether it is an English or Scottish company. Usually a Notice of Situation of Registered Office, giving the company's full address is sent to the Registrar together with the Memorandum. It must, in any event, be sent to him within fourteen days of incorporation of the company. The registered office is important since documents are effectively served on the company by posting or delivering them to this address. Thus a writ (a document used to commence legal proceedings) served on the company will be effectively served if delivered to the registered office.

The *objects clause* sets the contractual limits within which the company can validly operate, and is discussed more fully below.

The *liability clause* is a formality which merely states the nature of the shareholders' liability, that is whether it is limited by shares, by guarantee, or unlimited.

The *capital clause* sets out the amount of capital the company is authorised to raise by the issue of shares, and the way in which the shares are to be divided. This amount can be raised by the agreement of the shareholders without difficulty, although a reduction in the share capital, whilst possible, is more of a problem to achieve. It is a basic principle of company law that share capital should be maintained to protect the interests of the company's creditors.

The memorandum concludes with the names and addresses of those people agreeing to take shares in the company on its formation and indicating how many shares each will take. These people are called *subscribers*. The subscribers for the shares in the memorandum will often be appointed as directors. As the statutory minimum membership of a private company is one, a single subscriber to the memorandum will suffice to form the company. The minimum membership for a public company is two. Each subscriber will agree to take a certain number of shares on incorporation of the company, and the subscribers are therefore the first members of the company. Subsequently new members will join the company when it allots shares to them and their names are entered on the register of members which every company must maintain, and which is open to public inspection. Usually the subscribers will have been the promoters - the people engaged in setting up the company.

## Company name

Generally a company is free to choose the name it wishes to adopt, although as we have seen the word *limited* for a private company or *plc* for a public company must be inserted at the end of the company name. This is required by s.26 Companies Act 1985, which also provides that the name cannot be the same as one already held on the index of company names kept by the Registrar. Nor can a name be used which would in the opinion of the Secretary of State constitute a criminal offence or be offensive.

It is a tort for a person to represent his business as that of another and thereby obtain profit from that other's business goodwill. In such circumstances the injured business can claim under the tort of passing off against the business guilty of the deception and recover damages and obtain an injunction, by way of a remedy.

## The objects clause and the ultra vires doctrine

Being a corporate body the registered company can only lawfully do those things which its constitution allows it to do. As a condition of incorporation every registered company must include a statement in its memorandum which sets out what the company has been formed to do. The scope or extent of this statement, known as the company's *objects clause*, is initially decided by the people setting up the company, its promoters. They will often become the company's first directors following its incorporation.

The details contained in the objects clause provide shareholders with a description of the range of activities their company can legitimately undertake. It is right that, as investors, a company's shareholders should know the purpose for which their financial contribution can be used. A rational investor will want to establish how well the board of directors manages the company, something which can be achieved by looking at the company's trading performance in its particular line of business. An investor may be less willing to put money into an enterprise where the board has a wide freedom under the company's objects clause to pursue diverse commercial activities, some of which may fall well outside their experience as managers. This is particularly likely in the smaller private companies, for whereas the boards handling the affairs of public companies will include executive directors having wide commercial experience, in small private limited companies directors will sometimes have at best only a rudimentary knowledge of business management, and at worst none at all.

If a company acts outside the limits of its permissible activities as expressed in the objects clause it is said to be acting *ultra vires*, that is beyond its powers. At common law an ultra vires transaction has always been treated as a nullity, consequently an ultra vires contract entered into by a company was neither enforceable by it or against it. Even if the other contracting party was unaware that the company was exceeding its powers as expressed in the memorandum this would provide no relief, for under the doctrine of *constructive notice* a person dealing with a company was deemed to be aware of its public documents and hence of any restrictions on the company's capacity contained in them. Nor could the company subsequently ratify in general meeting an ultra vires transaction made on its behalf by the directors. Ratification has the effect of retrospectively validating a transaction, but in the case of an ultra vires contract this is not possible since the contract is a nullity.

When the United Kingdom became a member of the European Community on 1st January, 1973, the European Communities Act 1972, by which entry was effected, in a hurried attempt at providing for some measure of harmonisation between English company law and company law as it applied in the other member states, modified the ultra vires doctrine.

The present law on the subject is contained in s.35 Companies Act 1989 which states that, *"The validity of an act done by a company shall not be called into question on the ground of lack of capacity by reason on anything in the company's memorandum."* In other words it validates transactions which would otherwise be void on the grounds of breaching the company's constitution as expressed in the memorandum. The section adds that anyone making a transaction with the company is not obliged to check the memorandum to ascertain whether it authorises the transaction. The 1989 Act also abolishes the doctrine of constructive notice of matters which would be disclosed by a company search. Previously, as we have seen, a person dealing with a company was in some circumstances deemed to have knowledge of information contained in the public file of the company held at the Companies Registry. This principle no longer applies.

The changes introduced under the Companies Act 1989 do not however completely eliminate the application of ultra vires to registered companies, for:

(i)    a shareholder can still seek an injunction to restrain the company from entering into an ultra vires transaction, although this opportunity is lost once the transaction has been made, whether or not it has been carried out;

(ii)    directors are still obliged to act within their company's constitution. S.35(3) says, *"it remains the duty of the directors to observe any limitations on their powers flowing from the company's memorandum"*. They can be sued for breach of duty if they exceed their powers, however the company can now ratify action taken by directors in excess of their powers by special resolution, and an additional special resolution may be passed to relieve the directors of any liability for breach of duty already incurred as a result of exceeding the company's powers;

(iii) if a director exceeds his powers and the other party to the contract is a director of the company or the holding company, the company can if it chooses avoid the contract. This is an attempt at preventing directors defrauding the company using the provisions of the new s.35.

Whilst the powers of a company are found in its memorandum, the rules regulating the way in which these powers should be exercised are usually contained in the articles of association. Articles may, for example, cut down directors powers, by requiring transactions involving more than a certain amount of money to be approved by the members through an ordinary resolution passed at a meeting of the company. This can give rise to circumstances where an outsider enters into a transaction with a company which its memorandum authorises, but where the company's internal rules have not been complied with. Internal rules contained in a company's articles of association, being contained in its public file, came within the doctrine of constructive notice: the outsider was deemed to be aware of them. What he could not know was whether they had in fact been complied with when a company decision was made.

As a response to this difficulty the rule in *Royal British Bank v. Turquand* 1856 provided that an outsider was entitled to assume that the necessary rules of internal management had been complied with.

The rule in *Turquands Case* is affected by the Companies Act 1989, which provides that a third party dealing in good faith with a company can treat the company's constitution as imposing no restrictions on the power of the board of directors or persons authorised by them to bind the company. A third party is assumed to be acting in good faith, unless the contrary can be shown. Knowledge that the directors are acting beyond their powers does not, in itself, amount to bad faith.

## Alteration of the objects clause

S.4 Companies Act 1985 allows a company by special resolution alter its objects clause at any time and for any reason. The alteration is effective so long as no application is made to the court to cancel it within 21 days of the special resolution, and the company sends the Registrar within a further 15 days a copy of the altered memorandum. An application to cancel can be made by the holders of at least 15% of the issued share capital of any class, and the alteration is only effective in these circumstances where the court confirms it. A company can legitimately adopt a single object to carry on business as a general commercial company. A company formed with such an object will be able to carry on any business or trade, and do anything incidental or conducive to such a business or trade.

# The Articles of Association

The articles of association of a registered company must be supplied to the Registrar of Companies prior to incorporation. Like the memorandum the articles will then be publicly available in the company's file kept at Companies House in Cardiff.

The articles are concerned with the internal administration of the company, and it is for those setting up the company to determine the rules they consider appropriate for inclusion within the articles. The Companies Act 1985 does however provide a set of model articles which a company can adopt in whole or in part if it wishes. If a company fails to provide a set of articles then the model articles contained in the 1985 Act automatically apply to the company. They are known as *Table A* Articles. Matters which are normally dealt with in the Articles include the appointment and powers of the board of directors, the rules in relation to members' meetings and voting and the types of shares and rights attaching to the share categories. Additionally certain other documents must be supplied to the Registrar prior to incorporation, including a statutory declaration that all the requirements of the Act have been complied with.

# Test Questions

1.   What are the identifying characteristics of a partnership?

2.   What risks are associated with running a business as a sole trader or in partnership?

3.   Identify what consequences flow from a registered company being regarded as a legal person.

4.   List the circumstances in which the veil of incorporation of a company can be lifted.

5.   Are there any limitations placed upon the capacity of a company to make contracts?

6.   Distinguish between the functions of the memorandum of association and the articles of association of a registered company.

7.   Is any restriction placed upon the number of people who can belong to a company or a partnership?

# Financing the Company

For any company the raising of money for trading purposes is essential to its ability to carry on trade. The capital so acquired is a fundamental resource of the company.

Companies are able to raise the capital in different ways. The methods available and the legal rules and principles associated with them, are complex. Essentially companies can acquire capital through the issue of shares, and by means of borrowing through the issue of debentures. Shares and debentures are often referred to collectively as *company securities*. In a legal sense, capital is something positive. It is what the company has raised and can use for doing things, to buy business premises for instance, which are then referred to as fixed capital, or to purchase stock, which is referred to as circulating capital. In an accountancy sense, however, capital is something negative, appearing in a balance sheet under the heading of *liabilities*. Thus, to an accountant the money raised by issuing shares – (*share capital;*), issuing debentures - (*loan capital;*), as well as, the amount of money owed by the company to its trade creditors, is all regarded as part of the company's indebtedness. This is capital as a *debt*. All these items are owed.

The expression capital is such an important one that it has found its way into a variety of technical terms used in company law. The most important of these terms are:

- *Share capital* is capital raised by the issue of the company's shares, and is often used as a way of distinguishing capital gained in this way, from capital gained through borrowing.

- *Loan capital* is capital acquired by means of borrowing.

- *Nominal (or authorised capital)* refers to the value of shares a company is authorised to issue, and it appears in the capital clause of the memorandum of association.

- *Issued capital* is usually used to describe the value of capital in the form of shares which have actually been issued to the members.

- *Paid-up capital* is the amount which has been paid to the company by its members for the shares they hold. Companies do not always require immediate payment in full for issued shares. Under the Companies Act 1985, if a company makes a reference to share capital on its business stationery or order forms, this must be a reference to its paid up capital.

- *Unpaid capital.* If shares have been issued which have not been fully paid for, the amount outstanding is referred to as *unpaid capital*. For example, if 5,000 issued shares have a nominal value (that is a face value, sometimes referred to as *par* value) of £1 each and shareholders have been required to pay only 40 pence per share, then the paid up capital is £2,000 and the unpaid capital is £3,000. Shareholders may be required to pay up the outstanding amount on their shares by the company making a *call* on them to do so. The unpaid amount is the extent of the shareholders' liability to the company.

In company law references to capital are usually references to share capital.

# Share Capital

Issuing shares is one way of financing a company. How far a company is willing to use this method is likely to depend upon many factors. A private company may be willing to issue more shares because existing members are not in a position to invest further in the company, yet do not wish to dilute their control over the running of the company by issuing shares which grant votes to new members. A public company may avoid a share issue if its present investment potential is unlikely to attract the market. An alternative approach is to borrow money, that is raise loan capital, usually by means of the issue of debentures. Again, a company may be reluctant to use this approach, since it will have the effect of tying it down, and at times of high interest rates such borrowings may not be commercially advisable.

Further alternatives used by companies are: to obtain goods and services on credit; for instance, by leasing vehicles or obtaining machinery on hire purchase terms; and to retain profits - which simply involves holding back profits made by trading, the effects being borne by the shareholders whose *dividends*, (their return on their investment), will be reduced accordingly.

## Shares

Essentially a share is a unit of company ownership and a shareholder as a stakeholder in the organisation is a company member. Sometimes companies, particularly smaller ones, will issue only one type, or class, of shares. If they do all the shares will carry equal rights. But in larger companies different classes of shares are usually issued with varying rights attaching to them relating such matters as voting, payment of dividends and return of capital on liquidation. The two main types of shares are:

(a)   *Preference share*
      The main characteristic of a preference share is that it will carry a preferred fixed dividend. This means that the holder of a preference share is entitled to a fixed amount of dividend, e.g. 6% on the value of

each share, before other shareholders are paid any dividend. They are presumed to be cumulative which means that if in any year the company fails to declare a dividend, the shortfall must be made up out of profits of subsequent years. A preference share is therefore a safe investment with fixed interest, no matter how small or large is the company's profit. As far as return of capital on a winding up is concerned, the preference shareholder will rank equally with ordinary shareholders for any payment due, unless the preference shares are made preferential as to capital. Normally, preference shares do not carry voting rights and therefore the preference shareholder has little influence over the company's activities.

(b)   *Ordinary shares*
Ordinary shares are often referred to as the *equity share capital* of a company. When a company declares a dividend and the preference shareholders have been paid, the holders of ordinary shares are entitled to the remainder. It follows therefore that an ordinary shareholder in a well-managed company making high profits will receive a good return on his investment and consequently the value of his shares will rise. In this way a share can have a much higher market value than it's face value. Unfortunately, the reverse is also true and they may fall in market value so that ordinary shares inevitably carry a certain risk. This risk is reflected in the amount of control that an ordinary shareholder has over the company's business. While voting rights are not normally attached to preference shares, they are attached to ordinary shares enabling the ordinary shareholder to voice an opinion in a general meeting and vote on major issues involving the running of the company. Ordinary shareholders thus have the capacity to remove directors who have mismanaged the business of the company. An ordinary resolution is required in order to do so.

Where a company's share capital is divided into different classes, statutory provisions apply which limit the ability of the company to alter the rights attached to the classes of shares.

# The Shareholders in a Company

## Becoming a shareholder

There are two ways in which a person can become a company member (the words member and shareholder are for all practical purposes interchangeable). These are by subscribing to the company's memorandum, which involves the members name appearing in the subscription clause of the memorandum against the number of shares they agreed to take, or by their name being entered on the register of members under s.22 Companies Act 1985. This is of course the most common method.

The maintenance of this register is a statutory requirement. The register is kept either at the registered office or some other office used for this purpose and it must be available for public inspection. The Act prohibits trusts being entered on the register, so it is only the legal owner of the shares whose name appears. Normally a persons name is included on the register either because they have successfully applied to the company for shares in it, or because an existing shareholder has transferred ownership to them by selling them the shares.

The question of who may become a member is regulated by a combination of the general law and the articles. The articles may wish to exclude certain people from acquiring membership. The shareholders who make up the membership of public and private companies include both individual investors and institutional investors. The latter include organisations such as pension funds. Investors will usually be seeking a return on their investment in the form of dividend payments from the company to them. They will also be looking for the market value of their shares to increase. As we have seen directors manage companies for the benefit of the shareholders whilst auditors advise the shareholders of the financial health of their company. Whilst the principal obligation of shareholders is to pay for their shares, the rights they enjoy and general position they hold within the company is more complex.

## Transferring shares

Shares are the shareholders property. They can be transferred at any time to anyone the shareholder chooses. If a number of shares are held some can be transferred and some retained. The articles may however restrict this general right of transfer. The two most common ways in which this will be achieved are by granting the directors power to refuse to register a transfer, and by granting the members pre-emption rights.

When a member wishes to transfer shares the executed *transfer form* together with the share certificate must be sent to the company. On receipt the directors have two months within which to register the transfer and issue the transferee with a share certificate, or notify the transferee that the transfer is refused (s.183). Once the two month deadline has passed a transfer cannot be refused.

If the articles grant the board of directors the discretionary power to refuse a transfer, the fiduciary duty they owe to the company means they must exercise the power in good faith and in what they regard as the company's best interests.

Although the courts presume good faith has been present in the decision making (*Tett v. Phoenix Property & Investment Co. Ltd.* 1986), if there is evidence to the contrary the court can order the registration of the transfer to go ahead.

> In *Re: Smith and Fawcett Ltd.* 1942 a company article granted the directors the uncontrolled and absolute discretion to refuse to register any transfer of shares. Smith and Fawcett were the only members of the company. They were also its directors. They held 4001 shares each. Following Fawcetts death, Smith and a co-opted director refused to register the transfer of Fawcett's shares to his son, who was acting as his fathers executor. However Smith offered instead to register 2001 of the shares, and purchase the remaining 2000 shares at a valuation fixed by himself. The sons challenge against the refusal to register all the shares failed. The court could find no evidence of bad faith and was not therefore prepared to intervene. Lord Greene MR observed that small private companies are both commercially and at a personal level closer to partnerships than to public companies, and *"it is to be expected that in the articles of such a company the control of the directors over the membership may be very strict indeed"*.

If the power granted is not an absolute one, but permits refusal on specified grounds, then in the absence of anything to the contrary in the articles the court will compel the directors to specify the ground upon which their refusal is based (*Berry v. Tottenham Hotspur Ltd.* 1935).

## Pre-emption rights

If a company issues new shares the interests of existing members may be adversely affected in two ways. Firstly, the balance of power will shift if the shares carry voting rights and they are taken up by new members. Secondly, if the new shares are issued at a price below their real market value, the value of the existing shares will be diluted. S.89 Companies Act 1985 provides protection for existing shareholders by requiring that new equity shares be first offered to existing members so that their proportionate holding in the company can be maintained. This is known as a *rights issue*. There are however a range of exceptions to the statutory obligation. It does not apply for example to shares allotted for a non cash consideration. Moreover shareholders may waive the requirement using a special resolution, and in the case of a private company the right of pre-emption may be excluded by a suitable provision in the company's constitution.

A different form of pre-emption arrangement sometimes found in the articles of a private company is the requirement that if a shareholder wishes to sell his shares they must first be offered to the existing members at a fair value. This has the same effect as a rights issue for it grants the existing members a right of first refusal in respect of company shares which have become available and can be used to prevent the introduction of new members into the company. In very small private companies with perhaps three or four members it can be of great value to retain all the control of the company in the hands of the remaining shareholders when one of their number sells his or her interest. Case-law examples of this form of pre-emption rights can be found elsewhere in the chapter.

## Shareholders as company controllers

Shareholders collectively own the undertaking of the company. In effect the company is their agent. This agency role is performed by directors appointed by shareholders in company meetings, and directors are accountable to the company for the management of its activities.

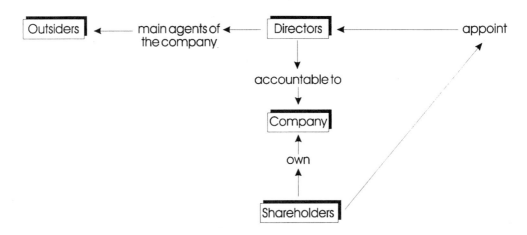

**Figure 4.2** *Shareholders as company controllers*

## Share certificates

A *share certificate* is a document issued by a company with provides evidence of title to the shares of the person named on it. S.186 Companies Act 1985 provides that the share certificate is *prima facie* evidence of the title the shareholder has to the shares. This means it is not necessarily conclusive evidence, however the onus is on the person challenging the certificate to prove a defective title.

The share certificate is treated as a representation by the company issuing it that the person named in it was the true owner of the shares at the date the certificate was issued. The company may therefore find itself liable to anyone relying on the information the certificate contains if that information turns out to be untrue.

In *Re: Bahia & San Francisco Railway Co.* 1868 case, brokers of a company member, Miss Tritten, transferred her shares to themselves by forging her signature on a share transfer form. They sent the form together with the share certificate they held for her to the company, and it duly issued a new share certificate in their names. They then sold the shares to two innocent parties, whose names were entered on the register of shareholders. Subsequently Miss Tritten discovered the forgery. The company was obliged to restore her name to the register, and remove the names of the innocent parties from it. They then sued the company. The court held that although the signature on the transfer was a forgery so that the transfer was of no effect, the company was still bound by the representations contained in the new share certificate which erroneously showed the brokers to be the owners of the shares. It was liable to pay the innocent parties damages equal to the value of shares at the time their names were removed from the register.

The effect of forgery needs to be carefully noted. In the *San Francisco Railway* case it was the share transfer which was forged. If someone forges a *share certificate* then the certificate is not issued with the authority of the company and the company is not liable for it. The only exception would be if the forgery has been done by a director of the company, since a director is someone having the authority of the company to issue share certificates.

## The statutory contract

S.14 of the Companies Act 1985 provides that the articles and the memorandum of a company constitute a binding contract between the company and its members under which the company and its members are bound to each other as though each shareholder has covenanted to observe the provisions of the memorandum and articles, the *statutory contract*.

The effect of the articles on shareholders can be summarised as follows:

- *The company is bound to the members in their capacity as members, and they are bound to it in the same way.*

In *Hickman v. Kent or Romney Marsh Sheepbreeders Association* 1915 the articles of the association stipulated that disputes between itself and its members should be referred to arbitration. The plaintiff, a member, brought court action against the association in relation to a number of matters. It was held that in accordance with the articles these matters must be referred to arbitration.

- *The members are contractually bound to each other, under the terms of the articles.*

Generally it is not possible for an individual member to enforce the contract in his own name against another member, although exceptionally this may be possible if the articles grant him a personal right.

The position is illustrated in the case of *Rayfield v. Hands* 1960. A clause in the articles of a private company stated, *"Every member who intends to transfer shares shall inform the directors who will take the said shares equally between them at a fair value."* The plaintiff notified the defendant directors of his intention to transfer his shares, however they denied any liability to take and pay for them. The court held they were obliged to do so, firstly because of their binding obligation indicated by the word "will" and secondly because the clause was a term of the contractual relationship between the plaintiff and the directors as company members.

• *The company is only bound to the members in their capacity as members.*

This proposition of law emerges from the following case.

In *Eley v. Positive Life Assurance Co Ltd.*, 1876, a provision in the articles of the company stated that the plaintiff should be the company's solicitor for life. He took up shares in the company. Sometime later the company removed him as its solicitor, and he sued the company for breach of contract. The action failed. The court said the statutory contract only granted him rights as a member, and what he was complaining of was breach of an article giving him rights as a legal advisor. Doubts have however been expressed about this decision, for it adds a rider to s.14 which the section does not contain, the phrase, *"in their capacity as members"*.

There is however no problem in using provisions contained in the articles as evidence of the contents of a separate service contract.

In *Re New British Iron Co Ltd.*, 1898, the articles provided that the directors, all of whom were members, were entitled to remuneration of £1000 p.a.. Their company went into liquidation, and they sought to recover from the liquidator the payment the company owed them for their services. The court held that the article was sufficient evidence of the terms of their contract as to payment, and they were able on this basis to recover the money owing to them.

A further important effect of s.14 results from its assertion that shareholders have entered into *covenants* with the company, for it means that they are bound to the company as if they had made a deed with it. The consequences of this arrangement can be seen in Figure 4.3. As well as resulting in the members being bound to each other, an idea already examined above, the company is bound to people who have become members by purchasing shares from existing shareholders rather than the company itself. Thus legal relationships are created which extend beyond the common law contractual relationship which only exists between the company and those members who have taken shares directly from it. In the figure, Z can enforce his rights as a shareholder against the company, for instance to secure his voting rights, whilst X and Z are bound to each other to the extent that they can enforce personal provisions in the articles. *Rayfield v. Hands* provides an example.

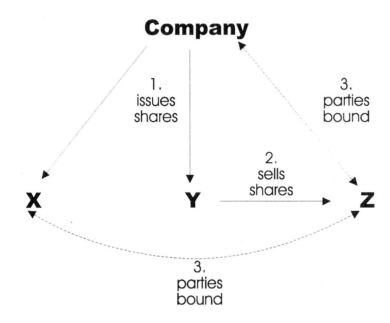

**Figure 4.3** *The effect of the statutory contract*

## Alteration of the articles

Although the constitutional documents of a company make up the terms of the contract between itself and its members, the memorandum and articles are not tablets of stone. The company does have the opportunity to amend them provided it does so lawfully. In the case of the articles they may be altered or added to by means of a special resolution which requires a 75% majority of the members voting in favour of it. No such resolution is necessary if there is unanimous agreement of the members to the proposed alteration. Alterations must however be made *bona fide,* that is in good faith, and for the benefit of the company as a whole. Clearly the ability of the company to change the terms of this contract at some future time may have the effect of placing individual members who might be harmed by such changes, in a disadvantageous position. Thus the courts reserve the power to refuse an alteration to the articles which has such an effect, unless there is a benefit to the company as a whole and the alteration has been made in good faith. This principle is best appreciated by looking at some of the caselaw on the subject.

In the leading case, *Allen v. Gold Reefs of West Africa* 1900 the articles of the company which already granted it a *lien* on partly paid shares to cover any liabilities owed to it by a member, were altered by extending the lien to holders of fully paid shares as well. A lien is simply a charge on shares, enabling the company to sell the shares in order to meet the debts owed to it by the members. Here a shareholder who at the time of his death held both fully and partly paid shares in the company and owed the company money for the partly paid shares, was also the only holder of fully paid shares. His executors challenged the alteration on the grounds of bad faith, but the court upheld the alteration. There was no evidence that the company was attempting to discriminate against the deceased personally; it was simply chance that he was the only holder of fully paid shares. In the words of Lord Lindley, *"The altered articles applied to all holders of fully paid shares and made no distinction between them."*

It seems that the test which should be applied is whether the proposal is in the honest opinion of those voting for it, for the benefit of the members. An alteration may be challenged if it is, *"so oppressive as to cast suspicion on the honesty of the persons responsible for it, or so extravagant that no reasonable men could really consider it for the benefit of the company."* (Bankes L.J. in *Shuttleworth v. Cox Bros. & Co. (Maidenhead) Ltd.* 1927). If it can be established that the alteration has the effect of discriminating between members, granting advantages to the majority which are denied to the minority then a challenge will normally be successful, although an alteration may be upheld as bona fide even though the members voting for it are improving their own personal prospects.

In *Greenhalgh v. Arderne Cinemas Ltd.* 1951 the articles of company, which prohibited the transfer of shares to a non member as long as an existing member was willing to pay a fair price for them, were altered to enable a transfer of shares to anyone by means of an ordinary resolution passed in a general meeting. The alteration was made because the majority shareholder wished to transfer his shares to a non member. This was held to be a valid alteration.

The courts will also uphold alterations which cause direct prejudice to individual members, as long as they are shown to be alterations made in good faith, and in the company's interest.

In *Sidebottom v. Kershaw Leese & Co.* 1920 an alteration was made enabling the directors, who were the majority shareholders, to request the transfer to their nominees at a fair value the shares of any member competing with the company's business. The court found this to be a valid and proper alteration for, in the words of Lord Sterndale M R, *"it is for the benefit of the company that they should not be obliged to have amongst them as members, persons who are competing with them in business and who may get knowledge from their membership which would enable them to compete better."*

In addition the following common law and statutory conditions apply to an alteration:

- *it must be lawful,* that is not be in conflict with the Act or with the general law;

- *it must not create a conflict between the memorandum and the articles.* If this does occur the provisions of the memorandum will prevail for it is the superior document;

- *it will require the leave of the court in certain circumstances.* These are where a minority of members have applied to the court for the cancellation of an alteration to the objects clause (s.5), where there has been an application for the cancellation of a resolution of a public company to re-register as a private company (s.54), or where a petition has been presented to the court on the ground that the affairs of the company are being conducted in a manner unfairly prejudicial to some part of the membership (s.461);

- *if it affects the rights attached to a particular class of shareholders.* If it does it is subject to the capacity of those disagreeing with the change, who may apply to the court for a cancellation, not exercising this power successfully. This power is available to 15% or more of the holders of the shares who did not give their consent, and it must be exercised within 21 days.

## Controlling the company – the powers of the members

A company has two principal sources of control over its affairs. These are the shareholders in general meeting and the directors. The most important matters affecting the company, for example changes in its constitution, rest with the shareholders in general meeting. Decisions reached at such meetings are arrived at through the putting of resolutions, which are then voted on. Generally a simple majority vote is sufficient to carry them, although some matters of special significance require a 75% majority. Since voting power plays such an important role in company matters the type of shares the company has issued is of considerable significance. Some shares, for example ordinary shares, usually carry full voting rights.

However other classes of share, such as preference shares, may carry no voting rights at all and therefore exclude shareholders of that class from effectively influencing the company in its decision making.

Since all public companies and many private companies consist of numerous members it is impractical to operate the company on a daily basis by means of general meetings. The articles will therefore provide for directors to be responsible for the daily running of the company and usually grant them the right to exercise all the powers of the company. They will remain answerable to the members in a general meeting although acts carried out by the directors within the powers delegated to them under the articles cannot be affected by decisions of a general meeting. So, if the directors have acted contrary to the wishes of the members, the ultimate sanction is to dismiss them or to change the articles and so bring in provisions that restrict the powers of the directors. In small companies the directors will often be the principal or only shareholders, so that such considerations will not be relevant.

## Shareholders' rights – majority rule, minority protection

As we have seen the rights enjoyed by a member of a company are primarily contractual, arising from the class of shares acquired and the rights attached to them as specified in the articles. Unlike a partner, who will usually possess the right to take part in the management of the firm, a shareholder will not always be involved in the daily management of the company, unless the organisation has a very small membership and its shareholders are also its directors. Companies' articles usually confer power on directors to operate the business, which they will perform on behalf of the members. The effect of such an arrangement is that ownership and management are separated. Nevertheless, ultimate control of the business is in the hands of the shareholders by the exercise of voting power in the general meeting. Where appropriate they can vote to remove a director.

In any vote which does not produce a unanimous outcome there will be two groups, the majority shareholders and the minority shareholders. In effect it is the majority that make the company decisions. Those who hold 75% or more of the voting shares are the ultimate company controllers. Under company legislation a three-quarter majority to secure changes to the constitution of the company itself. Thus the majority group can run the company almost as if it were their own. If the minority have a grievance, legally there is little they can do to redress it. The courts have been reluctant to assist minority shareholders who are claiming they have been oppressed or have had their interests prejudiced by the majority. Since it is the majority who rule the company it is not for the court to thwart their actions. If the minority are arguing that the majority have acted in breach of the memorandum or the articles, then it is a wrong which has been done to the company. The proper plaintiff is the company itself, not the minority shareholders. Of course they will find it impossible to pass a resolution that the company sue the majority, for the voting strength of the majority will be sufficient to block such a move. This leaves the minority in a very vulnerable position.

The case of *Foss v. Harbottle* 1843 laid down as a general principle that the courts will not interfere in the internal management of a company at the insistence of the minority shareholders. Here an action had been brought by the minority alleging that the directors were responsible for losses that had occurred when they sold some of their own land to the company, at what was alleged to be an over valuation. The court held that the action must fail as the proper plaintiff in such circumstances was the company itself. As the action to which the minority shareholders objected could have been ratified by the majority then it was the majority shareholders who should decide whether an action should be brought in the company name. The court saw no merit in interfering in the internal management of a company by passing judgment on its commercial decisions.

In *Pavlides v. Jenson and others* 1956, a company sold an asbestos mine for £182,000 when its real value was close to £1,000,000. A minority shareholder brought an action for damages against three directors who were responsible for the sale and against the company, alleging gross negligence. The court held that the action could not be brought by a minority shareholder because it was the company itself which should decide whether to redress the wrong that had been committed.

Thus the process of incorporation, having invested a company with a separate legal personality, dictates that the company and individual members are separate. If a wrong is committed against the company it is the company, by virtue of a decision made by the board of directors, that should seek redress for it.

The rule in *Foss v. Harbottle* does not however apply to every type of action taken by the majority. In certain situations the court will hear a claim brought by minority shareholders, even though the majority do not wish it. For example a single shareholder can bring legal proceedings to restrain proposed ultra vires activity, or to overcome a wrong which the shareholder has suffered in a personal capacity, such as having his votes refused (*Pender v. Lushington* 1877). A claim can also be brought when a fraud has been committed against the minority. This does not mean fraud in the criminal sense, rather conduct which is grossly unfair.

An example is provided by *Daniels v. Daniels* 1978.

The company was managed by Mr and Mrs Daniels. They were also the controlling shareholders. In 1970 they agreed to sell land belonging to the company to Mrs Daniels, at a price of £4250. In 1974 she resold the land for £120,000 and minority shareholders brought an action claiming that damages should be payable to the company. The court held that despite no allegation of fraud the action by the individual shareholders should be allowed to proceed. The trial judge, Templeman J, distinguished *Pavlides v. Jensen* on the grounds that the directors there had not benefited from their negligence. He stated *"to put up with foolish directors is one thing; to put up with directors who are so foolish that they make a profit of £115,000 odd at the expense of the company is something entirely different ... a minority shareholder who has no other remedy may sue where directors use their powers, intentionally or unintentionally, fraudulently or negligently, in a manner which benefits them at the expense of the company"*.

In addition to the common law, the Companies Act 1985 confers certain statutory rights on minority shareholders.

An important example of this is s.459 which gives a member the right to apply to the court for an order on the ground that the affairs of the company are being or have been conducted in a manner which is unfairly prejudicial to some members (including at least himself), or that an actual or proposed act or omission of the company is or would be prejudicial.

If the case is proved the court may issue an order to:

- regulate the company's affairs for the future;

- require the company to act or refrain from acting in a particular way;

- authorise civil proceedings in the name and on behalf of the company by a person; or

- require the purchase of any member's shares by the company or by other members.

In *Scottish CWS v. Meyer,* 1958, Meyer was a minority shareholder in a manufacturing company which was a subsidiary of the Scottish CWS. The CWS, as holding company, decided to close down the subsidiary, and took steps to cause it to cease trading. As a result Meyer's shares, which had been worth £3.75 each whilst the subsidiary was trading, fell in value to £1. The court ordered the holding company to purchase the shares of the minority members at their original value.

An example of a court order regulating a company's future affairs is seen in *Re H R Harmer Limited* 1959. The company was run by an elderly father acting as chairman and his two sons as directors. The father had voting control. He largely ignored the wishes of the board of directors and ran the business as his own. On an application by the sons as minority shareholders, alleging oppression, the court held that relief should be granted. The father was appointed life president of the company without rights, duties or powers and was ordered not to interfere with the company's affairs.

In *Re Elgindata Ltd.* 1991 the court held that in exceptional cases, serious mismanagement of a company could amount to unfairly prejudicial conduct under s. 459. Generally however the court should be reluctant to arrive at such a finding bearing in mind managerial decision making is matter of commercial judgment and that taking shares in a company carries the risk of their value being tied to the competence of the board of directors.

In *Re a Company, ex p Burr* 1992 Vinelott J discussed the possibility of a s.459 action where directors continue to run a company despite it operating at a loss and it having no realistic chance of becoming profitable in the future. He said: *"There can be no doubt that if the directors of a company continue to trade when the company is making losses and when it should have been apparent that there was no real prospect that the company would return to profitability, the court may draw the inference that the directors' decision was improperly influenced by their desire to continue in office and in control of the company and to draw remuneration and other benefits for themselves and others connected with them ... if that inference is drawn, the court may conclude that the affairs of the company are being conducted in a way which is unfairly prejudicial to the members or the members other than the directors and those who obtain such benefit."*

Non payment of dividends can amount to unfairly prejudicial conduct under s.459.

In *Re: Sam Weller & Sons Ltd.* 1990 the petitioners, who between them held 42.5% of the shares in their family business, complained that the company had not increased its dividend for 37 years, despite its profitability. In 1985 its net profit had been £36,000, but only £2,520 was paid out in dividends. The company was controlled by the petitioner's uncle, Sam Weller, who, together with his sons, continued to receive directors fees and remuneration. Peter Gibson J commented of the petitioners position, *"As their only income from the company is by way of dividend, their interests may be not only prejudiced by the policy of low dividend payments, but unfairly prejudiced."*

The s.459 remedy is often referred to as the *alternative remedy*, since it is an alternative to the more drastic step that minority shareholders can take of bringing the company to an end by petitioning the court to have it compulsorily wound up on just and equitable grounds under s.122 Insolvency Act 1986 (see later).

When an action is brought by a minority shareholder it may be in one of two forms. It will be a *derivative* action if the shareholder is suing in the name of the company. If the action is successful the remedy being sought will be awarded to the company. *Daniels v. Daniels* is an example. It will be a representative action if it is brought by a member to enforce a personal right, for instance as in *Pender v. Lushington*.

## Company Borrowing

As a legal person a company can borrow money. The term *loan capital* is applied to the funds the company raises in this way. The level of borrowing, and the procedures to be followed to exercise the power to borrow may be regulated by the memorandum and articles if the company so chooses. If these matters *are* regulated, and the company borrows in breach of them, the lender may still be able to hold the company bound through the application of the internal management rule (the rule in *Turquands Case*) and s.35 Companies Act 1989.

When a company borrows, the lender may require some form of security which the lender can realise in the event of the company defaulting on the loan. This is not a legal requirement, simply commercial common sense. The larger the borrowing, the more likely it is that the lender will demand protection in the event of a default. If security is not taken the lender is an unsecured creditor, and very vulnerable in the event of the company getting into financial difficulties, since secured creditors are able to realise their securities first, often leaving the unsecured creditors with virtually nothing left.

In larger companies there will be plenty of property which can be used as security, such as land and buildings, equipment, stock, together with non tangibles like book debts. In small companies however, with few assets, a lender such as a bank may require individual members to provide personal security. In this way the shareholders/directors of a company in which they are the only members can find that much of the benefit of limited liability is lost to them when they have to put up their homes as a security in relation to their company borrowing.

If a lender to a company takes no security the lender is simply an unsecured creditor, having the capacity to sue the company on the debt (and takes steps to enforce any judgment awarded), or petition as a creditor to have the company wound up if the debt is for £750 or more. A lender who has security is in a much stronger position, since if the company defaults the security can be used to meet the debt. Many types of company borrowing arrangements come within the umbrella term *debenture*. At its simplest a debenture can be merely a written note evidencing a debt, but in its usual commercial sense a debenture is regarded as a document expressing some secured obligation. This security will be in the form of a *charge* on property of the company. This is most important, for a secured debenture holder will normally have the power to appoint a *receiver* to protect the holders interests if the company defaults in any way, or if the property charged is felt to be in jeopardy. Debentures are issued in accordance with the articles of the company, and this usually means that their issue will be made following a board resolution.

## Charges

A charge is a security interest which the owner of the asset(s), the *chargor* agrees to create in favour of a creditor, the *chargee*. The agreement will provide that the asset charged may be sold by the chargee in the event of default by the chargor. There are two methods used to secure debentures by means of charges, the *fixed charge* and the *floating charge*.

## Fixed charges

A fixed or specific charge is like an ordinary mortgage taken out by an individual. It is created by taking out a legal or equitable mortgage on specific property, such as land or equipment. Its advantage is that it attaches to specifically identified assets, and thereafter these assets cannot be disposed of lawfully by the chargor without the chargee's permission. Moreover it should be possible to ascertain the value of the asset at the time the charge is created.

## Floating charges

A floating charge also requires the property subject to the charge to be identified, but the charge recognises that the chargor can deal with the property in the ordinary course of business without the permission of chargee. This is referred to sometimes as the *trading power*. A floating charge can only be an equitable charge, but it can apply to company property both present and future.

> In *Re: Yorkshire Woolcombers Association Ltd.* 1903 Romer LJ identified three characteristics of the floating charge. He said *"it is a charge on a class of assets of a company present and future; if that class is one which, in the ordinary course of the business of the company, would be changing from time to time; and if you find that by the charge it is contemplated that, until some future step is taken by or on behalf of those interested in the charge, the company may carry on its business in the ordinary way as far as concerns th' particular class of assets...."*

Floating charges are used to charge company property of a fluctuating are constantly in use or being turned over in the course of business. S' a common example. The company is free to acquire and sell ste charge, the trading power, unless the charge *crystallises*. Crys' the floating charge becoming a fixed charge, an event which will occur on any one of a number of grounds. These are where:

(i)     a receiver is appointed;

(ii)    the company goes into liquidation;

(iii)   the company ceases to trade (*Re: Woodroffes (Musical Instruments) Ltd.* 1986), or sells its business (*Re: Real Meat Co. Ltd.* 1996);

(iv)    the debenture enables the charge holder to convert the floating charge into a fixed charge by notice and the notice is given;

(v)     an event identified in the charge document as giving rise to automatic crystallisation has occurred. An example would be if a company creditor seeks to execute a judgment in his favour against the property charged. This last ground has been the subject of considerable controversy, since the crystallisation can occur without either the company or the charge holder being aware of it.

Once crystallisation takes place the directors can no longer deal with the assets charged. Of course it will not be known what the value of the assets actually is until crystallisation has occurred and the charge fixes to the assets in question. Whether a charge is fixed or floating depends upon the substance of the charge; express words identifying it as one or the other are not regarded as totally conclusive. In *Re: Brightlife Ltd.* 1987 Hoffmann J held that a charge over the book debts of a company, expressed as a fixed charge, was in reality a floating charge.

# Test Questions

---

1. What are the differences between ordinary shares and preference shares?

2. Consider why pre-emption rights are important to a shareholder.

3. What requirements must be satisfied for a company to alter its articles of association validly

4. Why is the statutory contract important both to a company and its shareholders?

5. Explain why the rule in *Foss v. Harbottle* can present a problem to minority shareholders?

6. Why is s.459 Companies Act 1985 such an important provision to a shareholder?

7. Consider whether a floating charge is a more valuable security for a company creditor than a fixed charge.

---

# Business Managers

All businesses, irrespective of size, need managers to run them; and to run an organisation requires the granting of powers to the managers. Managers, then, are key figures in the functioning of the business environment, and careful analysis of their legal role is central to grasping the way in which organisations work. We shall consider first the role of company directors as business managers, and conclude by looking at the position of partners as managers.

# Directors as Business Managers

One of the fundamental differences between a limited company and a partnership is seen in the management structure. In a partnership, ownership and management are in the same hands, for all partners are entitled to manage the firm and each is an agent of the firm and of the other partners. By contrast, in a company ownership and management are not automatically in the same hands. Shareholders own the company; directors manage it. Under company legislation all companies must have at least one director. For a public company there must be at least two directors – usually there will be several – and in private companies there are frequently more than the statutory minimum of one.

The function of company directors is crucial to the affairs of the organisation. Even in the smallest company there are three legally distinct components: the company *itself;* its *managers* (the directors); and its *owners* or proprietors (the shareholders). A complex legal relationship exists between the three. In a private company with few shareholders, it is common for each shareholder to act also as a director. In larger companies with many members, such an arrangement is not appropriate and consequently ownership and management will not be in the same hands. Public companies invariably appoint as directors people with proven track-records in the management of large organisations, and with commensurately high salaries. In contrast, directors of small private companies may be people with little if any commercial experience. Such experience, whilst clearly of considerable practical importance, is not a legal pre-requisite of directorship.

The following broad observations can be made concerning the relationship between the company, its directors and its shareholders. The directors have certain legal obligations or duties which they owe to the company. They control the company's business affairs and its assets, and in general meeting they are accountable to the company for the way in which they have exercised this control.

They are not accountable to the shareholders as proprietors other than in general meeting. This meeting is where the shareholders can exercise their powers. At it they can for example remove directors on the strength of an ordinary resolution (a single majority voting in favour). It is a meeting open to all the membership of the company. Although directors are not answerable to the shareholders as proprietors, directors must, under statute, provide them with a range of information to enable the shareholders to assess how the company is being, and has been operated.

Whilst shareholders are usually responsible for appointing directors, and can also remove them, they are not able to tell them how to exercise their powers. At best they can restrict powers available to the directors under the articles, and in respect of some matters it is now necessary for directors to seek approval to act from the general meeting. What this all amounts to is that directors act essentially as agents, not of the shareholders, but of the company itself.

# Directorship

## Definition of a director

The term director is applied to anyone entrusted with the management of a company who attends board meetings and takes part in their decision-making activities. There must be at least one director for a private company and two for a public one (s.282), but under the articles it is possible to provide for the appointment of more than the statutory minimum, and there is no statutory upper limit. Table A states that unless otherwise determined by ordinary resolution, the number of directors shall not be subject to any maximum but shall not be less than two.

Although the Act defines the term director to include, *"any person occupying the position of director, by whatever name called"* (s.741(1)), this is clearly not a helpful definition because it says nothing about what the nature of what such a position actually involves. Table A is more helpful however. It provides that subject to the provisions of the Act, and the memorandum and articles, and any directions given under the terms of any special resolution, *"the business of the company shall be managed by the directors who may exercise all the powers of the company"*. Thus the role of a director involves managing the company business, and as a consequence of s.741(1), it does not matter whether a person having such responsibility within the company is given the title of director or not. Furthermore, a director could include someone who has not actually been appointed to the board at all, but is acting as if he were a director; a *de facto* director.

## Shadow directors

A *shadow director* is a person who gives directions or instructions to the board which the board customarily acts upon. A person acting as a professional adviser to the board, such as a lawyer or an accountant, will not by reason of that capacity alone be regarded as a shadow director. A shadow director is thus someone who is able to exercise influence over the board, even though not formally appointed to sit on it himself. A shadow director could be a majority shareholder who tells the board members how to manage the affairs of the company, but for lack of time or for the avoidance of publicity chooses not to be a member himself. A person does not become a shadow director merely through the act of attempting to assert control. The board must do his bidding.

The possibility of shadow directors being associated with a company is important, since s.741 extends many of the provisions of the 1985 Act which apply to properly appointed directors, to *de facto* and to shadow directors as well.

A company is also required to keep a copy of any service contract it has with a shadow director. These contracts are usually held at the company's registered office.

## The company secretary

Every company must have a secretary, and the secretary has the power to bind the company in any contract of an administrative nature.

In *Panorama Developments (Guildford) Ltd. v. Fidelis Furnishing Fabrics Ltd.* 1971 the defendant's company secretary hired cars on behalf of the company on the understanding that the cars were being used to meet company customers. In fact he was using them for his own purposes. The court held the company to be bound to pay the hire charges. The transactions were of a kind a company secretary has the power to make, falling within the category of general administrative tasks.

Under Table A, directors have the power to appoint the secretary on such terms as they think fit, and they may also remove the secretary. In a private company the directors can appoint anyone they choose. However, in the case of a public company the directors must be satisfied that the secretary meets the criteria laid down under s.286, namely:

- appears to the board to have the requisite knowledge and experience to discharge the functions of secretary; and

- possesses one of the qualifications set out under the section. These range from holding a professional qualification as an accountant or lawyer, to having gained the appropriate experience through a previous position held.

## Appointment of directors

There are three methods by which a person may be properly appointed as a director. These are:

(i)     under the statement of first directors sent to the Registrar; or

(ii)    by being named in the articles; or

(iii)   under the provisions for appointment laid down in the articles.

Whichever means are used to appoint the first directors, that is either the subscribers making the appointment or the articles stipulating who shall act in this capacity, thereafter all subsequent appointments, and also terminations from office, are regulated by the articles.

Broadly, under the standard system contained in Table A, the following arrangements apply:

(i)     at the first annual general meeting after incorporation, all directors must retire. They may, of course, be reappointed at the meeting;

(ii)    at all subsequent annual general meetings one-third of the board must retire. This is referred to as retirement by rotation. Again, there is nothing to prevent a retiring director from being re-elected. Which directors are to retire is determined by length of office, but if they were all appointed at the same time, for instance at the first AGM, then the matter is decided by drawing lots;

(iii) a director retiring by rotation who is not replaced is automatically re-elected, unless it is resolved not to fill the vacancy or a resolution to re-elect the director is lost;

(iv) any member can by written notice give intention to propose a person for election with that person's written consent;

(v) *casual vacancies*, those occurring between annual general meetings where a director has died or has resigned during his or her term of office, can be temporarily filled by an appointment made by the existing board. They may also appoint additional directors between AGMs if they wish, for instance to replace a director who cannot attend board meetings through illness. The filling of casual vacancies by the board under the articles saves the need to summon a general meeting to do so. However, anyone appointed in this way must retire at the next annual general meeting of the company enabling the members to vote against such director if they wish to do so;

(vi) a director may appoint an *alternate director,* that is, someone to act as a temporary replacement. The alternate may be another director or some other person.

## Persons who cannot be appointed

Table A contains no restrictions on who may be appointed as a director, although articles may be drafted to include particular restrictions. For instance the company may seek to exclude minors from acting as directors, or perhaps another company.

Under statute, a person cannot be a company's sole director and secretary at the same time, nor its sole director and auditor.

Under the Company Directors Disqualification Act 1986 it is an offence for an undischarged bankrupt to act as a director without permission of the court. Articles may provide that anyone who has been bankrupt shall not be appointed as a director, and Table A more specifically states that a directors office becomes vacant on his bankruptcy. The 1986 Act also empowers the court to make a disqualification order against a named person. The person named is then prevented for the duration of the order except by leave of the court from acting as a company director or being involved in the promotion, formation or management of a company.

## Grounds for a disqualification order

Under the 1986 Act a number of grounds are identified under which the court may grant a disqualification order. Breach of an order renders the disqualified person liable to criminal proceedings carrying a maximum penalty of six months imprisonment, and it also renders the offender personally liable for the company's debts. These are formidable penalties. The imposition of personal liability, with its effect of lifting the corporate veil, is seen as an appropriate way to deal with someone who has had a disqualification order made against him because he has shown himself not fit to be a director, yet has continued in breach of the order to manage a company.

The grounds include:

(a)   *conviction of an indictable offence (s.2)*

One of the most common offences associated with company affairs is fraud. In *R v. Corbin* 1984 the defendant ran a business selling yachts through companies he owned. He was convicted of various fraudulent practices including borrowing from finance companies to buy yachts, falsely stating he had paid a deposit on them. He received two a half years imprisonment and a disqualification order for five years;

(b)   *persistent breaches of company law (s.3)*

Under s.3 the breaches in question involve the failure to provide any return account or documents required to be filed with the Registrar of Companies. There is a presumption that a person has been persistently in default if he has been convicted of a default three times in the past five years. The maximum period for disqualification is five years;

(c)   *fraud, fraudulent trading or breach of duty revealed in a winding up (s.4)*

(d)   *unfitness (s.6)*

When a company becomes insolvent the person involved in administering the insolvency such as the liquidator or administrative receiver must make a return to the Secretary of State regarding the conduct of the company's directors. On the basis of this information the Secretary of State may apply to the court for a disqualification order against an individual director on the grounds of his unfitness as evidenced in the return. The court must then satisfy itself as to the unfitness before it can make an order. Schedule 1 of the 1986 Act lists the factors to be considered by the court in reaching its decision. In broad terms these factors share a common feature, namely the way the directors have managed the company. The list is a long one, and it includes the following:

- any misfeasance or breach of duty by the director in relation to the company;

- any misapplication or retention of company money or property by the director;

- the directors responsibility for the company entering into transactions liable to be set aside in a liquidation;

- the directors failure to keep proper company records, or prepare or file annual company accounts;

- the directors responsibility for the company becoming insolvent;

- the directors responsibility for any failure by the company to supply goods or services which have already been paid for;

- the directors responsibility for failing to call a creditors meeting in a creditors voluntary winding up;

- any failure by the director to produce a statement of affairs as required in any insolvency proceedings concerning the company.

(e)   matters revealed following a DTI investigation (s.8)

If the DTI has investigated the affairs of the company and following an inspectors report, or information or documents obtained under powers to require production of documents and enter and search premises (s.447 and s.448 Companies Act 1985 respectively), it appears to the Secretary of State that a disqualification order should be made because a person is unfit to manage or in the public interest, he may apply to the Court. The maximum period for disqualification is fifteen years. This may give rise to a legal challenge against the Secretary of State where the Secretary decides not to proceed with an application. Such was the case in *R v. Secretary of State for Trade and Industry ex parte Lonrho plc* 1992, court proceedings which emerged out of the acrimonious public dispute between Lonrho, under the chairmanship of Tiny Rowland, and the Fayed brothers who had been successful in a take-over bid to acquire Harrods. DTI Inspectors who had criticised the brothers behaviour had not however recommended disqualification, and as a result the Secretary of State decided not to apply to the court for disqualification orders. The challenge against this decision was unsuccessful, the court concluding that it had been arrived at lawfully.

Unfitness under ss6 and 8 relates to management of companies generally rather than unfitness associated with a particular company, even though it will be as a result of specific malpractice that the issue of unfitness will emerge. Consequently disqualification will not be avoided by arguing that a director who is unfit to manage a public company may be fit to manage a private one, a proposition raised, and rejected, in *Re: Poly Peck International plc No.2* 1994. The company had experienced spectacular prosperity under the entrepreneurial direction of Asil Nadir, who held 25% of its shares, but it subsequently suffered an equally spectacular financial collapse. This was allegedly the result of large sums raised by the company from banks and shareholders being passed to subsidiary companies, who did not need it, and who deposited it in banks in the Turkish sector of Cyprus from which it could not be recovered. Facing criminal charges Mr Nadir fled the country. The Secretary of State then sought to commence disqualification proceedings against four remaining directors. This was outside the time limit for an application, which is two years from the date of the insolvency. The court would not waive the time limit. It found the Secretary's case against the remaining directors as *"speculative and very weak"* for they were a minority group on the board, and one of their number, the financial director, had worked hard to secure better financial management.

## Remuneration

There is no automatic right to payment for a director, but Table A allows for remuneration by way of an ordinary resolution, and grants the right to receive expenses incurred in the discharge of a director's duties (i.e. without the need for a resolution). Such a payment is treated as a gross taxable sum.

It should be remembered in the context of payments to directors that the nature of the relationship between a director and the company will depend upon a variety of factors, not least of which is the size and type of company involved. In some companies with very few members, it is not uncommon to find that each member of the company is also a director. Under such an arrangement the directors may well be satisfied to receive dividends from the company, which they gain in their capacity as members. Another possibility is that the director is someone contributing his or her time to the management of the company on a part-time basis. For instance a person could be a full-time accountant, who also acts as a company director of a company in which he or she holds no shares but receives fees for the advisory or supervisory work involved. Then there are the full-time executives or managers whose directorships are associated with the existence of a contract of employment between themselves and the company. Such a directors are company employees in receipt of a salary. If a director's remuneration is to be by way of payment of fees, the articles must expressly permit such payment. If they do not, the payment of fees is unlawful, even if the members have agreed to it by passing a resolution in general meeting (*Re George Newman & Co.* 1895).

Where a director works under a contract of service, a "service director", normal principles of employment law will apply under which the company is treated as the employer and the director the employee.

## Disclosure by Director

A director who has a direct or indirect personal interest in a contract of the company is required to declare the nature of the interest to the board at the first opportunity, so that the other directors are made aware of it (s.317). This is sometimes referred to as the *self-dealing rule*. Under Table A he may not vote at the meeting of the directors on any matter in which such an interest is held. The purpose of such provisions is to bring into the open any circumstance in which the director faces or is likely to face a conflict of interest. An example would be a situation where a director is a shareholder of another company which is in the process of negotiating a contract with the company of which he is a director. In effect, s.317 imposes a statutory duty of disclosure upon a director. In *Hely-Hutchinson v. Brayhead Ltd.* 1967 the Court of Appeal held that s.317 renders a contract voidable by the company if a director does not declare his interest.

One issue which emerges from s.317 is whether disclosure obligations apply to companies with a single director. The matter was tested in *Neptune (Vehicle Washing Equipment) Ltd. v. Fitzgerald* 1995. The plaintiff company had a sole director, Mr Fitzgerald. The company was later taken over. The new holding company did not appoint a director itself, but it took an active part in its management, and in due course Mr Fitzgerald decided to retire as his services were no longer needed. He caused the plaintiff company to pass a resolution authorising it to make a payment to him of £100,000 as compensation for the termination of his directorship. He retired, the payment was made, and then a new director was appointed to the plaintiff company, who immediately challenged the validity of the payment arguing there had not been formal disclosures of the personal interest of Mr Fitzgerald at a board meeting (of which he was the sole participating director). On its facts the action failed, however the court made clear that as a point of law s.317 does apply to a company with a sole director, with the result that the ordinary meaning of the word *meeting* which demands at least two participants is in these circumstances displaced.

## Property transactions involving directors

Further recognition of the powerful position enjoyed by directors over the companies they manage is found in the statutory rules which seek to regulate the transactions of directors by which they might gain personal advantage at the expense of the company. These rules cover substantial property transactions involving directors and loans to directors.

## Substantial property transactions involving directors

S.320 makes it unlawful for a company to enter into an arrangement with a director or connected person for the acquisition of a *non-cash asset of the requisite value,* without the prior approval of the company in general meeting. *Requisite value* means a non-cash asset whose value exceeds £50,000 or 10% or more of the company's net assets taken from the last accounts, subject to a minimum value of £1,000.

The aim of s.320 is to prevent directors purchasing company property at less than its true value, or selling the company their own property at above market value, without the approval of the members. Non-cash assets cover a wide range of property, from the tangible such as land to the non-tangible such as patents and debts.

Non-compliance renders the agreement avoidable at the option of the company. In other words, it may take steps to end the contract.

(a)    restitution is impossible, i.e. because the parties cannot be restored to their pre-contractual positions; or

(b)    the company has been indemnified; or

(c)    third party rights have been acquired; or

(d)    the company affirms the arrangement in general meeting within a easonable time.

## Loans to directors

In principle, although there are a number of exceptions, a company may not make loans or enter into similar transactions with or for the benefit of a director of the company or of its holding company: s.320. The provisions are complex, and apply mainly to what are called *relevant* companies; that is, public limited companies and private companies which form part of a group containing a public company.

# The Powers of Directors

In order to understand the significance of directors' powers we need to reflect on the way in which power is divided within a company. What this reveals is two potential power bases; the board of directors, and the members in general meeting. There are certain things which lawfully can only be done by a company in general meeting, for example, removing a director, and alterations to the objects clause. Moreover, it is necessary under the Companies Act to secure the passing of a special resolution, requiring 75% support of the voting shareholders, in order to make certain decisions in general meetings; alteration of the articles and the objects clause are both examples.

Most matters affecting companies however are not required to be decided in general meeting, and can be dealt with by the board of directors as part of the ordinary day-to-day running of the business. It will be recalled that Table A gives directors the power to manage the business of the company and exercise all its powers, that is, carry out the activities expressly or impliedly contained in the objects clause, subject to any restrictions under the Act, the memorandum and articles. The members can however control the activities of the board through any directions issued to the board under the terms of any special resolution they pass. This power-sharing arrangement recognises that a balance must be struck which enables the managers to manage effectively, whilst ensuring that ultimate control is vested in the proprietors of the organisation, the shareholders.

Despite the power sharing structure which applies to registered companies, real power undoubtedly rests in the hands of the board, partly because of Table A which, as we have seen, grants the board wide management powers, but also because in companies with a large membership, the board members are in close and regular contact with each other. The shareholders are unlikely to maintain such contacts amongst themselves, thus reducing their effectiveness as decision-makers in general meeting. Indeed, in larger companies the management is so firmly placed in the hands of the directors that the only occasion when members are likely to hear from them is when they receive notice of the Annual General Meeting. In such companies there is nothing artificial about the division of power; it is an appropriate practical way of conducting business.

## Members' control over the directors

This is achieved in two ways. Firstly, shareholders have the right in certain circumstances to take action on the company's behalf to prevent wrongdoing carried out by or committed against it. On this see *Foss v. Harbottle* 1843 and the various exceptions to it, and also the remedies under s.459 of the Act available where a member has suffered unfair prejudice considered earlier in the chapter. Secondly, the members have powers which they can exercise in general meeting to control the board. These are:

(a)   passing an ordinary resolution under s.303 to remove a director before his or her term of office expires;

(b)   not voting for the re-election of a director when he or she seeks re-election if the company's articles provide for retirement by rotation;

(c)   passing a special resolution to alter the articles to cut down the powers of the directors; and

(d)   passing a special resolution which gives the directors directions on how they should act in relation in a particular matter; in other words, giving them orders in advance.

## Delegation of functions

The larger an organisation is, the more valuable it becomes to have the capacity to delegate functions. This helps to avoid the need to hold frequent meetings involving all the managers in order to arrive at decisions which could more appropriately have been taken simply by one of them. In larger companies with boards having many directors on them, the ability to delegate is particularly useful. However, the general principle contained in both the Companies Act 1985 and Table A is that the board should act as a body, taking collective responsibility for its decisions. Article 72 of Table A does, however, allow for delegation of any of the directors' powers to a committee of any one or more directors, or to a *managing director* or any other director holding executive office (such as a finance director).

Commonly the boards of companies are headed by a managing director who by virtue of delegated powers is able to carry out executive functions alone, without the need to seek the approval of the board as a whole.

# The Duties of Directors

## The nature of a director's position

The relationship between a company and its directors is unique. They control the company, but cannot treat it as though it were their own. The expression *company* means the corporate body, the members, although it can sometimes be taken to include the creditors as well. Both these parties, shareholders, and creditors, have interests in the company and it is the responsibility of the directors to take account of the overall interests of the company, rather than particular sections of it.

A director does not have to be employed by a company to act as its director, thus his position is not necessarily that of an employee or servant. Even if the director is employed under a contract of service, his role as a manager, together with his custodianship of the interests of the company, mean that the duties he must discharge are not limited to those owed by an employee to an employer. Depending upon the particular circumstances he will act as the agent of the company and so will owe an agent's duties, however a director does not enjoy all the rights of an agent, and therefore examination of the law of agency does not provide us with a full account of the director's position either.

In some respects directors are in the position of trustees; they control the company's property and must manage it for the company's benefit. They owe the company a *fiduciary duty*, a duty associated with trusteeship, and must account for any breach of this duty. They are not true trustees, however, since they do not own the company's property. A true trustee must exercise considerable caution in managing the trust, but directors are engaged in commercial activities involving speculation and risk-taking and consequently their liability for the negligent management of the company's business is far less stringent than would be the case for a trustee. Thus, the nature of a director's position draws from a number of legally recognised roles, a clear illustration of the breadth and complexity of the post. It is worth recalling here that a person involved with a company does not need to be designated as a director to fall within the s.741 definition (see earlier) and, therefore may owe the company the same duties as those owed by a properly appointed director.

> There have been many judicial statements describing the general nature of directors' duties and Lord Cranworth's remarks in *Aberdeen Railway Co. v Blaikie Bros.* 1854 sum them up: *"The directors are a body to whom is delegated the duty of managing the general affairs of the company. A corporate body can only act by agents, and it is, of course, the duty of those agents to act as best to promote the interests of the corporation whose affairs they are conducting. Such agents have duties of a fiduciary nature towards their principal. And it is a rule of universal application, that no one, having such duties to discharge, shall be allowed to enter into engagements in which he has, or can have, a personal interest conflicting, or which possibly may conflict, with the interests of those whom he is bound to protect."*

## To whom are the duties owed?

### The shareholders

Directors owe their duties to the company as a whole. This is usually taken to mean the shareholders as a single body. This does not prevent directors from considering the interests of particular sections of shareholders, including themselves, when they make decisions. They do not have to see the company as something distinct from its members. Nor do they owe a general duty to individual shareholders.

> In *Percival v. Wright* 1902 the plaintiff, who wished to sell his shares in the company, entered into an agreement to sell them to the members of the board at a valuation he placed on them himself. The transaction went ahead, after which the plaintiff discovered that whilst his negotiations with the board were taking place, a third party was also negotiating a possible take-over of the company. These negotiations were never revealed to the plaintiff by the board, and in the event the take-over negotiations came to nothing. The plaintiff, however, sought to have the sale of his shares to the board set aside on the grounds of non-disclosure. The court held that the sale was binding. The directors were not trustees for individual shareholders who wished to sell their shares to them. They had not dealt unfairly with the plaintiff, since he had approached them and had named his price. Moreover, were the plaintiff to succeed, it would mean that the board should have disclosed to him prematurely the negotiations for the sale of the company which had been taking place, and this might well have damaged the company's interests. Under the Criminal Justice Act 1993, similar conduct on the part of a board could now give rise to criminal liability as insider dealing, although its provisions do not apply to private dealings in shares, and since in *Percival v Wright* the transaction was a private one, it would seem that even today no criminal liability would result.

If directors give advice to shareholders regarding a take-over bid for their company, an injunction may lie to prevent the bid going ahead if there is evidence that the directors have not been honest, as for example, by concealing the information that professional advisers have recommended rejection: *Gething v. Kilner* 1972.

No duty is owed to *individual* shareholders for any loss they have suffered through a fall in the value of their shares resulting from negligent mismanagement, since the loss is the company's. The company may however sue the negligent directors for breach of duty.

Exceptionally, a fiduciary duty may be owed to an individual shareholder on the particular facts of a case, such as those in *Coleman v. Myers* 1977 where the minority shareholders in a small family firm sold their shares to the managing director after he had made misrepresentations to them.

## The creditors

In a solvent company, the duty owed by the directors is a duty owed to the shareholders as a body. They are not responsible to the creditors. In the words of Lord Templeman in *Kuwait Asia Bank v. National Mutual Life* 1991: *"A director does not by reason only of his position as director owe any duty to creditors or trustees for creditors of the company.*" If however the company becomes insolvent the interests of the creditors arise. They control the company's assets by means of insolvency procedures (see later) and the assets, from a practical position, now belong to them rather than the shareholders.

In *Liquidator of West Mercia Safetywear Ltd. v. Dodd* 1988 the defendant was a director of two companies, West Mercia and A.J. Dodd. Both companies became insolvent. The liquidator of West Mercia brought a claim against the defendant on the basis of his breach of duty to the West Mercia creditors. The liquidator had instructed the directors not to operate the bank account of either company, but despite this instruction the defendant paid £4,000 from West Mercia's account into the other company's account to discharge a debt West Mercia owed it. This benefited the defendant personally, since it reduced his liability on a personal guarantee on the other company's overdraft. The Court of Appeal ordered him personally to repay the West Mercia liquidator.

## Specific duties owed

In broad terms, the duties of a director are:

* *fiduciary duties*, arising as a result of the equitable view of directors as quasi-trustees;

* *duties of care and skill*, arising under the common law through the operation of the tort of negligence; and

* *statutory duties*, arising out of the provisions contained in the Companies Act 1985.

### Fiduciary duties

Fiduciary duties owed by a director invlove the obligation to exercise powers bona fide and for the benefit of the company, and the obligation to avoid any conflict between their personal interests and those of the company, or as it is sometimes expressed, the duty not to make a *secret profit*. Case law illustrates the application of these duties in practice.

In *Howard Smith Ltd. v. Ampol Petroleum Ltd.* 1974 directors, acting honestly and within their powers, allotted shares to a company which wanted to make a take-over bid. By doing so, they aimed to prevent two shareholders who between them held 55% of the shares and had indicated they would reject any take-over bid, from being able to do so. It was held that the board had acted improperly. The issue of the shares would be set aside. The proper reason for the issue of shares is the raising of capital, and, *"it must be unconstitutional for directors to use their fiduciary powers over the shares in the company purely for the purpose of destroying an existing majority, or creating a new majority which did not previously exist"*.

Breach of the duty to act bona fide and in the interests of the company will also occur where the directors:

- *issue new shares to themselves, not because the company needs more capital but merely to increase their voting power;*

  In *Piercy v. S. Mills & Co. Ltd.* 1920 the directors used their powers to issue new voting shares to themselves, solely to acquire majority voting power. The court held that the directors had abused their powers and the allotment was declared void.

- *approve a transfer of their own partly-paid shares to escape liability for a call they intend to make;*

  In *Alexander v. Automatic Telephone Co.* 1900 the directors used their position to require all shareholders to pay 3s 6d on each share excluding themselves. The court held that his was a clear abuse of power and the directors were required to pay to the company the same amounts.

- *negotiate a new service agreement between the company and its managing director simply in order to confer additional benefits on him or his dependents;* ⁿ

  In *Re W and M Roith* 1967 it was held that a new service contract negotiated between a managing director and his company was unlawful as it was solely to make a pension provision for his widow and that no regard had been taken as to whether this was for the benefit of the company.

- *abdicate responsibility for the running of the company and appoint a manager with full powers who is not under the control of the board of directors, or obey the majority shareholder without exercising their own judgment or discretion.*

The following cases illustrate the position regarding the making of a secret profit. In a company law context the term "secret" is somewhat misleading, for a profit remains secret even if it has been disclosed by the director. The profit must be *approved* by the company in general meeting before it becomes lawful.

It is not surprising that a secret profit will arise when a director takes a bribe: *Boston Deep Sea Fishing Co. v. Ansell* 1888. However, a director will also be liable to account for a secret profit even though he could not have profited personally, or even though the company would have suffered no loss.

> In *Industrial Development Consultants v. Cooley* the defendant acted as the managing director of a design company and in this capacity he tried to obtain some work for the company from the Eastern Gas Board. The Board indicated to the defendant that they were not prepared to give his company the work. Realising that he might secure the work for himself, the defendant managed to leave his company on the pretence that he was close to a nervous breakdown. He set up his own company and secured the Gas Board contract. It was held that he must account to his former company for the profit he had made, despite the fact that it was most unlikely the company would ever have obtained the work for itself. Thus it seems a director will remain accountable even where the company has not sustained a loss.

A clear breach of duty occurs where directors negotiate a contract in the company's name, but then take the contract for themselves.

> This occurred in *Cook v. Deeks* 1916 where the directors of a company negotiated a construction contract which they took in their names, following which they called a company meeting where they were able to use their 75% shareholding in the company to pass a resolution that the company had no interest in the contract. This was held to constitute a fraud on the minority. It was of no effect, and the directors had to account to the company for the profit they made.

Breach may also occur where a director places himself in a conflict of interest situation.

> The case of *Guinness plc v. Saunders* 1990 provides an interesting example. In order to implement its objective of launching a take-over-bid for the Distillers company, the Guinness board appointed a committee comprising of three directors *"with full power and authority"* to settle the terms for the Distillers offer. The three directors were Mr Saunders, Mr Roux and Mr Ward. The committee made an agreement with Mr Ward that Guinness would pay him a sum amounting 0.2% of the ultimate value of a successful bid, for his advice and services. A successful bid was made, and an invoice for £5.2m representing the sum payable to Mr Ward was presented to the committee, and paid by them on behalf of Guinness. When however the full board discovered the payment the company sought to recover the money from Mr Ward. The House of Lords held it was entitled to do so. Under the articles a committee of the board had no power to make such an agreement; only the

board could authorise special remuneration to a director. It was a void contract for want of authority. No quantum meruit claim could be based upon an implied contract since the agreement itself was void. Nor was equitable relief available to grant Ward an allowance for his services because he had acted in breach of his fiduciary duty by putting himself in a position where his duty to the company and his personal interests conflicted irreconcilably. In Lord Templemans words the agreement prevented him *"from giving independent and impartial advice to Guinness."* However, in the absence of a firm contract, he was not in breach of the disclosure requirements under s.317.

## Duties of care and skill

As we saw earlier, there are common law duties applying to directors, which arise from the obligation of a director not to act negligently in managing the company's affairs. The question is essentially one of identifying the standard of care and skill owed by the particular director towards his or her company.

The leading case is that of *Re City Equitable Fire Insurance Co.* 1925. Here the company directors had delegated almost all responsibilities of management to the managing director. As a result, the directors failed to recognise a loss of over £1,200,000 from the company's funds, which was caused by the deliberate fraud of the managing director, described by the judge as, *"a daring and unprincipled scoundrel"*. The loss was discovered in the course of the winding-up of the company, and the liquidator successfully sought to make all the other directors liable for their negligence. Romer J. stated the following general propositions of law:

(i)    a director need not show a greater degree of skill than may reasonably be expected of a person with his knowledge and experience;

(ii)   a director need not give continuous attention to the affairs of the company. He is not bound to attend all meetings of the board, although he ought to attend whenever he is reasonably able to do so;

(iii)  a director may delegate duties to other officials in the company and trust them to be performed properly so long as there is no reason to doubt or mistrust them.

The judge commented *"It is indeed possible to describe the duties of directors in general terms ... The position of a director of a company carrying on a small retail business is very different from that of a director of a railway company. The duties of a bank director may differ widely from those of an insurance director, and the duties of a director of one insurance company may differ from those of a director of another."*

It is clear, therefore, that the duties of care and skill owed to a company by its directors are of a variable kind. Much higher standards of expertise will be expected of directors who are employed in a professional capacity in executive posts, for example, finance and engineering directors, than of directors who have nor claim to have such professional expertise. Yet even non-executive directors who have experience or qualifications in a field of relevance to the company's affairs may find that high objective standards appropriate to their specialist fields will be expected of them in law, despite their non-executive roles.

> This point emerged in the case of *Dorchester Finance Co. Ltd. v. Stebbing* 1989 where the company lost money as a result of the gross negligence of the actions of the company's one executive director. He failed to take out adequate securities on loans made by the company and the company found itself unable to recover the loans made. The two non-executive directors, who had little to do with the company, had signed cheques in blank at the request of the executive director. All three directors had considerable financial experience. The court held the two non-executive directors equally liable with the executive director in damages to the company.

## The effect of breach of duty

A director who is in breach of duty is jointly and severally liable with other directors who are similarly liable to make good the loss. He must account for any secret profit made, and in such cases the company is usually able to avoid a contract made with him. In appropriate circumstances the court may grant an injunction.

Relief from breach of duty is available in certain circumstances for example where the company by ordinary resolution waives the breach.

# Partners as Business Managers

## The background to the relationship of the partners

Unlike the management arrangements which operate in registered companies, in a partnership every partner is entitled to participate in the management of the business unless the partnership agreement provides otherwise. The partners are managing the business not for others, there are no shareholders, but for themselves. There are obvious problems inherent in attempting to reach the sort of joint decisions which are thus necessary to successfully manage a partnership, and it is not uncommon for partners to disagree. There are also risks involved, both in having unlimited liability, and in the fact that individual partners may be responsible for the acts and defaults of their co-partners. Each partner is an agent of the co-partners and as such has an agent's power to bind the partnership by his acts undertaken within the ordinary course of the business. It is crucial therefore that each partner has trust and confidence in his co-partners, the relationship being one of the utmost good faith. This is sometimes given its latin name and is known as a relationship *uberrimae fidei*. Each partner is therefore under a duty to make a full and frank disclosure to the firm of any matters affecting it that come to the partner's attention.

The power of a partner to bind the other members of the firm by his actions illustrates how important it is that each partner should trust and have confidence in his co-partners, not only in regard to their business ability but also as to their business ethics. In *Helmore v. Smith* 1886 Bacon V-C remarked that, *"mutual confidence is the life-blood"* of the firm, whilst in *Baird's Case* 1870 James LJ stated:

> *"Ordinary partnerships are by the law assumed and presumed to be based upon the mutual trust and confidence of each partner in the skill, knowledge and integrity of every other partner. As between the partners and the outside world (whatever may be their private arrangements between themselves), each partner is the unlimited agent of every other in every matter connected with the partnership business, or which he represents as the partnership business, and not being in its nature beyond the scope of the partnership".*

In the course of business, partnerships enter into transactions with other organisations and individuals and inevitably such transactions are negotiated and executed for the partnership by individual partners, rather than by the firm as a whole. It has already been noted that each partner is an agent of his co-partners. *"In English law a firm as such has no existence; partners carry on business both as principals and as agents for each other within the scope of the partnership business; the firm-name is a mere expression, not a legal entity"*, stated Lord Justice Farwell in *Sadler v. Whiteman* 1910.

Under the law of agency, the person who appoints an agent is called the principal. The principal is bound by contracts made within the agent's actual and apparent authority. If the agent acts within either of these two spheres the contract concluded between the agent and the third party becomes the principal's contract, and hence it is the principal and the third party who become bound to each other. The *actual* authority of an agent is the express power given by the principal. A firm may for instance expressly resolve in a partnership meeting that each partner shall have the power to employ staff. Authority may also arise where the agent's power to make a particular contract or class of contracts can be implied from the conduct of the parties or the circumstances of the case. The apparent, or ostensible authority of an agent is the power which the agent appears to others to hold. Of a partner's apparent authority s.5 Partnership Act, 1890, says:

*"Every partner is an agent of the firm and his other partners for the purpose of the business of the partnership; and the acts of every partner who does any act for the carrying on in the usual way business of the kind carried on by the firm of which he is a member bind the firm and his partners, unless the partner so acting has in fact no authority to act for the firm in the particular matter, and the person with whom he is dealing either knows that he has not authority, or does not know or believe him to be a partner".*

Whether a particular contract is one carrying on in the usual way business of the kind carried on by the firm is a question of fact.

In *Mercantile Credit Co. Ltd. v. Garrod* 1962 the court had to decide what would be considered as an act of a *"like kind"* to the business of persons who ran a garage. It was held that the sale of a car to a third party by one of the partners bound the other *partners*. This was despite an agreement between them that provided for the carrying out of repair work, and the letting of garages, but expressly excluded car sales.

A private limitation of the powers of an agent is not an effective way to bring the restriction to the notice of an outsider dealing with the agent, and the law recognises this. But if, for example, a partner has acted as an agent for his firm in the past with a particular third party, and he carries out a further transaction of a similar kind with the third party after the firm has taken away his express authority, the third party can nevertheless hold the firm bound, unless he knew at the time of contracting of the partner's lack of authority.

The exact scope of an agent's apparent authority under s.5 has been the subject of much litigation. In any partnership partners will usually have the apparent authority to: sell the goods or personal property of the firm; purchase in the firm's name goods usually or necessarily used in the firm's business; receive payments due to the firm; and employ staff to work for the firm. In a trading partnership (where the business is buying and selling goods) partners will additionally have authority to: borrow money for a purpose connected with the business of the firm; and deal with payments to and from the firm.

Since a partnership has no separate legal identity it is the individual partners who are ultimately accountable for all the firm's debts. Under the Partnership Act every partner is jointly liable with the other partners for all the debts and obligations of the firm incurred whilst being a partner. A legal action by a creditor seeking to recover money owed to him may be brought against any one or more of the firm's partners. However if the judgment obtained in the court does not satisfy the creditor he cannot then sue the remaining partners for having sued one partner, he is precluded from suing the others for the same debt. Nevertheless the creditor, if he had chosen to do so, could have sued the firm in its own name rather than suing an individual partner of the firm. This has the effect of automatically joining all the partners in the action, and means that the judgment will be met out of assets of the firm as a whole and, if there is a shortfall, out of the property of the individual partners.

## Changes in membership

The membership of a firm may alter from time to time. The firm may wish to expand its business by bringing in new partners to provide the benefit of additional capital or fresh expertise. Existing partners may leave the partnership to join a new business, or to retire. A changing membership poses the question of the extent to which incoming and outgoing partners are responsible for the debts and liabilities of the firm. Although partners are responsible for any matters arising during their membership of the firm, incoming partners are not liable for the debts incurred before they joined, nor outgoing partners for those incurred after they leave, provided the retiring partner advertises the fact that he is no longer a member of the firm. This involves sending notice to all customers of the firm while that person was a partner, and advertising the retirement in a publication known as the *London Gazette*. If this is not done a person dealing with the firm after a change in its membership can treat all apparent members of the old firm as still being members of the firm. With regard to existing liabilities the partner may be discharged from them when he retires through the agreement of the new firm and the creditors.

## Rights and duties of the partners

Ideally the partnership relationship should be regulated by a comprehensive partnership agreement. If it is not, the provisions of the Partnership Act will apply when the parties are in dispute as to the nature of their duties and are unable to reach agreement amongst themselves. In a business enterprise of this sort, where a member's entire wealth lies at stake, it is clearly of great value to execute a detailed agreement setting out in precise form the powers and responsibilities of the members. For instance it would be prudent for such an agreement to provide grounds for the removal of partners, since the Act makes no such provision. Because the members of the firm have the freedom to make their own agreement, without the statutory controls imposed upon other forms of business organisation, such as the registered company, the partnership stands out as a most flexible form of organisation.

The duties that the Act sets rest upon a single principle, namely that the relationship between the parties is of the utmost good faith.

In *Law v. Law* 1905, a partner sold his share in the business to another partner for £21,000, but the purchasing partner failed to disclose to his co-partner certain facts about the partnership assets, of which he alone was aware. When the vendor realised that he had sold his share at below its true value he sought to have the sale set aside. The Court of Appeal held that in such circumstances the sale was voidable, and could be set aside.

A partner is under a duty to his co-partners to render true accounts and full information of all things affecting the partnership. Personal benefits can only be retained with the consent of the other partners. This parallels the position directors are in.

In *Bentley v. Craven* 1853 one of the partners in a firm of sugar refiners, who acted as the firm's buyer, was able to purchase a large quantity of sugar at below market price. He resold it to the firm at the true market price. His co-partners were unaware that he was selling on his own account. When they discovered this they sued him for the profit he had made, and were held to be entitled to it. It was a secret profit and belonged to the firm.

A partner is under a duty not to compete with his firm by carrying on another business of the same nature unless the other partners have consented. If a partner is in breach of this duty he must account to the firm for all the profits made and pay them over. If the partnership agreement prohibits the carrying on of a competing business, the court may grant an injunction to stop a partner who disregards the limitation.

Further rights and duties are set out in the Act which states that, in the absence of a contrary agreement:

- all partners are entitled to take part in the management of the partnership business;

- any differences arising as to ordinary matters connected with the partnership business are to be decided by a majority of the partners, but no change can be made in the nature of the partnership business without the consent of all the partners;

- no person may be introduced as a partner without the consent of all existing partners;

- all partners are entitled to share equally in the profits of the business irrespective of the amount of time they have given to it, and must contribute equally towards any losses. The Act does not require the firm to keep books of account, although this will normally be provided for in the partnership agreement, together with specific reference to the proportions of the profit each partner is entitled to. If however there are partnership books they have to be kept at the principal place of business, where every partner is entitled to have access to them for the purpose of inspection and copying;

- if a partner makes a payment or advance beyond the agreed capital contribution he is entitled to interest at 5% p.a.;

- a partner is not entitled to payment of interest on his capital until profits have been ascertained;

- the firm must indemnify a partner in respect of payments made and personal liabilities incurred in the ordinary and proper conduct of the business of the firm, or in or about anything necessarily done for the preservation of the business or property of the firm (e.g. paying an insurance premium);

- a partner is not entitled to remuneration for acting in the partnership business.

In cases where the firm consists of active and sleeping partners the partnership agreement will often provide that as well as taking a share of the profits the active partners shall be entitled to the payment of a salary.

If any of the terms of the partnership agreement are broken, damages will be available as a remedy, and where appropriate an injunction may be granted.

## Partnership property

It can be of importance, particularly to the partners themselves, to establish which assets used by the partnership actually belong to the firm itself, rather than to themselves as individuals. Mere use of property for partnership purposes does not automatically transfer ownership in it to the business.

In *Miles v. Clarke* 1953 the defendant started up a photography business which involved him in acquiring a lease and photographic equipment. After trading unsuccessfully he was joined by the plaintiff, a free-lance photographer, who brought into the firm his business connection which was of considerable value. The partners traded profitably for some time, on the basis of equal profit sharing. Later, as a result of personal difficulties, it became necessary to wind up the firm. The plaintiff claimed a share in all the assets of the business. The court held that the assets of the business other than the stock-in-trade which had become partnership property, belonged to the particular partner who had brought them in.

The Act provides that all property and rights and interests in property originally brought into the partnership or subsequently acquired by purchase or otherwise on account of the firm, must be held and applied by the partners exclusively for the purpose of the partnership and in accordance with the partnership agreement. Such property is called *partnership property* and will normally be jointly owned by the partners. Because a partner is a co-owner of partnership property, rather than a sole owner of any particular part of the partnership's assets, he may be guilty of theft of partnership property if it can be established that his intention was to permanently deprive the other partners of their share.

Under the Act property bought with money belonging to the firm is deemed to have been bought on account of the firm, unless a contrary intention appears.

## Test Questions

| | |
|---|---|
| 1. | In what ways can someone become a company director? |
| 2. | Sate the categories of people who are unable to act as directors. |
| 3. | Identify the controls over the abuse by directors of their powers. |
| 4. | Who possesses real power in a company, the directors or the shareholders? |
| 5. | A company is owed fiduciary duties, and duties of care and skill, from its directors. How do these duties differ? |
| 6. | Why is the law of agency so important to anyone in partnership? |
| 7. | Identify what rights and what duties a partner has. |

## The Dissolution of Business Organisations

### Introduction

The life of a business organisation can come to an end for many reasons. It may have achieved what its members required of it, so that it no longer has any useful value. For instance a limited company may be set up to carry out a specific business venture, or it may insert a provision in the articles of association making it clear that the business is to last for a fixed period, or that it will expire on the happening of a certain event. A group of businessmen may contribute capital to a company they have formed, with the aim that the company will purchase, renovate and then sell certain industrial premises, or buy and then resell some other substantial asset. The company will end when the sale takes place if its sole purpose was the making of the sale.

A business may also come to an end because the commercial foundations upon which it was based have ceased to exist, or it has become no longer commercially viable to continue. If this occurs there is nothing to prevent the organisation from diversifying if this is acceptable to the members, thus prolonging the life of the business.

Most businesses which are terminated however, do not end their own lives out of choice, but because such action has been forced on them by their creditors. This occurs when the creditors lose confidence in the capacity of the organisation to repay them. It is a common feature of commercial life that when a business develops financial ill-health, its creditors will seek to reduce their losses by dissolving the business whilst there are still assets remaining in it.

Thus in considering the law as it affects the dissolution of businesses it is helpful to bear in mind the health of the organisation at the time it is being dissolved. The law, quite understandably, exerts far greater control over businesses which are terminated in circumstances of financial failure, than in cases where they are brought to an end fit and healthy, and nobody will lose money. Dissolution is important to the members of the business, who will be concerned as to what share of the assets they are entitled to, and for much the same reason it will be of concern to the creditors; they will want to know what the assets of the business are, and how they are to be distributed.

## The process of dissolution

The process laid down for terminating or dissolving a business depends upon two factors:

- what the type of business is; and

- what financial condition it is in.

We have seen that business organisations can be classified according to their legal status. Some are corporate bodies, some are unincorporated associations, whilst others are simple one man businesses. By now it should be clear that there are significant differences between these alternative business forms. This is reflected in the procedures for dissolving them. In the case of a limited company the procedure by which it is dissolved is referred to as a *winding-up. Bankruptcy* is the term used to describe the process by which an insolvent individual's assets are collected in, converted into money and distributed between his creditors. There is no technical term to describe the process for terminating a partnership. It is simply referred to as dissolution.

## Dissolution of a Partnership

When the commercial activity of a partnership ceases so does the business itself, for it is no longer being *"carried on"* as required under the Partnership Act 1890. In such circumstances the partnership will be dissolved, and its assets disposed of to those legally entitled to them. Alternatively, a partnership which is still in operation may be dissolved on any one of a number of different grounds.

Dissolution can occur either with or without the intervention of the court. Under the Partnership Act 1890 a partnership is dissolved *without* the intervention of the court,

- if it was entered into for a fixed term, which has now expired, or was entered into for a single venture, which has been completed;

- if entered into for an undefined time, by any partner giving notice to the other or others of an intention to dissolve the partnership. If such a notice is served then the partnership is dissolved from the date mentioned in the notice as the date of dissolution. If no date has been given, dissolution operates from the time the notice was received, subject to the partnership articles providing for some other date;

- by the death or bankruptcy of any partner. Partnership articles will often provide that in such an event the partnership will continue to be run by the remaining partners;

- if a partner's share of the business is charged to secure a separate judgment debt, the other partners may dissolve the business;

- if it becomes unlawful for the business of the firm to be carried on, or for the members of the firm to carry it on in partnership. This may occur, for example, where there is a partnership between a British partner and a foreign partner, the business is carried on in the United Kingdom, and war breaks out between the countries of the respective partners.

Dissolution can be granted by *the court* on an application to dissolve, made by a partner, in any of the following cases:

- where a partner is suffering from a mental disorder;

- where a partner other than the partner petitioning:

  (i)   becomes in any way permanently incapable of performing their part of the partnership contract, e.g. through physical illness, or

  (ii)  has been guilty of misconduct in business or private life, as in the opinion of the court, bearing in mind the nature of the partnership business, is calculated to be prejudicial to the carrying on of the business, or

  (iii) wilfully or persistently commits a breach of the partnership agreement, or otherwise behaves in a way in matters relating to the partnership business that it is impractical for the other partners to carry on in business with that partner.

Cases on dissolution on these grounds have included a refusal to meet for discussions on business matters, the keeping of erroneous accounts, persistent disagreement between the parties, and in *Anderson v. Anderson* 1857 where a father and son were in partnership together, by the opening by the father of all his son's correspondence;

- where the business of the partnership can only be carried on at a loss;

- if circumstances have arisen which, in the opinion of the court, render it just and equitable that the partnership be dissolved.

In *Re: Yenidje Tobacco Co. Ltd.* 1916 although the company was trading profitably the court held that it was just and equitable to wind it up, on the basis that its two directors had become so hostile towards each other that they would only communicate by means of messages passed to each other via the Secretary, and that this amounted to a position of deadlock. It was pointed out that a private limited company is similar to a partnership, and that had the directors been partners in a partnership, there would have been sufficient grounds for dissolution. Lord Justice Warrington stated *"... I am prepared to say that in a case like the present, where there are only two persons interested, and there are no shareholders other than those two, where there are no means of over-ruling by the action of a general meeting of shareholders the trouble which is occasioned by the quarrels of the two directors and shareholders, the company ought to be wound up if there exists such a ground as would be sufficient for the dissolution of a private partnership at the suit of one of the partners against the other. Such grounds exist in the present case."*

## The partnership and bankruptcy

Two distinct insolvency situations may arise which affect the partnership:

- one of the partners is declared personally bankrupt, whilst the remaining partners are personally solvent. This automatically brings the partnership to an end, although a new one may well be formed, without the bankrupt partner. The reason the firm automatically dissolves in such circumstances is because the bankrupt party's share passes to his trustee in bankruptcy, and thus in effect he is withdrawing his contribution and his stake in the business;

- the partnership itself is insolvent. If this is so, all the partners will normally have bankruptcy proceedings brought against them. It should be remembered that since a partnership does not grant limited liability to its members, they become personally liable for the debts which cannot be met by the assets of the firm.

## The administration and distribution of assets

If the partnership is dissolved its property is gathered in, and used to pay all debts and liabilities. If after this is done a surplus is left it is distributed between the partners. What they receive will depend upon what their partnership agreement says. If it makes no provision for such a situation, the position is regulated by the 1890 Act.

# Dissolution of a Registered Company

We have already seen that the process by which a registered company can be brought to an end is known as a winding up or a liquidation. The process is a detailed and complex one. It is regulated by the Insolvency Act 1986, a statute based upon the report of Sir Kenneth Cork. Shortly before the Royal Assent was granted, the Insolvency Bill as it then was, came back to the House of Lords for approval, where Lord Denning remarked, *"In 1977 Sir Kenneth Cork and his committee entered upon a review of the insolvency law. They sat for five years and heard the most expert evidence. It is the most technical subject you can imagine. Both lawyers and accountants hate it. Most of them know nothing about it."*

## Methods of dissolution

A company is created by incorporation through registration. It can therefore only come to an end when the registration is discharged. Once this happens the contractual relationship between the company and its members, based upon the memorandum and articles of the company, also comes to an end.

A company can be dissolved:

(a)    by proceedings brought by the Attorney-General for cancellation of the registration, on the grounds that the company's objects are illegal.

In *Attorney-General v. Lindi St. Claire (Personal Services) Ltd.* 1980 a lady, Miss St. Claire, formed the defendant company for the purposes of prostitution. The Registrar had granted it a certificate of incorporation, after refusing to register it under various names submitted by Miss St. Claire, including Hookers Ltd., Prostitutes Ltd. and even Lindi St. Claire French Lessons Ltd. The court however granted the cancellation on the grounds that the objects of the company were illegal;

(b)    by the Registrar, who under s.652 Companies Act 1985, may strike off the register a company that is defunct. A *defunct* company is one which is no longer carrying on business. The section lays down a procedure to be followed by the Registrar before he can validly exercise the power to remove the company from the register. This has become a very common method of dissolution, for it is cheap and easy;

(c)    by being wound-up, which may be either voluntary or compulsory. The legal provisions relating to company liquidations are contained in the Insolvency Act 1986. The title of this statute is perhaps rather misleading, since it contains provisions which regulate not only companies which are being dissolved on the basis of their insolvency, but also companies which, for a variety of reasons, are being wound up fully able to meet their liabilities.

## The process of winding up

Like a partnership, a limited company can be wound up either *voluntarily*, or *compulsorily* by order of the court. In either case the grounds are set out in the Insolvency Act 1986. They recognise that winding up is a step which may become necessary not only in cases of financial instability, but also because the company, which is of course a creature of statute, has failed to comply with the statutory provisions which bind it, or simply because the members no longer wish to trade together. When examining the operation of the limited company it is common to draw an analogy with natural persons. Thus the company is said to be born when its certificate of incorporation is granted, and henceforth its brain, the board of directors, guides its actions and formulates its decisions, which are executed through those it employs. Following this analogy through to its conclusion the process of winding up is akin to the process of administering the estate of a deceased person. Assets are collected and used to satisfy debts owing, after which any property remaining can be distributed to those lawfully entitled to them. In the case of a company this will be to its members. However the process of administering the estate of a deceased person commences with death, whereas winding up is a process which culminates in the dissolution of the company, the administration being completed before the life of the company ends. Statutory references below are to the Insolvency Act 1986 unless stated otherwise.

## Terminology

A number of technical expressions are used in liquidation and it is helpful to briefly identify and describe them before proceeding further.

A *petition* is an application to the court requesting the court to exercise its jurisdiction over company liquidations. A petition is presented where the liquidation is compulsory. In such cases the court has a major role to play. This is not so however in voluntary liquidations, where the liquidation is under the control of either the members or the creditors of the company.

A *contributory* is a person liable to contribute to the assets of a company if it is wound up. Existing members whose shares have not been fully paid fall within the definition of a contributory, and so do similarly placed past members, whose shareholding ceased within the year preceding the winding up. However a past member is not liable in respect of any debt contracted after his membership ceased.

A *liquidator* is a person appointed to take control of the company, collect its assets, pay its debts, and distribute any surplus to the members according to their rights as shareholders. The liquidator therefore holds a position of great responsibility, and it is important to ensure that only individuals of integrity are qualified to hold such a post. In recent years some disquiet has been felt as a result of company liquidations in which the liquidator has been found to be conducting the winding up for the benefit of directors, rather than the company's creditors. The Insolvency Act 1986 copes with this by requiring that only an *insolvency practitioner* can act in a winding up. He must be authorised by his own professional body (these include accountancy bodies and the Law Society), or by the Department of Trade and Industry. Certain people are completely excluded. To become an insolvency practitioner an applicant must be shown to be a fit and proper person, and must provide security.

Liquidators need to be distinguished from receivers. *Receivers* are appointed by the holders of secured debentures, under the terms of the debenture, when the company defaults in making a repayment or commits some other breach.

The *Official Receiver* is appointed by the Department of Trade, and is concerned both with personal insolvency and with corporate insolvency. Official receivers are attached to courts with insolvency jurisdiction, and they act in the capacity of liquidators in the case of compulsory liquidations, being appointed automatically when a *winding up order* is made, that is when the court issues an order that the company be wound up. The Official Receiver (OR) remains in this office until another liquidator is appointed.

Finally the *London Gazette* is an official publication used to satisfy the requirement of providing public notice of certain legal events, for example, in the case of a liquidation notice of a creditors' meeting.

## The Basic Aspects of a Company Liquidation

Once the process of winding-up has been completed the company will be struck off the register of companies and will cease to exist. No further claims can then be made against it. Consequently for anyone who is connected with the company, whether as an investor, creditor or employee, winding-up is of great significance.

Although statutory winding up provisions are detailed, and sometimes complex, there are basically three aspects to a liquidation:

- who has the ability to institute and control the winding up, and on what grounds;

- what are the legal provisions to be fulfilled during the procedure; and

- in what order are claims made against the company for payment met?

## Methods of Winding Up

Voluntary winding up is more common than compulsory liquidation. It is a less formal procedure, and is therefore quicker and cheaper.

### Voluntary winding up

Shareholders can at any time resolve to end the company, by passing a resolution to wind up, either a special resolution if the company is solvent, or, in the case of insolvency, an extraordinary resolution that it cannot continue in business by reason of its liabilities. An ordinary resolution is sufficient where the time period fixed in the articles for the life of the company has passed, or an event stipulated in the articles as giving rise to dissolution has taken place.

When the resolution is passed the liquidation procedure begins. The consequences are that:

- the company ceases to carry on business, other than to enable it to wind up;

- the company's corporate status remains intact until dissolution;

- transfers of shares, and changes in members' rights are void unless sanctioned by the liquidator;

- the directors' powers cease when the liquidator is appointed, although he, or in a creditors' voluntary winding up, they themselves, may permit the directors to continue; and

- if the liquidation is due to insolvency, company employees, who may include directors, will be dismissed. The liquidator may however employ them under a new contract.

Notice of the resolution must be advertised in the *London Gazette* within fourteen days of it being passed. If a majority of the directors within five weeks of the passing of the resolution make a statutory declaration that the company is solvent, then the company members are allowed to manage the winding up. This includes the appointment of their own liquidator. This is a valuable power for the person appointed will be under their control, rather than the control of the creditors or the court. The court can nevertheless remove a liquidator on the basis of unfitness for office. The declaration of solvency states that the directors have examined the company's affairs and formed the opinion that within a stated period (up to a maximum of twelve months) the company will be able to pay its debts in full. If a declaration of solvency is not made, the winding up is creditors' winding up. A creditors' meeting must be summoned by the company. Details of this meeting must be posted to creditors and members giving them at least seven days notice, and be advertised in the London Gazette and two local newspapers.

The business of the creditors' meeting is to receive from the directors a full statement of the company's affairs, to draw up a list of creditors with estimates of their claims, to appoint a liquidator who will insert a notice in the *London Gazette* notifying other creditors to send in claims and if considered necessary, appoint a liquidation committee. This committee oversees the liquidator's work.

## Compulsory winding up

A compulsory winding up is carried out by the court. This is either the High Court or, if the company's paid up share capital does not exceed £120,000, the County

Court in whose district the company has its registered office. Not all County Courts however, possess the necessary insolvency jurisdiction.

Proceedings are commenced by a person presenting a petition to the appropriate court. The petitioner may be the company itself, by resolution, the Secretary of State following an investigation or, in most cases, a creditor.

In *Re Othery Construction Ltd.* 1966 Lord Buckley stated that if a fully paid up shareholder is to successfully petition to wind up:

*"... he must show either that there will be a surplus available for distribution amongst the shareholders or that the affairs of the company require investigation in respects which are likely to produce such a surplus".*

A company may be wound up by the court on any one of the following grounds:

- the company has passed a special resolution requesting it;

- in the case of a company registered as a public company, the company has been registered for more than a year, but as yet no certificate of ability to commence business has been issued. This certificate, issued by the Registrar, can only be obtained when certain financial details have been given to him;

- the company does not commence business in the first year of its incorporation, or suspends business at any time for a whole year. An order will only be granted on this ground if the company has no intention of carrying on business again.

In *Re Middlesbrough Assembly Rooms Co.* 1880 a shareholder petitioned for winding up where the company had suspended trading for over three years, because of a trade depression. The majority shareholders opposed the petition on the basis that the company intended to recommence trading when the economic situation improved. It was held that in the circumstances the petition should be dismissed;

- in the case of a public company if the membership has fallen below two; or

- if the company is unable to pay its debts. This is the ground most commonly relied upon. The company is deemed to be unable to pay its debts if a creditor who is owed a sum exceeding £750 by the company has left a statutory demand for it at the company's registered office, and the demand has remained unpaid for a period of three clear weeks. The £750 figure can be made up by aggregating the debts of different creditors. The company is not however regarded as neglecting the debt if it disputes the payment of it. In such circumstances the petitioner would not be regarded as a creditor. It is also well established law that winding up proceedings are not to be used as a system for debt collection. In *Re a Company ex. p Fin Soft Holding SA* 1991 Harman J regarded the correct test in such cases to be *"is there a substantial dispute as to the debt upon which the petition is allegedly founded?"*. It follows that absence of good faith on the part of the company in disputing payment is irrelevant.

Alternatively the company is deemed unable to pay its debts if:

(i)     execution has been issued on a judgment in favour of a creditor which is returned either wholly or partially unsatisfied; or

(ii)    it is proved to the satisfaction of the court that the company is unable to pay its debts as they fall due.

In *Re a Company* 1986 it was held that a company can be regarded as unable to pay its debts under this ground, where it has funds but persistently fails or neglects to pay its debts unless it is forced to do so. Many companies have a deliberate policy of holding back payment for as long as possible, and for some this may be their means of survival; or

(iii)   where the court is satisfied that taking into account the company's present and future liabilities, the value of its assets is less than the amount of its liabilities; or

• the court is of the opinion that it is just and equitable that the company should be wound up. This ground covers a number of situations. For instance it covers cases in which the company has been formed for a fraudulent purpose; where the company is a sham, having no business or property; or where the rights of members are being flouted.

In *Loch v. John Blackwood Ltd.* 1924 a director with voting control refused to hold meetings, produce accounts or pay dividends. The court held that the company could be wound up.

In *Ebrahami v. Westbourne Galleries* 1972 two individuals E and N had operated successfully in partnership together for many years. Later they converted the business to a company, with themselves as sole shareholders and directors, and after a time N's son was allowed into the business. This was granted as a favour by the plaintiff, who transferred some of his shares to the son. Unfortunately his generosity was met by N and his son combining their interests to force the plaintiff out of the business. The court granted the plaintiff's application to wind up. Commenting on the expression *"just and equitable"* Lord Wilberforce said:

*"The words are a recognition of the fact that a limited company is more than a mere legal entity, with a personality in law of its own; that there is room in company law for the recognition of the fact that behind it, or amongst it, there are individuals, with rights, expectations and obligations ... which are not necessarily submerged in the company structure".*

The petition to wind up is presented to the district judge of the court who fixes a time and place for the hearing. The petition must be advertised in the *London Gazette* at least seven clear days (excluding Saturday and Sunday) before the hearing. Rules of Court set out the form in which this advertised information must be provided; if they are not complied with the petitioner may have to meet all the court costs. The aim of the advertisement is to invite interested parties, the company's creditors and contributories, to oppose or support the petition. A person intending to appear at the hearing must give notice of this to the petitioner. After presentation of the petition a provisional liquidator may be appointed who is generally the Official Receiver. In any event when the hearing takes place, and the court makes a winding-up order, the Official Receiver becomes provisional liquidator by statute, and continues as liquidator unless the meeting of the creditors and contributories agree to the appointment of some other liquidator. This person must be an insolvency practitioner. The 1986 Act sets out the liquidator's powers. Essentially his task is to collect and realise the company's assets, including unpaid sums due to the company from contributories for their shares, to settle the lists of creditors and contributories, pay the company's debts in a fixed order, and finally to adjust the rights of the contributories distributing any surplus assets among them. At meetings of creditors and contributories it may be decided to apply to the court to form a committee of inspection. Having fulfilled these responsibilities the liquidator applies to the court for an order that the company be dissolved, and is then released from his or her role. The court has a complete and unfettered discretion as to whether to make an order for winding up. It may as an alternative conditionally or unconditionally adjourn the hearing, make an interim order, or dismiss the petition altogether.

## Fraudulent and wrongful trading

The concept of *fraudulent trading* is a well known one in company law. It is a crime under the Companies Act 1985, and gives rise to civil liability under the Insolvency Act 1986. Civil liability can only occur when the company is being wound up. If in the course of the liquidation it appears to the liquidator that the company's business has been carried on with intent to defraud creditors or for any fraudulent purpose, the liquidator may apply to the court for an order that any person who has knowingly been a party to such conduct be liable to contribute to the assets of the company. The court can order such a contribution as it thinks proper in the circumstances. In this way the creditors as a whole are compensated in the winding up for any serious wrongdoing committed by the directors, or any other party, in their management of or dealings with the company.The expression *fraudulent* is not defined by statute, however the courts have provided some indication of what must be established.

In *Re William C. Leitch Brass Ltd.* 1932 it was said that a company will be acting fraudulently by incurring debts either knowing it will be unable to meet them when they fall due, or reckless as to whether it will be able to pay them at such time. An important qualification to liability was given in *Re Patrick & Lyon Ltd.* 1933 where it was said that the behaviour of the directors had to demonstrate real moral blame, and it is this feature of fraudulent trading which presents the major limitation upon its effectiveness as a civil remedy. So long as the directors can satisfy the court that, even when the company was in an insolvent situation, they genuinely and honestly believed that the company would be able to meet its debts when they fell due, then it is unlikely that they will be held personally accountable. Clearly the less business competence and experience they possess the easier it will be for them to avoid liability.

It was because of this difficulty in establishing fraudulent trading that additional liability based upon negligence was introduced under s.214 Insolvency Act 1986, and known as wrongful trading. Only a director can incur liability for wrongful trading, and as with s.213 action can only be taken by the liquidator of the company. The liquidator needs to establish that the person was at the time a director, that the company had gone into insolvent liquidation, and that at some time before the proceedings to wind up commenced, the person against whom they were being brought knew or ought to have concluded that there was no reasonable prospect that the company would avoid going into insolvent liquidation. If these criteria are met the court may declare the person concerned liable to contribute to the assets of the company. The section is particularly demanding on directors in a number of aspects. Under s.214 insolvent liquidation means that the assets as realised in the liquidation are insufficient to meet not only the company's debts and other liabilities, but also the costs of the winding up itself, which are generally substantial. The standard of skill expected of the director is based upon two sets of criteria, that is not only the general knowledge, skill and experience which that particular director holds, but also the skill and experience that can be reasonably expected from a reasonably diligent director. The test is an objective rather than a subjective one. Even the defence available under the section operates in a rigorous fashion towards directors. It provides that no order may be made by the court if it is satisfied that the person in question took every step with a view to minimising the potential loss to the company's creditors as he ought to have taken. The expression *every step* is clearly very stringent.

> The wrongful trading provisions were applied in *Re Produce Marketing Consortium Ltd.* 1989 where two directors had continued to trade when the accounts showed their company to be insolvent, in the honest but unrealistically optimistic belief that the company's fortunes would change. They were ordered by the court to contribute £75,000 plus interest to the assets of the company.

It seems that s.214 is a more potent weapon in the hands of liquidators than s.213. Establishing fraud is more difficult than establishing negligence, and this together with the rigorous standards demanded by s.214 suggests that wrongful trading is likely to be regarded increasingly by liquidators as a more attractive remedy than fraudulent trading. Even so there may still be reasons why a claim under s.213 may be brought by a liquidator. Orders made under s.213 can be punitive, for example, but perhaps the most significant reason is where a contribution is being sought from someone other than a director, for unlike s.214, s.213 catches anyone 'knowingly' a party to the fraud.

In *Re Gerald Cooper Chemicals Ltd.* 1978 the court held that a creditor who accepts money from the company knowing it has been procured by carrying on business with the intent to defraud other creditors by the act of paying him, will be liable under s.213. Templeman, J. stated *"A man who warms himself with the fire of fraud cannot complain if he is singed"*.

## The order of priorities

On dissolution there are likely to be many claims against the assets of the company, and if it is insolvent the question which arises is how to handle the shortfall. Do all the company's creditors absorb the loss according to the proportion of credit they have provided, or do some creditors rank before others, so that whilst those at the top of the list may be repaid in full, those at the bottom could find themselves with nothing?

The answer is that the Insolvency Act 1986 lays down an order of priorities for the distribution of assets. The relevant provisions are contained in ss.175 and 176, which lays down the following order:

(a)    the costs of winding up (for example the liquidator's fees);

(b)    preferential debts. These include: income tax deducted from the pay of company employees under the PAYE system over the past year; VAT payments owed by the company that have accrued over the past six months; wages and salaries of employees outstanding for the previous four months, up to a present maximum figure of £800 per employee. A director may be a salaried employee, and thus qualify under this head, however a director's fee rather than a salary will not rank as a preferential debt. If assets are sufficient, preferential debts are paid in full. If not, the available assets are distributed rateably between the preferential creditors, and in these circumstances property subject to a floating charge must be applied first in the payment of preferential debts, the holder being entitled only to the balance. Creditors who have the security of a fixed charge over assets of the company are, of course, able to realise the assets charged to meet the company's liability towards them;

(c)     ordinary unsecured debts, such as sums owing to trade creditors. If these cannot be paid in full they are paid rateably amongst the creditors;

(d)     the members according to their rights under the memorandum and articles. It may be that one class of shareholders is entitled to repayment of a certain amount of the surplus before the others, thus preference shareholders may receive repayment of their paid up capital in priority to ordinary shareholders.

# Alternatives to Winding Up

Whilst as we have seen, a company may be dissolved for reasons other than financial difficulty, most dissolutions are the result of a financial crisis. Directors faced with this situation may have the future affairs of the company taken out of their hands in a compulsory or creditors' liquidation, the result of which will be that the life of the company will come to an end, and some creditors at least will be left with their debts unsatisfied. One of the aims of the Insolvency Act 1986 was to provide alternatives to this drastic outcome, which would act as financial rescue packages for companies in difficulty. These rescue packages come in the form of compositions with creditors, and the use of administration orders.

# Choosing the Legal Form for a Business

This chapter has explored in detail the legal characteristics of the two principal forms of private sector business organisation, the partnership and the registered company. It is clear that the differences between them are significant, not only from a legal standpoint but also from a commercial one. We can conclude our examination of business organisations by examining the basis upon which the decision may be taken whether to operate in partnership or form a registered company, that is whether or not to incorporate.

## Partnership or registered company?

There are two circumstances in which the opportunity for choosing the legal form of the business is illusory.

(i)    Sometimes people drift into business relationships rather than discuss and plan them in advance. Perhaps what began as a mere hobby pursued by two friends develops into a money making venture, and they find themselves in a business relationship without any conscious decision on their part. If their relationship satisfies the definition of a partnership contained in s.1 Partnership Act 1890, then the law will regard them as partners. They do not need to have entered into a written agreement. They many not even be aware of their legal status. In law however they are now operating as a firm.

(ii)   If professional people, such as accountants, architects, doctors or lawyers seek to carry out their work in combination with co-professionals, the law prevents them from incorporating their business. It is only permissible for them to carry out their work collectively in partnership so the opportunity of incorporating is denied them.

Assuming however that like-minded people are anxious to establish a joint business venture, what factors are likely to influence them in deciding whether or not to incorporate? The following checklist of points covers all the major factors, and illustrates the essential legal and commercial differences between the partnership and the registered company.

## Registered companies and partnerships compared

(i)    *Legal status*
A registered company is a corporate body once its certificate of incorporation is granted to it. It is an artificial entity and is required to establish its nationality, a registered office where it can be served with formal notices, and provide itself with a name which it must use for the purpose of conducting business. It is legally separate from its members, who may make contracts with it, for example by selling to it a business previously operated as a partnership or on a sole trader basis.

A partnership is not a corporate body. It is no more than the sum total of the individuals who make it up. Although it must register under the Business Names Act 1985 any name it uses to trade under which does not consist of the surnames of all the partners, this name (e.g. Smith and Co.) does not give it any special persona, although for practical convenience Rules of the Supreme Court enable proceedings by and against the firm to be brought in the firms name.

(ii)   *Members' liability*
In a company, the financial liability of the members for any legal liabilities of the business such as trading debts ends when they have fully paid for their shares. There are however particular circumstances where members may still face personal liability, although these are restricted. An example is the potentialpersonal liability of directors who continue to run the company in circumstances where they know or ought to realise the company is unlikely to avoid an insolvent liquidation, and it subsequently goes into an insolvent liquidation (wrongful trading). Essentially however a shareholder has limited liability.

The liability of partners for the debts of a firm is unlimited. If the assets of the firm are insufficient to meet the liability the creditor can look to the personal property of the individual partners. They may have bankruptcy proceedings brought against them. Limited liability is however available in a limited partnership, a special form of partnership which may be established under the provisions of the Limited Partnership Act 1907. There are however very few limited partnerships in operation.

(iii)   *Agency*
In a company, mere membership does not of itself invest the shareholder with the power to act as an agent for and on behalf of the company. Agency powers are contained in the articles of association of the company and these powers are the principal agency source. Articles normally grant full powers as agents to the board of directors. In a firm however each partner is an agent of the other partners and of the partnership as a whole (s.5 Partnership Act 1890).

(v)   *Management*
Whereas companies are managed by those granted the power to do so under the articles – the directors of the company, in a firm all the members have the full right to take part in its management. Denial of this right would entitle the aggrieved partner to petition to have the firm dissolved. Thus whilst ownership and management are often in separate hands in the case of a registered company, this is never the position in a firm. Consequently the means available to company members to require directors to account for their actions are of crucial importance, and company law provides that certain decisions, such as alterations to the

articles, can only legitimately be carried out at a general meeting of the company where all the membership is entitled to be present.

(v)  *Membership*

There is no limit placed on the number of members a registered company may have. New members can join the company with little restriction, although the directors may have the power to refuse a share transfer in some cases. In a firm however a new partner can only join with the consent of all the existing members, emphasising the close commercial relationship of the partners. Moreover normal trading partnerships are restricted to a maximum of twenty partners. There is no limit however placed on the size of a professional partnership. A private company can have a single member but a firm must have two members.

(vi)  *Taxation*

A company pays corporation tax on a flat rate basis on its profits. Shareholders are taxed on the dividends the company pays them. In a partnership partners pay income tax on the apportioned profits they receive from the business.

(vii)  *Borrowing*

Companies, particularly larger ones, have much greater borrowing capability than partnerships. They can raise loan capital by issuing debentures and provide security by way of floating charges, neither of which partnerships can do.

(viii)  *Formalities and public inspection*

Whereas a firm can maintain complete secrecy over its affairs (other than providing details of its proprietors where the Business Names Act 1985 applies) a registered company must provide the Registrar of Companies with a wealth of detail about itself on a regular basis. All of this information is held on its file and is available for public inspection. Thus its membership, its annual accounts, and details of the property it has charged, are amongst the long list of details which the Registrar must be provided with. There are also fees to be paid when such documents are delivered e.g. £25 on filing a copy of the annual return, and also of course a considerable internal administration burden for the company in satisfying the extensive information demands of company legislation. Financial penalties can be exacted against companies in default. Moreover company legislation in general is highly prescriptive, demanding particular procedures to be followed, and forms to be used, if a company is to lawfully conduct its affairs.

# Test Questions

1. In what circumstances can a partnership be brought to an end?

2. How does a voluntary winding up differ from a compulsory winding up?

3. Under what circumstances is a company said to be unable to pay debts?

4. Why must directors take great care if their company gets into financial difficulties?

5. In an insolvent liquidation some creditors will be better placed than others to recover what they are owed. Identify which creditors this observation applies to.

6. Why might people going into a business choose to form a partnership rather than a registered company?

7. What are the main attractions of a company over a partnership as a means of conducting a business?

# Assignment - Trouble at Mills

In 1992 Mark Mills, together with his cousin Bryan and an accountant called Peter Marshall, decided to form a company to deal in personal insurance services. The company received its certificate of incorporation at the end of 1992. It was called Mills & Co. (Insurance Services) Ltd. and its premises were in Leeds. Mark and Bryan took up 35% of the shares each, Peter took the remainder. The company objects stated that it could carry on the business of providing *"personal insurance of any kind"*. In 1995 Peter was anxious that his wife should join the company, and each of the existing shareholders agreed to transfer some of their shares to her. As a result she obtained a 25% stake, Mark, Bryan and Peter's shareholding being reduced to 25% each.

Mark was happy with the company structure, since Peter's wife brought to the business considerable commercial expertise, and he received a large sum for the shares he transferred to her. Within a year however, the relationship between the shareholders had deteriorated. In particular Mark felt increasingly isolated. He was anxious that the company expand its insurance business. The other shareholders however were of the view that the company, which was increasingly unprofitable, should diversify, and move into the lucrative field of marketing, where Peter's wife had expertise.

By 1998 Mark had decided to form a separate business to offer a complete range of insurance facilities. He formed a partnership with James Blake-Smith, an old schoolfriend, to carry on the additional business. He did not reveal the existence of this business to his fellow shareholders in Mills & Co. Ltd., assuming that since it was based in Barnsley, a town twenty miles away from the company's place of business in Leeds, it had nothing to do with them. No partnership articles were drawn up. The other members of Mills & Co. Ltd. recently discovered the existence of Mark's new firm. They responded by calling a company meeting, at which, they resolved to alter the company articles to enable it to pursue marketing work, to sell off the company's present business undertaking at a figure well below what Mark believes to be its true value, and to remove him as a director. In addition they are threatening to take away his voting rights. Mark's problems have been compounded by problems in the partnership. He has discovered that James Blake-Smith has been in financial difficulties, and that bankruptcy proceedings have been commenced against him this week. He has also purchased, in the firm's name, an expensive computer system, despite a recent partnership meeting at which it was agreed to defer the expenditure until the next financial year.

## Task

Acting as Mark's legal advisor draft an outline report that expresses your considered legal opinion on his present business problems.

# Chapter 5

# The Statutory Regulation of Employment

As the title of this chapter indicates its purpose is to examine some of the key statutory provisions relating to employment. To fully appreciate the legal position of full and part-time employees and independent contractors however you should also appreciate how the common law regulates employment relationships, in particular the formation and content of the contract of employment. As the majority of statutory rights apply to employees and not to contractors it is important to be able to distinguish between the two relationships. In the majority of cases of course it is relatively easy to identify an employee working under a contract of employment but there are always borderline cases where the distinction is not straightforward, particularly where contractors are supplying personal services. There has been a major shift in recent legislation to confer rights not on employees but on 'workers' and this would include contractors providing personal services. This means that many self employed workers are protected by new rules on working time and holidays, the minimum wage and the protection given to whistle blowers.

The table on the following page contains the main statutory rights, their statutory source and the category of worker who is protected. You will notice that some statutory rights arise only after a period of continuous employment but this notion is still subject to a challenge in the European Court of Justice. In the present government's proposals for reform in employment law, fairness at work, the qualifying period to qualify for the most significant statutory right, unfair dismissal, is to be reduced from two years to one year from June 1999.

The main statute is the Employment Rights Act 1996 but this has now been amended by the fairness at work reforms contained in the Employment Relation Act 1999.

## Table of Key Statutory Employment Rights

| Statutory Right | Statutory Source | Individuals Protected |
|---|---|---|
| Not to suffer discrimination in recruitment and employment on the grounds of race sex or disability | Sex Discrimination Act 1975 Race Relations Act 1976 Equal Pay Act 1970 Equal Treatment Directive Disability Discrimination Act 1995 | Full-time and part-time employees. Contractors providing personal services |
| To be provided with a safe working environment | The Health and Safety at Work Act 1974 The Health and Safety (Work Place) Regulations 1992 | Full-time and part-time employees Contractors providing personal services |
| To have a written statement of employment terms To have an itemised pay statement Not to suffer unlawful deductions To have maternity leave where appropriate To notice on the termination of employment | The Employment Rights Act 1996 | Full-time and part-time employees |
| To have preferential status against an iinsolvent employer | Insolvency Act 1986 | Full-time and part-time employees |
| Not to suffer discrimination in recruitment and employment on the grounds of Trade Union Membership or activities | The Trade Union and Labour Relations (Consolidation) Act 1992 | Full-time and part-time employees |
| To be paid a minimum wage and to work a limited number of hours | The National Minimum Wage Act 1998 The Working Time Regulations 1998 | Workers |
| Not to be unfairly dismissed To be paid a redundancy payment where appropriate To receive maternity absence where appropriate To receive a written statement of the reasons for dismissal where appropriate | The Employment Rights Act 1996 | Full-time and part-time employees who have one years continuous service with the same employer (subject to exceptions) |
| Not to suffer a detriment or be dismissed for revealing a protected disclosure | Public Interest (Disclosure) Act 1998 | Workers |

# Employees and Contractors

There are an infinite variety of terms and conditions under which one person may do work for another. The requirements of employers will range from the need to engage full-time or part-time employees where a long standing relationship with their workers is envisaged, characterised by mutual trust and confidence between the parties, to the use of temporary workers engaged to complete a particular task. It may be that the temporary worker, such as the accountant or solicitor, provides a specialist skill which is required by the employer only on an intermittent basis. Alternatively temporary and casual employment only may be offered, because of economic necessity or the expansion or contraction of the size of the workforce in line with demand. Independent contractors (or self employed workers) are now well established as a substantial proportion of the workforce of some industries, for instance, the media, catering and construction. Of the million or so construction workers, well over half a million are self employed. The changing face of employment patterns in Britain is shown by official figures which reveal that while 62.3% of household income is earned from wages and salaries, over 10% is now derived from self-employment. This form of employment has many advantages for both sides. The employer *gets the job done* and the contractor is normally well paid in return. A criticism of the system is that it provides no support for the older or infirm worker, no security of employment, and may lead to a general reduction in health and safety standards. The increasing use of the self employed in business to execute work and provide services both in the public and private sectors makes the basic division between the employed and self employed a matter of considerable importance.

A large number of legal and economic consequences stem from the distinction between employed and self employed status. For this reason it is necessary to be able to identify the status of the employment relationship that has been entered into. Employment legislation and the common law both recognise the distinction between employment under a *contract of service* and self employment under a *contract for services*. The distinction is a relatively straightforward one to make in the majority of cases. It is only in a small proportion of cases that difficulties arise, often where employers, or those they employ are seeking to achieve contractor status for economic advantage or in order to evade legal responsibilities. The table on the following page provides a summary of the major legal and economic consequences of the employment classification.

# Legal and Economic Consequences of Employment Classification

Contract of Service (Employed Persons)      Contract for Services (Self-employed)

## Liability

An employer may be made vicariously liable for the wrongful acts of employees committed during the course of their employment.

As a general principle an employer may not be made liable for the wrongful acts of contractors he employs other than in exceptional cases.

## Common Law Employment Terms

Numerous terms are implied into a contract of employment by the common law to regulate the relationship of employer and employee e.g. trust and confidence.

The common law is much less likely to intervene in the relationship of employer and contractor.

## Health and Safety

A high standard of care is owed by an employer both under statute and the common law with regard to the health and safety of his employees.

While both the common law and statute recognise the existence of a duty of care by an employer in relation to the contractors he employs, at common law it is of a lesser standard than the duty owed to employees.

## Statutory Employment Rights

A large number of individual employment rights are conferred on employees by statute which generally arise after a period of service e.g. the right to unfair dismissal protection; to redundancy payments; to security of employment after maternity leave; etc.

Contractors are effectively excluded from the mass of individual employment rights conferred by statute. One notable exception however is the legislation in relation to sex and race discrimination, which protects the self-employed when they are providing personal services.

## Income Tax

The income tax payable by an employee is deducted at source by the employer under the PAYE (pay as you earn) scheme. An employee is referred to as a Schedule E tax payer.

The income tax of a self employed person is payable by the taxpayer and not his employer, on a lump sum preceding year basis (Schedule D). From 1994 however the self employed are gradually being moved to a 'current year basis' of assessment. They do however retain more favourable treatment in claiming reasonable expenses when assessed for tax. Furthermore an independent sub-contractor may have to charge VAT on services.

## Welfare Benefits

Under the Social Security Act 1975 both employer and employee must contribute to the payment of Class 1 National Insurance contributions assessed on an earnings related basis, entitling the employee to claim all the available welfare benefits e.g. Job Seekers Allowance, statutory sick pay, industrial disablement benefit, state retirement pension.

Under the Social Security Act 1975 a self-employed person is individually responsible for the payment of lower Class 2 National Insurance contributions and has only limited rights to claim welfare benefits e.g. statutory sick pay.

# Distinguishing between the Employed and Self Employed

Once again while it should be stressed that in the vast majority of cases it is easy to recognise a contract service and a contract for services the distinction between the contracts in borderline cases is not so straightforward. It does seem that all legal systems find the distinction between the two contracts a difficult one to make. The definition of an employee in the Employment Rights Act 1996 is "an individual who has entered into or works under a contract of employment". A contract of employment is defined as a "contract of service or apprenticeship, whether express or implied and if express oral or in writing

In the final analysis the determination of whether an individual is an employee or a contractor is a question of law for the courts rather than a question of fact involving placing sole reliance on the description of the contract given by the parties to it. Over the years a number of tests have been formulated by the courts to attempt to determine any given worker's status. Originally the courts would only consider the level of control over a worker by an employer. If an employer could tell his workers not only *what* to do, but also *how* and *when* to do it, then the workers would be regarded as employees, employed under a contract of service. Today the courts adopt a much wider approach and take account of all the circumstances to determine a worker's status. This is not to say that control is no longer a significant factor, for it would be difficult to imagine a contract of service where the employer did not have the ultimate authority to control the work performed by the employee.

The present approach of the courts, which involves viewing all of the circumstances of the case to determine status, has been described in various ways as the mixed, multiple or economic reality test. It has its origins in the following case.

In *Ready Mixed Concrete Ltd. v. Ministry of Pensions* 1968 MacKenna J, a single judge of the Queens Bench Division of the High Court, sat as the final appellate court to decide the employment status of a driver for the plaintiff company. This was in order to determine the employer's responsibility in relation to the National Insurance contributions of its drivers. The Ministry of Pensions had rejected the employer's contention that its drivers were self employed, despite the existence of written contracts of employment (30 pages long) which had attempted to create a contract for services rather than contracts of service. The declaration that the driver was self employed was not decisive and all aspects of his job were considered, for instance the fact that the driver purchased the lorry from the company; had to maintain it; that pay was calculated on the basis of the driving work performed. All these factors pointed to the driver being a contractor. Others pointed to his status as an employee. He had to paint the lorry in the company colours, he had to use it exclusively for company business and he was required to obey reasonable orders. McKenna J stated that there is a contract of service if an individual agrees to provide his own work, submits to his employer's control and in addition the majority of the contractual provisions are consistent with a contract of service. This approach has since been referred to as the mixed or multiple test. On the facts the power to delegate work was regarded as a decisive indication that the drivers were self employed under a contract for services.

The status of self employment cannot be achieved simply by including an express provision in a contract. The courts will look to the substance of an employment relationship rather than the label applied by the parties in order to decide a worker's status.

> In *Ferguson v. John Dawson Ltd.* 1976 the plaintiff, a builder's labourer agreed to work as a *self employed labour only sub contractor* an arrangement commonly known as the *lump*. When working on a flat roof he fell and suffered injuries. No guard rail had been provided, in breach of the duty to employees owed under the Construction (Working Places) Regulations 1966. The High Court decided that the employer was in breach of this statutory duty towards the plaintiff and damages of over £30,000 were awarded. On appeal the employer argued that as the plaintiff was self employed the statutory duty was not owed to him. It was the plaintiff's responsibility to ensure that the guard rail was in place. The Court of Appeal held, by a majority, that the plaintiff was in reality an employee and so entitled to the compensation awarded. The *lump* was no more than a device to attempt to gain tax advantages and whilst a declaration as to employment status may be relevant, it is not the conclusive factor to determine the true nature of the employment relationship.

By asking the question whether the worker is *in business on his own account* or under the control of an employer under a continuing business relationship, the courts have found it possible to conclude that a relationship traditionally regarded as self employment, namely that of a homeworker, was in reality a contract of service. Questions posed in applying this entrepreneurial test would include whether the individual was in business on his own, provides his own equipment, employs other workers and has a financial stake in the business.

Reliance on a pool of casual workers has long been a tradition in some sectors of business including the catering industry.

> The legal status of so called *'regular casuals'* was put to the test in *O'Kelly and Others v. Trusthouse Forte plc* 1983. Here a banqueting department run by the employer was staffed in part by full time employees but mainly by so called *'casuals'*. Among the casuals were *'regulars'* who were given preference when work was available, were often expected to work very long

hours and consequently had no other employment. The applicants in this case were *regulars* but when they became trade union shop stewards they were told by the employer that their services would no longer be required. In a claim for unfair dismissal brought by the applicants, the first issue the industrial tribunal had to deal with was whether they were employed under a contract of service and so protected by the law relating to unfair dismissal. In determining their employment status the tribunal acknowledged that its role was to *"consider all aspects of the relationship, no feature being itself decisive, each of which may vary in weight and direction and, having given such a balance to the factors as seem appropriate determine whether the person was carrying on business on his own account"*. Applying this mixed or multiple test the tribunal isolated factors consistent with a contract of service including the lack of mutual obligations on the part of the employer to provide work and on the part of the worker to offer services (referred to as *mutuality of obligation*). In addition there was the custom and practice of the catering industry to employ large numbers on a casual basis. By placing most emphasis on the inconsistent factors the tribunal found that the applicants were not employees and therefore not entitled to statutory protection. The Court of Appeal later found it unable to interfere with the tribunal's decision given that the correct legal approach has been adopted.

This decision has been the subject of a great deal of criticism mainly because it ignores the economic reality of working in such a relationship. A leading commentator, Gwyneth Pitt wrote in 1985 *"can it really have been the intention of Parliament that casual workers, frequently at the bottom of the employment heap, should not receive the basic protection of the law"*.

A more liberal interpretation of the requirement that there should be a mutuality of obligations existing between employers and employees was taken in *Carmichael v. National Power plc* 1998. Here the Court of Appeal considered the employment status of power station tour guides employed on a casual basis "as and when required". The court found that here there was an implied term containing mutual obligation on the employer to provide work when it became available and on the guides to take on a reasonable amount of work when offered. The guides were therefore classified as employees and entitled to the full range of statutory employment rights. There is no doubt that applying this approach to the requirement of mutuality of obligation the Court of Appeal would have found that the casual workers in *O'Kelly* were in reality employees.

In the final analysis in a borderline case the determination of a worker's status can only be made by asking a number of questions relating to the main features of the relationship such as the extent to which the employee is:

- providing personal services;

- under the employer's control;

- regarded as an integral part of the organisation;

- in business on his own account;

- providing tools and equipment;

- sharing in the profit and contributing towards the losses;

- able to delegate work;

- in agreement as to his status.

The fact that there has been such litigation on the employed/self employed distinction suggests that in the borderline cases in particular, decisions are by no means clear cut. The courts are faced with the difficult task of maintaining a balance between the freedom of employers to offer employment on the terms that best suit their interest and the rights of workers, for the most part in an unequal bargaining position, to obtain the benefits of status as an employee. Under European Union employment law rights and duties tend to be conferred and imposed on *'workers'* which would include employees or contractors providing personal services. This approach is now being adopted in the UK so that contractors providing personal services are brought within protective legislation. The Working Time Regulations, the Minimum Wage Act and the Public Interest (Disclosure) Act all apply to *workers* rather than employees.

## Formation of the Contract of Employment

Having identified the main employment relationships it is now possible to focus attention on the process by which an employer recruits his staff, both full-time and part-time. A significant trend of employment over the last decade has been the growth of reliance on part-time workers. While as a general rule self employed workers tend to work longer hours than employees, there are nevertheless over a half a million (9.5% of the total workforce) self employed part-timers in Britain.

## The Recruitment Process

The recruitment process will normally begin when the employer places an advertisement indicating that staff are required. Statements of fact in the advertisement may be classified as representations and if they prove to be false and having induced a contract of employment an innocent employee could seek a remedy for misrepresentation. In rare cases statements in the advertisement maybe given the status of contractual terms or at least used as evidence to determine the express terms of employment.

> In *Holliday Concrete v. Woods* 1979 the job advertisement indicated that a fifteen month contract was available. This was regarded as the period of employment rather than the employer's view that there was an understanding that the job would last as long on the project continued.

A job advertisement may also place clear obligations on an employee so that if they are not fulfilled this will be a factor in determining the reasonableness of the employer's decision to dismiss as a result.

## The Application form

Advertisements for job applications normally indicate that a prospective employee should complete an application form to assist in the selection process. While a significant feature of the employment contract is that it involves a relationship of trust and confidence it is not a contract uberrimae fidei (utmost good faith) such as partnership or insurance. This means that there is no duty on an applicant to volunteer information which is not requested during the recruitment process, which includes the completion of the application form.

> In *Walton v. TAC Construction Materials Ltd.* 1981 the complainant was dismissed after working for thirteen months when the employer discovered that he was a heroin addict. During a medical inspection prior to employment the employee had answered "none" when asked to give details of serious illnesses and failed to reveal that he was injecting himself with heroin. Both the tribunal and the EAT held that it was fair to dismiss the applicant firstly because of his deception and secondly in accordance with their policy not to employ anyone who was addicted to drugs. Although not relevant for the case the EAT considered whether the complainant should have disclosed his addiction for the purposes of employment and decided that *"it could not be said that there is any duty on the employee in the ordinary case, though there may be exceptions, to volunteer information about himself or otherwise than in response to a direct question"*.

In determining the fairness of an employer's decision to dismiss after discovering an employees mis-statement on an application form all the circumstances must be considered including the significance of the mis-statement, the length of employment and whether the work was satisfactory. To willfully give false information on a job application could also give rise to a criminal prosecution for obtaining a pecuniary advantage by deception.

## Job interviews

The primary objective of the job interview from the employer's viewpoint is to assist in the selection process. It should be stressed however if a decision to employ an applicant is made it may be at this point that a formal offer is made and accepted and a contract concluded. Even in cases where an understanding is reached, subject to a formal written offer at a later stage, statements or promises made during the interview may be used to interpret the contractual terms or constitute express terms of the contract in themselves. Certainly it makes sense to ensure at the interview stage that a prospective employee is given a realistic picture of the terms and conditions of employment and what the job entails. Even statements such as promotion prospects could be regarded as a term of employment if they later prove to be unrealistic. Certainly a clearly worded job offer will override conflicting statements made in the job advertisement. In the event of conflict between oral statements and writing the writing will normally have primacy but it is the intention of the parties which must be determined.

Quite often an offer of employment is made *conditional,* for instance *"subject to the receipt of satisfactory written references"* or the *"passing of a medical examination"*.

> In *Wishart v. National Association of Citizens Advice Bureaux Ltd.* 1990 The Court of Appeal considered a case where the plaintiff had been offered the post of information officer "subject to satisfactory references" and then when the employer discovered his past attendance record withdrew the job offer. The issue before the Court of Appeal was whether the employer's decision to treat the references as unsatisfactory could be viewed objectively and tested by the standard of the reasonable person in the position of the employer. In fact the court decided that unlike medical opinion as to the employee's fitness which could be tested objectively, there was no obligation in law on the employer other than to decide in good faith whether the references were satisfactory. *"The natural reading of a communication, the purpose of which is to tell the prospective employee that part of the decision on whether he is firmly offered the post has yet to be made, is that the employer is reserving the right to make up his own mind when the references have been received and studied. "*

If the acceptance of the job offer is *conditional* the normal contractual rules apply and it will be taken as a rejection and amount to a counter offer capable of acceptance or rejection.

It is in the interests of both the employer and the employee that the express terms of employment are precise and clearly understood. It is then less likely that legal problems will arise in the future when contractual terms are possibly subject to change or it becomes necessary to bring the employment relationship to an end.

Once a contract of employment is concluded there is legal redress available if either party decides to back out of the contract in breach. The unilateral withdrawal by an employer of an offer of employment, once accepted, will constitute a breach of contract. Here the damages awarded could in exceptional cases exceed the wages due under the contractual notice period.

It should be stressed however that the above scenario is rare and damages available against an employer in breach will normally be restricted to the wages due under the notice period Also the courts will not, other than in exceptional cases, order specific performance of a contract of employment. The remedy for breach by the employee is damages. In practice unless an employer has incurred substantial recruitment costs the cost of litigation would make an action against an employee in breach unwise. There is no right to bring an unfair dismissal claim without two years continuous employment (now a year) unless the reason for dismissal is shown to be inadmissible such as related to trade union membership, statutory rights or health and safety.

## Test Questions

1.  Name five statutory rights that apply to employees and two statutory rights that apply to workers.

2.  What is meant by a contract of service and a contract for services?

3.  How do employees and contractors differ in relation to income tax, national insurance and welfare benefits.

4.  What is meant by vicarious liability and how does it apply to employees?

5.  Compare the control test and the multiple test.

6.  Are contracts of employment of 'utmost good faith'?

7.  What is meant by a conditional offer of employment?

# Equal Opportunities in Recruitment and at the Workplace

As a general principle, employers are free to pick and choose to whom they offer employment and can reject an applicant for all manner of reasons including qualifications, attitude, references or suitability. A limitation on the freedom to employ is embodied within the Disabled Persons (Employment) Act 1958 which provides that an employer with twenty or more employees must in the absence of an exemption certificate, have a minimum of three percent of the workforce registered as disabled persons. Indeed in certain jobs, disabled persons must be given priority. Furthermore, rather than stigmatising an individual for life because of his past conduct, the Rehabilitation of Offenders Act 1974 allows past offenders who have criminal convictions to regard them as 'spent' in certain circumstances. Imprisonment for 30 months or more can never be spent and in a number of professions even spent offences must be disclosed for instance medicine, the law and teaching. If the offence is spent then on a job application the past conviction need not be mentioned and the failure to disclose it is no ground for an employer to discriminate against individuals by refusing to employ them or by dismissing them for past offences. It is reasonable of course for an employer to expect full disclosure of information on a job application and this would most certainly include a prospective employee providing details of criminal convictions which were not spent. A failure to fully disclose details of previous employment or trade union activities however may not be regarded as fatal to the validity of the contract of employment.

Also under the Trade Union and Labour Relations (Consolidation) Act 1992 it is unlawful to refuse employment because a person is or is not a trade union member. Also under the Act if a job advertisement indicates that trade union membership is a requirement and, then employment is refused it will be presumed to be for that reason if the applicant is not a trade union member.

Unfortunately you should appreciate that despite the superficial emphasis given to equal opportunities in business, industry and the professions, numerous studies have shown that discriminatory practices are still widespread in staff recruitment in the UK. Prospective employees are discriminated against for various reasons including racial origin, sex, sexuality, religion, age and disability. In an attempt to reduce and hopefully eradicate these practices, legislation has been passed in the UK to make sex, race and disability discrimination unlawful in employment.

As yet there is no legislation covering age and sexuality but following increasing pressure to make discrimination against the disabled unlawful. The Disability Discrimination Act was passed in 1995.

As a consequence of discriminatory recruitment practices we have a workforce in the UK divided by sex and race. Members of racial and ethnic minority groups generally occupy a low position in the occupational structure, concentrated in unskilled manual jobs and unrepresented in skilled manual jobs, managerial and professional occupations. They are found mainly in low paying industries such as clothing and textiles, in service sector jobs and in hospitals, shops and catering. Furthermore male black workers earn considerably less than male white workers and suffer a much higher rate of unemployment. Female workers are similarly concentrated in low paid unskilled jobs in a relatively small number of occupations including mainly clerical and related jobs and industries such as cleaning, catering and manufacturing. Because of child care responsibilities many women take part-time or casual work, often unskilled with poor pay and conditions. Economic trends in the labour market indicate an increase in the use of wage payment systems which encourage overtime, shift work and bonus payments, which necessarily discriminate against women. In addition to UK legislation on discrimination there is also European Community law which is directly applicable in UK Courts and also incorporated into United Kingdom law by Statute and by Statutory Instruments.

The right not to be discriminated against on the grounds of sex, race or marital status is one of the few individual employment rights that has not been weakened but rather strengthened over recent years. This has been mainly due to the impact of Community law and judgments of the European Court of Justice particularly in relation to gender.

The tendency to stereotype sexes and races and also perceive jobs to have male or female characteristics means that discrimination in Britain is still widespread. Nevertheless there are still relatively few complaints brought and success rates are consistently low. Studies have shown that there are numerous reasons for this, ranging from ignorance as to legal rights, insufficient support for complainants, difficulties of proof, low levels of compensation, and fear of victimisation. On the positive side however, there have been some notable successes recently which have caused change in employment practices. Unlawful discrimination has been found in a number of important equal pay cases, in relation to part-time workers, in unnecessary demands for British qualifications, in maximum age limits and in stringent language tests. There is no doubt that there is a change in attitude, for there is increasing evidence that employers are adopting equal opportunity employment practices. Equal opportunity is an important issue in industrial relations, and the law can act as an important stimulus to ensure that organisations adopt employment practices designed to combat discrimination.There is increasing pressure in Britain to extend the law to protect those in our society who are less favourably treated in employment because of their age, sexuality and religion.

# Sex and Race Discrimination

The *Race Relations Act* 1976 and the *Sex Discrimination Act* 1975 as amended, identify similar categories of unlawful acts in relation to discrimination, namely direct discrimination, indirect discrimination, and victimisation. It is convenient to set out these unlawful acts of discrimination in tabular form as a means of comparison.See the table below.

| Race Relations Act 1976 | Sex Discrimination Act 1975 |
|---|---|
| **Direct Discrimination** | |
| This occurs where one person: Treats another less favourably on racial grounds e.g. by segregating workers by race. | This occurs when one person: Treats another less favourably on the grounds of sex or marital status e.g. by providing women with different working conditions or selecting married women first for redundancy. |
| **Indirect Discrimination** | |
| This occurs where one person: Requires another to meet a condition which as a member of a racial group is less easily satisfied because: (a) the proportion of that group who can comply with it is smaller; and (b) the condition is to the complainant's detriment and is not justified. There would therefore be indirect discrimination if an employer required young job applicants to have been educated only in Britain. | This occurs where one person: Requires another to meet a condition which as a member of a particular sex or as a married person is less easily satisfied because: (a) the proportion of that sex or married persons who can comply with it is smaller; and (b) the condition is to the complainant's detriment and is not justified. There would therefore be indirect discrimination if an employer advertised for a clerk who is at least six feet tall. |
| **Victimisation** | |
| This occurs where one person: Treats another less favourably because the other has given evidence or information in connection with, brought proceedings under, or made allegations under the Act against the discriminator. | This occurs where one person: Treats another less favourably because the other has given evidence or information in connection with, brought proceedings under, or made allegations under the Act against the discriminator. |

The fact that both pieces of legislation are drafted in a largely similar fashion means that case-law involving the *Sex Discrimination Act* will also serve as an aid to the interpretation of the provision of The *Race Relations Act*. It is proposed to consider the provisions of both Acts in unison.

The *Sex Discrimination Act* 1975 is concerned with discrimination on grounds of gender either by males against females, or vice versa, and on grounds of marital status by treating a married person less favourably than an unmarried person.

In *Nemes v. Allen* 1977 an employer in an attempt to cope with a redundancy situation dismissed female workers when they married. This was held to be unlawful direct discrimination on the grounds of sex and marital status.

The *Race Relations Act* 1976 is more complex in relation to those it protects and is concerned with discrimination on racial grounds which, is based upon colour, race, nationality, or ethnic or national origin.

In *Race Relations Board v. Mecca* 1976 an individual telephoned to apply for a job but when the employer discovered the applicant was black, he put the telephone down. This was held to be unlawful direct discrimination as the applicant had been denied the opportunity to apply for a job on racial grounds.

While the definition of racial grounds is wide there is no reference to discrimination based on religion. It does seem however that some religions would normally be covered by the definition *colour, race, nationality, or ethnic or national origins.*

In *Seide v. Gillette Industries* 1980 the EAT held that the term *"Jewish"* can mean membership of a particular race or ethnic group as well as a religion. Also in *Mandla v. Dowell Lee* 1983 the House of Lords held that Sikhs were a racial group within the meaning of the Act.

In *Crown Supplies PGA v. Dawkins* 1993 the Court of Appeal held that Rastafarianism is no more than a religious sect and not an ethnic group for the purposes of the Race Relations Act.

In *Northern Joint Police Board v. Power* 1997 the EAT held that discrimination against an English person or a Scottish person based on national origins is discrimination on racial grounds within the meaning of the Race Relations Act. National origins in the definition has a different meaning from nationality which points to citizenship.

In relation to employment, any discriminatory practice which comes within any of the three categories (direct, indirect or victimisation) is unlawful and could occur in the recruitment process, at the workplace or in relation to the termination of employment.

It is therefore unlawful for a person in relation to employment by him to discriminate in the arrangements he makes for the purposes of deciding whom should be offered employment, the terms on which it is offered or by refusing to offer employment. Also where there is an existing employment relationship it is unlawful for an employer to discriminate in the way he gives access to opportunities for promotion, transfer, training or any other benefits, or refuses to afford such access. Furthermore, it is unlawful to discriminate by dismissing the complainant or subject him to any other detriment.

The Equal Treatment Directive has had considerable impact on UK discrimination law and in *Johnston v. Chief Constable of the RUC* 1987 it was confirmed that the Directive was unconditional and sufficiently precise to be used by an individual against a member state or in a national court. An individual could not enforce the Directive against a private employer however.

While it is clear that UK domestic law, particularly the *Sex Discrimination Act*, provides no redress to a person who suffers discrimination in employment because of sexual orientation there is a possibility that European Union law may provide a remedy.

In *P v. S* 1996 the European Court of Justice considered whether the Equal Treatment Directive applied to the case where a transsexual had been dismissed for a reason related to a sex change. Following the complainant's announcement that he intended to undertake gender reassignment, and the commencement of initial surgery, he had been dismissed. The European Court held that the Directive's principle of equal treatment required no discrimination on the grounds of sex and its scope should not be confined to a person's gender status but also to gender reassignment. A comparison should be drawn in such a case with the treatment the applicant received before undergoing the reassignment and after.

## Disability Discrimination

Disability discrimination legislation was introduced in 1995 in the form of the Disability Discrimination Act in force from December 1996 in relation to employment.

The extent of the Act has been the subject of much criticism particularly from groups representing the disabled.The Act applies to employers who have 20 or more employees,making it unlawful to discriminate against someone who has or who had a disability in recruitment or at the workplace.Disability is defined as *"a physical or mental impairment which has a substantial and long term adverse affect on the persons ability to carry out normal day to day activities"*.The unlawful forms of discrimination created under the legislation are *less favourable treatment*and *failure to make adjustments* both of which are potentially justifiable. Less favourable treatment is equivalent to direct discrimination with which we are already familiar.

In *Goodwin v. The Patents Office* 1999 the EAT reversed the tribunal's decision and found that a paranoid schizophrenic who was dismissed because of his behaviour was a disabled person under the 1995 Act. The EAT laid down helpful guidelines in determining disability stressing the need to interpret the Act with its object in mind.

An employer discriminates against a disabled person

For a reason which relates to the disabled person's disability;

- *the employer treats that person less favourably than he treats or would treat others to whom that reason does not or would not apply; and*

- *if, and only if, the employer cannot justify the less favourable treatment.*

- *An employer also discriminates against a disabled person if:*

- *the employer fails to comply with any duty to make adjustments imposed by the 1995 Act; and*

- *if, and only if, the employer cannot justify the failure to comply with the duty.*

A significant feature of both forms of unlawful discrimination is that they may be justified. Justification must however be by reference to a reason which is both substantial and material to the circumstances of the particular case.

There would be a prima facie case if failure to make adjustments when an employer makes arrangements or his premises have a feature which places the disabled person at a substantial disadvantage in comparison with non-disabled persons. In such circumstances the employer is under a duty to take such steps as are reasonable to stop the arrangements or remove the feature, for instance adjust the premises or alter terms and conditions of employment. In deciding whether it is reasonable for the employer to make the adjustments all the circumstances including cost and disruption should be taken account of.

## Time limits

Complaints of unlawful discrimination are made to the industrial tribunal and the time limit for presenting a complaint is three months from the act or last act of discrimination. The tribunal has power to permit a claim presented out of time if it is just and equitable in the circumstances. While time begins to run from the date of the last act complained of, the statutes also provide that *"any act extending over a period shall be treated as done at the end of the period"*.

In *Barclays Bank v. Kapur* 1991 an employer's refusal to give its Asian employees the same favourable pension terms as its European employees was held to be a continuing discriminatory act extending over the period of employment until the employment terminated.

Both the *Commission for Racial Equality* and the *Equal Opportunities Commission* have a role to play in encouraging, advising and providing financial assistance to prospective litigants. Furthermore only the Commissions may bring proceedings in respect of certain unlawful acts including discriminatory advertising, unlawful instruction to discriminate and unlawful inducements to discriminate.

## Direct Discrimination

Direct discrimination occurs where one person treats another less favourably on the grounds of sex, race or marital status. It may occur during the recruitment process, in a continuing employment relationship or on its termination. In an allegation of direct discrimination the formal burden of proof is on the complainant. The difficulty is of course that often direct evidence of discrimination is not available and consequently it is sufficient if the complainant can establish primary facts from which inferences of discrimination can be drawn. Evidence is necessary therefore to draw comparison with some person, actual or hypothetical who falls outside the relevant racial group or gender who was or would be treated differently by the employer.

A good example of this approach is provided by *Humphreys v. St. Georges School* 1978. Here a complainant woman teacher established the following primary facts. As an experienced teacher along with two less experienced and less well qualified male applicants, she had applied for two vacant posts within a school. These facts, along with the fact that both male applicants were appointed, were sufficient to raise a prima facie (on the face of it) case of sex discrimination. The Court of Appeal stressed that it is only in an "exceptional or frivolous case" that the complainant will fail to establish a prima facie case.

Once the primary facts indicate a prima facie case of discrimination therefore *"the employer is called on to give an explanation and, failing a clear and specific explanation being given by the employer to the satisfaction of the industrial tribunal, an inference of unlawful discrimination from the primary facts will mean the complaint succeeds"*.

Certainly there is no burden on an employer to disprove discrimination but once a prime facie case has been made out a tribunal is entitled to turn to an employer for an explanation of the facts.

While there is no legal obligation as a employer to give reasons for not selecting a candidate for a job the legislation provides that an employer could be required to complete a questionnaire in which reason for decision making are asked. The questionnaire is admissible in evidence and evasive responses by the employer in the questionnaire will influence the tribunal's findings.

Direct discrimination extends not only to acts based on sex but also decisions made on gender-based criteria. The intention of the alleged discriminator is immaterial and tribunals should focus simply on whether the act or decision satisfies the *"but for"* test. Would the complainant have received the same treatment but for his or her sex?

In *Ace Mini Cars Ltd. and Loy v. Albertie* 1990 the EAT held that there was unlawful direct discrimination by an employer who refused to employ a black female minicab driver because he believed that she would be the subject of racial attacks.

In *Horsey v. Dyfed CC* 1982 the act complained of was a refusal by the employer to recommend a married female social worker for secondment in London. The reason for the refusal was the fact that the wife's husband was already working in London and the employer believed that on completion of her secondment she would not return. This assumption the EAT held was one based on sex and in the circumstances constituted direct discrimination.

If the employer puts forward a number of reasons for his conduct, some valid and some discriminatory, then provided the discriminatory reason was an important factor, there is unlawful discrimination.

In *Owen & Briggs v. James* 1982 a case involving race discrimination, the complainant was a young black girl who had applied for a job as a shorthand typist with a firm of solicitors. She was interviewed for the job but rejected. When the post was re-advertised some months later she re-applied, but when she arrived for her interview the employer refused to see her. The same day a young white girl was appointed to the post despite the fact that her shorthand speed (35 words per minute) was far inferior to the complainant's (80 words per minute). It was also established that one of the partners of the firm had said to the successful candidate *"why take on a coloured girl when English girls were available"*. The applicant's unlawful direct discrimination on the grounds of race was upheld in the industrial tribunal and on appeal in the Employment Appeal Tribunal. On further appeal to the Court of Appeal by the employer, it was argued that there could be no unlawful discrimination unless the sole reason for the conduct was the racial factor. This argument was rejected, the court deciding that it is sufficient if race is an important factor in the employer's decision and accordingly the appeal was unsuccessful.

## Proof of Discrimination

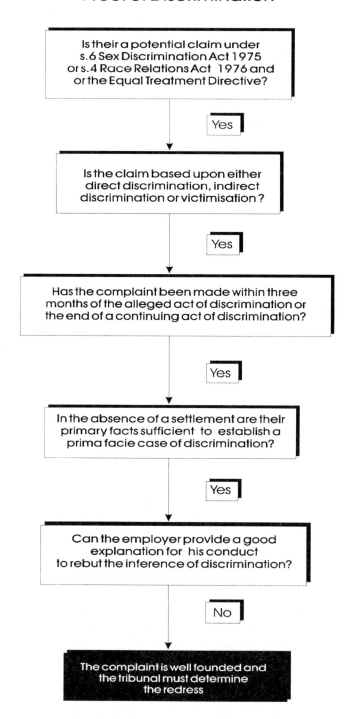

**Figure 5.3** *Proof of discrimination*

A useful tool to attack the credibility of the employer's denial of discrimination is statistical evidence. This is particularly so when the management decisions on matters such as promotion or access to benefits are based upon subjective criteria such as *excellence, potential* or *efficiency*. In *Owen & Briggs v. James* 1982 if the firm of solicitors could have shown that they had other black employees, this could have gone a long way towards enabling the tribunal to reach a contrary decision.

The types of questions asked in interviews may be of relevance to determine whether there has been discrimination.

> In *Saunders v. Richmond on Thames LBC* 1978 the EAT confirmed that it is not in itself unlawful to ask a question of a woman which would not be asked of a man. Here in an interview for a job as a golf professional, the female applicant was asked whether there were other female golf professionals and whether she thought that men would respond as well to a woman golf professional as to a man. Her claim of unlawful discrimination when she was not appointed did not succeed. The existence of direct discrimination depended upon whether she was treated less favourably on the grounds of sex than a man. Here, while the questions demonstrated an out of date attitude, the industrial tribunal was entitled to find that they were not asked with the intention of discriminating.

> In *Smith v. Safeways plc* 1996 the Court of Appeal provided guidance as to the circumstances in which an employer's dress and appearance code would constitute sex discrimination. Here the employer had adopted an appearance code which applied to delicatessen staff but which operated differently for men and women particularly in relation to length of hair. The complainant was dismissed for refusing to have his ponytail shortened claiming that a woman in a comparable position would surely be required to keep her hair clipped back. The majority of the EAT thought that the hair length rule was discriminatory and unlike a dress code it was a rule which extended beyond working hours. In an important judgment the Court of Appeal disagreed with EAT and emphasised that *"there is an important distinction between discrimination between the sexes and discrimination against one or the other of the sexes. Discrimination is not failing to treat men and women the same. If discrimination is to be established, it is necessary to show not merely that the sexes are treated differently, but that the treatment accorded to one is less favourable than the treatment accorded to another"*. Appearance codes should be even handed and will not be discriminatory if their content is different *"if they enforce a common principle of smartness or conventionality, and takes as a whole and not garment for garment or item by item, neither gender is treated less favourably in enforcing that principle."*

It is also unlawful to show an intention to commit an act of discrimination in relation to employment. Therefore the publication of an advertisement which invites applicants for the post of salesman or barmaids would constitute unlawful discrimination.

Under the EC *"Equal Treatment Directive"* the UK is required to implement the principle of *"equal treatment for men and women as regards access to employment"*. *The directive also provides that "there shall be no discrimination whatsoever on grounds of sex in the conditions, including selection criteria, for access to all jobs or posts".*

> In *Dekker v. Stichting Vormingscentrum voor Jonge Volwassenen Plus* 1991 the European Court of Justice held that it is a breach of the directive to refuse to employ a woman because she is pregnant despite the fact that this could mean grave financial consequences for the employer. If a woman receives less favourable treatment because she is pregnant this is direct discrimination and there is no need to establish that a man in comparable circumstances would not have been treated better.

EC law does not refer specifically to race discrimination but does provide that there should be no discrimination based on nationality within the Community in Article 48 of the Treaty of Rome Nationality is under the Race Relations Act 1976 included within the protection against discrimination on racial grounds.

## Sexual harassment

Sexual harassment while not referred to specifically in the Sex Discrimination Act has been held to constitute unlawful direct discrimination for which an employer could be made vicariously responsible. The EC Resolution on the Protection of the Dignity of Men and Women at Work defines sexual harassment as conduct of a sexual nature, or other conduct based on sex affecting the dignity of men and women at work which is

- unwanted, unreasonable and offensive to the recipient;

- used as a basis for employment decisions; or

- such as to create an intimidating, hostile or humiliating work environment for the recipient.

The code recommends that employers should facilitate a climate of opinion at work which inhibits sexual harassment. This could involve the issuing of a policy statement which is communicated and promoted through training. Also employers should adopt clear and precise procedures for dealing with complaints including sympathetic counsellors and incorporating independent and objective investigations.

A range of conduct which could constitute sexual harassment emerges from the case-law including:

- physical attacks;

- brushing against the victim;

- making suggestive statements or telephone calls;

- pressurising the victim to enter into a sexual relationship;

- sending the victim suggestive material.

An employer may be made vicariously liable for the action of his employees committed during the course of employment and this would include sexual harassment constituting unlawful discrimination. In relation to sex and race discrimination the expression "course of employment" is given an everyday meaning following the decision in *Jones v. Tower Boot 1997*. Sexual harassment constitutes less favourable treatment for the purpose of direct discrimination and also amounts to a detriment. Liability for sexual harassment is imposed vicariously on the employer. An action against the harasser could of course be brought in tort and if his conduct constitutes a criminal offence there could be a prosecution. Under the Sex Discrimination Act however he may only be made liable as a secondary party. This means that if the harasser is acting outside the course of employment the victim could not claim against him under the Sex Discrimination Act. Alternative actions in tort for the victim include assault and battery and more significantly the increasing recognition of a separate tort of harassment. The victim of sexual harassment at the workplace has a potential claim for unlawful direct sex discrimination, victimisation or even unfair dismissal where appropriate.

In *Insitu Cleaning Co Ltd. v. Heads* 1995 the EAT considered whether a single act of verbal sexual harassment is sufficient to found a complaint of direct sex discrimination. Here the complaint related to a derogatory remark made by a young male manager in a meeting and directed at the complainant, a female area supervisor. Despite the fact that the remark referred to complainant's breasts the employer argued that it was not sex related and therefore could not amount to direct discrimination. The EAT agreed with the tribunal that the employer was vicariously liable for the sexual harassment which constituted direct sex discrimination. *"The appellant's argument that the remark was not sex-related in that a similar remark could have been made to a man, for example, in relation to a balding head or beard, was absurd. A remark by a man about a woman's breasts cannot sensibly be equated with a remark by a woman about a bald head or a beard. One is sexual, the other is not. The industrial tribunal was entitled to find that the respondent suffered a detriment as a result of the remark." The EAT confirmed that one incident of verbal sexual harassment can constitute direct discrimination depending on its seriousness.*

It is inevitable that in a claim for sexual harassment the industrial tribunal will award compensation for hurt feelings and decide the level that is appropriate whether or not compensation is payable under any other head.

## Indirect Discrimination

Indirect discrimination, a more subtle form of discrimination than direct discrimination, is designed to cover overt yet not blatant acts of discrimination. A complaint of indirect discrimination could be brought under the UK legislation or the Equal Treatment Directive if applicable. Indirect discrimination occurs where a person requires another to meet a requirement or condition which as a member of a particular sex, race or marital status is less easily satisfied. This is because the proportion of those of that type who can comply with the requirement or condition is smaller, and it is to the complainant's detriment and not justifiable. It was held in *Perera v. Civil Service Commission* 1981 that in an allegation of indirect discrimination it is necessary to show that the requirement or condition is mandatory rather than one of a number of criteria which the employer would take into account.

> In *Meer v. London Borough of Tower Hamlets* 1988 the requirement was alleged to be job selection criteria, one of which was to have experience working in Tower Hamlets. The fact that this particular criteria was not mandatory meant that it could not constitute a requirement for the purposes of indirect discrimination.

For the purposes of showing that the proportion of the complainant's type who can comply with the condition is smaller there is no need to produce elaborate statistical evidence, but rather a common sense approach is to be encouraged. Nevertheless to succeed it is necessary to show that the proportion who can comply is considerably smaller.

> In *Price v. Civil Service Commission* 1978 the complainant alleged indirect discrimination on the grounds of sex because far fewer women than men could comply with the age limits of seventeen and a half to twenty eight to qualify as an eligible candidate for the executive officer grade. By comparing the proportion of qualified women with the proportion of qualified men, it is obvious that as a larger number of women of that age group will be likely to

be having or bringing up children, then the proportion who can comply with the age requirement is less. The EAT held that as the proportion who can comply in practice is less and the requirement was not justifiable, there was unlawful indirect discrimination.

Even where indirect discrimination is established there are no damages payable if it is shown to be unintentional. Where the fundamental purpose of the claim is to secure compensation for the victim there is little point in presenting a complaint where there was no intention to discriminate.

The definition of indirect discrimination also requires the complainant to have suffered a detriment and the requirement or condition must not be justifiable. The fact that the complainant has been adversely affected by the condition is sufficient to establish a detriment. It is open however for the defendant to show as a question of fact that in all the circumstances the requirement is justifiable.

In *Singh v. Rowntree Mackintosh* 1979 the complainant objected to a *no beard rule* operated by confectioners, which was alleged to be indirectly discriminatory against Sikhs. Here the EAT held that while the rule was discriminatory, it was a justifiable requirement on the grounds of hygiene, supported by medical advice, and therefore not unlawful. The burden of proof was on the employer to justify the requirement or condition and here the tribunal recognised that in adopting standards the employer must be allowed that independence of judgment as to what he believes is a common expedient in the conduct of his business. Certainly the requirement must be more than convenient but need not be necessarily essential.

# Victimisation

Unlawful discrimination in the form of victimisation is rarely alleged but is intended to protect employees at the work place who are given less favourable treatment by the employer for bringing a complaint under the legislation or giving evidence on behalf of a complainant. It is of course the fear of victimisation that often prevents employees from taking or supporting legal action against an employer. Possible victimisation and sensational reporting are reasons why many employees who suffer sexual harassment from a superior decide not to seek legal redress.

In *Northampton County Council v. Dattani* 1994 the complainant's employers promised to investigate a complaint that she has not been selected for a period of paid study leave. When the employer received notification of her claim under the Race Relations Act the investigation was dropped. The EAT upheld the tribunal's ruling of unlawful victimisation.

Both the *Equal Opportunities Commission*and the *Commission for Racial Equality* have issued Codes of Practice to provide guidance to employers as to how to avoid sex and race discrimination particularly in recruitment. While the Codes are not law they are admissible in evidence in any proceedings under the legislation. An employer who complies with the Codes is more likely to avoid liability. One recommendation that employers should adopt is to monitor their recruitment processes, for resultant statistics could be used to overturn an inference of discrimination. Certainly this would be useful information to enable an employer to comply with the questionnaire procedures available to an individual considering or having brought proceedings under the discrimination legislation.

## Lawful Discrimination in Recruitment

Both the *Sex Discrimination Act* 1975 and the *Race Relations Act* 1976 identify circumstances where it is lawful to discriminate in the recruitment of staff. They are referred to as instances of *genuine occupational qualification (goq)*.It should be stressed from the outset that goq defence only applies to the making of a job offer or access to promotional, training or other benefits.

The categories of genuine occupational requirements under the Sex Discrimination Act are as follows.

- where the job requires a man or woman for physiological reasons other than physical strength, or in dramatic performances or other entertainment for reasons of authenticity, e.g. female stripper or male model;

- where there are considerations of decency or privacy because the job is likely to involve physical contact with men in circumstances where they might reasonably object to it being carried out by a woman, e.g. male toilet attendant;

- where there are statutory requirements, e.g. woman may not work underground in coal mines. Following the Sex Discrimination Act1986 there are few statutory restrictions that survive;

- where the work location makes it impracticable to live elsewhere than the employer's premises and it is unreasonable to expect the employer to provide separate facilities for sleeping or sanitation;

- where the personal service is most effectively provided by a man or woman, e.g. a female social worker dealing with unmarried mothers;

- where the nature of the establishment within which the work is done requires the job to be held by a man because it is a hospital, prison or

other establishment for males, requiring special care, and it is reasonable
that the job should not be held by a woman;

- where the job needs to be held by a man because it is likely to involve the
  performance of duties outside the United Kingdom, in a country whose law
  and customs are such that the duties could not be effectively performed by
  a woman, e.g. Saudi Arabia;

- where the job is one of two to be held by a married couple.

The decency or privacy genuine occupational can only be raised if in the
circumstances it is not practical to employ a man or a woman.

In *Secretary of State for Scotland v. Henley* 1983 the decency or privacy goq
was raised as a defence to recruit a male as a hall governor in a men's prison
on the grounds that the job holder might have to be present in the toilet areas
or where the men might be in a state of undress. The fact that no objection
had been raised by the men helped the tribunal decide that the goq did not
apply.

The categories of genuine occupational requirement in race discrimination set out in
the Race Relations Act 1976 are

- drama and entertainment where the person of that racial group is required
  for reasons of authenticity, e.g. employing only a black actor to play the
  part of Martin Luther King;

- artist's or photographic models in order to achieve authenticity, e.g. a
  photograph depicting a national scene;

- bar or restaurant work where the setting requires an employee from a
  particular race, again for reasons of authenticity, e.g. Chinese Restaurant;

- the holder of the job provides persons of that racial group with personal
  services promoting their welfare and those services can most effectively be
  provided by a person of that racial group, e.g. a Bangladeshi social
  worker.

# Enforcement and Remedies

Discrimination law in employment may be enforced by individual complaint to an
industrial tribunal. Also both the *Commission for Racial Equality* and *Equal
Opportunities Commission*have a role to play in the enforcement of the law and
where certain unlawful acts are alleged, their role is an exclusive one. The process

and time limits relating to the presentation of a complaint were considered earlier. If despite the attempts at conciliation the complainant decides to go ahead, there is a special pre-tribunal procedure to assist in the effective presentation of the complaint and access to information.

The remedies available to a tribunal who felt that a complaint has been made out are:

- an order declaring the rights of the parties;

- an order requiring the respondent to pay the complainant damages subject to the upper limit for unlawful dismissal claims;

- a recommendation of action to be taken by the respondent to reduce the adverse effect of discrimination.

A failure by the respondent without reasonable justification to comply with a recommendation may lead to an award of increased compensation. In the case of indirect discrimination if the respondent proves that the requirement or condition was applied without any intention to discriminate then no compensation will be awarded.

The *Sex Discrimination and Equal Pay (Remedies) Regulations* 1993 formally removed the ceiling on compensation for unlawful sex discrimination and set out the method of calculating the interest. In 1993 it was also recognised that thousands of women who had been dismissed from the armed forces because they were pregnant can claim sex discrimination. The fact that the ceiling on compensation was lifted dramatically increased the significance of the potential claims and tens of thousands of pounds have been awarded. Tribunals have recognised that injury to feelings in such cases can include the emotional effect of discharge from the services evidenced by feelings of humiliation, isolation, loss of status and career aspirations and personal hurt.

The statutory ceiling of £11,000 on a compensatory award for race discrimination has also been lifted under the *Race Relations (Remedies) Act* 1994. If a complaint is well founded then the tribunal must decide whether it is *"just and equitable"* to award damages. The damages should reflect a sum of injury to feelings and the pecuniary loss subject to the ceiling. Damages for injury to feelings should compensate the complainant for the insult and humiliation suffered. In *Browne v. Cassell* 1972 Ld Diplock said that *"where salt is rubbed into the wound by high handed malicious insulting or offensive conduct additional compensation may be awarded by way of aggravated damages"*.

Pecuniary loss which is quantifiable includes the loss of wages, the loss of opportunity to work and the loss of advantage on the labour market.

In *British Gas Plc v. Shama* 1991 the Employment Appeal Tribunal confirmed that there are limits to the extent that tribunals have power to make recommendations to reduce the adverse affects of unlawful discrimination. While the tribunal had found that the complainant had been the victim of direct racial discrimination when she was not promoted, the tribunal had no power to recommend that she should be promoted to the next suitable vacancy.

If it does little else, discrimination law should stimulate equality of opportunity and act as a framework within which to identify barriers facing women and ethnic minority workers at work. As was suggested earlier, there is a view that there should be similar laws to protect people who are discriminated against because of their sexuality or age. Ethically, job applicants should be judged on the basis of their ability rather than their gender or racial origin.

## Test Questions

1.   What forms of discrimination are unlawful under UK law?

2.   What is meant by:
     *   direct discrimination?
     *   indirect discrimination?
     *   victimisation?

3.   When is there discrimination on racial grounds?

4.   How is disability defined under the Disability Discrimination Act?

5.   How does a complainant prove direct discrimination?

6.   Could an employee's dress code constitute sex discrimination?

7.   What type of conduct could constitute sexual harassment?

8.   Give five examples of lawful sex discrimination.

9.   What is the level of compensation for sex and race discrimination?

# Legal Formalities and the Contract of Employment

Contrary to popular belief, apart from merchant seamen and apprentices, there is no legal requirement that a contract of employment be in writing. While there are problems associated with identifying the terms of an oral agreement, nevertheless given the fluid nature of a contract of employment there is no guarantee that a requirement to reduce the original contract to writing would solve all the problems of interpreting its content. A contract of employment is unenforceable if it is illegal under statute or its objects are contrary to public policy at common law. *Illegality* can arise in the formation or during the continuance of the contract.

> In *Napier v. National Business Agency* 1951 the plaintiff was employed on a salary of thirteen pounds per week with six pounds a week expenses.Both parties were aware that genuine expenses would never exceed one pound. Following her dismissal the plaintiff claimed damages for wrongful dismissal. The Court held that the contract was unenforceable as contrary to public policy. By contracting as they had *"the parties to it were doing that which they must be taken to know would be liable to defeat the proper claim of the Inland Revenue and to avoid altogether, or at least to postpone, the proper payment of income tax"*.

# Statutory Statement of Terms and Conditions of Employment

Under s1 of the *Employment Rights Act* 1996 there is a statutory requirement on employers to provide their employees within two months of the commencement of employment with a written statement of the main terms of employment. The section originally applied to full-time employees (those engaged under an employment contract for sixteen hours or more a week) or part-time workers (engaged between eight and sixteen hours) after five years employment. Under the *Employment Protection (Part-time Employees) Regulations* 1995 the hours threshold has been removed and part-time employees are entitled to a statutory statement. Certain classes of employees are excluded from s.1 including registered dock workers, Crown employees and employees who work wholly or mainly outside Great Britain. The objective of s.1 is to ensure that employees have written confirmation and a source to scrutinise at least the main terms of their employment contracts. Employers can issue the statement in instalments but within the two months limit and the principal statement should contain certain information prescribed by section 1.

Particulars which must be included in the statutory statement include:

- reference to the parties and the dates on which the period of continuous employment began (stating whether a previous period of employment is included as part of continuous employment);

- the scale of remuneration and the method of calculation;

- the intervals at which remuneration is paid (whether weekly or monthly or some other period);

- the terms and conditions relating to hours of work;

- the terms and conditions relating to holidays and holiday pay (sufficient to enable the employee's entitlement to accrued holiday pay on the termination of employment to be precisely calculated);

- the terms and conditions relating to sickness or injury and sickness pay;

- the terms and conditions relating to pension and pension scheme;

- the length of notice which the employee is obliged to give and entitled to receive;

- the title of the job which the employee is employed to do or a brief description of the work;

- in addition every statement given shall include a note containing a specification of any disciplinary rules or reference to an accessible document containing such rules;

- the name of the person to whom the employee can apply if he is dissatisfied with any disciplinary decision relating to him;

- the name of the person to whom the employer can apply to seek the redress of any grievance;

- any collective agreement which directly affects terms and conditions of employment.

A section 1 statement may refer to other documents such as a staff handbook or written policy for the purposes of sickness provisions and pensions and a collective agreement for the purposes of notice provisions provided the employee has either a reasonable opportunity of reading such documents during the course of employment or they are readily accessible. It would also be permissible to include a disciplinary and grievance procedure in separate documents provided they are reasonably accessible.

There is no requirement to include a note on disciplinary proceedings in the written statement where the employer (together with any associated employer) has less than twenty employees on the date when the employee's employment began.

To satisfy the requirements of s.1 it is not sufficient simply to be told or shown the above particulars of employment. The employer must present the employee with a document containing the information or at least make such a document available for inspection (e.g. a collective agreement and a rule book). It should be stressed that a statutory statement is not the contract of employment but rather strong prima facie evidence of its terms. Certainly the mere acknowledgment of its receipt does not turn the statement into a contract.

Contractual terms we shall discover, are often the subject of change, in which case an employer is obliged to notify the employee of changes in the statement within one month of the change. An employer who fails to comply with obligations in relation to the statutory statement could be the subject of a complaint to the industrial tribunal. With no effective sanction available for employers who fail to comply with s.1, complaints to tribunals are rare, and only arise usually in connection with other complaints, for instance in relation to unfair dismissal. Finally it should be mentioned that those employers who provide their employees with a written contract of employment which covers all the matters which must be referred to in the statutory statement, do not have to supply their employees with a separate statutory statement. The writing should of course reflect what has been orally agreed by the parties.

## The Contents of a Contract of Employment

A contract of employment is composed of its *terms,* the mutual promises and obligations of the parties to it. Contractual terms may be 'express' and become part of the contract through the express agreement of the parties. Usually of course, there is simply agreement by the prospective employee to the standard terms dictated by the prospective employer or terms previously agreed between the employer and a trade union. Alternatively, contractual terms may be implied into the contract of employment by an external source. The major sources for implication we shall discover, are the courts and tribunals but occasionally terms are implied into contracts of employment by statutory provisions or through custom. Such mutual obligations have legal significance and a failure to comply with the requirement of a term of the contract could provide the innocent party with the option of securing legal redress. An action for breach of contract may be brought to secure damages against the party in breach of a contractual term. If damages would not suffice to provide a remedy, an injunction could be sought to restrain the breach of contract. In such circumstances an interlocutory (temporary) injunction is often sought as a remedy. One rarely used option for an employee who feels that his employer is unreasonably requiring him to do work which is not part of his contractual obligations is to seek an injunction to maintain the status quo at work. A further option for an employee in these circumstances is to apply to the High Court for a declaration as to the legal position.

In the majority of cases of conflict or dispute between the employer and employee, the true legal position can only be assessed by identifying and analysing the express terms of employment and any implied terms which have become incorporated into the contract.

# Express Terms

Earlier in the chapter we saw that the express terms of a contract of employment are those expressly agreed by the employer and employee, and may be in writing or may be purely oral. The statutory statement of the main terms and conditions of employment will normally provide sound evidence of the express terms. Even a job advertisement, an application form or a letter of appointment could contain contractual terms, as well as matters orally agreed in the interview. Express terms relate to matters such as *wages, hours, holidays, sick pay, job description, restraints, etc.* Of course, what has expressly been agreed by the parties may often require interpretation in the courts and industrial tribunals.

It is the ordinary courts that generally but now not exclusively deal with disputes surrounding the interpretation of the terms of a contract of employment based upon an action for breach of contract. The majority of employment disputes however relate to statutory employment rights such as unfair dismissal, redundancy and discrimination and they are heard by Employment Tribunals and on appeal by the Employment Appeal Tribunal.

Express terms must not be drafted so widely that all eventualities are covered and they become meaningless. An appropriate form of words should be used in order to achieve a realistic expectation of the employer's requirements. Express terms covering matters such as a staff mobility should be interpreted in a reasonable and humane way.

## Work rules

It is common practice in many spheres of employment for the employer to issue work rules by printing notices or handing out rule books. Such rule books often contain instructions as to time-keeping, meal breaks, disciplinary offences and grievance procedure, sickness and pension rights, job descriptions, and the employer's safety policy. Although there is still some doubt as to the legal status of work rules, the present view is that such documents are unlikely to contain contractual terms. One school of thought is that work rules should be regarded as *'conditions'* rather than *'terms'* of employment, hence the expression, *"terms and conditions of employment"* and as such they should be subject to unilateral change by the employer. For example, while the number of hours worked would normally be the subject of express agreement and constitute a contractual *'term'*, instructions as to when these hours should be worked will normally be contained in a rule book and as a *condition* be liable to unilateral change.

> In *Dryden v. Greater Glasgow Health Board* 1992 the EAT held that an employer was entitled to introduce a rule imposing a smoking ban at the workplace and the staff has no implied right to smoke. *"An employer is entitled to make rules for the conduct of employees in their place of work within the scope of the contract and once it was held that there was no implied term in the contract which entitled the employee to facilities for smoking, the rule against smoking was a lawful rule"*.

## Implied Terms

A contract of employment is composed of contractual terms which have been expressly agreed or incorporated into the contract by an external source such as a collective agreement, the custom and practice of a particular trade or business, or the common law. To have a full appreciation of the content of a contract of employment you should be aware of the role of the common law in defining rights and duties of employers and employees. In addition to a large number of common law rights and duties relating to such matters as good faith, confidentiality, health and safety, and obedience, there is an increased willingness of the courts and tribunals to imply terms into employment contracts to deal with issues such as trust and confidence, mutual respect and sexual harassment. Later when we consider the termination of employment, you will discover that the need to point to a clear breach of the contract of employment to establish a constructive dismissal has encouraged judicial ingenuity in incorporating implied terms which the court then declares that the employer has broken.

Apart from one notable exception in relation to equal pay, statute is not a major source of implied terms of employment. On the creation of a contract of employment, however, a number of statutory rights arise immediately, most of which are non-excludable and further rights attach to the contract after a period of continuous employment.

The fact that common law implied terms confer rights and impose duties on both parties to the employment relationship, suggests that they can be more meaningfully examined by considering each of them in turn in relation to both the employer and the employee. Most of the implied terms can be categorised under broad headings such as the wage/work bargain, health and safety, good faith, confidentiality, fidelity, and trust and confidence.

> In *Jones v. Associated Tunnelling Ltd.* 1981 the EAT held a contract of employment cannot simply be silent on the place of work. If there is no express term, it is necessary to imply some terms into each contract of employment laying down the place of work in order to give the contract *business efficacy.* The term to be implied in that which in all the circumstances the parties, if reasonable, would probably have agreed if they had directed their minds to the problem.

The role of the courts and tribunals in implying contractual obligations into contracts of employment is a fundamental feature of employment law. Employment conflicts sometime occur in determining whether a particular job function carries the status of a contractual duty even where job descriptions have been agreed by the parties. This conflict often arises during industrial action.

> In *Sim v. Rotherham Metropolitan Borough Council* 1986 the High Court had to decide whether the requirement of school teachers to provide cover for absent colleagues during normal school hours was an implied contractual obligation or merely a matter of goodwill. Refusing to provide such cover during a period of industrial action had led the employer to deduct an appropriate sum from the teacher's monthly salary. The High Court recognised that school teachers are a member of a profession and as such you would not expect their contracts to detail the professional obligations under their contracts. *"The contractual obligations of persons employed in a profession are defined largely by the nature of their profession and the obligations incumbent upon those who follow that profession. Teachers have a contractual obligation to discharge their professional obligations towards their pupils and their school. Cover arrangements, the court decided, are part of a teacher's professional obligations and the refusal of teachers to comply with them was a breach of contract".*

In a contract of employment there is an implied duty on the employee to provide personal service for which the employer is obliged to provide a wage. At the appointed time therefore, an employee is required to present himself for work and be ready and willing to perform at the direction of the employer. Absence from work without good reason would clearly constitute a breach of contract which would entitle the employer to adjust the wage accordingly. If the absence is due to industrial action there is an increasing tendency for the courts and tribunals to deal with conflict over entitlement to a wage or a partial wage by applying strict contractual principles.

The principle of *no work no pay* was reaffirmed by the House of Lords in *Miles v. Wakefield MBC* 1987. Here industrial action taken by Registrars involved them in refusing to carry out a proportion of their work, that of performing marriages, on Saturday mornings. While the Registrars attended for work on Saturdays and performed other duties the employer made it clear that wages would be deducted for Saturday morning hours if the employees were unwilling to perform the full range of their duties. The House of Lords upheld the employer's position that they were entitled to withhold the Saturday wage despite the fact that a substantial part of the work was performed. Lord Templeman said that *"in a contract of employment, wages and work go together, in an action by an employee to recover his pay he must allege and be ready to prove that he worked or was willing to work"*.

# Health and Safety

At common law an employer is obliged to provide his workers with a safe system of work. This common law duty encompasses an obligation to ensure that workers are provided with safe plant and appliances, appropriate safety equipment, safe work methods and safe fellow workers.

In *British Aircraft Corporation v. Austin* 1978 the employer was held to be in breach of his implied duty of safety when he failed to investigate a complaint relating to the suitability of protective glasses for an employee. This conduct was held to be a repudiatory breach of the contract of employment sufficient to entitle the employee to terminate the contract and regard himself as constructively dismissed.

More recently in *Waltons & Morse v Dorrington* 1997 the EAT held that an employer was in fundamental breach of a contract of employment by requiring a non smoking employee to work in an environment affected by the smoking habits of others.

Employees themselves are under a duty to co-operate in relation to their own safety and that of their work colleagues. An employee who is unduly negligent in the performance of his work will be in breach of his employment contract and while he is unlikely to be sued by his employer, this could be used as a justifiable reason for dismissal.

In *Lister v. Romford Ice and Cold Storage Co. Ltd.* 1957 the House of Lords held that an employee who caused injury by negligently reversing his lorry, was in breach of an implied term of his contract of employment.

Health and safety is covered in more depth later in the chapter.

# Employees duty of good faith (mutual trust and confidence)

Of all the implied duties, the duty of good faith and mutual respect is the most difficult to define precisely. This is because good faith is such a wide ranging concept and involves an obligation on the employee to respect confidences, obey reasonable instructions, take care of the employer's property, account for money received in the performance of duties and not disrupt the employer's business. An employer on the other hand must treat his workforce with respect, indemnify them for expenses incurred in the performance of their duties and when providing a reference, ensure that it is accurate and fair.

Any attempt by an employee to use his position for undisclosed personal gain, for instance by accepting bribes or making a secret commission, will constitute a breach of the employment contract. The origins of this implied duty can be traced back to nineteenth century case-law.

In *Boston Deep Sea Fishing and Ice Company v. Ansell* 1889 an employee who received secret commissions from other companies for placing orders with them was held to be in breach of this implied duty of his contract of employment.

Part of the obligation of good faith requires an employee to submit to his employer's control and this involves obeying reasonable orders. What would constitute a reasonable instruction depends upon an objective interpretation of the employee's contractual duties both express and implied.

In *Pepper v. Webb* 1969 the head gardener who responded to the request to plant some flowers with the words, *"I couldn't care less about your bloody greenhouse or your sodding garden"* was held to be in breach of the implied duty to obey reasonable instructions.

Even if an instruction is within the scope of an employee's duties, it may not be reasonable if it involves a risk of serious injury or a breach of the criminal law. Certainly the duty of good faith would require an employee to be flexible and move with the times, so that an instruction to adopt work techniques involving new technology, after proper training has been given, would normally be regarded as reasonable.

In *Cresswell v. Board of Inland Revenue* 1984, Walton J said that *"there can really be no doubt as to the fact that an employee is expected to adapt himself to new methods and techniques introduced in the course of employment"*.

It is important to distinguish however, between a change in work methods and change in the job itself which if not authorised or agreed to, could not be unilaterally imposed without a possible claim for a redundancy payment or compensation for unfair dismissal. A wilful refusal to obey a reasonable order could lead ultimately to a dismissal for misconduct.

Employees have an implied obligation to take care of their employer's property. An employee who negligently allows his employer's property to be stolen or causes it wilful damage will be in breach of his employment contract and liable to dismissal.

Good faith most certainly includes respecting confidences so there would be a clear breach of the contract of employment if the employee revealed confidential information relating to any aspect of his employer's business to a competitor, or made use of such information for his own purposes.

## Employer's duty of good faith

It is only relatively recently that the courts and tribunals have recognised that an employee's duty to trust and respect his employer is in fact a mutual obligation in an employment relationship.

> In *Woods v. W H Car Services (Peterborough) Ltd.* 1982 the EAT recognised that in every employment contract there is an implied term of great importance, that of trust and confidence between the parties. Such a term requires that employers *"will not, without reasonable and proper cause, conduct themselves in a manner calculated or likely to destroy or damage the relationship of trust and confidence between employer and employee"*.

Employers who have been guilty of conduct such as verbal or physical abuse of their employees or unilateral attempts to impose unreasonable changes in employment terms have found themselves in breach of this implied term.

> In *Hilton International Hotels (UK) Ltd. v. Protopapa* 1990 the complainant resigned from her job as a telephone supervisor in one of her employer's hotels when she was severely reprimanded by her manager. The reason for the reprimand was her failure to obtain permission before making a dental appointment and the fact that it was *"officious and insensitive"* constituted a repudiatory breach of her contract of employment. The EAT confirmed that she was *"humiliated, intimidated and degraded to such an extent that there was a breach of trust and confidence which went to the root of the contract"*.

> In *Malik v. BCCI* 1997 the House of Lords held that employees could recover damages from their employer because of the stigma attaching to their reputation as former employees of BCCI put them at a disadvantage on the labour market. An employer which operates a business in a dishonest and

corrupt manner is in breach of the implied contractual term of trust and confidence.

The notion that an employee is under the control of his employer carries with it an obligation to indemnify the employee for expenses incurred in the performance of his duties. Furthermore an employer may be made vicariously liable for the wrongs committed by an employee during the course of his employment.

> In *Scally v. Southern Health and Social Services Board* 1991 the House of Lords held that there is an implied term in a contract of employment imposing a duty on the employer to take reasonable steps to provide an employee with certain information. Here the information in question related to pension rights which had been negotiated on the employee's behalf but they had not been informed of the benefits they conferred. Four junior doctors sued their employer for loss sustained by them because of the failure of their employer to give them notice of the right to purchase added years of pension entitlement. *"It is necessary to imply an obligation on the employer to take reasonable steps to bring a term of the contract of employment to the employee's attention so that he may be in a position to enjoy its benefit where the terms of the contract have not been negotiated with the individual employee but result from negotiation with a representative body".*

## Payment of Wages

The main statutory rights in relation to the payment of wages are:

- the right to a minimum wage

- the right to an itemised pay statement

- the right not to suffer unlawful deductions of wages.

The right to a minimum wage was introduced into the UK law by the National Minimum Wage Act 1998. The minimum hourly rate was set at £3.60, and for workers between the ages of 18 and 21 £3.00. The Act applies to 'workers' rather then just 'employees' and so extends to contractors providing personal services. The aim is to *"provide workers across Britain for the first time with a floor below which their wage will not fall, regardless of where they live or work, the sector or size of company in which they work".*

While there is no legal requirement that an employment contract be in writing, under s.1 of the Employment Rights Act 1996, an employee is entitled to be supplied with a written statement of the main terms and conditions of employment. The 1996 Act further provides that every employee has the right to be given a written itemised pay statement at the time or before wages or salary are paid. Following the Employment Protection (Part-time Employees) Regulation 1995, part-time employees are also entitled to a written itemised pay statement. Certain particulars must be included on the statement:

- the gross amount of the wages or salary;

- the amount of any variable and fixed deduction and the purpose for which they are made;

- the net amount of the wages or salary; and

- where different parts of the net amount are paid in different ways, the amount and method of each part-payment.

In relation to fixed deductions a further option is for the employer to provide his employees with a standing statement of fixed deductions. If this statement is kept up to date on an annual basis then the employee need only include the aggregate amount of fixed deductions in the pay statement. If an employer fails to comply with the obligation to provide a complete and accurate itemised pay statement, the remedy for an employee is to make an application to the industrial tribunal within three months for a declaration to that effect.

Under the 1996 Act an employer shall not make any deduction from any wages of any worker employed by him unless the deduction is authorised:

(a)    by statute or a provision of the worker's contract; or

(b)    the worker has previously signified in writing his agreement or consent to the making of the deduction.

Lawful deductions are those which are:

- authorised by statute; or

- covered by a contractual term; or

- previously consented to in writing.

Statutory authorisation would cover deductions for income tax, national insurance and attachment of earnings orders. Contractual authorisation means a written contractual term transferred to the worker prior to the deduction. The term must authorise the deduction so that a tribunal could be called on to determine whether it is justified.

## Time off for Trade Union Officials to carry out Trade Union Duties

The right to paid time off for trade union officials is now contained in the Trade Union and Labour Relations (Consolidation) Act 1992. Under s.168(1) An employer shall permit an employee of his who is an official of an independent trade union recognised by the employer to take time off during his working hours for the purpose of carrying out any duties of his, as such an official, concerned with

- negotiations with the employer related to or connected with matters relating to collective bargaining in relation to which the trade union is recognised by the employer, or

- the performance on behalf of employees of the employer of functions related to or connected with matters falling within that provision which the employer has agreed may be so performed by the trade union.

The type of matters which an offical may have to deal with relate to:

- terms and conditions of employment, or the physical conditions in which any workers are required to work;

- engagement or non-engagement, or termination or suspension of employment or the duties of employment, of one or more workers;

- allocation of work or the duties of employment between workers or groups of workers;

- matters of discipline;

- a worker's membership or non-membership of a trade union;

- facilities for officials of trade unions; and

- machinery for negotiation or consultation, and other procedures, relating to any of the above matters, including the recognition by employers or employers' associations of the right of a trade union to represent workers in such negotiation or consultation or in the carrying out of such procedures.

In *Ryford Ltd. v. Drinkwater* 1996 the EAT considered the operation of s.168 in relation to the right of a trade union official to take time off for the purpose of trade union duties. To establish a breach of s.168 the EAT prescribed that the official had to establish on the balance of probabilities, that a request for time off was made, that it came to the notice of the employer's appropriate representative, and that they either refused it, ignored it or failed to respond to it. Obviously the employer must be aware of the request before he can "fail" to *"permit"* time off.

## Time off for Trade Union Members to take part in Trade Union Activities

A member of a recognised independent trade union has the right to be given reasonable time off during working hours to take part in a trade union activity.

Under s.170(1) An employer shall permit an employee of his who is a member of an independent trade union recognised by the employer in respect of that description of employee to take time off during his working hours for the purpose of taking part in–

- any activities of the union, and

- any activities in relation to which the employee is acting as a representative of the union.

Following the Employment Protection (Part-Time Employees) Regulations 1995 this right applies to all employees whether or full-time or part-time.

Specifically excluded from the expression 'trade union activity' is industrial action whether or not in contemplation or furtherance of a trade dispute.

An employee, whether full-time or part-time, is entitled by virtue of the Employment Rights Act 1996 to take time off during working hours to undertake certain public duties such as in the capacity of a Justice of the Peace or a local councillor. Once again the amount of time off must be reasonable bearing in mind the amount of time off needed to perform the public duty and the effect of the absence on the employer's business.

## Time off to look for work, arrange for training or deal with a domestic incident

If an employee is dismissed by reason of redundancy rather than being warned of impending redundancy, he is entitled, before his notice period expires, to be allowed to have a reasonable amount of paid time off during working hours to search for new employment or make arrangements for training for future employment. If such time off is unreasonably refused, the employee may within three months present a complaint to an industrial tribunal who may declare that fact if they feel the claim is well founded, and award compensation. To qualify for this right the employee must have been employed for a continuous period of two years at the time the notice period expires. There is a new right under the Employment Relations Act 1999 for employees to be given reasonable (unpaid) time off during working hours "in order to deal with a domestic incident". This is an incident which occurs in the employee's home or which affects a member of the family. Death or illness would certainly qualify as a domestic incident where an employee would be entitled to leave.

## Test Questions

1. What is the requirement of s.1 of the Employment Rights Act 1996?

2. Give eight examples of particulars which must be included in the statutory statement.

3. What is meant by:
   * express terms of employment?
   * implied terms of employment?

4. Why is it necessary to imply terms into a contract of employment?

5. What is meant by:
   * employee's duty of good faith?
   * employer's duty of good faith?

6. What are the employees statutory rights in relation to the payment of wages?

7. When is:
   * a trade union official entitled to time off work?
   * a trade union member entitled to time off work?
   * an employee entitled to time off work?

## Health and Safety at Work

Certainly a high priority should be given to the aim of securing a safe working environment. While health and safety law is embodied within the UK legislation and common law it is an area of law that has been subjected to dramatic change due to our membership of the European Union.

In the United Kingdom legal intervention in the field of health and safety has a long history and the earliest examples of employment legislation, the nineteenth century Factories Acts, were designed to ensure that a slender cushion of legislative protection was provided for those categories of workers at particular risk. The criminal codes in relation to health and safety law were contained in numerous statutes and statutory instruments e.g. the Factories Act 1961, the Office Shops and Railway Premises Act 1963. Eventually in 1972 the Robens Committee on Safety and Health at work criticised this fragmented state of the law. As a result of the Robens Committee recommendations the Health and Safety at Work Act 1974 was passed.

The aims of the Act were to:

- lay down general duties applicable across the industrial spectrum;

- provide a unified system of enforcement under the control of the Health and Safety Executive and local authorities;

- create the Health and Safety Commission to assist in the process of changing attitudes and producing detailed regulations applicable to each industrial sector backed up by codes of practice designed to give guidance as to how general duties and specific regulations could be satisfied.

By imposing legal duties on employers, employees, contractors, manufacturers and others backed up by criminal sanctions, the 1974 Act is designed to achieve minimum standards of conduct and so minimising the risk of injury and enhancing the welfare of those at the workplace. In addition to criminal sanctions however the possibility of civil redress must also be considered so that those injured at the workplace have a further avenue of redress to secure compensation by relying on common law principles relying on the tort of negligence and breach of statutory duty.

As previously stated UK businesses also operate in a European legal framework and health and safety issues are an established part of European Community social policy. Since the adoption of the Single European Act 1986 the regulation of Health and Safety at work in the UK as been refined by European Community law initiatives. In 1990 the Chairman of the Health and Safety Commission said that *"the European Community has now to be regarded as the principal engine of health and safety law affecting the UK not just in worker safety but also major hazards and most environmental hazards"*. Article 22 of the Single European Act 1986 added a new Article 118A to the Treaty of Rome and so introduced a new concept *"the working environment"*.

Article 118A provides that *"Member States shall pay particular attention to encouraging improvements especially in the working environment, as regards the health and safety of workers and shall set as their objective the harmonisation of conditions in this area, while maintaining the improvements made"*.

## Working Time Regulations

The Working Time Directive had been passed under the qualified majority procedure as a health and safety measure and this was challenged by the UK government which had voted against it. In November 1996 the European Court of Justice ruled that the directive was lawfully introduced and should be incorporated into UK law. (This has now been achieved by the Working Time Regulations 1998.)

The 1998 regulations apply to 'workers' which include not only employees but contractors providing personal services such as agency workers. The new rights include:

- a limit of 48 hours on average weekly working time (from which a worker can voluntarily opt out),

- a minimum of three weeks paid annual leave (rising to four weeks in November 1999) subject to a 13 week qualifying period,

- a right to a daily rest period after 11 consecutive hours,

- a weekly rest period of 24 hours,

- a daily rest period of 20 minutes when the working day is more than 6 hours,

- a limit of an average eight hours work in each 24 hour period for night workers,

- a right to a "health assessment" before being required to perform night work.

There are a number of exemptions of course including transport, sea fishing and doctors in training. The Act encourages employers and trade unions to collectively agree how the regulations are to apply in their own particular circumstances. The regulations are enforceable by individual complaint to the Employment Tribunal and in some cases action may be taken by the Health and Safety Executive.

# Health and Safety Regulations

In order to implement numerous European directives a number of regulations have been produced clarifying new law and repealing out of date law. In addition, practical guidance in the form of codes of practice have also been produced to ensure compliance with the regulations which have been in force from the beginning of 1993.

The regulations apply to virtually all work activities and place duties on employers in relation to their employees and in some circumstances to the public and self employed contractors in relation to themselves and others who may be affected by their acts or omissions. The regulations are very comprehensive however it should be stressed that the main focus is initially to promote awareness and enforcement is not likely unless:

- *the risks to health and safety are immediate and evident, or*

- *employers appear deliberately unwilling to recognise their responsibilities to ensure the long term health, safety and welfare of employees and others affected by their activities.*

## Management of health and safety at work regulations 1992

These regulations are aimed at improving health and safety management and apply to almost all work activities in Great Britain and offshore. Under them employers are required to adopt a well organised and systematic approach to comply with their statutory duties in relation to health and safety. In pursuing this objective employers are required to:

- carry out a risk assessment of health and safety so that preventive and protective measures can be identified. While there is an existing obligation in the Health and Safety at Work Act for employers of five or more employees to prepare a written health and safety policy there is now an additional obligation on them to record the findings of the risk assessment.

- make arrangements for putting into practice the health and safety measures that follow from the risk assessment. These arrangements will include planning, organisation, control, monitoring and review and must be recorded by employers with five or more employees.

- appoint competent people to help devise and implement the appropriate measures and ensure that employees including temporary workers are given appropriate health and safety training and understandable information.

- provide appropriate health surveillance for employees and set up emergency procedures where the risk assessment shows it to be necessary.

- consult employees safety representatives, provide facilities for them and co-operate with other employers sharing the same working environment.

## Provision and use of work equipment regulations 1992

Under the regulations general duties are placed upon employers in relation to equipment used at work and minimum requirements are identified to apply to all industries.

The general duties will require an employer to:

* assess working conditions in particular risks and hazards when selecting work equipment.

* ensure that equipment is suitable for its use and that it conforms with EC product safety directives.

* give staff adequate information, instruction and training and maintaining equipment in efficient working order and a good state of repair.

* In addition to the general duties the regulations also contain specific requirements in relation to equipment which will replace existing regulations. They include:

* guarding of the dangerous parts of machines.

* protection against specific hazards such as articles or substances, fire risks and explosion.

* ensuring adequate lighting, maintenance, warnings, stability, control systems and control devices.

## Manual handling operations regulations 1992

These regulations are aimed at preventing injuries which occur at the workplace due to the mishandling of loads by incorrect lifting, lowering, pushing, pulling, carrying or simply moving them about. Such operations should have been identified in the risk assessment. The regulations require an employer to ensure that:

* there is a genuine need to move a load and that manual handling is necessary rather than mechanical means

* the weight size and shape of the load is assessed along with the working environment and the handler's capabilities

- in so far as is reasonably practicable the risk of injury is reduced by for example reducing the load, employing mechanical means or training the handler.

## Workplace (health safety and welfare) regulations 1992

The aim of these regulations is to replace numerous parts of existing legislation including the Factories Act 1961 and the Office Shops and Railway Premises Act 1963. They cover many aspects of health safety and welfare at the workplace in particular the working environment which includes temperature, ventilation, lighting, room size, work stations and seating. Facilities at the workplace are covered which includes toilets, washing, eating and changing facilities, drinking water, clothing storage, rest areas and facilities along with the need for cleanliness and effective removal of waste. Specific aspects of safety are included in particular relating to safe passage of pedestrians and vehicles, windows and skylights, doors, gates and escalators and floors.

## Personal protective equipment at work regulations 1992

By these regulations some old law relating to PPE is replaced but more recent legal rules, in particular the Control of Substances Hazardous to Health or Noise at Work Regulations, remain in force. Personal protective equipment includes protective clothing, eye foot and head protection, harnesses, life jackets and high visibility clothing. Where risks are not adequately controlled by other means there is a duty to provide PPE free of charge for employees exposed to risks. The PPE provided must provide effective protection as appropriate to the risks and working conditions, take account of the worker's needs and fit properly. Further regulations are necessary to comply with a separate EC directive on the design certification and testing of PPE. The present regulations require an assessment of risks to determine the suitability of PPE; the provision of storage facilities; adequate training information and instruction; appropriate methods of cleansing maintenance and replacement and effective supervision to ensure its proper use.

## Heath and safety (display screen equipment) regulations 1992

These regulations apply where an individual habitually uses display screen equipment as a significant part of normal work. Duties are imposed on employers if equipment is used for the display of text, numbers and graphics but some systems are excluded including transport systems for public use, cash registers, window typewriters and portable systems not in prolonged use. The duties require employers to:

- assess display screen work stations and reduce risks revealed.

- ensure that minimum requirements are satisfied in relation to the display screen, keyboard, desk and chair, working environments and task design and software

- plan the work so that there are changes of activity and appropriate breaks and

- provide information and training for display screen users, eye testing and special spectacles if needed.

There is no doubt that under these regulations in particular, employers will have to incur considerable expense to ensure that equipment meets the basic minimum requirements. Existing work stations must be brought up to and the costs of eye testing spectacles and insurance must all be borne by the employer.

## Enforcement of Health and Safety Law

Enforcement of the safety legislation is in the hands of the *Health and Safety Executive* and local authorities which have a number of powers at their disposal. The main power is to appoint inspectors who have authority to enter premises, take samples and require information to be given. The breach of a general duty or a specific regulation under the Health and Safety legislation is a criminal offence. This can lead to a prosecution in the criminal courts. Less serious offences are dealt with summarily in the Magistrates Court and those of a more serious nature are tried on indictment in the Crown Court. Conviction in *summary* proceedings carries a fine of up to £5000, or for an *indictable* offence, an unlimited fine and/or up to two years imprisonment. The fundamental aim of those enforcing the law is to encourage a positive attitude to health and safety at the workplace rather than to take numerous employers through the criminal courts. There is no doubt however that some employers resent the economic cost of health and safety and it may only be the threat of criminal prosecution, that will cause the more recalcitrant employers to respond. There is no doubt however that enforcement remains inadequate due to under resourcing of the inspectorate.

One of the major innovations of the Health and Safety at Work Act was the introduction of *constructive sanctions*. A Health and Safety Inspector who believes that an employer is contravening one of the statutory provisions may serve on that person an *improvement notice* requiring that the contravention be remedied within a specific period of not less than twenty one days. The notice will specify the provision which is contravened and state how it is being broken. In cases where the contravention involves an immediate risk of serious injury, the inspector may serve a *prohibition notice* which will direct that the particular activity is terminated until the contravention is rectified. Such a notice may take immediate effect or be deferred for a specified time. Failure to comply with a prohibition notice, for example by using a machine which has been identified as a serious source of danger, is an offence triable on indictment in the Crown Court.

While liability is generally associated with fault the courts have recently confirmed that even where there was little evidence of personal blame, an occupier of factory premises may still be held liable under the Factories Act 1961 if he fails to make his premises as safe as is reasonably practicable for all persons who may work there, even if they are not employees.

## General duties

Most of the general duties contained in the 1974 Act impose on a number of different categories of person, a standard of care based on the idea of reasonable practicability. The most important general duty is that contained in s.2(1). Section 2(2) identifies matters to which the duty extends:

*Under s.2(1) It shall be the duty of every employer to ensure, so far as is reasonably practicable, the health, safety and welfare at work of all his employees.*

*Under s.2(2) This duty extends to*

(a)    *the provision of such information, instruction, training and supervision as is necessary to ensure, so far as is reasonably practicable, the health and safety at work of his employees;*

(b)    *so far as is reasonably practicable as regards any place of work under the employer's control, the maintenance of it in a condition that is safe and without risks to health and the provision and maintenance of means of access to and egress from it that are safe and without such risks;*

(c)    *the provision of such information, instruction, training and supervision as is necessary to ensure, so far as is reasonably practicable, the health and safety at work of his employees;*

(d)    *so far as is reasonable practicable as regards any place of work under the employer's control, the maintenance of it in a condition that is safe and without risks to health and the provision and maintenance of means of access to and egress from it that are safe and without such risks;*

(e)    *the provision and maintenance of a working environment for his employees that is, so far as is reasonably practicable, safe, without risks to health, and adequate as regards facilities and arrangements for their welfare at work.*

The scope of the general duty, contained in s.2, qualified by the words *"reasonably practicable"* is difficult to determine and little guidance has been provided by the courts. However the meaning of this phrase is obviously crucial in determining the scope of an employer's duty. It would be wrong to assume that it imposes a standard of care comparable with the duty to take reasonable care at common law. The statutory duty requires the employer to take action to ensure health and safety unless, on the facts, it is impracticable in the circumstances. This has been taken to mean that in determining the scope of general duties cost-benefit considerations must be taken account of.

In *Associated Dairies v. Hartley* 1979 the employer supplied his workers with safety shoes which they could pay for at £1 per week. An employee who had not purchased the shoes suffered a fractured toe when the wheel of a roller truck ran over it. There was an obvious risk to workers from roller trucks in the employer's warehouse. Accordingly an improvement notice was served on the employer requiring him to provide his employers with safety shoes free of charge (estimated cost £20,000 in the first year and £10,000 per annum thereafter). The Court of Appeal held that while such a requirement was practicable in all the circumstances of the case, it was not reasonably so, bearing in mind the cost in relation to the risk of injury. The improvement notice was therefore cancelled, the court confirming that in relation to the general duty, practicability alone is not the test, for it is qualified by the term *"reasonable"*.

More recently there is evidence that the courts have adopted a more positive approach to the interpretation of the general duties under s.2(1) and s.2(2).

In *R. v. Associated Octel Co. Ltd.* 1994 the Court of Appeal gave further guidance as to reasonable practicability stressing the subjective nature of the concept *"what is reasonably practicable for a large organisation employing safety officers or engineers contracting for the services of a small contractor on routine operations may differ markedly from what is reasonably practicable for a small shopkeeper employing a local builder on activities on which he has no expertise"*

## Duty to non-employees

Both employers and those who are self employed are required, in the words of s.3(1), to *"conduct their undertakings in such a way, in so far as is reasonably practicable, to protect persons other than their own employees from risks to their health and safety."* This would require an employer to give anyone who may be affected, information relating to health and safety risks arising from the way in which the business is run.

> In *Carmichael v. Rosehall Engineering Works Ltd.* 1983 an employer was found to be in breach of his duty under s.3(1) when he failed to provide two youths on a work experience programme with suitable clothing for carrying out a cleaning operation using flammable liquid. The failure to give proper instruction and information, as to the possible risks to their health and safety, was a factor which led to the death of one of the boys when his paraffin soaked overalls burst into flames.

Those to whom an employer owes a duty under s.3(1) include contractors and employees of independent contractors.

In determining reasonable practicability under s.3(1) it is necessary to consider the extent of control over the contractor, the requirement of instruction as to work methods and safety measures, the degree of risk and the competence and experience of the workmen.

Under the Act proceedings may be taken against a director of a company which, with his consent or due to his negligence committed an offence. In a prosecution brought against Mr Chapman in 1992 whose company had contravened a *prohibition notice*, the Crown Court used its powers under the Company Directors Disqualification Act 1986 to ban him from being a company director for two years in addition to a £5,000 fine and a £5,000 fine on the company.

## Duty for premises and machinery

By virtue of s.4 a general duty is imposed on those who control work premises to ensure *so far as is reasonably practicable the safety of the premises, any means of access and exit from the place of work, and of any plant or substance provided for use on the premises.*

The duty extends to persons in control of non-domestic premises which are made available as a place of work and is owed to those who are not their employees.

A successful prosecution under s.4(2) requires the proof of:

- unsafe premises and a risk to health;

- the identity of the individual having control of the premises; and

- the fact that the person in control ought reasonably to have taken measures to ensure safety.

A further general duty imposed on those who control work premises is to *use the best practicable means to prevent the emission of offensive substances and to render harmless and inoffensive those substances emitted.*

Those who design, manufacture, import or supply any article for use at work are required under s.6 in so far as is reasonably practicable to ensure the article's safety, to carry out necessary testing and examining and provide sufficient information about the use of the article at work to render it safe and without risks to health.

Finally there is a general duty on every employee while at work under s.7 to take reasonable care for the health and safety of himself and of other persons who may be affected by his acts or omissions at work and to cooperate with employers in the discharge of their health and safety duties. Those employees who act in disregard of health and safety should be counselled but in the end dismissed if they are a danger to themselves or others. Wilful breaches of a safety rule, for instance a no smoking policy was has been held to be a justifiable reason for dismissal.

Certainly there is no room to be complacent about compliance with health and safety law for of the 5000 or so deaths at the workplace over the last ten years in the UK, the Health and Safety Executive estimated that over 70% are due to the failure of companies to provide workers with adequate safety equipment, training, supervision and instruction as they are bound to do under the legislation. Lack of enforcement, particularly against individual directors or managers is a particular cause for concern and the small number of prosecutions that are brought against companies only result in a limited fine in the Magistrates Court.

## Civil Redress

A further major objective of the law relating to health and safety at the workplace is to provide a means by which those who have suffered injury may recover compensation. Since the mid 1960s, state benefit has been available for employees who suffer injury from accidents arising out of and in the course of employment or contract prescribed industrial diseases. If injury is caused through fault however, whether of the employer or a fellow worker, an injured person can bring a claim for damages through the courts. If it can be shown that injury has occurred as a result of a failure to comply with a regulation under the Health and Safety at Work Act 1974 or some other statutory obligation, for instance under the Factories Act 1961, then a claim could be brought for damages under a civil action for breach of statutory duty. This action has the status of a separate tort and can provide a means of redress for persons who suffer harm as a result of a breach of a duty imposed by statute.

An alternative course of action for an employee who has suffered harm due to the fault of his employer or a fellow employee is to base a claim on common law negligence. Under the common law, an employer owes a legal duty of care to ensure the health and safety of his employees and this duty takes effect on an implied term of the contract of employment. An employer is required to take reasonable care with regard to the safety of his employees by providing a safe system of work. The provision of a safe system of work involves an obligation to provide safe fellow employees, safe plant and equipment, safe working premises and safe working methods. If an employer is in breach of his common law duty to take reasonable care, and damage in the form of injury is caused as a result, he will be liable.

As far as safety equipment is concerned, the contemporary view seems to be that the common law duty to make it available and ensure that employees are aware of it does not necessarily carry with it any further obligation to inspect it or insist that it is worn. Obviously there is some obligation on the employee to take some responsibility for his own safety by ensuring that safety equipment is renewed when necessary.

In *Pape v. Cumbria County Council* 1991 the plaintiff had been employed as a cleaner by the council for many years and her job involved the use of chemical cleaning materials and detergents. While rubber gloves were supplied they were rarely used the employer failing to point out the dangers of frequent contact of the skin with cleaners or encouraging the use of gloves. In 1982 the plaintiff was diagnosed as suffering from dermatitis and told by a consultant to protect her skin at work. This she did but her medical condition deteriorated so that all her skin became infected and in 1989 she gave up her job as a result. Mrs Pape claimed damages against her employer for negligence in that her dermatitis resulted from exposure to chemicals in the course of her employment and the employer was in breach of a clear duty to warn of the dangers and persuade staff to take preventative measures. The High Court awarded her £58,000 in damages stating that *"there is a duty on an employer to warn cleaners of the dangers of handling chemical cleaning materials with unprotected hands and to instruct them as to the need to wear gloves all the time. The argument on behalf of the defendant that an employer's duty to his office cleaners is fully discharged when he provides them with gloves could not be accepted."* The risk of dermatitis was not an obvious risk to the cleaners but should be appreciated by a reasonable employer.

The common law duty encompasses an obligation to provide safe plant and appliances. If an employer was aware that machinery or tools are not reasonably safe, and an employee is injured as a result, the employer will be in breach of his duty under the common law.

In the past an employer could satisfy his duty to provide safe equipment by showing that he purchased the equipment from a reputable supplier and that he had no knowledge of any defect. Under the Employers Liability (Defective Equipment) Act 1969, injury occurring to an employee under those circumstances may be attributed to the deemed negligence of the employer. If damages are awarded against the employer then it is up to him to seek a remedy from the supplier of the defective equipment.

The obligation to provide a safe system of work also encompasses a requirement to provide safe fellow employees. If there are untrained or unskilled people employed at the workplace then a higher standard of care is owed by the employer to ensure their safety and the safety of those who work with them.

The conduct of fellow employees of contributing to an unhealthy working environment by smoking could be the responsibility of the employer in relation to an employee who suffers damage to health through passive smoking.

The duty to provide safe fellow employees exists irrespective of any issue of the employer's vicarious liability for the actions of his employees. If an employee is injured through the negligence of some third party then the court must decide in the circumstances whether this constitutes a breach of the employer's duty of care and so imposing liability.

The employer's common law duty also imposes an obligation to provide safe working methods and safe working premises. To determine whether an employer is providing safe working methods, it is necessary to consider a number of factors including:

- the layout of the work place;

- training and supervision;

- warnings; and

- whether protective equipment is provided.

It should be stressed that the common law duty on an employer is to take reasonable care, and if he gives proper instructions which the employee fails to observe then the employer will not be liable if the employee is then injured. The common law duty is not one of strict liability but rather a duty to take reasonable care in the circumstances.

In *Dixon v. London Fire and Civil Defence* 1993 the fire authority was held not to be in breach of its common law duty of care to an officer who slipped and fell as a result of a wet floor. The fact that water had leaked on to the floor of the fire station from an appliance did not constitute negligence for such an occurrence was endemic in the fire service and appeared to be insoluble.

If the plaintiff is a trained professional it may be reasonable to allow the employer to rely on the plaintiff's expertise without the need for warnings or instruction.

The courts have recognised that to require an employee to work long hours, which is related to health problems, could put an employer in breach of his common law duty. Although only a majority decision, the Court of Appeal in *Johnstone v. Bloomsbury Health Authority* 1991 recognised that the implied objective of health and safety in an employment contract may override a clear express contractual right in relation to the hours of work.

There is an increased recognition that individual employees may suffer stress as a direct result of their work. If an employer has reason to believe that this is the case and takes no steps to alleviate the problem there is now authority to suggest he could be in breach of duty.

In *Walker v. Northumberland CC* 1995 the High Court held that a local authority was in breach of duty if care to a senior social worker who was required to cope with an increased workload despite the fact the employer was aware of his susceptibility to mental breakdown. Mr Justice Coleman said that *"An employer owes a duty to his employees not to cause them psychiatric damage by the volume or character of the work which they are required to perform. Although the law on the extent of the duty on an employer to provide an employee with a safe system of work and to take reasonable steps to protect him from risks which are reasonably foreseeable has developed almost exclusively in cases involving physical injury to the employee, there is no logical reason why risk of injury to an employee's mental health should be excluded from the scope of the employer's duty. The standard of care required for performance of that duty must be measured against the yardstick of reasonable conduct on the part of a person in the employer's position. What is reasonable depends on the nature of the relationship, the magnitude of the risk of injury which was reasonably foreseeable, the seriousness of the consequences for the person to whom the duty is owed of the risk eventuating, and the cost and practicability of preventing the risk. The practicability of remedial measures must take into account the resources and facilities at the disposal of the person or body who owes the duty of care, and purpose of the activity which has given rise to the risk of injury".*

It should be noted that a material fact in deciding liability in the Walker case was that the plaintiff complained of his employers breach of duty in relation to a second nervous breakdown which was reasonably forseeable.Previously Mr Walker had suffered a breakdown due to the stress caused by his heavy workload which was not reasonably foreseeable and for which there would have been no breach of duty. By allowing Mr Walker to be exposed to the same workload as before however the employer should have appreciated that he was as a result of the first breakdown more vulnerable to psychiatric damage.

While repetitive strain injury is now a recognised complaint brought on by excessive typing the House of Lords in 1998 took a less than sympathetic view to establishing liability.

> In *Pickford v. Imperial Chemical Industries* 1998 a secretary who suffered *repetitive strain injury* due to her secretarial duties claimed that her employer had been negligent in failing to instruct her about the need for rest breaks and work organisation to alleviate the need for long periods of typing. By a majority decision the Court of Appeal reversed the decision of the High Court and found that the employer was in breach of the duty of care he owed to his employee. A majority of the House of Lords however reversed the court Appeal and confirmed the decision of the High Court and dismissed the claim. They felt that Ms Pickford as a general secretary had a number of duties other than typing and would have organised her own rest periods from the word processor. In addition they thought that the medical evidence was insufficient to prove that her condition was caused by repetitive movements while typing.

# Test Questions

1. What are the general aims of the Health and Safety at Work Act 1974?

2. State the main provision of the Working Time Regulations 1998.

3. What is the purpose of a risk assessment?

4. How is health and safety law enforced?

5. State the general duties under the Health and Safety at Work Act 1974.

6. What is the significance of *Walker v. Northumberland CC* 1995?

7. What is the employer's duty in relation to safety equipment?

# The Termination of Employment

Legal conflict between employer and employee arises most usually when the employment relationship comes to an end. Important statutory rights, such as unfair dismissal and redundancy, and common law rights, such as a wrongful dismissal all depend upon showing that the employment relationship was terminated by means of a dismissal. For this purpose therefore, it is necessary to explore the various modes of termination of the employment relationship and identify when a dismissal, whether express or implied has occurred.

# Dismissal and Notice

If an employer or an employee wishes to terminate a contract of employment they are required to comply with the employee's contractual requirements in relation to notice. Generally the length of the notice period will depend upon the nature of the employment and may increase in relation to the number of years' service. In addition, there are statutory minimum periods of notice that apply where the contract is silent or provides for less favourable periods. The statutory statement of the main terms and conditions of employment supplied under of the Employment Rights Act 1996 will stipulate the minimum notice period to which the employee is entitled.

| After continuous employment for: | Minimum notice required |
|---|---|
| 4 weeks up to 2 years | 1 week |
| 2 years up to 12 years | 1 week for each year |
| 12 years or more | 12 weeks |

If the contractual notice period is less than the statutory minimum period then the statutory minimum period will apply. Following the Employment Protection (Part-Time Employees) Regulations 1995, the right to a statutory minimum period of notice extends to part-time employees regardless of their hours of work.

There is nothing to prevent an employee from waiving his right to notice or, in fact, accepting a lump sum payment in lieu of the notice period to which he is entitled. Failure by the employer to comply with notice requirements would entitle the employee to bring an action for damages in the county courts or the employment tribunal based on breach of contract. Such a claim is known as 'wrongful dismissal' referring to the wrongful manner in which the contract of employment has been terminated.

# Wrongful Dismissal

Summary dismissal occurs when the contract of employment is terminated instantly without notice and it is prima facie wrongful. Such a dismissal is justifiable under the common law, however, if it can be shown that the employee is guilty of a serious or repudiatory breach of the contract of employment because of his 'gross misconduct'. By summarily dismissing, the employer is accepting the repudiatory breach of the employee and treating the contract as discharged. Whether the alleged misconduct may be classified as gross is a question of fact and degree, but it would normally include conduct such as disobedience, neglect, dishonesty, or misbehaviour. Certainly early cases must now be viewed with caution. The summary dismissal of a housemaid in *Turner v. Mason* 1854 because she went to visit her sick mother in contravention of her employer's instructions was held not to be wrongful but would be unlikely to constitute gross misconduct in the present day. Until recently an action for wrongful dismissal was a common law claim for breach of contract and could only be dealt with in the ordinary courts. Now employment tribunals also have jurisdiction to hear an action for wrongful dismissal.

A fundamental question that is often asked is whether the employment relationship can survive the nature of the misconduct.

> In *Pepper v. Webb* 1969 the action of the head gardener in wilfully disobeying a reasonable order was sufficient to amount to gross misconduct and provide grounds for summary dismissal, despite the contract of employment providing for three months' notice. It should be stressed, however, that the reaction of the gardener in this case represented the culmination of a long period of insolence, and the isolated use of choice obscenities by an employee to an employer may not amount to gross misconduct if there is provocation.

> In *Denco Ltd. v. Joinson* 1991 the EAT felt that if an employee uses an unauthorised password in order to enter a computer known to contain information to which he is not entitled that of itself is gross misconduct which could attract summary dismissal. In such cases the EAT thought it desirable that the management should stress that such dishonesty will carry with it severe penalties.

The remedy for a successful claim of wrongful dismissal is an action for damages amounting to the loss of wages payable during the notice period. It seems therefore that if an employer pays the employee an appropriate lump sum on summary dismissal, which represents a full payment of pay in lieu of notice, there would be little point in bringing a claim for breach of contract as no further damages would be payable. Of course since 1971 an aggrieved employee who is qualified has the further option of complaining to a tribunal that the instant dismissal is unfair. *Raspin v. United News Shops* 1999 is the first case where an award of damages was made against an employer to reflect the fact that a wrongful dismissal prevented an employee acquiring the necessary service to qualify to make a complaint of unfair dismissal. The damages awarded reflected the loss of opportunity to bring an unfair dismissal complaint.

In cases where a fixed term contract is prematurely brought to an end by the employer's repudiatory breach, a claim for damages for breach of contract may be the more appropriate avenue for redress, for the sum due under the unexpired term of the contract may be well in excess of the possible compensation available for unfair dismissal.

There is an increasing practice for senior post holders in organisations to negotiate long periods of notice to terminate their contracts of employment. Inevitably a substantial sum would become payable if an employer wishes to terminate such a contract without giving the notice to which the employee is entitled under the contract.

> In *Clark v. BET Plc* 1997 following a takeover the chief executive of BET was dismissed without the three years notice to which he was entitled under his contract. Liability for wrongful dismissal was not denied by the employer but the parties litigated in the High Court over the level of damages. The plaintiff's contract of employment provided that his considerable salary should be reviewed annually and increased at the boards discretion. In addition the contract stated that "The executive will participate in a bonus arrangement providing a maximum of 60% basic salary in any year". For the previous five years the plaintiff was given a 10% salary increase and the maximum bonus. The High Court held that the damages for wrongful dismissal should reflect a 10% salary increase over the three year notice period, for the plaintiff had a contractual right to an annual upward adjustment in salary. A 50% bonus of salary for each of the three years was also payable as a realistic assumption of the plaintiff's position had he stayed with the company, The figure of 2.85 million paid in damages demonstrates the need for careful drafting in the contracts of high earners.

## Dismissal

For the purposes of unfair dismissal the meaning of *'dismissal'* is defined in s.95(1) of the Employment Rights Act 1996. The section envisages a dismissal arising expressly, impliedly on the expiration of a fixed term contract of employment and constructively in response to the employers conduct.

# Express Dismissal

Under s.95(1)(a) an express dismissal occurs where the employer terminates the contract of employment with or without notice.

We have already said that an employer is normally required to give the employee notice in accordance with the terms of the contract or least the statutory or common law minimum period. For a dismissal with notice, therefore, there is normally no room for any misunderstanding in relation to the employer's intentions. In cases of alleged summary dismissal, however, where there is no notice, there have been claims by the employer that it was not his intention to dismiss but rather merely to discipline. While the words, "you're dismissed, fired, sacked", etc. leave little doubt as to the employer's intentions, if he uses more ambiguous language, perhaps to register his discontent with the employee, the argument that there has been no express dismissal could have some merit.

> In *Futty v. Brekkes Ltd.* 1974 the tribunal was called on to place an interpretation on the quaint language used on the Hull dock. During an altercation with his foreman the complainant fish filleter was told, *"If you do not like the job, fuck off "*. The complainant took this as a dismissal, left, and found a job elsewhere. For the purposes of an unfair dismissal claim the employer argued in his defence that there had been no dismissal. Here the words were to be considered in the context of the fish trade, and in these circumstances were taken to mean that if you do not like the work you are doing, clock off and come back tomorrow. The custom of the fish trade was that, for a dismissal, the language used was clear and formal. The tribunal agreed with the employer's view and held that the complainant had terminated his own employment by deciding on this occasion that he would leave and subsequently find himself alternative employment.

# Implied Dismissal

If a fixed term contract is terminated by either party prematurely without good reason or authorisation under the contract then an action may lie for damages for breach of contract. If the contract runs its course however there is an implied dismissal when the term expires. Potentially therefore if the fixed term contract is not renewed the employee is entitled to present a complaint of unfair dismissal. Under the Employment Rights Act 1996 an employer under a fixed term contract of one year or more can expressly exclude unfair dismissal and redundancy rights. This right to remove unfair dismissal rights has been removed by the Employment Relations Act 1999 but still applies in relation to redundancy

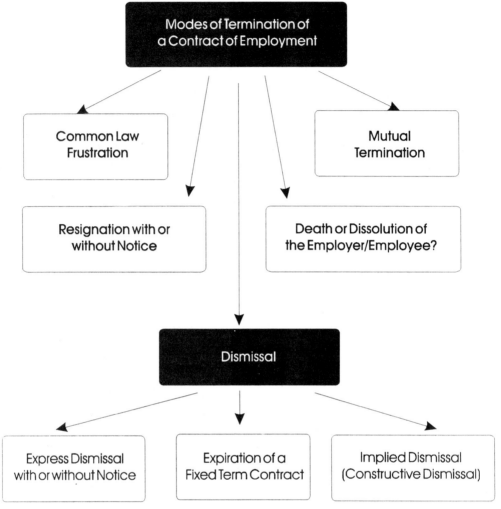

**Figure 5.1** *Modes of Termination*

## Constructive Dismissal

In a large number of cases it may seem superficially that the contract of employment has been terminated by the employee's conduct in *walking out* and treating the contract as at an end. Where however, the reason for leaving was due to the conduct of the employer or those under his control, it may be that the employee could show that the employer is responsible for the contractual termination. In such circumstances an employee could argue implied dismissal. Such a dismissal is commonly referred to as a constructive dismissal.

Originally the test for determining whether a constructive dismissal had taken place was to judge the reasonableness of the employer's conduct. Since *Western*

*Excavating (ECC) Ltd. v. Sharp*    1978 however, the Courts have rejected that approach as being too vague and now the so called 'conduct test' is to be applied based upon strict contractual principles. The aim of the conduct test is to bring some degree of certainty to the law by requiring the employee to justify his leaving as a response to the employer's repudiatory conduct. *"If the employer is guilty of conduct which is a significant breach going to the root of the contract of employment, or which shows that the employer no longer intends to be bound by one or more of the essential terms of the contract then the employee is entitled to treat himself as discharged from any further performance."*

A breach by the employer of the express terms of the contract of employment covering such matters as wages, job location, contractual duties and job description, normally comes about when the employer unilaterally attempts to impose a change on the employee without his consent.

By demoting an employee and failing to provide him with suitable office accommodation an employer could be held to be in fundamental breach of the contract of employment. Such an employee could accept the repudiatory breach and regard himself as constructively dismissed.

This was the case in *Wadham Stringer Commercials (London) Ltd. & Wadham Stringer Vehicles Ltd. v. Brown*    1983 where a fleet sales director was effectively demoted to no more than a retail salesman. At the same time he was moved from reasonable accommodation to an office 8ft x 6ft with no ventilation, next to the gentleman's lavatory. As a consequence the employee eventually resigned and claimed a constructive dismissal which was unfair. The EAT agreed that there had been a fundamental breach of contract, accepted by the employee, and following *Western Excavating (ECC) Ltd. v. Sharp* , a constructive dismissal. The employer's argument that their actions were the result of economic necessity were relevant, but only in deciding the reasonableness of their conduct for the purposes of the test of fairness or for the purpose of assessing the level of compensation in an unfair dismissal claim.

The need to look for a clear breach of a contractual term has encouraged both tribunals and courts in the absence of relevant express terms to imply terms into a contract of employment. It is the need therefore to accommodate the doctrine of constructive dismissal that has encouraged judicial ingenuity in applying the business efficacy test to find implied obligations in employment contracts. An excellent example is provided by the need to maintain trust and confidence in the employment relationship.

In *Courtaulds Northern Textiles Ltd. v. Andrew*    1979 the EAT stated that *"there is an implied term in a contract of employment that the employers will not, without reasonable and proper cause, conduct themselves in a manner calculated or likely to destroy or seriously damage the relationship of confidence and trust between the parties"*. Here a comment made to the complainant by his assistant manager that "you can't do the bloody job anyway" which was not a true expression of his opinion was held to justify the complainant in resigning and treating himself as constructively dismissed. While criticism of a worker's performance would not necessarily amount to repudiatory conduct so as to lead to constructive dismissal, here telling the employee that he could not do his job, when that was not a true expression of opinion, was conduct which was *"likely to destroy the trust relationship which was a necessary element in the relationship between the supervisory employee and his employers"*.

Failing to treat an employee fairly in relation to a disciplinary matter could constitute repudiatory conduct for the purposes of constructive dismissal.

In *Greenaway Harrison Ltd. v. Wiles* 1994 the EAT held that a telephonist who refused to accept a radical change in her shift pattern and was threatened with dismissal was entitled to leave and regard herself as constructively dismissed. The threat of dismissal constituted an anticipatory breach of contract by the employer.

An employer is of course vicariously responsible for the actions of his employees within the scope of their employment so that if a supervisor in reprimanding an employee does so in a reprehensible manner this can be taken to be the *employers' conduct* for the purpose of constructive dismissal.

# Frustration

There is no dismissal if it can be shown that the contract of employment has been brought to an end through the operation of the common law doctrine of frustration. Frustration occurs where, due to a change in circumstances, performance of the contract becomes impossible or radically different than the performance envisaged by the parties when they made the contract. The specified events upon which a claim of frustration could be based are limited generally to long illness, and imprisonment. Certainly the distinction between the termination of a contract of employment by dismissal and termination by frustration is of critical importance.

In *Shepherd & Company Ltd. v. Jerrom* 1986 the Court of Appeal considered the position of an apprentice plumber who was sentenced to Borstal training for a minimum period of six months. Failure to dismiss him in accordance with standard procedures for apprentices led the tribunal and the EAT to find that he had been constructively dismissed unfairly and so entitled to compensation. The Court of Appeal disagreed however and held that the four year apprenticeship contract had been frustrated by the six month sentence.

It is difficult in any given case to say whether the circumstances of an illness are such that it is no longer practical to regard the contract of employment as surviving. Obviously the seriousness and length of the illness are crucial factors but generally all the circumstances are relevant, including the nature of the job, the length of employment, the needs of the employer and obligations in relation to replacement, and the conduct of the employer.

# Resignation

There is no dismissal if the employee expressly terminates the contract of employment by resigning.

In *Sothern v. Franks Charlesley* 1981 the Court of Appeal held that an office manager who formally said in a meeting *"I am resigning"* had used unambiguous language and had brought her contract of employment to an end.

In *Kwik-Fit v. Lineham* 1992 as a direct consequence of issuing a written warning to a depot manager in accordance with the company's disciplinary procedure, he walked out in protest. While the employer took the view that the manager had resigned he nevertheless presents a complaint of unfair dismissal. The EAT held that where words or action of resignation are unambiguous an employer can accept them as such unless there are 'special circumstances'. *"Words spoken or action expressed in temper or in the heat of the moment or under extreme pressure, or the intellectual make-up of an employee may be such special circumstances"*. In a case such as this, where there are special circumstances, an employer is required to allow a reasonable period to elapse, perhaps a matter of days, before accepting a resignation to determine an employee's true intention. The correct question to ask in deciding whether a resignation constitutes a dismissal is *"Who really terminated the contract of employment"*.

There will normally be a contractual provision as to the length of notice to be given and, in addition, there is a statutory minimum period of one week where the employee has at least one month of continuous employment. Failure to comply with notice requirements is a breach of contract for which the employee could be made liable in damages. Employers rarely sue in these cases due mainly to the problem of quantifying their loss which would include the additional cost of advertising for and hiring a replacement during the notice period.

The unilateral act of resigning must be distinguished from the consensual termination of employment which normally involves an exchange of consideration

# Mutual Termination

If the parties to a contract of employment, without duress and after taking proper advice, enter into a separate contract, supported by good consideration, with the objective of terminating the employment relationship by mutual consent, the contract will be valid and enforceable.

# Unfair Dismissal

The introduction of the right not to be dismissed without good reason in the Industrial Relations Act 1971 was a recognition that an employee has a stake in his job which cannot be extinguished simply by serving contractual notice. In the same way that a tenant may acquire security of tenure in his home and resist the enforcement of a notice to quit unless it is reasonable in the circumstances, an employee, through continuous employment, can acquire security in his job. The right not to be unfairly dismissed is intended to act as a constraint on employers who feel they have the authority to hire and fire as they please. The extent to which the law of unfair dismissal achieves the objective of constraining management prerogative is arguable. Over the last twenty years unfair dismissal has developed into a highly complex area of law recognised as such as early as 1977 by Philips J in *Devis & Sons Ltd. v. Atkins* 1977, when he said, *"the expression 'unfair dismissal' is in no sense a common-sense expression capable of being understood by the man in the street"*. The present unfair dismissal law is contained in the Employment Rights Act 1996 which is the main source of statutory employment rights. Under s.94(1) in every employment to which the section applies, every employee shall have the right not to be unfairly dismissed by his employer.

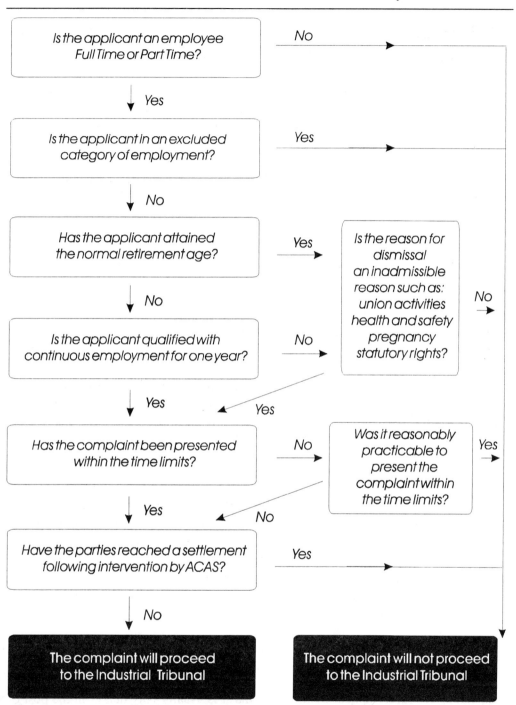

**Figure 5.2**  *Unfair Dismissal Complaint*

## Qualifications

To fall within unfair dismissal then an employee had to show continuous employment in a job which is not an excluded category of work. The minimum period of continuous employment is not less than one year ending with the effective date of termination. This is the date that the contract of employment actually comes to an end and if a summary dismissal is unjustified it may be necessary to add the statutory period of notice onto the date of dismissal.

A further requirement is that if on, or before, the effective date of termination, the employee has reached the 'normal retiring age' or, if more than the age of 65 (whether male or female), then there is no right to present a claim.

In addition to qualifying through service, an employee must not fall within one of the excluded categories of employment. Such as the police or members of the armed forces.

It was possible for employees with fixed term contracts of one year or more to expressly waive unfair dismissal rights but this has now been repealed by the Employment Relations Act 1999.

To initiate a complaint of unfair dismissal the Act provides that a tribunal will not have jurisdiction unless it is presented within three months *"beginning with "* the *"effective date of termination"*. The expression *"effective date of termination"* means for most purposes the date that the employment actually terminates. It seems that for a summary dismissal, whether or not in breach of contract, the effective date of termination is the date of dismissal.

> In *Stapp v. The Shaftesbury Society* 1982 the Court of Appeal held that the *'effective date of termination'* means the actual date of termination of the employment whether or not the employee was wrongfully dismissed. Here the effect of a summary dismissal with wages paid in lieu of one month's notice was to make the effective date of dismissal the date of termination of employment and so the employee had insufficient continuous employment to bring a claim for unfair dismissal.

An employment tribunal may hear a complaint presented outside the time limits if it is satisfied that it was not reasonably practicable to present the claim in time.

Such claims are rarely upheld by tribunals and it is usually only delays in the post or deceit by the employer which would provide a reasonable excuse for the delay

## Conciliation

A copy of the IT1 having been sent to ACAS, a conciliation officer is appointed to get in touch with both parties in an attempt to resolve the conflict and reach an amicable settlement. It should be stressed that in many cases an agreement is reached because of the intervention of the conciliation officer. While he is under a statutory duty to endeavour to promote a voluntary settlement of the complaint by encouraging an agreement to reinstate the employee, or make a payment of compensation, there is no requirement for the parties to co-operate or even communicate with him.If the complaint proceeds to a full hearing, the burden of proof is on the complainant to show that he has been dismissed unless that is conceded.

The Employment Rights (Dispute Resolution) Act 1998 encourages the use of internal procedures and voluntary arbitration developed by ACAS.

Having established that a dismissal has occurred, it then falls to the tribunal to determine the reason for dismissal, whether it is a reason categorised in the statute and, if so, whether the dismissal is fair or unfair and redress where appropriate.

## Reason for dismissal

To assist the complainant in a claim for unfair dismissal the complainant is entitled to be provided with a written statement of the reason or reasons for dismissal within fourteen days of a written request. The written statement provided under this section is important evidence of the employer's reason or reasons for dismissal. Following the  Employment Protection (Part-Time Employees) Regulations 1995  the right applies to part-time employees regardless of their hours of work. The right to a statement of the reason or reasons applies where the dismissal is express or the non-renewal of a fixed term contract, but not if the complaint is based on a constructive dismissal. If an employer unreasonably fails to comply with a request the employee may present a complaint to the tribunal who may declare what it finds the reasons for dismissal are and also compensate the employee with an award of two weeks' wages.

**Statutory Reasons for Dismissal**

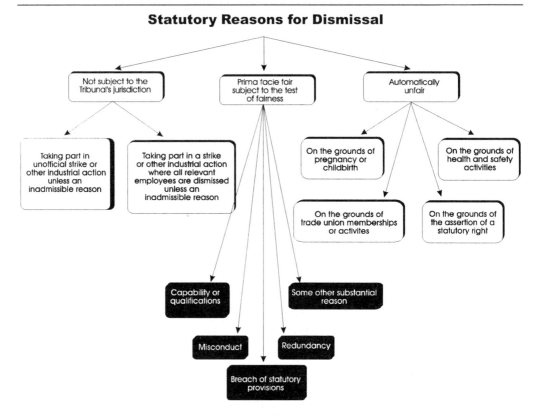

**Figure 5.3** *Statutory Reasons for Dismissal*

The heart of unfair dismissal law is contained in s.98 and it is to this section we must devote attention.

Under the section therefore it clearly states that it is the employer who must show the reason or principal reason for the dismissal, and that the reason falls within one of the four categories of reasons identified in s.98(2) or is a substantial reason under s.98(1) of a kind such as to justify the dismissal of an employee holding the position which that employee held. If the employee establishes the true reason for dismissal, and that it falls within one of the five statutory reasons identified in s.98, then the dismissal is prima facie fair. The final determination of fairness is achieved by applying the test of reasonableness contained in s.98(3).

The five statutory reasons are:

- capability or qualifications,

- misconduct,

- redundancy,

- breach of a statutory provision,

- some other substantial reason.

The burden of proving, on the balance of probabilities, the real reason for dismissal, and that it is a statutory reason falling within s.98, is upon the employer. Failure to establish this true reason will make the decision to dismiss automatically unfair.

# The Test of Fairness

Once the employer has shown that the principal reason for dismissal is on the face of it fair it is then necessary for the industrial tribunal to determine the heart of the issue, whether the employer acted reasonably in the circumstances.

> The test of fairness is contained in s.98(3) which provides that the determination of the question of whether the dismissal was fair or unfair, having regard to the reason shown by the employer, shall depend on whether in the circumstances (including the size and administrative resources of the employer's undertaking) the employer acted reasonably or unreasonably in treating it as a sufficient reason for dismissing the employee, and that question shall be determined in accordance with equity and the substantial merits of the case.

Where there are multiple reasons for dismissal it must be determined which is the principal one for the purposes of applying s.98(3).*Fairness* then has to be judged by the industrial tribunal acting as an industrial jury applying the words of s.98(3). The tribunal is not an arbitrator and has no jurisdiction to substitute its own views of reasonableness for the employer's but must adjudicate upon what a reasonable employer would have done in the circumstances.

Useful guidelines in relation to the approach to be adopted in applying s.98(3) were provided by the EAT in *Iceland Frozen Foods v. Jones* 1982. Here Brown Wilkinson J. suggested that the approach which should be adopted by tribunals was to start by considering the words of the section and then determine the reasonableness of the employer's conduct, not whether they believe the conduct to be fair. The tribunal must resist the temptation to substitute its own views as to the right course for the employer to adopt and recognise that there is a *band of reasonable responses* to the employer's conduct. Within this *'band'* reasonable employers could take different views. The role of the tribunal is to decide whether the decision of the employer in the case before it comes within the band of reasonable responses which the employer might have adopted. If the dismissal is within the band of reasonable responses which the employer might have adopted it is fair, otherwise it is unfair. This approach has been widely adopted.

As the test of fairness is based upon the actions of a reasonable employer it is possible to find an employer acting within his contractual authority nevertheless acting unfairly for the purposes of unfair dismissal. A decision to dismiss based purely on economic considerations may fall within the band of reasonable responses of a reasonable employer.

> In *Saunders v. Scottish National Camps* 1980 the complainant, a handyman employed at a children's holiday camp, was dismissed when the employer discovered that he was a homosexual. The reason for dismissal was that the employee indulged in homosexuality and it was unsuitable to employ someone of that tendency in children's camps. Both the industrial tribunal and the EAT found the dismissal to be fair. They decided that a large proportion of employers in this situation would perceive that the employment of a homosexual should be restricted where there is close contact with children. This is despite the fact that such a view may not be rational or supported by evidence which is scientifically sound. There is no doubt however that the continued employment could have proved to be an economic liability for the employer, bearing in mind the views of certain parents.

If the reason for dismissal is connected with the employer's belief in the culpability of an employee, then to act reasonably the employer must have made due investigation and enquiry in order to equip himself with sufficient information to arrive at an "*honest belief*" in the employee's guilt.

> In *British Railways Board v. Jackson* 1994 the complainant, a buffet car steward, who had fourteen years service with British Rail, was summarily dismissed when he was discovered to have bread and bacon in his possession at the beginning of his early morning shift without a satisfactory explanation. The reason for dismissal was contravening the BR rule relating to the possession of goods for the purposes of engaging in trade or business for his own benefit. Following a disciplinary hearing the complainant was summarily dismissed for gross misconduct. Both the tribunal and the EAT felt that the employer had "jumped the gun" in that the complainant was challenged in the locker room and had not taken the food onto the train. This conclusion was held to be flawed by the Court of Appeal who stated that the "*question which the tribunal had to determine was whether it was reasonable for the employers to find that the employee intended, in breach of the rules, to trade for his own advantage in the goods found in his possession. It was the wrong approach to adopt a legalistic stance and ask whether technically the BR rule had been infringed and conclude: that the employer had 'jumped the gun'.*" To determine whether dismissal was a reasonable response the employer was entitled to take into account:

- the prevalence of this type of conduct among stewards;

- the need to deal with it severely as a deterrent;

- the conduct of the employee in not owning up and put forward unconvincing explanations.

Despite the facts that there was no completed act of dishonesty and the complainant had a long period of service with a good record, there was no basis that the tribunal could conclude that the decision to dismiss was not a reasonable response to the misconduct.

If an employee is dismissed for alleged misconduct the employer is normally obliged to investigate the circumstances and this is the case even where an employee is already under a final written warning.

# Statutory Reasons

## Capability or qualifications

For the purposes of this reason *capability' is assessed by reference to skill, aptitude, health or any other physical or mental quality*. The majority of cases where capability is the reason relied upon relate to incompetence or ill health. Where an allegation of incompetence is established through evidence, in determining the reasonableness of the employer's decision to dismiss it is also necessary to examine the reasons for the alleged incompetence. This could involve a consideration of the employer's appraisal processes, the amount of training and supervision required, and the extent to which employees are given the opportunity to improve their performance. Obviously there are degrees of incompetence, but even one serious lapse could be sufficient to justify a dismissal.

> In *Taylor v. Alidair Ltd.* 1978 the applicant pilot was dismissed when as a result of an error of judgment, the passenger plane he was flying landed so hard that serious damage was caused to the plane. The Court of Appeal held that *"the company has reasonable grounds for honestly believing that the applicant was not competent "*. As a result of this serious act of incompetence the belief was reasonably held, and the dismissal was consequently a fair one.

If incapability is alleged, due to the ill health of the employee, once again reasonableness of the employer's decision to dismiss must be viewed by the extent to which it is an informed judgment bearing in mind the various options available. Earlier in the chapter we considered the extent to which a long illness can amount to a frustration of the contract of employment.

If the reason for dismissal is related to 'qualifications' of the employee this is taken to mean *"any degree, diploma or other academic, technical or professional qualification relevant to the position which the employee held."*

## Misconduct

Misconduct as a reason for dismissal covers a wide range of circumstances including such matters as lateness, absenteeism, insubordination, breach of safety rules and immorality. Of course the gravity of the misconduct, and the steps taken by the employer to address it, are crucial factors in determining whether the decision to dismiss for misconduct is a reasonable one or not. Misconduct at work has been held to include:

- stealing from the employer;

- a breach of safety instructions;

- refusal to obey reasonable instructions;

- immorality;

- drunkenness; and

- absenteeism.

If the misconduct of the employee is of a sufficiently serious nature it may be reasonable for the employer to dismiss the employee with immediate effect.

In *Hamilton v. Argyll & Clyde Health Board* 1993 the complainant was a chief hospital technician who was dismissed following an allegation that she had torn up a request card for a respiratory test on a patient so that the test was not carried out. Following an investigation the employer concluded that she had committed the guilty act and dismissed her for gross misconduct. The misconduct complained of, the employer believed, fell within the definition of misconduct set out in the employer's disciplinary procedure. The finding of a fair dismissal in the tribunal was challenged on appeal on the grounds that the employer had, in response to a union request, considered the employee for employment within some other sphere within the organisation. As the employment relationship had not been destroyed by the misconduct, the misconduct could not be classified as "gross" within the definition. This argument was rejected by the EAT which upheld the tribunal's decision. *"Willingness by an employer to offer re-employment is not inconsistent with a conclusion that an employee has been guilty of gross misconduct. What is gross misconduct must be considered in relation to the particular employment and the particular employee ".*

## Redundancy

The employer may show that the reason for dismissal was that the employee was redundant. Essentially a redundancy situation arises when an employer closes part or all of his business operation, the purposes for which the employee was employed, or alternatively the requirements of the business for workers of a particular kind have ceased or diminished. For the purposes of unfair dismissal however, not only must the dismissal be by reason of redundancy but the selection of the employee in question must also be fair.

In a redundancy selection the employer failed to observe agreed industrial practice, this could render a decision to dismiss on grounds of redundancy unfair.

> Guidance in relation to the approach to be adopted by industrial tribunals in determining the fairness of redundancy selections was provided by the Employment Appeal Tribunal in *Williams v. Compair Maxim Ltd.* 1982. Here the complainants had been dismissed for redundancy, the employer having failed to consult with the recognised trade union. Selection had been left to departmental managers, one of whom gave evidence that he had retained those employees whom he considered would be best to retain in the interests of the company in the long run. Length of service was not a factor taken into account. The industrial tribunal's finding of fair dismissal was reversed by the EAT which held the decision to be perverse. Measuring the conduct of the employer in question with that of a reasonable employer, a tribunal taken to be aware of good industrial practice, could not have reached the decision that the dismissals were fair. The employer's decision to dismiss was not within the range of conduct which a reasonable employer could have adopted in these circumstances. While accepting that it was impossible to lay down detailed procedures for a selection process, the EAT felt that reasonable employers would attempt to act in accordance with five basic principles and should depart from them only with good reason.
>
> • As much warning as possible should be given of impending redundancies to enable the union and employees to inform themselves of the facts, seek alternative solutions and find alternative employment.
>
> • The employer will consult with the union as to the best means of achieving the objective as fairly and with as little hardship as possible. Criteria should be agreed to be applied in selection and the selection monitored.

- The criteria agreed should not depend upon subjective opinion of the person selecting but it must be capable of objective scrutiny and include such matters as attendance record, job efficiency, experience or length of service.

- The employer must seek to ensure that the selection is made fairly in accordance with these criteria and consider union representations.

- The employer should examine the possibility of finding suitable alternative employment.

Certainly the need for consultation in a redundancy situation is one of the fundamentals of fairness and it is only in exceptional cases that a failure to consult can be overlooked.

Consultation with an employee in the context of dismissal for redundancy and conducted in a fair and genuine way *"by giving those consulted a fair and proper opportunity to understand fully the matters about which they are being consulted. The obligation to consult is separate from the obligation to warn"*.

## Employment in contravention of the law

For the purposes of this limited category it must be shown that it would be illegal to continue to employ the employee in question. A good example is where driving is an integral part of the employee's work and he is disqualified from driving. As usual the reasonableness of the employer's decision to dismiss must be viewed in the light of the particular circumstance, not least the availability of alternative work.

In *Gill v. Walls Meat Company Ltd.* 1971 to have continued to employ the complainant, who worked on an open meat counter would have infringed Food Regulations, for he had grown a beard. After refusing to shave it off and also an offer of alternative work, the tribunal held that the decision to dismiss was a fair one.

## Some other substantial reason

This final category of reason is used to include reasons for dismissal which do not fall neatly into the previous categories.

A clash of personalities in the office was held to be a substantial reason of a kind to justify dismissal in *Treganowan v. Robert Knee & Company Ltd.* 1975. Here the complainant was dismissed because the atmosphere in the office where she worked had become so hostile that it was seriously affecting the employer's business. The prime cause of the trouble was the complainant, whose constant reference to her private life seriously upset her colleagues who felt that they could not work with her.

If the reason for dismissal is related to unacceptable periods of absence because of illness then it could fall into this category as the reason for dismissal.Certainly the refusal of an employee to accept an alteration in terms of employment has been held to fall within this category. This could be classified as an economic dismissal following a reorganisation and regarded as fair.

## Procedural fairness

In addition to examining the reason relied upon, the process of determining the reasonableness of the employer's decision to dismiss necessarily involves a consideration of the procedure implemented by the employer in relation to the dismissal. There exists a Code of Practice drawn up by ACAS on *"Disciplinary Practice and Procedures in Employment"*. The Code provides that employees should be fully informed of disciplinary rules and procedures and the likely consequences if the rules are broken. Also the Code identifies the essential features of a disciplinary procedure so that in cases of misconduct, the procedure should have built in a process involving formal and informal, oral and written warnings. In particular, at some point, the employee should be given the opportunity of putting his side of the case accompanied by a representative from a trade union or otherwise. *In Lock v. Cardiff Railway Company* 1998 the EAT confirmed that the *"Code forms the basis on which an employee's conduct should be judged"*.

One important point in relation to procedures is that the graver the misconduct the less requirement there would be to implement a system of warnings. Also, where warnings are given for less serious matters they should be recorded but then after a period of satisfactory conduct eventually disregarded.

> In the important case of *Polkey v. A E Dayton Services Ltd.* 1987 the complainant, a van driver, employed by the defendants for over four years, was without warning or consultation, handed a letter of redundancy. His claim of unfair dismissal was based on the employer's failure to observe the statutory code of practice which provides for warning and consultation in a redundancy situation. Despite there being a *"heartless disregard"* of the code, the tribunal, EAT and the Court of Appeal all found that the dismissal was fair. Applying the *"no difference principle"*, if a fair procedure had been adopted, the employer could still have reasonably decided to dismiss. This approach was rejected by the House of lords who held that the employer's decision to dismiss had to be judged by applying the test of reasonableness. There was no scope for deciding what the employer might have done had he adopted a different procedure. Where the employer fails to observe the code,

he will only be acting fairly if the tribunal is satisfied that *"the employer could reasonably have concluded in the light of circumstances known at the time of dismissal that consultation or warning would be utterly useless"*.

The House of Lords held in Polkey therefore that a failure to follow an agreed procedure in dismissing an employee is likely to result in a finding of unfair dismissal. This is subject to the exception where it is obvious that use of the proper procedure would be futile. The Court of Appeal has recently provided guidance as to when as employer can rely on this exception.

## Dismissal in Connection with Business Transfer

The Transfer of Undertakings (Protection of Employment) Regulations 1981 provides some degree of protection to employees who are dismissed on the transfer of a business undertaking. The aim of the regulations is to ensure that on the transfer of a business the contractual rights of the employees are preserved. Under reg 5 the transfer of an undertaking shall not operate to terminate the contract of employment of any person employed but such contracts shall have effect as originally made by the transferee.

Under the regulations it is provided that the dismissal of an employee before or after a relevant transfer is to be regarded as unfair if the reason is connected with the transfer. The dismissal is prima facie fair however, if it is for an 'economic, technical or organisational reason' entailing change in the workforce and so regarded as 'some other substantial reason'. If the decision to dismiss is regarded as reasonable it is fair.

> Guidance in relation to the interpretation of economic, technical or organisational reason was provided by the EAT *in Wheeler v. Patel & J. Golding Group of Companies* 1987. Here the unfair dismissal claim by a sales assistant against the purchaser of the shop where she worked was rejected because she had been dismissed before the contractual date set for completion of the sale. In relation to the phrase an *"economic reason"* for dismissal the EAT felt that like technical or organisational *reasons "it must be a reason which relates to the conduct of the business"*. A desire to obtain an enhanced price for the business or to achieve a sale is not a reason relating to the conduct of the business. This limited meaning given to the *phrase "economic reason"* reflects the fact that if a broad literal interpretation were given to it, the majority of dismissals by transfers in such circumstances would be regarded as for an *"economic reason"*. Here the dismissal, in order to comply with the requirement of an intending purchaser, was not for *an "economic reason"*, for it did not relate to the conduct of the business, rather the vendor's desire to sell. As the vendor had not shown that the dismissal was for

an economic technical or organisational reason, the unfair dismissal claim against the vendor was upheld.

A dismissal caused by or connected with the transfer of a business for the purpose of the regulations will be fair if the reason for dismissal is an *"organisational one"* entailing changes in the workforce.

The changes imposed upon the complainant *in Crawford v. Swinton Insurance Brokers* 1990 on the transfer of business were held to be so radical that when she resigned as a result of them she could regard herself as constructively dismissed. From a clerk/typist who worked mainly at home, she was offered other work, with the changed function of selling insurance. The tribunal further held however that the changes imposed were dictated by the new employer's organisational requirements, and to offer new standard conditions to existing staff was a *"change of the workforce"* for the purpose of the regulations . Such a finding was approved by the EAT which held that there can be a *"change in the workforce"* if the same people are kept on but given different jobs. In the case of a constructive dismissal following an organisational change however, it is the tribunal's function to *"identify the principal reason for the conduct of the employer which entitled the employee to terminate the contract and then determine whether the reason is an economic, technical or organisational one entailing changes in the workforce"*.

An important transformation of the law relating to liability for dismissals on a business transfer was brought about by the House of Lords' decision in *Lister v. Forth Dry Dock and Engineering Company Ltd.* 1989. Here the Lords held that liability for a dismissal by the vendor prior to the transfer, will pass to the purchaser, if the employee has been unfairly dismissed for a reason connected with the transfer. In order to give effect to the EEC Employee Rights on Transfer of Business Directive, Regulation 5(3) which provides that liability is to be transferred only where the employee *is "employed immediately before the transfer"* is to have the words *added "or would have been so employed if he had not been dismissed"* in the circumstances described in the regulation. The effect of this change is that an employee who is dismissed solely because of a transfer is automatically passed to the transferee but if the employee is dismissed for an economic, technical or organisational reason then liability will not pass unless the employee was still employed at the time of transfer. Without such an interpretation, employees in cases like this would be left with *"worthless claims for unfair dismissal"* against an insolvent employer.

In cases where there is a relevant transfer for the purposes of the regulations and a dismissal before the transfer by the transferor, under regulation 5(2) the act of dismissal is deemed to have been done by the transferee who would be responsible for the dismissal.

> In *Stirling DC v. Allan* 1995 the Court of Session held that on the completion of a relevant transfer all the transferor liabilities in connection with contracts of employment are under reg 5 automatically transferred to the transferee business

# Remedies for Unfair Dismissal

If a complaint of unfair dismissal is successful, the tribunal has authority to make an order for *reinstatement or re-engagement* or make an award of *compensation*. Irrespective of whether they have been requested, the tribunal is obliged to explain the remedies of reinstatement and re-engagement to a successful complainant and discover whether he wishes to apply for such an order.

An order for reinstatement requires the employer to treat the complainant in all respects as if he had not been dismissed. By such an order, the employer would be required to make good any arrears of pay or any rights or privileges which would have accrued but for the dismissal. If the employee would have benefited from improvements in terms and conditions but for the dismissal, then the order must reflect the improvement from the date it was agreed. In exercising its discretion to make an order of reinstatement the tribunal must take account of:

- the wishes of the complainant;

- whether it is practicable for an employer to comply with such an order; and

- whether the complainant contributed to the dismissal and whether it would be just to make such an order.

If the tribunal decides not to make an order for reinstatement it must then consider the possibility of re-engagement. An order of re-engagement requires the employer, his successor, or an associate to employ the complainant in comparable work or other suitable employment and on making such an order the tribunal must specify the terms upon which the re-engagement is to take place. Such would include the identity of the parties, the nature of the employment remuneration. An amount payable for arrears if pay rights and privileges restored and the date the order must be complied with.

For re-engagement the tribunal must take account of the following considerations:

- the wishes of the employee;

- whether it is practicable for the employer to comply with an order for re-engagement; and

- where the employee contributed to some extent to the dismissal and whether it would be just to order re-engagement and if so, on what terms.

If a tribunal decides not to make either order it must make an award of compensation. But even if either order is made, a tribunal has no power to ensure that it is complied with. Failure to comply or fully comply with an order of reinstatement or re-engagement can only lead to an award of compensation subject to the maximum limit.

## Compensation

The most common form of redress for unfair dismissal is compensation.

An order for compensation as redress for unfair dismissal may consist of a *basic award*, a *compensatory award* , and an *additional award*.

## Basic award

The basic award is payable in all cases of unfair dismissal irrespective of loss and is calculated with reference to the complainant's continuous employment and average week's wage. It should be noted however that if it can be shown that the complainant contributed to the dismissal through his own fault, or has unreasonably refused an offer of reinstatement, the amount of the basic award can be reduced by a just and equitable proportion. The computation of the basic award is the same as for a redundancy payment, so the present maximum is £6,600.

The amount of the basic award is calculated by reference to the period the employee has been continuously employed, ending with the effective date of termination. By reckoning backwards from the effective date of termination the number of years employment can be determined allowing:

*one and a half weeks' pay for each year of employment in which the employee was not below 41 years of age;*

*one week's pay for each year the employee was not below 22 years of age;*

*a half week's pay for each year of employment between 18 and 21 years of age.*

To calculate the basic award therefore it is necessary to determine the employee's gross pay up to a maximum of £220, his length of service up to a maximum of 20 years and his age. The maximum award payable therefore is for an employee who is dismissed after 20 years' service, over the age of 41, with a gross wage in excess of £220. He will be entitled to a basic award of 20 x 1½ x £220 = £6,600.

In many cases the employee's period of continuous service will cover more than one age rate barrier. In such circumstances it is necessary to calculate the entitlement at the relevant rate, e.g. for an employee who is made redundant at the age of 44 who, after 15 years' service has a gross wage of £160, is entitled to:

| | | |
|---|---|---|
| 3 years x 1½ x £160 | = | £620 |
| plus | | |
| 12 years x 1 x £160 | = | £1920 |
| | | £2540 |

## Compensatory award

In assessing the amount of the compensatory award, up to the present maximum of £11,400 a tribunal must have regard to the loss sustained by the complainant in consequence of the dismissal. The maximum will be raised to £50,000 under the Employment Relations Act 1999.

The amount of a compensatory award should take account of any failure by the employee to mitigate his loss, for instance by refusing an offer of suitable alternative employment. The Court of Appeal held in *Babcock Fata v. Addison* 1987 that any money paid in lieu of notice should be deducted from a compensatory award as should any ex gratia payment made. Heads of compensation that are assessable include the loss of fringe benefits attached to the job, expense incurred in seeking alternative work, net wages lost up to the hearing, estimated future earnings, the termination of continuous employment which necessarily limits future rights and the loss of pension rights.

As a general rule the compensatory award is limited to financial loss and cannot extend to hurt feelings. Although unfair dismissal may be traumatic, no damages are available for the distress caused by the employer's action. It would be possible however to compensate for financial loss resulting from the manner of the dismissal, rather than injury to feelings, particularly when it affects future prospects of employment. Injury to feelings are recognised for the purposes of compensation in discrimination legislation so that if a dismissal is proved to be sex or race discrimination then the distress suffered by the applicant can be compensated.

The compensatory award, like the basic award, may be reduced because of the complainant's contributory fault.

### Additional award

Previously there were also Additional awards which could be made against an employer who refused to comply with reinstatement or reengagement orders and Special awards for dismissals in connection with trade union or health and safety matters. The Employment Relations Act 1999 abolishes the special award and creates a new additional award increased to an amount not less then 26 nor more than 52 weeks pay. The new additional award will not cover the special award categories and applies when an employer fails to show that it was not reasonably practicable to comply with an order of reinstatement or reengagement.

## Test Questions

1. What is the statutory minimum period of notice?

2. Explain what is meant by wrongful dismissal.

3. State the three forms of statutory dismissal.

4. Explain what is meant by constructive dismissal.

5. Who is qualified to present a complaint of unfair dismissal?

6. State the statutory reasons for dismissal that are presumed to be fair.

7. State the statutory reasons for dismissal that are automatically unfair.

8. What is the test of fairness?

9. State the remedies for unfair dismissal.

## Redundancy Payments

Redundancy occurs when an employee is dismissed because an employer has closed his business or the business is closed in the place the employee works. Alternatively there is redundancy if the employer no longer requires or has a reduced requirement for employees to carry out work of a particular kind. In both cases there must be no suitable alternative employment. As far as unfair dismissal is concerned a dismissal by reason of redundancy is a statutory reason for dismissal and provided the employer consults when he need to and adopts rational criterion for selection, such a dismissal may be classified as fair.

The right to a redundancy payment for workers dismissed because there is no longer a demand for their services was first introduced in 1965 under the Redundancy Payments Act. The 1965 Act represented a major statutory intervention in the individual employment relationship, for while redundancy/severance payments have always been contractually agreed, the Act made the State redundancy payment a statutory requirement for qualifying employees. It was the first example of any State provision for compensation for workers who lost their jobs through no fault of their own. The complex provisions of the Act are now found in the Employment Rights Act 1996.

The object of redundancy provision is to compensate a worker for the loss of a long term stake he has in his job. Employment tribunals have jurisdiction over disputes relating to entitlement and the amount of any redundancy payment and also where the complaint is one of unfair dismissal due to unfair selection for redundancy.

Originally to qualify for the right to a redundancy payment it was necessary to establish two years continuous employment with the same employer as a full-time employee over the age of eighteen, and now part-time employees regardless of their hours can also qualify for a payment with two years continuous employment.

## Redundancy Dismissal

The right to a redundancy payment arises when a qualifying employee has been dismissed by reason of redundancy. The reason for dismissal must therefore be redundancy, a presumption of which arises in favour of the applicant unless the contrary is proved. It is for the employer to rebut the presumption of redundancy on the balance of probabilities by showing that the dismissal was for some reason other than redundancy.

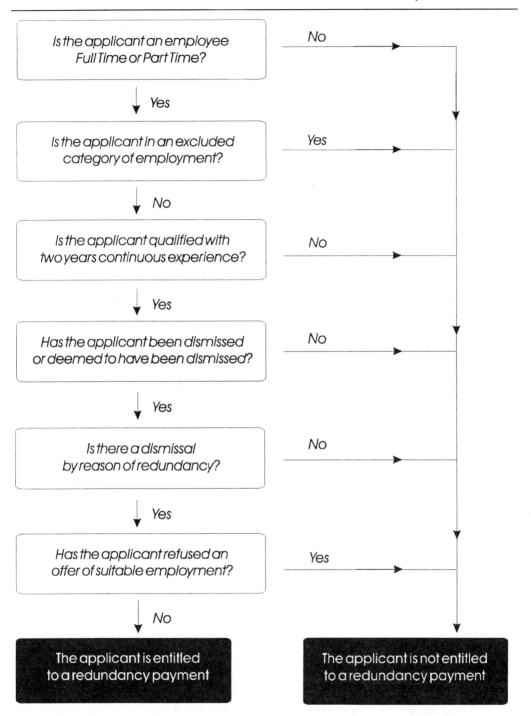

**Figure 5.5** *Entitlement to a Redundancy Payment*

Redundancy could occur because the business is closed or it is intended that it will be. Such a closure could relate to the whole business or just a part of it and be permanent or temporary. In addition redundancy could arise if the business is closed in the place where the employee works. If, however, the employee's contract provides that he could be required to move to a new work location, and the employer attempts to trigger the clause, then there is no redundancy. Even without an express clause there is an implied term in the contract of employment that the employee may be moved to a new work location within reasonable commuting distance from home.

There is also a redundancy situation where the requirements of the business for employees to carry out work of a particular kind have ceased or diminished or expected to do so.

The fact that the dismissed employee has been replaced by another employee will not normally lead to a finding of redundancy for it cannot be said that the requirements of the business for an employee have ceased or diminished. There would be a redundancy, however, if it could be shown that the replacement employee was moved because of a reduction in requirements. Here an employee is being dismissed to make way for an employee who would otherwise be surplus to requirements and so the dismissed employee is entitled to a redundancy payment.

In situations where the employee's skills have become outdated because of changes in working methods to which he cannot or is not prepared to adapt, there have been conflicting views as to whether, if he is dismissed, it is by reason of redundancy or incapability.

The contemporary approach to change seems to be that so long as the job function remains, there is no redundancy. If an employee is given a very wide job function, that is likely to mean where there are technological or social changes in the way that a job is performed, that does not make it a different kind of work for the purposes of redundancy. In cases where an employee has an express flexibility clause in his contract that would not prevent a finding of redundancy where there is a clear reduction in requirements for him to carry out his primary job function. *In Johnson v. Peabody Trust* 1996 the claimant was employed for a number of years as a roofer by a housing association however a term in his contract provided for flexibility in that if there was no roofing work he could be redeployed on other building operations such as plastering. In 1993 the claimant was, along with others, selected for redundancy due to a down turn in roofing work. The tribunal felt that the claimant was employed as a roofer and the fact that the employers requirements for roofing work had diminished meant that he was redundant. On appeal it was argued that under the contract test, as the claimant could be required to carry out multi trade operations, which had not diminished, he could not be classified as redundant. The EAT rejected this argument and held that here there was a fair dismissal by reason of redundancy despite the flexibility clause in the roofer's contract. The essential nature of the claimant's contract was that of a skilled roofer and the fact that he could be required to do other work did not alter that fact.

## Suitable Alternative Employment

If, before employment terminates, the employer makes the employee an offer either to renew the contract of employment or re-engage the employee under a new contract which constitutes suitable alternative employment, then provided the new contract is to commence within four weeks of the previous one terminating, an unreasonable refusal to accept such an offer will mean that the employee will not be entitled to make a claim for a redundancy payment. Failure to take up an offer of a new contract on identical terms and conditions of employment therefore would normally constitute an unreasonable refusal to accept re-engagement and, as a consequence, an employer will lose the right to make a claim for payment. If the offer is of alternative employment, it is necessary to determine its suitability in relation to the previous employment. For the new employment to be 'suitable' it must be substantially similar to the previous job and not employment of an entirely different nature at the same salary. The question is one of fact and degree and one which the tribunal must examine in the light of the particular circumstances of the case including such matters as the nature of the work, the rates of pay, the place of work, the new status, and fringe benefits. Personal factors affecting the employee may also be considered such as social and family links, accommodation, and the children's education.

## Redundancy Procedure

The Trade Union and Labour Relations (Consolidation) Act 1992 contains a number of rules relating to the procedure to be invoked in a redundancy situation where an independent trade union is recognised in relation to the class of employees involved. In *Commission of the European Communities v. United Kingdom of Great Britain and Northern Ireland* 1994, the European Court of Justice has ruled that by failing to ensure worker representation in the work place where there is no recognised trade union the UK has failed to comply with Community law obligations to ensure that workers representatives are informed and consulted on collective redundancies. It seems that the UK government will respond by providing for worker representation in future legislation. The primary duty imposed on the employer is to consult with trade union representatives.

The Trade Union Reform and Employment Rights Act 1993 amended the redundancy consultation procedures to bring the UK in line with the EC Collective Redundancies Directive. Under the Act the information to be given to union representatives when redundancies are proposed is expanded to include the proposed method of calculating payments. The consultation should consider how redundancy dismissals may be avoided and how the consequences of dismissal may be mitigated.

If an employer fails to comply with the consultation requirements then the trade union could seek a remedy by presenting a complaint to an employment tribunal. The tribunal can make a declaration as to non-compliance and also make a protective award requiring the employer to pay the specified employees their wages for the "protected period", specified not to exceed the consultation period to which they were entitled, 90, 30 or 28 days. An employer who fails to comply with a protective award can be required to do so on an individual complaint to a tribunal by an employee.

Whether or not there is an independent trade union involved, the Act also requires an employer to notify the Secretary of State in writing of proposed redundancies. The notification period is at least 90 days if it is proposed to dismiss 100 or more employees within 90 days or less, or 30 days if it is proposed to dismiss 10 or more employees within a 30 day period. Copies of the notice must be given to trade union representatives where there is a recognised independent trade union. Failure to notify the Secretary of State can lead to a fine on summary conviction.

Finally, mention should also be made of the fact that an employee with two years' service who is given notice of dismissal by reason of redundancy has the right, during the notice period, to be given reasonable time off during working hours, to look for new employment or make arrangements for future training. The employee is also entitled to be paid at the appropriate rate during the period of absence and can present a claim to a tribunal if his rights are denied.

## Redundancy Calculation

If an employee believes that as a qualifying worker he has been dismissed by reason of redundancy, the onus is upon him to make a claim to his employer for a redundancy payment. If the employer denies the claim or simply refuses to make a payment, the remedy of the employee is by way of complaint to an industrial tribunal. If a redundancy payment is made (otherwise than in compliance with an order of the tribunal specifying the amount), then an employer is guilty of an offence if he fails without reasonable excuse to give the employee a written statement indicating how the payment was calculated. The sum is calculated in the same way as a basic award by reference to the age of the claimant, the length of continuous employment and the weekly pay of the claimant.

## Amount of the payment

| Age (inclusive) | Amount of week's pay for each year of employment |
|---|---|
| 18 – 21 | ½ |
| 22 – 40 | 1 |
| 41 – 65 | 1½ |

Given that the aim of the payment is to provide a lump sum for the employee while he is seeking new employment, the fact that he will soon qualify for state retirement pension is also a factor in calculating the amount. Accordingly, for each month that the claimant is over sixty-four at the relevant date, the amount is reduced by one twelfth.

Another feature of the calculation is the fact that each year the maximum week's pay is adjusted to reflect the current average wage which is presently £220. Consequently the maximum redundancy payment is 20 years x 1½ (for employment between the ages of (41-65) x £220 = £6,600. For employees on a weekly fixed rate then the contractual rate is the current average wage. In cases where the wage does vary, however, a week's pay is calculated by reference to the average hourly rate of remuneration over the last twelve weeks of employment.

## Test Questions

1. Explain what is meant by redundancy.

2. Why were redundancy payments first introduced?

3. Who qualifies for a redundancy payment?

4. What happened in *Johnson v. Peabody Trust* 1996?

5. What is the effect of an offer of suitable alternative employment in a redundancy situation?

6. When is an employer required to consult in a redundancy situation?

7. How is a redundancy payment calculated?

# Assignment - Brecknall College

Brecknall College is a large institution of further and higher education located in the West Midlands. Last year a Business School was set up within the college by merging a number of departments. While the Business School has been successful in attracting students there have been a number of staffing problems.

1. A staff deployment problem has emerged in the area of accountancy and finance in the Business School. Ernie Quinn, a Lecturer in accountancy with twenty three years service at the University was asked by his Resource Director to take responsibility for the development of a course on managing finance in small businesses. This duty was to commence in the next academic year and involved a minimum of eight hours class contact. Over the years Ernie has built up a solid reputation for his opposition to change and has only recently co-operated in the team approach necessary for the operation of vocational courses with their emphasis on student centred learning. "Ernie's the name and accountancy is my game" he has said repeatedly in meetings and to classes over the years.

A major problem faced by the resource director is the dramatic diminution of accountancy courses and courses where accountancy forms an element. For a large part of the present academic year Ernie has operated a timetable which was eight hours short of his contractual teaching requirement with no additional responsibilities. True to form Ernie refuses the offer of course development work point blank, despite the attempt by his Head of Department to persuade him to take on this "challenging work". Subsequently Ernie sent a copy of his statement of terms of employment to the Director of the Business School where he is described as a Lecturer in Accountancy. He has also verbally threatened to leave and take the college to the Employment Tribunal.

2. Last month David Royle, a deputy director of the Business School, despite having eighteen years loyal service walked out of the College after a meeting of the Senior Management Team. In a heated discussion over departmental budgets the Principal had called David an "intellectual pigmy" and he had responded by telling her to *"stuff her job"* and walked out. In the interim there had been no communication between the parties and at the next meeting of the Senior Management Team the Principal to the Director of the Business School, said that *"she was glad to see the back of him"*. She also indicated that she intended to write to Mr. Royle to confirm his resignation and to *"sort out any payment of salary that was due to him"*.

3. A difficult issue has arisen in relation to three lecturers in the Business School who were originally recruited by the College as specialists in economic and social history. Following the reorganisation of the College they found themselves

deployed in the Business School in the economics section. Unfortunately while there is a call for a historical perspective in some areas of the Business School, the subject of economic history no longer features as part of the curriculum in any of the courses within the Business School. The three members of staff affected by the closure have been interviewed by the Director of the Business School and various suggestions have been made in relation to their future.

- Michael Johnstone is fifty seven a senior lecturer in economic history who has worked at the College for twenty seven years. He has been offered early retirement with a lump sum and pension relating to his years of service and a sum equivalent to treble the state redundancy payment. Michael's present salary is £24,728 per annum.

- William James is thirty seven, a lecturer in economic and social history, who has worked at the College for eleven years. Foreseeing the diminution in his area of work the Director of the Business School decided to relocate William last year in the management section of the Business School. William agreed in his meeting with the Director to "give it a go for a term". William resigned last month stating that despite retraining he found it "difficult to cope as a lecturer in management".

- Alex Grey is thirty one, a part-time lecturer in economic history who has worked at the College for the last four years on average between five and seven hours per week over a thirty six week academic year. He has been told by the Director that his services will no longer be required.

## Task

Your task is to produce an informal report in which you set out the legal position in relation to the preceding issues.

# Index

## A

Acceptance  36, 37 ,43-47
Advertisement 38, 60, 129, 139
Advisory Conciliation and Arbitration Service
  (ACAS) 25, 301
Agency 176, 190, 208, 209, 229
Anticipatory breach 91
Application form 241
Arbitrator 55
Arbitration 11, 25, 54, 55, 107
Articles of Association 177-181
Award
  additional 315
  basic 313
  compensatory 313

## B

Bankruptcy
  bankruptcy definition 215
  insolvency partnership 217
  trustee in bankruptcy 120, 217
Barrister 23
Barter 110
Basic award 313
Business
  arbitration 11, 54, 55
  choice of form 154, 228-230
  definition 2, 152
  firm 155
  form of 152-154, 228-230
  free market 29
  importance of law to 6, 7
  laissez faire 29
  managers 7, 8, 167, 189, 207
  market needs 29
  morality 7, 28, 31, 32
  negotiations 31, 37, 58, 59, 84
  reputation 7, 129, 40
...self regulation 2, 129
Business organisations
  accountability 3
  advertising 129, 134
  agency ( see Agency )
  aims and objectives 151, 152
  assets 7
  bargaining 29, 31
  classification 152, 153
  criminal offences 56
  corporation 56, 154
  debts 32, 222, 223
  ethics 27, 31, 32
  financing 214
  insolvency (see Bankruptcy, Company)
  insurance 4, 24
  legal advisers 22
  legal skills 8
  liabilities of (see Liability)
  private sector 152, 153
  profit 7
  public sector 152, 153
  publicity 7, 170, 230
  registered companies (see Company)
  relationships 2, 3, 190, 200, 207, 216
  rights of (see Company, Partnership)
  sole trader 154, 155
  tax 5, 230
  termination of 213-215
Business transfer 310

## C

Capacity to contract 55-57
Capital 164 (and see Company)
Caveat emptor 66
Caveat venditor 117
Citizens Advice Bureau 22
Civil Law 3, 285-289
Codes of practice 15, 132, 133, 136, 142
Collective agreements 55
Common law 12
Commission for Racial Equality 250, 259
Company
  administration order 227
  alternative remedy 185
  annual general meeting 199
  articles of association 165, 169, 177-181
  auditors 174, 193
  borrowing 186-189, 230
  capital 159, 166, 171-173, 186
  charges 187, 188, 230
  class rights 173, 181, 182
  contracting 167-169
  contributory 219

corporate personality 56, 159-163
creditors composition 227
criminal liability 159-160
debentures 186
debts 32, 222, 223, 226, 227
defunct 218
derivative action 186-188
directors ( see Directors )
disqualification orders (see Directors)
dividend 172, 173, 185, 196
Foss v. Harbottle, rule in 183, 199
fraudulent trading 163, 224, 225
guarantee 158, 159
incorporation 7, 165
information 230
insider dealing 202
insolvency practitioner 219
liability 158
liquidator 120, 219, 221, 224
loans 171
meetings 181, 206
membership 163
memorandum of association 164-170
name 164, 167
objects 166-170
officer 163, 165
pre-emption rights 164, 175, 176
private limited 164
privatisation 159
promoters 165, 166
prospectus 39
public limited 159, 164
purchase of shares by 184
receiver 187, 188
registrar 165, 166
registration 165, 217
resolutions 181
rights issue 165, 175
secretary 163, 191, 192
securities 171
share capital 171
share certificate 176
share transfer 34, 174, 175
shareholders 173-176, 181-186, 190, 199,
        230
shares 40, 110, 164, 171-173
single member 165
statutory contract 177-179
subscribers 166, 173
subsidiary 162
Table A 170
ultra vires 167-169
unlimited 158, 159

wrongful trading 163, 225
winding up 215, 218-224
compulsory 7, 221-224
Compensation 313-315
Compensation Order 5, 145
Compensatory award 314
Competition 20
Conciliation 301
Conciliation officer 301
Conditional fee 24
Confidentiality 270
Consideration 48-52
Constructive dismissal 294-296
Consumer, dealing as 2, 118
Consumer credit agreements 6
A.P.R. 140
cancellation 141
credit cards 140
default notice 140
definition of 140
extortionate credit bargains 141
form and content 34, 140
licensing 5
protected goods 140
termination 141
Consumer Protection 108, 126
Consumer Protection Advisory Committee
        142, 143
Contract
acceptance - 36, 37, 43-47, 242
accord and satisfaction 89
adhesion 31
agency (see Agency)
agreement -35-37
anticipatory breach 91
arbitration 54, 55
auction 38
bargaining power 29, 31
breach of 29, 85, 94-102
capacity - 55-57
collective agreement 55
competition 6
condition 75, 112, 125
consensus 30
consideration 48-52, 110
damages 85, 95-98
deeds 33
definition 28
discharge 86-94
divisible 86, 87
duress 31, 32, 72-74
employment of 34, 35
equitable estoppel 90

exclusion clauses 79, 80, 84, 85, 114
fixed term 293
formalities 33, 34
freedom of 29, 30
frustration of 91-94, 112, 296
hire purchase 140
honour clauses 53
illegality 262
implied terms 31, 78-80, 266-268
intention 53, 54
invitation to treat 38, 40
land 34
letters of comfort 54
minors 56, 57
misrepresentation 37, 58-66, 241
mistake 66-71
monopoly 31
negotiation 31, 37, 58, 59, 84
offer 37-43, 242
partnership (see Partnership)
partial performance 87, 88
penalty 85
price 41, 85, 111, 124, 135-137
privity of 52
public interest 28
quantum meruit 101, 102, 206
remedies 84, 85, 94-102
representation 59
speciality 33
specific performance 100, 101
standard form 84, 85, 120
substantial performance 86-88
tender 39
terms 74-85
uberrimae fidei 61, 208, 241
undue influence 31, 32, 72-74
unenforceable 34
unfair terms 144
vitiating elements 30, 58
void 30
voidable 30
warranty 75, 112, 125
writing 33, 34, 262
Contract of Employment
  breach of contractual term 264
  disciplinary procedures 263
  document, details of 234
  express terms 265
  formation 34, 35, 240
  frustration of 296
  implied terms 266-268
  of service 197, 235
  recruitment 240

termination of 290
terms and conditions 262, 263
written particulars of 262
Copyright 34
Corporations (see Company)
Costs 6, 11, 22 24
Courts 100-14
  Chancery 10
  Court of Appeal 10
  County 11
  Crown 10
  European 10
  hierarchy 12
  High Court 10
  House of Lords 10
  Magistrates 10
  Restrictive Practices 6, 143
Credit sale 140
Criminal law 3-6
Crown Prosecution Service 5

**D**

DTI 5, 6, 141, 163, 195, 196
Damages 7, 112, 124
Data Protection 146-148
Debenture 186
Debt 32, 222, 223, 226, 227
Defective goods (see Product Liability)
Direct discrimination 246, 250
Directives 21
Directors
  alternate 193
  appointment 192, 193
  breach of duty 207
  casual vacancies 193
  conflict of interest 197, 205
  contract of services 196
  controls over 181, 182, 199, 200
  definition 160, 191
  delegation 200, 206
  disclosure 197
  disqualification order 193-196
  duties, care and skill 185, 206, 207
  duties, fiduciary 201, 203-206
  duties, statutory 168, 203
  duty to creditors 202-203
  duty to shareholders 201, 202
  fees 196, 197
  loans 198
  managing director 200
  position of 160, 169
  powers of 199

property transactions of 198
removal of 173,,182, 190, 200, 221
remuneration 196, 197
secret profit 203-205
shadow 191
Table A 190, 193
Director General of Fair Trading 6, 136, 142,
144
Disability discrimination 244, 248, 249
Disabled persons 244, 248
Dismissal
constructive 294
express 293
fair 298
implied 293, 294
notice 290
summary 291
unfair 298
wrongful 291
Duress, undue influence (see Contract)

**E**

Employment
casual labour 235, 238
collective agreement 55
contract for services 235
contract of service 235
dismissal 290
health and safety 268
recruitment 240
redundancy 307
vicarious liability 13, 255, 287
Employment Appeals Tribunal 25, 26
Employment Tribunal 16, 25
Equal Opportunities Commission 250, 259
Equal pay 20
Europe 17-21
European Commission 7, 19
Council of Ministers 20
Court of Justice 20
directives 21, 126
European Union 9
health and safety 18
institutions 19-20
Maastricht 18
regulations 21
secondary legislation 20
Single European Act 1986 18
Treaty on European Union 1992 18
Treaty of Rome 1957 18
Types of Community Law 19
Exclusion clauses 79, 80, 84, 85

Express dismissal 293
Express Terms 77, 78, 84, 85, 265
Extortionate credit bargains 141

**F**

Fault (see Liability)
Fixed term contract 293
Food Safety 145, 146
Frustrated Contract (see Contract)

**G**

Genuine occupational requirement 258, 259
Gross misconduct 291, 292
Goodwill 2
Good faith 269, 270

**H**

Health and Safety 5, 236, 268, 275-289
Health and Safety Commission 15, 276
Health and Safety Executive 5, 281
Hire, contracts of 109
Hire-purchase agreements 109, 140

**I**

Implied dismissal 293
Implied terms (see Contract)
Income tax 230, 236
Independent contractors 235
Indirect discrimination 256
Industrial action 267
Injunction 7, 98-100
Improvement notice 281
Insurance 4, 61
Interviews 242, 253

**L**

Land 139
Law Society 24
Lawyers 22, 23
Legal advice and information 22
Legal System 1, 3, 4, 11-19
Act of Parliament 14
common law 12
criminal law 3-6
EU (see Europe)
lawyers 22, 23
legislation 14, 15, 19, 20
obiter 13, 14
Parliament 15

precedent 11, 12
ratio 13
statutory interpretation 15, 16
Liability in business
  contractual 5, 119, 120
  corporate 158
  criminal 5
  fault 4
  generally 56
  strict 137
  tortious 285-288
  vicarious 236, 255
Licensing 5
Local authority 5, 39, 135, 144, 153

# M

Magistrates Court 9, 10
Market economy 2
Memorandum of association 164-179
Merchantable quality 115-117
Minors 10, 56, 57, 193
Misconduct 306, 307
Misleading price indications 135-137
Misrepresentation (see Contract)
Mistake (see Contract)
Mutual termination 298

# N

Negligence 4, 285-288
Nemo dat quod non habet 111
Notice 290

# O

Obiter dicta 13, 14
Offer (see Contract)
Overruling 14

# P

Partnership
  agency 208, 209, 229
  definition 157
  description of 144, 208
  dissolution 215-217
  firm 155
  formalities 155, 156, 230
  liability of 209, 229
  membership 156, 210, 230
  name 156, 228
  partner's rights and duties 182, 210-212,
                           229

property of 212, 213
  sleeping partners 157, 212
  unlimited 156, 229
Part-time employment 235, 262, 272, 290
Passing off, tort of 167
Pay 234
Precedent 11, 12
Pregnancy 302
Pre-hearing assessment 25
Privity of contract 52
Product liability 115-117, 126
Professional negligence 127, 128
Prohibition notice 281, 284
Promoters (see Company)
Public interest 28

# Q

Qualifications 305
Quantum meruit 101, 102, 206

# R

Race discrimination 244-261
Ratio decidendi 13
Recruitment 240
Redundancy 307, 316-321
Re-engagement 312
Reference 241
Reinstatement 312
Repudiatory breach 295
Resignation 297
Restrictive practice 6
Reversing 14
Risk assessment 278

# S

Safe goods 5, 126
Sale of goods 109-133
  definition 109
  delivery 113, 121, 124
  description 114, 129-133
  exclusion of liability 114, 118
  fitness for purpose 116, 177
  implied terms 113-117
  merchantable quality 115-117, 144
  nemo dat 111
  payment 41, 111, 124
  remedies 123-125
  retention of title 85, 111
  risk 111, 120
  romalpa 85, 121
  sale or return 122

satisfactory quality 115-117
specific goods 120-122
title 110
transfer of title 85, 111, 123
unascertained goods 122, 123
Satisfactory quality 115-117
Self employed 235
Services, supply of (see Supply of..)
Sex Discrimination 244-261
Sexual harassment 254-256
Shares (see Company)
Small claims 11
Solicitors 22
Specific performance (see Contract)
Statutory
employment rights 236
interpretation 15, 16
reasons 302, 305
statement 234, 262
Strict liability 116, 130
Summary dismissal 291, 292
Supply of Goods and Services 109, 127, 128,
137-139

**T**

Time limits 249
Time off 273-275
Tort 4, 285, 286
Trade associations 141
Trade descriptions 40, 129-139, 144
Trading standards 5, 108
Trial 13
Tribunals 11, 22, 24
Trust and confidence 259, 270

**U**

Ultra Vires (see Company)
Unfair dismissal
automatically unfair 302
compensation 313
complaint 295
continuous employment 300
excluded employees 300
fair 303
fixed term contracts 293
health and safety 302
pregnancy 302
reasons 301, 302
redundancy 307
remedy 312

**V**

Vicarious Liability 13, 236, 255, 287
Victimisation 246, 257

**W**

Wages 271, 272
Welfare benefits 236
Work rules 265
Workers 240
Working time 277
Wrongful dismissal 291, 292